Experiments in Focus

Linguistische Arbeiten

Edited by
Klaus von Heusinger, Agnes Jäger,
Gereon Müller, Ingo Plag,
Elisabeth Stark and Richard Wiese

Volume 571

Experiments in Focus

Information Structure and Semantic Processing

Edited by
Sam Featherston,
Robin Hörnig,
Sophie von Wietersheim
and Susanne Winkler

DE GRUYTER

ISBN 978-3-11-076598-4
e-ISBN (PDF) 978-3-11-062309-3
e-ISBN (EPUB) 978-3-11-062228-7
ISSN 0344-6727

Library of Congress Control Number: 2019941345

Bibliographic information published by the Deutsche Nationalbibliothek
The Deutsche Nationalbibliothek lists this publication in the Deutsche Nationalbibliografie;
detailed bibliographic data are available on the Internet at http://dnb.dnb.de.

© 2021 Walter de Gruyter GmbH, Berlin/Boston
This volume is text- and page-identical with the hardback published in 2019.
Typesetting: Integra Software Services Pvt. Ltd.
Printing and binding: CPI books GmbH, Leck

www.degruyter.com

Contents

Robin Hörnig, Sam Featherston, Sophie von Wietersheim and Susanne Winkler
Markedness in context: An approach to licensing —— 1

Sophia Döring and Sophie Repp
The modal particles *ja* and *doch* and their interaction with discourse structure: Corpus and experimental evidence —— 17

Kordula De Kuthy and Britta Stolterfoht
Focus projection revisited: Pitch accent perception in German —— 57

Jutta M. Hartmann
Focus and prosody in nominal copular clauses —— 71

Andreas Konietzko, Janina Radó and Susanne Winkler
Focus constraints on relative clause antecedents in sluicing —— 105

Robin Hörnig and Caroline Féry
Markers of discourse status in descriptions of altered spatial layouts —— 129

Thomas Weskott, Robin Hörnig and Gert Webelhuth
On the contextual licensing of English locative inversion and topicalization —— 153

Markus Bader and Jana Häussler
How to get from graded intuitions to binary decisions —— 183

Alexander Dröge, Jürg Fleischer and Ina Bornkessel-Schlesewsky
Scrambled Wackernagel! Neural responses to noncanonical pronoun serializations in German —— 209

Balázs Surányi and István Fekete
Logical and pragmatic meaning in the interpretation of disjunction: Contextual relevance and scalar implicatures —— 251

Andreas Konietzko and Karen Lidzba
The processing of argument structure: A comparison between patients with early left-hemispheric brain lesions and healthy controls —— 279

Hannah Gerbrich, Vivian Schreier and Sam Featherston
Standard items for English judgment studies: Syntax and semantics —— 305

Index —— 329

Robin Hörnig, Sam Featherston, Sophie von Wietersheim and Susanne Winkler

Markedness in context: An approach to licensing

This volume is a collection of selected papers that adopt an experimental approach to questions of information structure and processing. The concept of information structure we employ here includes, but is not limited to, theories of focus, issues of markedness, and contextual licensing. Since these features are used by the parser to guide incremental interpretation, it is of great interest to consider not only how these factors are represented in the language, but also how they contribute to processing. The major research questions that these papers address are as follows:

- What are the various devices with which the grammar encodes information-structural concepts such as unmarked (wide) focus or marked (narrow or contrastive) focus?
- How do lexical phenomena such as discourse particles and syntactic constructions interact with information structure?
- How do such discourse status factors as givenness, parallel vs. non-parallel focus, and common ground management interact?
- How can the differences between marked and unmarked word orders be described? And how does context influence the licensing of these structures?
- What approaches can linguists adopt to help them disentangle the different factors that play a role in processing sentences in context?

The papers in this volume address these questions and propose answers. These papers are unified in their interest in the representation and implementation of aspects of interpretation and processing, and the conviction that experimental methods can yield insights. Within this unity, they vary in their methodological approach, theoretical concerns, and linguistic aims. In the following, we show how empirical studies can address such mental processes as the extraction of meaning from linguistic forms in context, but we shall begin by sketching the papers in their relationship to the common heading of the *markedness of a linguistic form* and, related to it, the idea of *contextual licensing*.[1] We consider *contextual licensing*

---

[1] We have greatly benefitted from an ongoing and always stimulating exchange with Thomas Weskott on information structural issues such as markedness of forms and contexts as licensors. Our thanks go also to Andreas Konietzko for more recent pertinent discussion.

https://doi.org/10.1515/9783110623093-001

both as a theoretical and a methodological notion that can be made use of in experimental designs. With the markedness of a linguistic form we follow Höhle's (1982) inquiry into the nature of normal accentuation ('normale Betonung') and normal constituent order ('normale Wortstellung'). The reader may tentatively equate *normal* with *unmarked*; Höhle speaks of *relatively unmarked* ('relativ unmarkiert').

Pairs of linguistic forms that are similar, but not identical, usually have differences of meaning that are specific to the differences in form, so differences in form without a corresponding difference in meaning call for a justification. Sometimes the solution seems to be that the forms then differ in information-structural function. One such function is focus. The goal is to establish a systematic form-function mapping for those cases where differences in form correlate with a difference in function. One way of signaling a difference in focus is prosody. In English and German, for instance, speakers can do this by a differential placement of the most prominent pitch accent, illustrated in (1a) versus (1b) (the syllable in bold and small capitals carries the pitch accent).

(1) a. The woman burnt the **BOOK**.
    b. The **WO**man burnt the book.

(2) a. What did the woman burn?
    b. Who burnt the book?

Superficially, (1a) and (1b) do not differ in meaning, in the sense that they arguably share the same truth conditions; however, they can function as the answers to different questions. This difference does not depend upon an issue of the facts in the world, but rather depends upon what the questioner already knows about the facts. Question (2a) is more likely to be answered with (1a), whereas question (2b) is more likely to be answered with (1b). Native speakers probably do not consider (1a) a felicitous answer to (2b). They will perhaps consider (1b) an even less felicitous answer to (2a).

When we consider the assertions (1a) and (1b) as possible answers to questions, we see that the questions differ in the requested information, whereas the answers differ with respect to the constituent carrying the pitch accent. The felicity of a question-answer pair depends upon their matching in terms of focus. The content of the question word determines the focus in the question; the pitch accent signals which part of the answer the speaker considers to be the focus. This correspondence of focus in questions and answers is called *question-answer congruence*.

This congruence relation provides a nice way to illustrate how very similar sentence forms may differ in their information-structural qualities, for instance, in their focus quality. An equally important research issue is how to determine the focus of an utterance, which is part of an ongoing discourse rather than the answer to an explicit question. A first guess would be that the utterances (1a) and (1b) would be part of different discourses. More generally, the encoding of focus in a linguistic form signals a set of contextual requirements on the surrounding discourse. The constraints on the preceding context can, as in (1) and (2) above, be fulfilled by a question, but need not be. The intuitive appeal of questions in an alternative semantics approach to focus is pointed out by Zimmermann & Onéa (2011:1652): "Intuitively, focus marking on the subject in (1) [= *PE\ter went to Paris*] indicates that alternative propositions of the form *x went to Paris* are relevant for the interpretation of (1); for instance, (1) would constitute an ideal answer to the *wh*-question *Who went to Paris?*" In any event, if the two linguistic forms (1a) and (1b) signal different contextual requirements by virtue of their difference in linguistic form, they are expected to be uttered in different contexts, and it is this sort of external evidence of focus within linguistic examples that permits an experimental approach to these questions.

This is then the empirical perspective on these issues taken in this volume. If we take (1a) and (1b) as being uttered in the contexts (2a) and (2b) respectively, then they would make up a coherent story; we can experimentally test whether the story is not only coherent but accurately reflects the behavior of speakers. We present, for instance, (1a) or (1b) together with the alternative contexts (2a) and (2b) to native speakers and ask them to choose the context that better fits the assertion. If our hypothesis is correct, they will behave in the way that we predict. If they don't, we'll have to revise our theory and test again.

One restriction on the evidence of experimental studies is that a well-designed experiment will deliver exactly the answer to the question that it was designed to answer, but not necessarily anything beyond that. If this hypothesis is only partially correct, or if it is merely a part of a larger generalization, an economically designed experiment will not reveal this to us. Based on this study alone we cannot rule out that there are other contexts that fulfil the contextual requirements of (1a) or (1b), or that there are other contexts that would fulfil the requirements of both (1a) and (1b) felicitously. To this extent such a study offers only a partial view.

The reason why this limited view can become problematic is that the repertoire of available distinctions in form is insufficiently rich to capture the full range of possible differentiations in information structure. This is why we do not find a simple bijective mapping from focus-related forms to focus functions, as the term *form-function pairs* might suggest. In (1a) and (1b) we have distinguished two different examples of narrow focus, *the woman* and *the book*. There is a third possible narrow focus in the same example, a verb focus – *The woman* **BURNT** *the book.*, which would be a felicitous response to the question *What did the woman do with the book?*

However, it is also possible to focus on larger constituents: focus projections. One of them is VP focus: *The woman [burnt the* **BOOK***]*$_F$, as a response to the question *What did the woman do?* There is also the form known as broad focus, [*The* woman burnt the **BOOK**]_F, which is the response to the general question *What happened?* Attentive readers will note that the pitch accent in these last two cases is on exactly the same syllable as in the example with narrow focus on the object. Both of these, as well as the narrow focus on [*the* **BOOK**]_F, have the form: *The woman burnt the* **BOOK**. How can that be?

It turns out that there are some regularities, for instance, in German a pitch accent is usually placed finally in an intonation phrase. Since we assume that the focus projection of an utterance corresponds to an intonation phrase, we can say that the minimal intonation phrase corresponding to the narrow focus [*the* **BOOK**]_F forms the final part of the larger intonation phrase corresponding to the VP focus [*burnt the* **BOOK**]_F. The same is true of the even larger intonation phrase corresponding to the broad focus [*The woman burnt the* **BOOK**]_F. In all three instances, the pitch accent is placed at the coincident end of the intonation phrase, on **BOOK**. Since the perceptible feature of the intonation phrase is the pitch accent, we thus end up with a non-bijective mapping and consequently with an ambiguous signal for focus in case of (1a), which we repeat here for convenience, extended by the VP focus question (2c) and the broad focus question (2d).

(1) a. The woman burnt the **BOOK**.
　　b. The **WO**man burnt the book.

(2) a. What did the woman burn?
　　b. Who burnt the book?
　　c. What did the woman do?
　　d. What happened?

As (1a) is thus compatible with more than one focus, (2a), (2c), and (2d), its contextual restrictions are less strict than the contextual restrictions of the linguistic form in (1b), the focus of which does not project to a larger constituent (but see the contribution of De Kuthy & Stolterfoht, this volume, below). We can therefore state, following Höhle (1982:102, Definition (78)), that the linguistic form with the least strong contextual restrictions among the set of alternative forms is (contextually) *unmarked* or *least marked* (Höhle 1982: *relatively unmarked*). The quantitative concept of markedness inherent in the term *least marked* refers to types of context rather than instances and is a feature of the ambiguity in the information structural signal. This use of the term *markedness* does not permit us to say that a given linguistic form is marked in a context of type A but unmarked in a context of type B. It is possible, however, that a type of context meets the contextual requirements of a marked form. Basically, if a context type meets the contextual restrictions of a marked linguistic form the context type is expected to license the marked form.

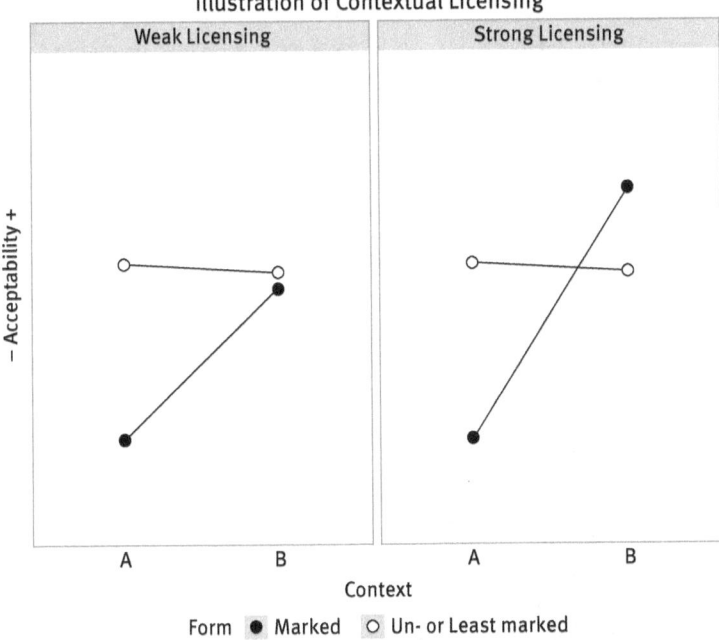

Figure 1: Illustration of weak versus strong contextual licensing. Left panel: Marked form is judged equally or less acceptable than unmarked form. Right panel: Marked form is judged significantly more acceptable than least marked form.

Here we speak of contextual licensing as a methodological term applicable to experimental evaluation. We can experimentally demonstrate that a context B meets the contextual requirements of a marked form if it licenses the form; a type of context can be said to license the form if it is judged more acceptable in the licensing context type B compared to a non-licensing context type A. We distinguish a weak and a strong version of contextual licensing, which we will explain here in experimental terms. The two patterns of contextual licensing are illustrated in Figure 1.

The weak version of contextual licensing assumes the existence of an *unmarked* form, not a *least marked* form. We call it unmarked because either this form will have no contextual restrictions at all, or else all types of context employed in the study meet the restrictions of this form. Let's assume that we gather acceptability judgments on how well the form fits a context type or, in other words, how well a context type fulfils the contextual restrictions of a form. Since the contextual restrictions on this form are equally compatible with all the types of contexts tested, its acceptability should be unaffected by the embedding context types A and B. The marked form is said to be contextually licensed by context type B if it is judged more acceptable in context type B than in context type A. In terms of a factorial design with the factors FORM and CONTEXT, contextual licensing thus needs to be confirmed by a significant ordinal interaction of FORM and CONTEXT.

The strong version of contextual licensing also needs to be confirmed by an interaction of FORM and CONTEXT, though a disordinal one. Strong contextual licensing employs the concept of a least marked form, rather than an unmarked form. A type of context B licenses a marked form strongly if the marked form is more acceptable in context type B than in context type A and the marked form is more acceptable in context type B than the least marked form. Let us see what that means for (1) and (2): (1a) is the least marked form and (1b) is a marked form. Context type (2b) strongly licenses (1b) if (1b) is judged more acceptable in context type (2b) than in context type (2a), and it is judged more acceptable in context type (2b) than (1a) is.[2]

The contrast of unmarked and least marked thus entails that there is no type of context for the unmarked form that meets the contextual restrictions of the unmarked form to a lesser degree than those of a marked form; in order for this to hold the unmarked form must be free of contextual requirements. For a least marked form there exists a type of context that meets the contextual requirement of a marked form to a greater degree than those of the least marked form, that is, a least marked form must be associated with contextual requirements.

Contextual licensing can also be readily applied to types of experiments gathering other dependent variables such as reading time experiments, and language production and corpus frequency studies. Here, a context of type B would weakly license the production of a marked linguistic form if the frequency of production of the marked form significantly increases from context type A to context type B and the marked form occurs in context type B about as often as the unmarked form. A context of type B would strongly license the production of a marked linguistic form if in context type B the marked form is produced more frequently than the least marked form. It is not unlikely that strong contextual licensing is more often observed in production than in comprehension (e.g., by gathering acceptability judgments) because in production the linguistic forms directly compete with one another (Featherston 2005, 2019).

While we have so far illustrated our discussion of focus and markedness using prosody, it can equally well be applied to other phenomena such as word order, and several papers in this volume do exactly this. Höhle (1982) observes

---

[2] Strictly speaking this contrast does not suffice to establish a particular form as least marked due to our quantitative definition of least marked. We therefore need to establish (1a) as least marked form independent of the outlined experiment or we must extend the experimental design by an additional condition, for instance, with a broad focus condition.

that an intuitively marked constituent order restricts the set of possible types of contexts. Again, a type of context corresponds to a possible focus. We provide an English example in (3).

(3) a. John has burnt the **BO**ok.
    b. The **BO**ok, John has burnt.

(4) a. What has John burnt?
    b. What has John done?
    c. What has happened?

(5) Has John burnt the book **AND** the painting?

Example (3a) shows a sentence with unmarked constituent order and unmarked accentuation. It is a possible answer to all three of the questions in (4)–(4a) with a narrow focus, (4b) with a VP focus, and (4c) with a broad focus. Again we use questions to instantiate focus variants here, but it will be clear that these questions could be represented by other contextual material that would yield the three focus types.

Example (3b) is a variant of (3a) with an alternative constituent order. Although the pitch accent in (3a) and (3b) is on the same constituent, (3b) cannot felicitously answer any of the questions in (4), not even the narrow focus question (4a), which focuses the constituent which bears the pitch accent in (3b). This English constituent order variant is thus very strongly marked and has very specific contextual licensing requirements, which might be illustrated in the question in (5).

Analogously to the markedness of accentuation, Höhle identifies the constituent order with the least restricted set of possible context types as least marked or relatively unmarked; note that this concept of a least marked constituent order is intended to apply irrespective of accentuation. Höhle observes that the sets of focus projections associated with two form variants stand in a set-subset relation of one another and concludes that a linguistic form that is licensed by a broad focus is least marked. Accordingly, a constituent order like (3a) is least marked if its accentuation is least marked and it fits an all-new context. Since (3a) meets these requirements it is the English least marked constituent order.

It then follows that there are sentences with a least marked constituent order together with a least marked accentuation. Such a sentence identifies exactly one narrow focus that can be expressed with a least marked accentuation and a least marked constituent order. Every other narrow focus must be expressed with a marked form of the sentence. The sentence in (6a) (adopted from Dröge et al, this volume, their example (1)) is least marked with respect to both constituent order and accentuation. Example (6a) is a felicitous answer to the narrow focus question (7a).

(6) a. *Gestern* hat *der Assistent* dem Geschäftsführer den **KA**ffee
 b. *Gestern* hat *der Assistent* dem Ge**SCHÄFTS**führer den Kaffee
 yesterday has [the assistant]$_{NOM}$ [the CEO]$_{DAT}$ [the coffee]$_{ACC}$
 gebracht.
 gebracht.
 brought

 c. *Gestern* hat *der Assistent* den Kaffee dem Ge**SCHÄFTS**führer
 d. *Gestern* hat *der Assistent* den **KA**ffee dem Geschäftsführer
 yesterday has [the assistant]$_{NOM}$ [the coffee]$_{ACC}$ [the CEO]$_{DAT}$
 gebracht.
 brought
 'Yesterday, the assistant has brought the coffee to the CEO.'

(7) a. *Was hat der Assistent gestern dem Geschäftsführer gebracht?*
 'What has the assistant brought to the CEO yesterday?'
 b. *Wem hat der Assistent gestern den Kaffee gebracht?*
 'To whom has the assistant brought the coffee yesterday?'

It will be clear that the least marked form (6a) is not a felicitous answer to the narrow focus question (7b), so question (7b) needs a marked form of the sentence as a reply. One possibility is to displace the pitch accent onto the requested constituent, *dem Geschäftsführer* 'the CEO'. Due to the displacement of the pitch accent from the least marked position on the last nominal constituent to a marked position on an earlier nominal constituent, example (6b) becomes marked, but only the accentuation is marked, not the constituent order. If a speaker wants to avoid a marked accentuation she can switch the order of indirect and direct object from IO$_{DAT}$–DO$_{ACC}$ to DO$_{ACC}$–IO$_{DAT}$, as in (6c). The pitch accent in (6c) is placed on the last nominal constituent and is thus least marked, but the constituent order is marked. Since the answer to (7b) can be marked either in its accentuation or its constituent order, we can find out whether accentuation or constituent order are more flexible in a language, by investigating how native speakers answer such questions.

There is, however, another interesting question which relates to example (6d). Given a narrow focus, the pitch accent in (6d) determines *den **KA**ffee* 'the coffee' as focus; thus (6d) should be an adequate answer to question (7a). If so, this question should license (6d) and there should be two alternative forms as a reply to (7a): the least marked form (6a) and the doubly marked form (6d). One could speculate that (6d) will be preferred to (6a) because (6a) is ambiguous, whereas (6d) is not.

But probably nobody would bet on (6d): we expect speakers to prefer least marked forms over marked forms. Example (6d) may not even be contextually licensed, as previously observed in our English example (4a)–(3b). For instance, in an experiment on language production, we may find that doubly marked forms like (6d) are produced equally infrequently as answers to (7a) or (7b). Would it then be possible to conclude that doubly marked forms like (6d) are dispensable in a language because the least marked form already does the job? Given that this form can be produced by the normal generative mechanisms, but is in fact functionally superfluous, should we expect it to be grammatical and fully acceptable, ungrammatical and unacceptable, or grammatical but poorly acceptable? Such paradigms can thus deliver interesting test cases for the interaction of focus and grammar.

The papers that make up this collection have been selected from the very active field of information structure research on the basis of several criteria. The first is that they should be centrally placed within the academic discourse of empirical and theoretical linguistics. This means that mere descriptions of phenomena are less highly valued; there is a requirement that the paper address the question of the causation of the observed effects, ideally locating them within a larger model of grammatical, discourse, or psycholinguistic explanation. The second priority is empirical support. While there is a tradition of armchair research in linguistics, the papers selected here all assign a high value to the gathering and analysis of replicable data that provides a robust evidential base for claims made. The collection also aspires to breadth of coverage of the various factors that demonstrably interact with syntactico-semantic patterning. Several papers look at the phonological reflexes of information structural effects, such as pitch accent placement and prosody. Others deal with linearity contrasts among sentence constituents. The particular value of the papers in this collection is that they utilize the added explanatory advantage of combining both firm data and the insights of linguistic theory.

We have put the papers in this collection together on the basis of the questions that they address and the approaches that they adopt. They have the common factor that they examine issues of the morphological, prosodic, and syntactic means with which languages signal information-structural status such as focus and discourse givenness.

Sophia Döring and **Sophie Repp** study the German modal particles *ja* and *doch* and their interaction with discourse structure. According to Döring and Repp, modal particles have a coherence-creating function. In the case of *ja*, the speaker signals to the hearer that – contrary to the usual expectation interlocutors entertain – the proposition that *ja* takes scope over is already part of the common ground, that is, it is already known to the hearer. The presence of the modal particle renders the form of the utterance marked. Döring and Repp claim that the use of the modal particle is obligatory and thus advocate a strong contextual licensing in our sense. They propose that the particle's function is to remind the hearer of the proposition in order to raise its salience. Likewise, the particle *doch* makes the proposition that it takes scope over and which is part of the common ground salient in the mind of the hearer. Moreover, it signals that the proposition in question is in conflict with another proposition in the common ground. In addition to a corpus study, Döring and Repp conducted an experiment showing that the modal particles *ja* and *doch* are associated with different discourse relations. The contextual requirements thus not only include requirements on the preceding context establishing the proposition that the particle takes scope over as part of the common ground; they also include forward requirements concerning that proposition and how it relates to the forthcoming discourse.

Kordula de Kuthy and **Britta Stolterfoht** challenge one of the claims that we put forward above: that a pitch accent placed at the end of an intonation phrase corresponding to a narrow object focus is indistinguishable (i.e., instantiates the same form) from a pitch accent placed at the end of an intonation phrase corresponding to a VP focus. They recorded spoken utterances of two female speakers in two contexts: a narrow object focus question and a VP focus question. Acoustic analyses showed significant differences between the utterances produced in the different conditions. In a subsequent perception experiment participants listened to matching and mismatching question-answer pairs and judged the fit of the answers to the questions. De Kuthy and Stolterfoht found that the fit of matching answers to VP focus questions was rated better than mismatching answers; however, the fit of matching and mismatching answers to narrow object focus questions was judged equally good. Consequently, they distinguish the two forms of focus with the pitch accent on the object and characterize the VP focus answer as less marked than the answer with narrow object focus. Nevertheless, the set-subset relation between broader and narrower focus seems to be intact and this supports the dependency between instantiations of VP focus and narrow focus.

The interaction of syntax and focus is the core topic of **Jutta M. Hartmann**'s paper. She investigates specificational copular clauses (*The winner is Susan*) in comparison to predicational copular clauses (*Susan is the winner*) and predicts that specificational copular clauses will resist pre-copular (contrastive) focus even if contextually licensed, while predicational copular clauses will accept pre- or post-copular (contrastive) focus just as licensed by the context. Hartmann reports two rating studies using auditory stimuli, manipulating firstly the intonation contours (among them a neutral post-copular focus) and additionally the presence or absence of prior context questions. The results confirm a highly restricted focus structure for specificational copular clauses, but not for predicational copular clauses. Hartmann explains the difference in terms of the interaction of syntax and information structure: specificational copular clauses are inversion structures as a result of focus assignment to the post-copular DP. Their focus assignment is thus not flexible but determined by their syntactic form. Predicational copular clauses are not restricted in this way. The comparison of judgments gathered with and without context shows that narrow focus without context is marked but not licensed, that is, it is always judged worse than the neutral focus.

The following paper makes use of the distinction between accented and deaccented constituents. **Andreas Konietzko**, **Janina Radó**, and **Susanne Winkler** investigate the interpretation of complex sluicing structures in German, in which the antecedent of the *wh*-remnant of the elliptical construction occurs either in the preceding matrix correlate or relative correlate clause. Complex sluicing is only licensed if the *wh*-remnant and its antecedent express a contrastive relationship, expressed in the focus parallelism requirement that differs from the characteristics of regular unstressed pronouns, as for example discussed in Dröge et al. (this volume). The central observation is that in similar contexts that either focus the grammatically appropriate antecedent (parallel focus) or not (nonparallel focus), it matters whether the antecedent of the *wh*-remnant occurs in the matrix correlate clause, or in an in situ relative clause, or an extraposed relative clause. The authors argue that the judgment differences have their origin in information structure. This hypothesis is supported in two acceptability rating studies that compared the focus status of the antecedent (parallel vs. nonparallel) with the structural position (in the matrix clause, and different types of relative clauses). The experiments show how contextual licensing conditions and specific structural licensing conditions of relative clause extraposition interact.

The work of **Robin Hörnig** and **Caroline Féry** explores how German speakers mark the discourse status of entities involved in linguistic descriptions of spatial layouts. In a production study participants specified the relative location of toy animals. The target entities had either the discourse status new or given. The recordings of the target localizations were checked for three possible signals of discourse status: constituent order, definiteness of the target, and the contour of the pitch accents on the target expression. Speakers made use of all three signals to tell apart given from new targets. They tended to multiply signal the discourse status of targets; often all three signals were used together: New targets often came with a marked constituent order paired with an unmarked falling pitch accent on the phrase final new target and an indefinite determiner.

The frequent production of marked constituent orders speak in favor of a strong licensing in response to the discourse status of the target – which confirms what has been found previously for comprehension.

It has often been observed that English word order in root sentences is relatively rigid compared to the word order of German. **Thomas Weskott, Robin Hörnig,** and **Gert Webelhuth** address the question whether English marked word order constructions improve in appropriate contextual conditions in the same way as has been shown for the corresponding German structures (Weskott et al. 2011). They refer to this phenomenon as contextual licensing: given the right kind of context, sentences with marked word order do not show the usual markedness effects of degraded acceptability and increased processing time. In four experiments, they tested to what extent English locative inversion and English topicalization can be contextually licensed. The results of these studies show similarities to the corresponding results on German. They thus claim that English word order, despite being generally regarded as fairly rigid, nevertheless shows effects of context sensitivity. The weaker effects of context on English marked forms confirm that they are associated with stronger contextual requirements than the corresponding marked forms in German.

Markus Bader and **Jana Häussler** go beyond the consideration of specific phenomena to consider how the causal factors of perceived well-formedness interact more generally. They are interested in the correlation of gradient and binary grammaticality judgements, but also in the relationship between grammaticality and frequency more generally. They describe the Grammar First Model that combines the advantages of the Decathlon Model (Featherston 2005) on the one hand and the Direct Mapping Model (Bader & Häussler 2010) on the other hand. The Grammar First Model makes two predictions: first, binary and gradient judgment data should correlate highly; second, the grammaticality of a structure and its frequency should only interact loosely. The authors report an experiment that tests whether grammaticality or frequency determine the choice between two linguistic forms during production, the unmarked form (active voice) versus a marked form (*bekommen* passive). The transitive verbs figuring in the target sentence pairs were divided into three categories dependent on their acceptability if combined with the *bekommen* passive (high, middle, degraded). Contexts presented prior to the choice between the two forms manipulated whether the agent or the recipient were established as topic. Bader and Häussler showed that the unmarked form was highly preferred with the agent (= subject) as topic; the *bekommen* passive was highly preferred with the recipient (= subject) as topic as long as the verb was fully acceptable with the *bekommen* passive. The worse the general fit of a verb with a *bekommen* passive the less is the ability of the context to license the marked form. The results also show that judged well-formedness is the determining factor, whereas frequency only has a minor effect.

Alexander Dröge, Jürg Fleischer, and **Ina Bornkessel-Schlesewsky** investigate pronoun serializations in the German middlefield using event-related brain potentials. In Standard German, unstressed personal pronouns appear at the left edge of the middlefield in the order accusative before dative. However, some historical and dialectal evidence, especially from southern variants, shows that dative before accusative is possible and sometimes even preferred (e.g., Fleischer 2012). The central question is whether the non-canonical pronoun orders are only marked, and thus susceptible to contextual licensing, or whether they should be classed as ungrammatical. Acceptability ratings show a general preference for the canonical order, but the judgments for all four tested serializations are within the upper third of the four-point scale and can hardly considered ungrammatical. Dröge, Fleischer, and Bornkessel-Schlesewsky discuss in detail their claim that the observed ERP signatures do not support the ungrammaticality of non-canonical orders of unstressed personal pronouns.

The paper of **Balázs Surányi** and **István Fekete** is in the tradition of experimental pragmatics. They report two experiments in Hungarian on the interpretation of the disjunction *or*. The influential claim has been that this expression automatically gives rise to the exclusivity implicature *but not both* by default (e.g., Levinson 2000). They first report a picture verification task that tests whether the implicature is drawn if processing is shallow, as predicted by a defaultist approach. The results do not support the defaultist view. Their second experiment investigates whether the probability of drawing an exclusivity implicature in ordinary processing is sensitive to narrow focus on the disjoined NP. Surányi and Fekete take advantage of a marked (or 'non-canonical') syntactic construction in Hungarian in which the constituent being placed in immediately preverbal position is identified as focused. The authors suppose that the syntactically marked narrow focus, rendering the alternatives mentioned in the disjunction more salient, does its job without context. The authors find no effect of focus.

The research of **Andreas Konietzko** and **Karen Lidzba** discusses the language competence of patients with left-hemispheric brain lesions, revealing deficits in non-canonical word orders, such as object topicalization, passivization, and non-canonical argument realizations such as psych-verbs. The authors propose a Default Mapping Hypothesis, which states that the patients prefer direct linking of syntax to argument structure, locating the deficits in the patients' morphosyntactic processing. They propose, however, that these deficits need not be absolute, but can be dependent on how morphosyntactic cues interact: either the cues function cumulatively (Cumulativity Hypothesis), or each factor has a certain weighting that contributes toward the processing of the relevant structure (Cue

Strength Hypothesis). The three experiments yield evidence for both hypotheses, showing that case marking is an effective cue even for patients. We learn that the processing of marked or non-canonical forms is impaired compared to the canonical or unmarked form but that the processing of different marked forms is not equally impaired. Given the tight relationship between markedness of forms and information structural functions, we may assume that the impaired processing of marked forms indicates that patients have particular difficulties in processing information-structural cues. It is possible, however, that information structure, once available in the patients' language processing, helps them to arrive at the correct interpretation of marked forms in an adequate context.

The paper by **Hannah Gerbrich**, **Vivian Schreier**, and **Sam Featherston** is methodological in that it offers a set of standard items for use in linguistic studies. These standard items provide an anchored scale of well-formedness, which allows example sentences to be assigned an absolute well-formedness rating. The scale distinguishes five degrees of well-formedness, and is designed to be simple enough to be accessible even to the intuition of a single person, while at the same time providing a clear advantage in detail over the traditional good, bad, question mark categories applied in the literature. The authors further discuss whether such a scale, which was originally designed for use in syntactic studies, can also be used for work on semantic and pragmatic factors. They conclude that it can, but point out an apparent difference between judgments of syntactic form and interpretational felicity. The collection of more finely gradient data is an important methodological step toward further study of the nuances in acceptability that markedness and focus phenomena trigger.

This volume came about in Tübingen in the intellectual and linguistic context of the Collaborative Research Center SFB 833 *The Construction of Meaning*, which is funded by the Deutsche Forschungsgemeinschaft, without which this work would not have been possible. Many colleagues have contributed to the work reported here and have generously supported us in the selection of the papers and the production of the book. In particular, we should like to thank Sigrid Beck, the chair of the SFB, Marga Reis, for her role in promoting linguistic study in Tübingen over decades, and Beate Starke for making our lives easier on a daily basis.

We should also like to express our profound gratitude to all those who have participated in the review process through which all the papers have gone. Their comments and constructive criticism have greatly aided our optimization of the quality of the papers.

The student assistants have also provided invaluable help in both formatting and manuscript preparation. Finally, we would emphasize our appreciation of the helpful approach and tolerance of the authors, who have been excellent cooperation partners, even when things took a little longer than anticipated.

References

Bader, M. & J. Häussler. 2010. Toward a model of grammaticality judgments. Journal of Linguistics 46(2): 273–330.
Featherston, S. 2005. The Decathlon model of empirical syntax. In (M. Reis & S. Kepser, eds) Linguistic evidence. Empirical, theoretical and computational perspectives, 187–208. Berlin: de Gruyter.
Featherston, S. 2019. The Decathlon model. In (A. Kertész, E. Moravcsik, & C. Rákosi, eds) Current approaches to syntax – a comparative handbook, 155–186. Berlin: de Gruyter Mouton.
Fleischer, J. 2012. Pronominalsyntax im nordwestlichen Niederdeutsch: eine Auswertung des Wenker-Materials (mit Einbezug der friesischen und dänischen Formulare). Niederdeutsches Jahrbuch 135: 59–80.
Höhle, T. 1982. Explikation für "normale Betonung" und „normale Wortstellung".
    In (W. Abraham, ed) Satzglieder im Deutschen, 75–153. Tübingen: Günther Narr Verlag.
Levinson, S.C. 2000. Presumptive Meaning: The Theory of Generalized Conversational Implicature. Cambridge, MA: MIT Press.
Weskott, T., R. Hörnig, G. Fanselow & R. Kliegl. 2011. Contextual licensing of marked OVS word order in German. Linguistische Berichte 225: 3–18.
Zimmermann, M., & E. Onéa. 2011. Focus marking and focus interpretation. Lingua 121: 1651–1670.

Sophia Döring and Sophie Repp
The modal particles *ja* and *doch* and their interaction with discourse structure: Corpus and experimental evidence

1 Introduction

German modal particles have been in the center of linguistic research for several years, the main focus lying on their semantic and pragmatic properties (e.g., Thurmair 1989; Lindner 1991; Jacobs 1991; Waltereit 2001; Karagjosova 2004; Zimmermann 2004, 2012; Gutzmann 2009; Egg 2013; Repp 2013; Rojas-Esponda 2014). Modal particles are usually thought to operate at the semantics-pragmatics interface. The meaning contributions that they have been claimed to make, roughly fall into three types. The first is a modification of the sentence type or the illocution (ary operator) of the utterance they occur in (e.g., Lindner 1991; Jacobs 1991; Waltereit 2001; Karagjosova 2004). For instance, in an assertion a particle may indicate that the speaker is uncertain about committing to the proposition that is asserted, that is, the particle signals that the speaker modifies or cancels a felicity condition of the speech act assertion. The second is that modal particles relate the proposition they scope over to another proposition in the common ground CG (e.g., Karagjosova 2004; Egg 2013; Repp 2013). The other proposition can be a proposition that was at issue in the previous utterance, a felicity condition of the previous utterance, or it can be a proposition that was entailed or implicated by earlier discourse. The third type of meaning contribution is more generally interaction-directed: Modal particles serve as meta-pragmatic instructions (König & Recquart 1991) or as interaction-regulating instructions (Karagjosova 2004) to the hearer (also cf. Franck 1980). The purpose of such instructions is to integrate an utterance into the current discourse context (also cf. Thurmair 1989).

What these meaning types have in common is that they essentially concern common ground management (cf. Repp 2013). Modal particles indicate how a proposition relates to the common ground, and how the common ground is to be developed – by pointing to common or individual knowledge, to epistemic

---

Acknowledgments: This work was supported by the German Research Foundation DFG as part of the Collaborative Research Centre (Sonderforschungsbereich, SFB) 632 *Information Structure* at the Humboldt-Universität zu Berlin. Part of this research was carried out within the PhD project of one of the authors.

https://doi.org/10.1515/9783110623093-002

states, and to expectations of the interlocutors. Common ground management creates and/or enhances discourse coherence and thus serves smooth communication.

For discourses to be coherent they must have a structure. Discourse structure is usually assumed to be hierarchical, and it is assumed that discourse units must be related to other discourse units by discourse relations in a meaningful way (Mann & Thompson 1988; Asher & Lascarides 2003; Hobbs 1985; Sanders, Spooren & Noordman 1992). If, and if so how, modal particles interact with, and contribute to, discourse structure is largely unknown.[1] The goal of the present chapter is to explore the interaction of modal particles and discourse structure by investigating the interplay of modal particles and discourse relations, and thus to contribute to a better understanding of the role that the particles fulfil in the creation of discourse coherence.

To develop an initial idea of the coherence-creating function of modal particles, let us consider the particle *ja*, which occurs in assertions. Assertions come with the preparatory condition that it is not obvious to both speaker and addressee that the addressee knows the asserted proposition *p* (Searle 1969). In other words, the proposition that is asserted must be new. Now, *ja* is generally taken to indicate (roughly), that the speaker assumes that the proposition *ja* scopes over is already part of the common ground, that is, that it is not new (see many of the references above). So by using *ja* in an assertion, the speaker signals that the relevant preparatory condition is cancelled (Waltereit 2001). One may ask why a speaker might want to cancel this preparatory condition. One answer to this question is that the speaker wants to remind the listeners of the proposition (Karagjosova 2004) so that the proposition is retrieved from memory and re-activated in the addressee's mental model of the discourse (Repp 2013). A re-activation can serve coherence purposes in discourse. Consider (1), a discourse consisting of two utterances.

(1) Ann: Peter hat ja seine Geburtstagsfeier abgesagt. Da können
 Peter has JA his birthday.party cancelled then can
 wir am Sonntag einen Ausflug machen.
 we on.the Sunday a trip make
 'As you know, Peter has cancelled his birthday party. So we can go on a trip on Sunday.'

---

[1] But see Rojas-Esponda (2014) for a question-under-discussion approach for *doch*.

The first utterance contains the modal particle *ja*, which suggests that the speaker, Ann, thinks that the proposition *ja* scopes over – p_{ja} – is already in the common ground. If this is indeed the case, *ja* is obligatory in this assertion: without the particle the preparatory condition mentioned above would be violated. The addressee could complain with good cause that Ann's discourse move is redundant. A reaction like *I know that* would be quite natural. In (1), however, Ann is signaling that she chose to violate the preparatory condition and that she wishes to remind the addressee of p_{ja}. We propose that the effect of bringing up p_{ja} in (1) is that p_{ja} is placed in a particular position in the discourse structure. The speaker mentions known information in her first utterance – that is, in the first discourse unit – so that she can attach a second discourse unit. The result is a more coherent discourse because the second unit is not presented in isolation. The two units are in a CAUSE relation: the first unit gives the reason for why it is now possible to go on a trip. We propose that the purpose of relating the two discourse units is the speaker's pre-emption of a rejection of the second assertion by the addressee. Ann probably thought that the addressee might have forgotten that Peter has cancelled his birthday party. As a consequence, the addressee would probably not agree that the proposition *that they can go on a trip on Sunday* should become part of the common ground. The *ja*-utterance facilitates the addition of that proposition to the common ground, where *facilitation* means that the addressee will accept the addition more readily than without the *ja*-utterance.

In the present chapter, we explore how the German modal particles *ja* and *doch* are used by speakers to create discourse coherence and 'smooth' communication (a) by indicating the status of a proposition with respect to the common ground, and (b) by highlighting a proposition's function as a discourse unit in its relation(s) with other discourse units in the current discourse structure. We present evidence from a corpus study and from a forced choice experiment where the former shows for *ja* and *doch* (a) that these particles preferably occur in certain discourse relations while 'avoiding' others, and the experiment reveals (b) that when given the choice between the two particles – whose meaning is closely related – native speakers choose the particle depending on the discourse relation. We argue that these findings can be explained in a model that conceives of modal particles as common ground managing operators that serve the creation and enhancement of discourse coherence. In the next two sections we present our theoretical assumptions about common ground management (Section 2.1) and about discourse structure (Section 3.1) in relation to the meaning contribution of modal particles. In Section 4 we present the corpus study, in Section 5 we present the experiment. Section 6 offers a general discussion and concludes.

2 The meaning and use of *ja* and *doch*

2.1 Common ground and common ground management

To make our ideas about modal particles as common ground managing operators more precise we will formulate them in a model of common ground development that is an adaptation of the model proposed by Farkas & Bruce (2010). The common ground in Farkas & Bruce (2010) is that of Stalnaker (1978), that is, the set of propositions that the interlocutors mutually assume to be true. In addition, there are sets of individual discourse commitments, which keep track of what each interlocutor has publicly committed to during a conversation (cf. Ginzburg 1995; Asher & Lascarides 2003 for similar proposals). Discourse commitments can be understood as the current mental states of the discourse participants. The common ground is the intersection of the individual discourse commitments of all interlocutors plus assumed shared background knowledge. The model furthermore contains a component called *Table*, which records what is currently under discussion. Interlocutors place syntactic objects paired with their denotations on the Table. What is on the Table is *at issue*. Moving an issue to the common ground happens via so-called *projected sets*, which contain future developments of the common ground, and which are projected according to default rules about expected moves by the interlocutors. In the case of assertions, the default move of the addressee is the acceptance of the information on the Table, so after the assertion of a proposition p all possible future common grounds contain p. For polar questions, in contrast, the future common grounds may contain p or $\neg p$.

Farkas & Bruce assume that conversation is driven by two motors. One is to increase the common ground, that is, to increase shared knowledge. The other is to empty the Table and thus to reach a stable state. As a consequence, a discourse move that rejects an interlocutor's utterance is more marked than a move that accepts a previous move. Acceptance leads to the removal of the respective proposition from the Table and to its addition to the common ground, whereas a rejection requires a retraction of a discourse commitment by one of the interlocutors. Rejections therefore are considered to create conversational crises, that is a conversational state, where settling the issue cannot be reached via canonical acceptance. Retraction is a more 'dramatic', non-canonical move. Interlocutors try to avoid conversational crises.

2.2 Proposal for the meaning of *ja* and *doch*

Applying this model to example (1) from the introduction, we can observe two things. The first is that the first utterance is a redundant discourse move since the addition of the proposition p_{ja} does not result in an increased common ground. We will come back to this issue further below. The second observation is that – if we enrich the model in a way to be specified instantly – we correctly predict that making the first discourse move, that is, uttering the *ja*-utterance and reminding the addressee of p_{ja}, is well-motivated because a conversational crisis can be avoided: it is unlikely that the addressee will erroneously reject the second proposition p_2 because s/he believes that $\neg p_{ja}$, which would be inconsistent with p_2: after all s/he has just been reminded of p_{ja}.

Starting with the second observation, note that Farkas & Bruce do not intend their model to account for the development of mental discourse representations that are subject to memory restrictions – which are relevant for forgetting and remembering, and for the mental saliency or non-saliency of knowledge. As a matter of fact, Farkas & Bruce explicitly restrict the model's scope to the Heimean context change potential and exclude aspects that go beyond truth-conditional meaning. However, recall that we argued above for *ja* that in addition to imposing on the common ground the condition that it entails the proposition p_{ja}, *ja* has a reminding function. In other words, *ja* requires p_{ja} to be non-salient prior to the assertion of p_{ja}. If p_{ja} were salient, it would not necessary to remind the listener of p_{ja}. The reminder *makes* the proposition p_{ja} salient, which, as we suggested above, can have the effect of avoiding a conversational crisis. Therefore, it seems that a model of common ground management must incorporate attributes like saliency. This is what we will assume from now on (also cf. Karagjosova 2004 on the differential accessibility of propositions in the set of discourse commitments depending on the mental activation status of the propositions).

Returning to the first observation mentioned above, namely that the *ja*-utterance in (1) is redundant because p_{ja} is taken to be already in the common ground, one might wonder whether in the model of Farkas & Bruce p_{ja} is placed on and removed from the Table like a new proposition. The answer to this question must be *yes* because an interlocutor might not agree with the speaker's assumption that the proposition is already in the common ground, or s/he might altogether disagree with the truth of the proposition. Indeed, discourses like (2) – which is a continuation of (1) – are felicitous: the addressee in (2), Ben, rejects p_{ja}, by publicly committing to $\neg p$ and placing $\neg p$ on the Table. As a consequence, the projected set is inconsistent. A conversational crisis arises. One of the speakers must retract his/her commitment.

(2) Ann: Peter hat ja seine Geburtstagsfeier abgesagt. Da können wir am
Sonntag einen Ausflug machen. (= (1))
'As you know, Peter has cancelled his birthday party. So we can go on
a trip on Sunday.'

Ben: Peter hat seinen Geburtstag NICHT[2] abgesagt. Maria hat
Peter has his birthday not cancelled Maria has
das nur behauptet, um ihn zu ärgern.
that only claimed in.order him to annoy
'Peter hasn't cancelled his birthday. Maria only said that to annoy him.'

There is a question here whether the rejection is a rejection of the presupposition or of the assertion that p. Note that Ben might also react to Ann's first utterance by saying: *What? How I am supposed to know that Peter has cancelled his party!?*, thus rejecting the presupposition. Alternatively, his utterance might be preceded by a simple *No!*, which would indicate that he rejects the assertion. This observation can be taken as further evidence for our proposal above that attributes like saliency must be part of the common ground: the distinction between a proposition being in the common ground vs. not being in the common ground is not sufficient to describe the meaning contribution of *ja*. The utterance of p_{ja} changes the internal make-up of the common ground with respect to saliency. If, after a *ja*-utterance, the addressee confirms p_{ja} – by explicitly committing to it or by just remaining silent, s/he accepts this update of the common ground.

Turning to the modal particle *doch*, consider the discourse in (3). Ann places the proposition that *Maria is coming to Peter's birthday party* (=p_1), on the Table. Then, Ben places the proposition that *Peter has cancelled his party* (=p_2) on the Table, which results in inconsistent projected sets. p_1 comes with the presupposition q, *that there is a birthday party for Peter*. Since presuppositions are placed on the Table like any other non-at-issue information (Döring 2016),[3] all projected sets contain q as well as p_2, which cannot both be true because p_2 entails $\neg q$. The result is a conversational crisis. One of the speakers has to retract his/her commitment.

---

2 Small caps indicate prosodic stress.
3 This assumption is in conflict with Farkas & Bruce's (2010) proposal that what is on the Table is *at issue*, as presuppositions etc. are obviously not at issue. However, considering that denials can target non-at-issue content (Horn 1989, Van der Sandt 1991), and considering that the Table is the locus for negotiations about what is in or will be in the common ground, this proposal needs a qualification. We assume with Döring (2016) that non-at-issue content is placed on the Table but is marked for being not at issue.

(3) Ann: Maria kommt auch zu Peters Geburtstagsfeier.
　　　　 Maria comes also to Peter's birthday.party
　　　　 'Maria is also coming to Peter's birthday party.'

Ben: Peter hat die Feier doch abgesagt.
　　　 Peter has the party DOCH cancelled
　　　 'But Peter has cancelled the party – you should know that.'

Now, Ben uses *doch* in his reply, which similarly to *ja* signals that the speaker assumes that the respective proposition, $p_2 = p_{doch}$, is already in the common ground,[4] and in addition signals that p_{doch} is in conflict with a proposition in the discourse, that is, that a common ground containing both propositions would be inconsistent. Thus, *doch* signals the cancellation of the same preparatory condition as *ja*. However, different from *ja*, *doch* signals that p_{doch} in (3) is marked as being in the common ground against the evidence that the speaker has just received: Ann cannot be committed to p_{doch} – she has put q on the Table – so p_{doch} cannot be in the common ground – according to Ann. So why does Ben use *doch*? We suggest that *doch* is used in (3) to resolve a conversational crisis in a quick and efficient way, 'quick' meaning that Ann will retract her commitment to p_1 without further discussion. If Ann is reminded by Ben that she is already committed to a proposition that is inconsistent with p_1, and if Ann accepts the reminder as correct, she might be more easily inclined to retract p_1, and the Table can be cleared.[5] Note that Ben's utterance without the particle would be coherent: *doch* is not required to mark the inconsistency in the projected sets. However, without *doch*, Ben's utterance would not be a reminder. Ben would be signaling that he is conveying new information, which would have to be negotiated between the two interlocutors, like any other new information.

The examples that we have discussed up to now involve dialogues with affirming and rejecting moves, and we have sketched our ideas of how modal particles may contribute to pre-empting or resolving conversational crises, and thus making discourses (more) coherent. As modal particles can also occur in monologues, the question arises of what their function in these contexts is. We propose that the particles essentially have the same coherence-creating function

---

[4] There may be examples in which *ja* or *doch* seem to be used out-of-the-blue. For cases in which the addressee indeed did not know $p_{ja/doch}$ before, we argue that the proposition is accommodated.

[5] Note that *doch* cannot be replaced with *ja* in (3). Since the stricter discourse conditions of *doch* (i.e. that the common ground entails, presupposes or implicates $\neg p_{doch}$) are met in this discourse, *doch* has to be used.

as in dialogues. For instance, the conflict-marking meaning contribution of *doch* may be used to make explicit the kind of discourse relation the speaker intends the (quiet) addressee to extract from the monologue, which will enable the addressee to construct a coherent discourse structure and pre-empt or quickly resolve a(n implicit) conversational crisis and/or incomprehension. In the next section we will discuss in what way modal particles may interact with discourse structure and discourse relations.

3 Predictions for discourse structure

3.1 Discourse structure and discourse relations

A general assumption in theories of discourse structure and discourse coherence (e.g., Hobbs 1985; Grosz & Sidner 1986; Mann & Thompson 1988; Sanders & Spooren & Noordman 1992; Carlson & Marcu 2001; Kehler 2002; Asher & Lascarides 2003) is that discourses consist of discourse units, which are connected to each other by meaning relations. Elementary discourse units, *EDUs*, basically correspond to clauses. They combine to larger units such that units and relations form a hierarchical structure. A basic assumption shared by all discourse theories is that most relations are asymmetric in the sense that one unit is more central to the overall topic of the discourse than the other, so that deleting the less central unit would alter the discourse in a less substantial way than deleting the more central unit. In Rhetorical Structure Theory (RST) (Mann & Thompson 1988; Mann & Taboada 2005–2015) – the theory which serves as the theoretical background for the corpus study to be presented further below – the more central unit is called the *nucleus*. The less central unit is called the *satellite*. The satellite has a specific function relative to the nucleus, which depends on the particular discourse relation. For instance, in a BACKGROUND relation[6] the satellite provides background information, which is supposed to facilitate the comprehension of the information given in the nucleus. The order of nucleus and satellite is flexible in most relations. In addition to asymmetric relations, there are symmetric relations, which consist of two or more nuclei and hence are called *multinuclear* relations (as opposed to the asymmetric *mononuclear* relations). In multinuclear relations, two or more units of the same importance are related.

---

[6] See the Appendix for definitions and examples of the RST discourse relations discussed in this chapter.

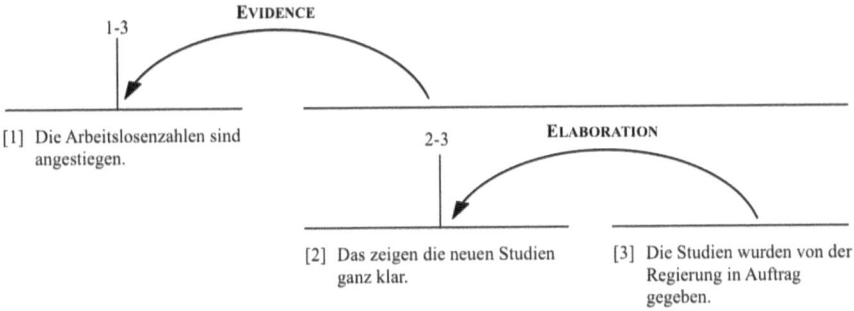

Figure 1: Discourse structure for (4).

The discourses in (4) and (5) illustrate the hierarchical organization of discourses, the relation between nuclei and their satellites, and the variable directionality of the relation between nucleus and satellite. Both discourses consist of three sentences, which correspond to three EDUs, but they differ both in the relations they involve and in the structure they have. In (4), EDU [3] elaborates on the information provided in EDU [2], so the two are in an ELABORATION relation. [2] and [3] form a larger unit which is related to EDU [1] by an EVIDENCE relation, cf. Figure 1. The vertical lines in Figure 1 mark the EDUs that are nuclei. The numbers indicate the sequence of units that make up the discourse relation containing the nucleus, for example, [2] in Figure 1 is the nucleus of the relation holding between [2] and [3].

(4) [1] Die Arbeitslosenzahlen sind angestiegen.
      the unemployment.figures are risen
  [2] Das zeigen die neuen Studien ganz klar.
      that show the new studies very clearly
  [3] Die Studien wurden von der Regierung in Auftrag gegeben.
      The studies were by the government in order given
  '[1] The unemployment rate has risen. [2] The new studies show this very clearly. [3] These studies have been commissioned by the government.'

In (5), EDU [1] provides the CAUSE for what is described in EDU [2]. EDU [3] is attached to EDU [2] by an EVALUATION relation. Thus, EDU [2] serves as the nucleus for two relations, cf. Figure 2. The satellite of the CAUSE relation precedes the nucleus, and the satellite of the EVALUATION relation follows the nucleus.

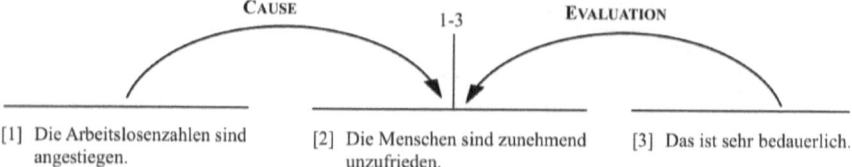

[1] Die Arbeitslosenzahlen sind angestiegen. [2] Die Menschen sind zunehmend unzufrieden. [3] Das ist sehr bedauerlich.

Figure 2: Discourse structure for (5).

(5) [1] Die   Arbeitslosenzahlen   sind angestiegen.
         the   unemployment.figures   are   risen
    [2] Die   Menschen   sind   zunehmend   unzufrieden.
         the   people   are   increasingly unhappy
    [3] Das   ist   sehr   bedauerlich.
         this   is   very   deplorable
    '[1] The unemployment rate has risen. [2] People are more and more unhappy. [3] This is deplorable.'

The number and characteristics of the relations proposed in existing discourse theories differ considerably. Grosz & Sidner (1986) propose a basic distinction of two relations, Mann & Thompson (1988) introduce a set of 23 relations, and Carlson & Marcu (2001) define over 70 relations. The number of relations assumed in these theories is largely a result of the different research questions pursued and the ensuing methodology that is employed for classification, for example, a bottom-up strategy starting from a classification of connectives or a top-down strategy starting from very basic cognitive categories. The set of relations in Mann & Thompson's (1988) RST (including later modifications; Mann & Taboada 2005–2015), is a medium-sized set of relations that has been developed on the basis of corpus work, see Section 4 for details.

3.2 Predictions for *ja* and *doch*

Turning to the interplay of the modal particles *ja* and *doch* with discourse relations and discourse structure, we first consider the meaning component that the two particles share, namely that of marking the proposition they scope over as already being in the common ground. From this meaning component we predict that *ja* and *doch* often occur in discourse relations where one of the discourse units is likely to contain known information. For instance, as already mentioned, the satellite in the BACKGROUND relation provides information that helps the addressee to understand the information given in the nucleus. We may assume that if the satellite presents information that is already known this will be useful in understanding the nucleus. If, in addition, the information presented in the satellite is *marked* as known by *ja/doch* this might further contribute to the acceptance of the nucleus. Note, however, that BACKGROUND relations have also been attributed a wider meaning in the sense that the satellite may give a definition of a concept or information to 'set the stage' for an event or another argument (cf. Asher, Prévot & Vieu 2007). In principle, the satellite can thus offer known or new information.

There are also discourse relations where the satellite by definition contains new or non-factive information, so we predict that *ja* and *doch* do not occur in the satellite of such relations. The ELABORATION and CONDITION relations are a case in point. (6) illustrates the infelicitous use of *ja* in the satellite of an ELABORATION relation. ELABORATION is defined in a very general way in RST, viz. as presenting additional information. Mann & Thompson (1988) propose that adding information can take many forms so that nucleus and satellite constitute pairings like *generalization – specific, process – step, object – attribute*, among others. We may assume that speakers provide additional information because it is new.

(6) [1] Maria fährt dieses Jahr nach Österreich.
     Maria goes this year to Austria
   [2] Sie geht (#ja) in Kitzbühel wandern.
     she goes JA in Kitzbühel hike
   'Maria is going to Austria this year. She is going hiking in Kitzbühel – as you should know.'

Next recall that *doch* has the additional meaning component of indicating that a proposition in the context is inconsistent with the proposition that *doch* scopes over, that is, that of indicating a conflict. Because of this meaning component we expect *doch* to occur in discourse relations that involve conflict or contrast. Prima facie these are CONTRAST, CONCESSION, and ANTITHESIS. CONTRAST is a multinuclear relation where there are similarities and differences between the two nuclei. A connector typically occurring in CONTRAST relations is *but*. (7)B shows that *doch* can occur in a CONTRAST relation (EDUs [1]–[2]). Note, however, that the contrast expressed by the relation does not correspond to the contrast/conflict that *doch* hints at: *doch* indicates that EDU [2] is in contrast with something speaker A insinuated before, namely that both of Peter's parents are tall – which B expected A to know. Without the context, B's second utterance (EDUs [1]–[2]) would be an infelicitous discourse.

(7) A: Peter ist sehr groß. Das ist kein Wunder bei seinen Eltern.
     Peter is very tall that is no wonder with his parents
   'Peter is very tall. This is not really surprising, looking at his parents.'

B: Warum?
   why
   [1] Peters   Vater   ist   groß,
       Peter's   father   is   tall
   [2] aber   seine   Mutter   ist   doch   klein.
       but   his   mother   is   DOCH   short
   'Why? His father is tall but his mother is short.'

We tentatively suggest that the failure of *doch* to point to the same contrast as the CONTRAST relation is due to the CONTRAST relation being a multinuclear, that is, symmetric discourse relation. There is no satellite whose function – such as that of enabling the addressee to better understand the nucleus in the BACKGROUND relation – can be enhanced/highlighted by the modal particle. We will see presently that this problem does not arise in the other, mononuclear contrastive discourse relations. With respect to the occurrence of *doch* in CONTRAST we suggest that the particle does not actually occur in CONTRAST more often than in other, non-contrastive relations, due to the symmetry of the relation.

In a CONCESSION relation, which is a mononuclear contrastive relation that often is signaled by connectors like *although* or *even though*, the speaker acknowledges that there is a potential or apparent incompatibility between nucleus and satellite but expresses that this incompatibility is not genuine: s/he endorses the nucleus and expresses that the satellite is no real obstacle for accepting the nucleus (cf. Mann & Thompson 1992). The discourse in (8) contains a CONCESSION relation; the second clause is the satellite.

(8) Alle   Kandidaten   hatten   Schwierigkeiten.   Dabei   ist   die   Aufgabe
    all   candidates   had   difficulties   although   is   the   task
    (doch)   nicht   schwer.
    DOCH   not   hard
    'All candidates had difficulties – even though the task is not hard.'

We suggest that one effect of adding *doch* to the satellite in this example is to increase the degree of the apparent incompatibility between nucleus and satellite, that is, the contrastiveness between the discourse units is increased. The speaker seems to express his/her wonderment at the fact that all candidates had difficulties with a certain task in view of the known fact that the task was not difficult. So, *doch* here seems to highlight that adding the nucleus to the common ground is not a matter of course: the speaker signals that the acceptance of the nucleus might be difficult. Still s/he expects the hearer to accept the nucleus. We propose that the particle helps the listener to recognize the discourse relation as one involving a conflict, which might prompt the listener to discuss a possible conflict resolution in the subsequent discourse but will not lead to a rejection of the proposition(s) at issue.

We will see later in the discussion of the corpus results that (8) is actually an untypical example for the occurrence of *doch* in a CONCESSION relation: in CONCESSIONS, *doch* typically occurs in the nucleus rather than in the satellite. We will come back to this issue further below.

In an ANTITHESIS relation, there is a 'genuine' incompatibility between nucleus and satellite. We will concentrate here on ANTITHESES whose satellite contains a negation, see (9).[7] In the discussion section we provide a detailed analysis also of an example with a non-negative satellite. In example (9), the 'genuine' incompatibility between nucleus and satellite is an incompatibility between the proposition denoted by the nucleus and the non-negated proposition in the satellite. In the satellite, the speaker rejects the idea that Peter could take the place of Andrew. We assume that like in the CONCESSION relation in (8), *doch* helps the listener to recognize the discourse relation as one involving conflict. As in the previous example, nucleus and satellite (which – including the meaning contribution of the negation – conveys given, and thus uncontroversial information), are expected to be accepted by the listener more easily if the speaker draws particular attention to the conflict (and thus pre-empts protest).

(9) Wir sollten Andrew nehmen. Peter kommt (doch) nicht in Frage.
    we should Andrew take   Peter comes DOCH not in question
    'We should take Andrew. Peter is out of the question.'

In the next section we will see that there are other discourse relations where *ja* and *doch* occur frequently, although in view of the meaning contribution that has been suggested for the two particles these relations at first sight are no prime candidates for hosting the particles. Still, we will see that, overall, particles serve to increase the acceptance of propositions into the common ground.

4 Corpus study: Modal particles in political speeches

The corpus study served to verify our ideas about the occurrence of the modal particles *ja* and *doch* in particular discourse relations and their function for the

---

[7] This example also is felicitous with stressed *doch*, which has a different meaning from unstressed *doch* (Egg & Zimmermann 2012). We are only interested in the variant with unstressed *doch* here.

establishment of discourse coherence in our model of common ground management by a quantitative analysis of naturally occurring discourses. The corpus chosen for the study was a corpus of the official transcripts[8] of 28 speeches (126.112 word tokens) by Helmut Kohl, who was the chancellor of Germany from 1982 to 1998. The speeches were given in the German Federal parliament (*Bundestag*) in the period from 1996 to 1999.[9] This corpus was chosen for three reasons. First, it contained sufficiently long contributions to individual topics such that the discourse structure could be determined with suitable consistency during annotation. Second, it was a corpus of spoken language, which in the case of modal particles – which occur more frequently in spoken than in written language – ensured the occurrence of a sufficient number of modal particles. Finally, speeches are directed at a concrete audience, so that they are closer to dialogues than are other monologic text types (such as novels and newspaper texts).

4.1 Data annotation

The corpus is annotated for *part of speech*, automatically analyzed by *TreeTagger* (Schmidt 1994) using the *Stuttgart Tübingen Tagset* (STTS; Schiller et al. 1999). Within STTS, modal particles are assigned the label ADV, that is, they are not distinguished from adverbs and from other particles. Since *ja* and *doch* have homographs that are answer particles or conjunctions, they were distinguished manually from these homographs and were annotated as 'MP'. There were 364 occurrences of *doch* and 112 occurrences of *ja*.[10]

For the annotation of the discourse relations which the EDUs containing a modal particle (=EDU_{MP}) had with other discourse units, the 23 discourse relations of RST (Mann & Thompson 1988; Mann & Taboada 2005–2015) were used as a tag set.[11] As there is no one-to-one correspondence between linguistic cues

---

8 Slips of the tongue, interjections, truncations are removed by the official transcribers. An exemplary comparison of an audio file and the respective manuscript shows that some of the originally contained modal particles are removed, too.
9 Parliament speeches in general are available via the German *Bundestag*, the corpus used here is a subcorpus of a large corpus of parliament speeches from various speakers (> 36 million tokens), which has already been annotated for part of speech by the Department for German Studies and Linguistics at Humboldt-University and is freely available via a corpus search interface (https://www.linguistik.hu-berlin.de/en/institut-en/professuren-en/korpuslinguistik/korpora/cqp).
10 Particles occurring in interjections by the audience are ignored in the analysis.
11 We did not distinguish between volitionality and non-volitionality in CAUSE and RESULT. CAUSE and RESULT are in fact 'flip versions' of each other: the nucleus in CAUSE would be the

and discourse relations (except for certain conjunctions, e.g., *because* signals CAUSE relations), a close inspection of the surrounding context was required to assign the appropriate relation. To identify the discourse relation that an EDU$_{MP}$ had with other discourse units a step-wise procedure was applied. First, the relation that the EDU$_{MP}$ had with its adjacent EDUs was determined provided there was such a relation. If there was none, for instance, in cases where the EDU$_{MP}$ occurred at the end of a speech so that there was no right context and the EDU$_{MP}$ did not attach to the EDU on its immediate left, further context was taken into consideration. The nearest (in terms of hierarchical closeness) elementary or non-elementary discourse unit with which the EDU$_{MP}$ had a discourse relation was the one that was annotated. Typically, such a unit was identified in the left context. Furthermore, each EDU$_{MP}$ was annotated for its role as nucleus vs. satellite of the respective discourse relation. Although EDUs can be involved in more than one discourse relation (see above), only one discourse relation was counted for each EDU$_{MP}$ for the statistical analysis of the data that we report below. In most cases, this was the relation in which the EDU$_{MP}$ was the satellite. The reasoning behind this decision was that our goal was to find out what function the particle in EDU$_{MP}$, and by extension what function the EDU$_{MP}$ itself has in relation to the nucleus of the relation. In this sense it is more 'informative' to consider the satellite in a discourse relation.

4.2 Data analysis

Since not all discourse relations occur with the same frequency, a baseline was needed to assess the frequency of occurrence of the modal particles relative to the overall distribution of the discourse relations. As the annotation of discourse relations is extremely time-consuming, a sub-corpus of the corpus was used to create this baseline: three of the Parliament speeches (27.000 tokens)[12] were annotated in their entirety for discourse relations, that is, for all discourse units irrespective of the presence or absence of a modal particle. We refer to this sub-corpus as the *reference corpus*. The distribution of relations in the reference corpus is given in Figure 3.

---

satellite in RESULT and vice versa. It is the task of the annotator to decide which EDU is more central to the overall discourse topic, and thus which EDU is the nucleus and which EDU is the satellite.

[12] Speech #1: session 86, Bonn, February 8, 1996; speech #4: session 121, Bonn, September 11, 1996; speech #16: session 206, Bonn, November 26, 1997.

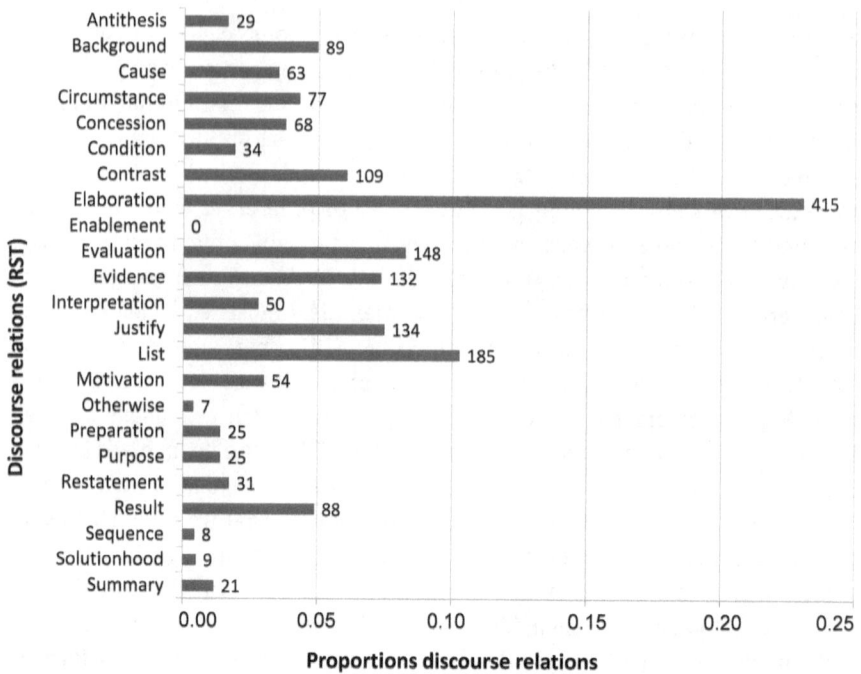

Figure 3: General distribution of RST relations based on the analysis of three speeches, reference corpus (1801 discourse relations). The numbers at the end of each bar are the raw frequencies.

Figure 3 shows that the frequency of occurrence of the individual relations is quite variable. The relation ELABORATION occurs extremely frequently. We assume that this is not necessarily due to the text type of the present corpus, parliament speeches, but rather that it is a consequence of the fact that ELABORATION is defined in a very general way in RST (cf. Section 3.1). SEQUENCE, in contrast, is a relation hardly used in the corpus. We assume that this is text type specific. A SEQUENCE describes a temporal order of events (*first X happened, then Y*), and is more likely to occur in narratives than in argumentative parliament speeches.

With respect to the distribution of modal particles relative to the distribution of discourse relations, the null hypothesis is that modal particles occur equally often in all relations. The *expected frequency* n_{exp} of occurrence of a particle in a discourse relation is therefore the number of occurrences of the discourse relation in the corpus relative to the overall number of discourse relations in the corpus multiplied by the number of occurrences of the respective particle in the corpus (e.g., $n_{ja} = 112$), for example:

(10) Expected frequency of occurrence n_{exp} for *ja* in the BACKGROUND relation
$n_{exp.(ja/B)} = n_B/n_{total} \times n_{ja} = 89/1801 \times 112 = 5.53$

4.3 Results

Table 1 shows the expected and observed frequencies for the occurrence of *ja* and *doch* for the discourse relations in which the discourse unit containing the modal particle, EDU_{MP}, occurred. It also indicates for each mononuclear discourse relation how often the EDU_{MP} was the satellite in the respective discourse relation (counts and proportions). Figure 4 illustrates the distribution of *ja* in the discourse relations that are most relevant for our discussion further below, Figure 5 does the same for *doch*.

The statistical analysis of the observed frequency of occurrence of the two modal particles in the different discourse relations revealed that they are not equally distributed. We present the results first for *ja*, and then for *doch*. For *ja*, an exact multinomial goodness of fitness test[13] (R package EMT; Menzel 2013) showed that the observed frequencies differ significantly from the expected frequencies ($p < .0001$). Subsequent exact binomial goodness of fit tests conducted for each discourse relation (with Holm-Bonferroni corrected α-levels for multiple comparisons) revealed significantly higher observed frequencies than expected for the relations BACKGROUND ($p < .001$) and EVIDENCE ($p < .05$), and significantly lower observed frequencies than expected for the relations ELABORATION ($p < .001$) and List ($p < .001$). In all mononuclear relations, the modal particle occurred exclusively or almost exclusively in the satellite.

For *doch*, an exact multinomial goodness of fitness test showed that the observed frequencies differ significantly from the expected frequencies ($p < .0001$). Subsequent exact binomial goodness of fit tests conducted for each discourse relation (with Holm-Bonferroni corrected α-levels for multiple comparisons) revealed significantly higher observed frequencies than expected for the relations ANTITHESIS ($p < .05$), CONCESSION ($p < .05$), EVIDENCE ($p < .01$), INTERPRETATION ($p < .01$), JUSTIFY ($p < .001$), and MOTIVATION ($p < .001$), and significantly lower observed frequencies than expected for the relations CIRCUMSTANCE ($p < .001$), CONDITION ($p < .05$), CONTRAST ($p < .01$), ELABORATION ($p < .001$), and LIST ($p < .001$). In the relations ANTITHESIS, CAUSE, CONCESSION, and MOTIVATION, *doch* occurred more often in the nucleus than in the satellite.

---

[13] Due to the high number of categories and the concomitant memory limitations for the computation the multinomial tests reported above were run with a Monte Carlo simulation with 106 withdrawals.

Table 1: Expected and observed frequencies of *ja* and *doch* in the corpus.

Discourse Relation	Discourse relation in reference corpus			*ja* in corpus			*doch* in corpus		
	Frequency n	Proportion	n_{exp}	n_{obs}	n_{obs} and ($prop_{obs}$) in satellite	n_{exp}	n_{obs}	n_{obs} and ($prop_{obs}$) in satellite	
ANTITHESIS	29	.02	1.8	1	0	5.9	14	4	(.29)
BACKGROUND	89	.05	5.5	32	32 (1.0)	18.0	22	21	(.95)
CAUSE	63	.03	3.9	10	10 (1.0)	12.7	13	11	(.85)
CIRCUMSTANCE	77	.04	4.8	0	–	15.6	0	–	
CONCESSION	68	.04	4.2	5	4 (.8)	13.7	26	4	(.15)
CONDITION	34	.02	2.1	0	–	6.9	0	–	
CONTRAST	109	.06	6.8	3	n.a.	22.0	7	n.a.	
ELABORATION	415	.23	25.8	3	3 (1.0)	83.9	16	16 (1.0)	
ENABLEMENT	0	.00	0.0	2	2 (1.0)	0.0	2	2 (1.0)	
EVALUATION	148	.08	9.2	10	10 (1.0)	29.9	23	23 (1.0)	
EVIDENCE	132	.07	8.2	19	19 (1.0)	26.7	47	47 (1.0)	
INTERPRETATION	50	.03	3.1	4	4 (1.0)	10.1	23	23 (1.0)	
JUSTIFY	134	.07	8.3	15	15 (1.0)	27.1	86	86 (1.0)	
LIST	185	.10	11.5	0	n.a.	37.4	0	n.a.	
MOTIVATION	54	.03	3.4	5	4 (.8)	10.9	59	13	(.28)

Table 1 (continued)

Discourse Relation	Discourse relation in reference corpus			ja in corpus			doch in corpus		
	Frequency n	Proportion	n_{exp}	n_{obs}	n_{obs} and $(prop_{obs})$ in satellite	n_{exp}	n_{obs}	n_{obs} and $(prop_{obs})$ in satellite
OTHERWISE	7	.00	0.4	1	1 (1.0)	1.4	0	–
PREPARATION	25	.01	1.6	0	–	5.1	0	–
PURPOSE	25	.01	1.6	0	–	5.1	1	1 (1.0)
RESTATEMENT	31	.02	1.9	0	–	6.3	4	3 (.75)
RESULT	88	.05	5.5	1	1 (1.0)	17.8	20	20 (1.0)
SEQUENCE	8	.00	0.5	0	n.a.	1.6	0	n.a.
SOLUTIONHOOD	9	.00	0.6	0	–	1.8	2	2 (1.0)
SUMMARY	21	.01	1.3	1	1 (1.0)	4.2	1	1

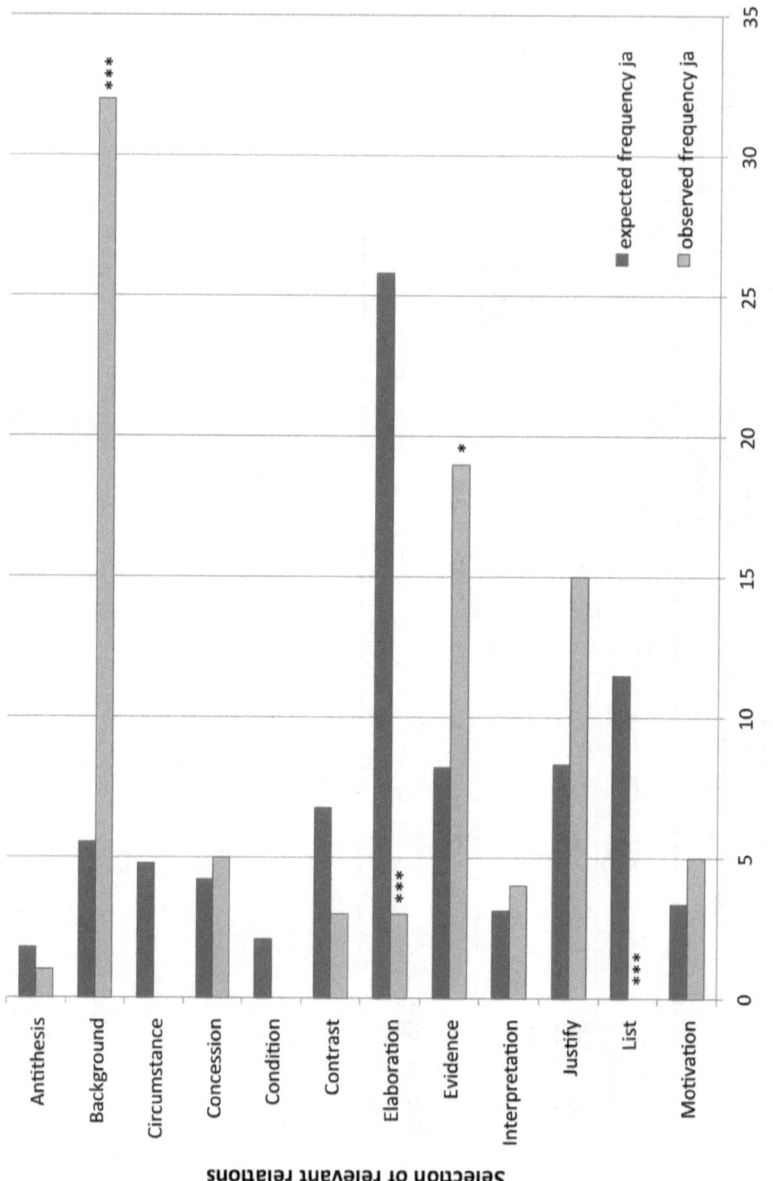

Figure 4: Expected and observed frequencies of *ja* in selected DRs. (* = α-level < .05, corrected; *** = α-level < .001, corrected).

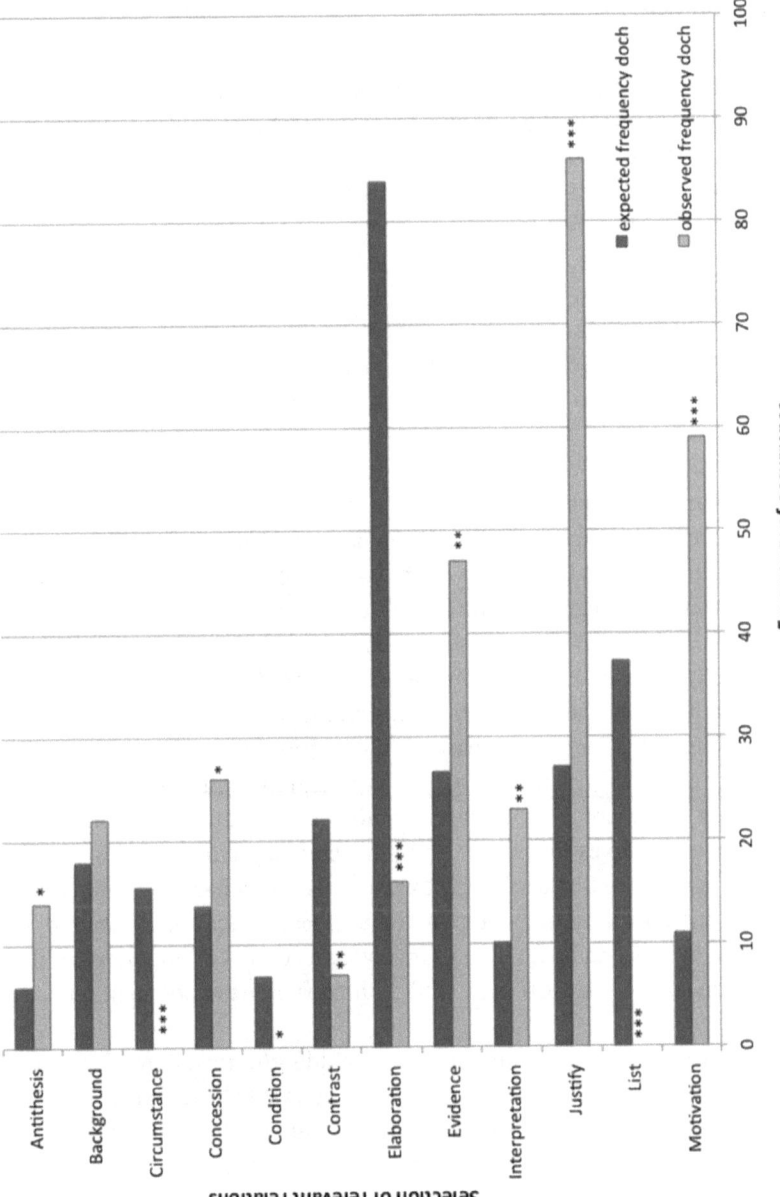

Figure 5: Expected and observed frequencies of *doch* in selected DRs. (* = α-level < .05, corrected; *** = α-level < .001, corrected).

4.4 Discussion

The corpus analysis showed that the frequency of occurrence of the modal particles *ja* and *doch* varies with the discourse relation in which the EDU$_{MP}$ occurs. For *ja*, we found that the particle occurs more often than expected in BACKGROUND and in EVIDENCE relations, and less often than expected in ELABORATION and LIST relations. For *doch*, we found that it occurs more often than expected in ANTITHESIS, CONCESSION, EVIDENCE, INTERPRETATION, and MOTIVATION relations, and less often than expected in ELABORATION, CONDITION, CONTRAST, CIRCUMSTANCE, and LIST relations. Some of these findings confirm our predictions. No finding is at odds with our predictions but we had not made predictions for all the discourse relations that the analysis revealed to preferably host or not host *ja* and *doch* respectively.

For both *ja* and *doch* we predicted that due to their function to indicate that the proposition they scope over is already in the common ground, they should occur particularly often in the satellite of the BACKGROUND relation. This prediction was confirmed for *ja* but not for *doch*. There might be two reasons for why *doch* does not occur frequently in the BACKGROUND relation. The first is that *ja* is preferred over *doch* because *ja* only has the reminding/retrieval function whereas *doch* is more complex and involves an additional meaning component so that if the intention of the speaker is merely to remind the addressee, *ja* is 'enough' to express this intention. The second reason is the nature of the additional meaning component of *doch*: it is plausible that the conflict-indicating function of *doch* is not actually that smoothly compatible with a BACKGROUND relation, where the satellite merely serves the easier comprehension of the nucleus. Rather, the conflict that is indicated by *doch* might always also be reflected in the type of discourse relation involved, for example, the presence of *doch* might lead to the interpretation of a discourse relation as involving a conflict or apparent conflict like ANTITHESIS or CONCESSION (also cf. the findings of the experiment reported in Section 5).

We furthermore predicted that due their reminding/retrieval function *ja* and *doch* should be incompatible with discourse relations that by definition provide new information or present non-factive content, that is, information that is not in the common ground and for which reminding therefore is not possible. The corpus analysis revealed that, as predicted, the two particles occur less frequently than expected in the ELABORATION relation. We also found that *doch* occurs less often than expected in the CONDITION relation. For *ja* we did not obtain this latter result. However, note that the expected number of occurrences for *ja* in the CONDITION relation was four, and the observed number of occurrences was zero.

Thus, we may assume that the statistical null effect is a consequence of a lack of statistical power. The raw number goes in the right direction and it represents the lowest number possible.

Staying with *ja*, which only has the reminding/retrieval function, the corpus analysis also revealed that the particle occurs frequently in the EVIDENCE relation, which is a result that we had not predicted. The EVIDENCE relation differs from the BACKGROUND relation in that the satellite is not used to increase the addressee's ability to understand the information conveyed in the nucleus, but to increase the addressee's belief in the information conveyed in the nucleus: the speaker provides a piece of evidence that may serve as proof for what is said in the nucleus. We may plausibly assume that if a piece of evidence is, or is signaled to be, already in the common ground its effect as proof might be more efficient. Thus, we propose that the speaker exploits the meaning of *ja* to strengthen his/her argument: the proposition *ja* scopes over is signaled to be already in the common ground and thus uncontroversial and unassailable. Therefore, it can serve as a very good argument for whatever the speaker wishes to say in the nucleus. So the EVIDENCE relation like the BACKGROUND relation involves a satellite that enhances the chance that the addressee accepts the proposition denoted by the nucleus into common ground.

Another non-predicted finding for *ja* was the low number of occurrences of the particle in the LIST relation. We suggest that in this multinuclear relation, an EDU$_{MP}$ with *ja* cannot (or cannot easily) fulfil its role of enhancing the acceptance of another proposition because the two EDUs that are involved are of equal importance, that is, are symmetric, whereas the common ground managing function of *ja* seems to rely on an asymmetric discourse relation. A similar observation can be made for *doch* which neither occurs in the LIST relation. We assume that the symmetry of the LIST relation is not compatible with the common ground managing function of *ja* and *doch*. This proposal essentially is the same as the one that we made for the CONTRAST relation in Section 3.1. CONTRAST also is symmetrical and does not seem to be easily compatible with *doch*. We will see instantly that the corpus results corroborate this assumption for *doch*.

Turning to the other findings for *doch*, we observe that the two contrastive discourse relations that we predicted *doch* to occur in, CONCESSION and ANTITHESIS, indeed frequently contained *doch*. And just as we suspected, the symmetric CONTRAST relation does not often contain an *EDU$_{MP}$* with *doch*. As a matter of fact, *doch* occurs very infrequently in the CONTRAST relation. We interpret this finding as support for our hypothesis, that *ja* and *doch* preferably occur in asymmetric relations. We will elaborate on this issue in the discussion session.

With respect to CONCESSION and ANTITHESIS, it is quite surprising that contrary to what we hypothesized in Section 3.1, *doch* did not occur particularly often in the *satellite* of CONCESSION and ANTITHESIS relations but in the *nucleus*. For instance, in (11) EDU [1] is the satellite of the CONCESSION relation with EDU [2], the nucleus, which contains *doch*.

(11) [1] Wenn ich es auch bejahe, dass wir es im Augenblick tun,
      if   I it also approve that we it at.the moment do
    [2] so kann es aber langfristig doch nicht so bleiben.
      so can it but long-run   DOCH not so stay
    '[1] Although I approve of our current practice, [2] things cannot stay like this in the long run.' (Speech #22, 109358)

Recall that in a CONCESSION the speaker acknowledges that there is a potential or apparent incompatibility between nucleus and satellite but considers the satellite no real obstacle for accepting the nucleus. We argued earlier that placing *doch* in the satellite of a CONCESSION helps the listener to recognize the conflict that is expressed in this discourse relation, with the effect that both speaker and listener agree that accepting the nucleus might be difficult but should nevertheless be done. The corpus findings suggest that placing the particle in the nucleus is more effective. We propose that *doch* still marks the conflict, but by indicating that the proposition denoted by the nucleus (rather than the one denoted by the satellite) is already in the common ground, the particle helps dismissing the 'difficulty' presented in the satellite. Thus, it is not generally the case that *ja* and *doch* always "do their work" in the satellite of a discourse relation. Rather, this seems to depend on the precise discourse semantics of the relation and the concomitant intentions of the speaker.

Turning to ANTITHESES, first consider (12). EDU$_{MP}$ [2] with *doch* is the nucleus for two satellites (complex [1], and [3]), both relations being ANTITHESES. We assume that, as in the CONCESSION example above, *doch* marks the proposition denoted by the nucleus as uncontroversial, thus highlighting the incompatibility with the conflicting satellite(s). Note that the satellite in the ANTITHESIS [2]–[3] contains a negation whereas the satellite in [1]–[2] does not. The conflict in [2]–[3] is a conflict with the non-negated proposition denoted by [3] (*Someone else overthrew Helmut Schmidt*). The conflict in [1]–[2] is a conflict with the listener's claim in 1982 (*that the Free Democrats were involved in the overthrow of Helmut Schmidt*). So in neither ANTITHESIS the conflict targets the proposition denoted by the entire satellite. Rather the conflict targets propositions that may be inferred from the satellite ([1]), or that are just implied to be present in the context ([2]).[14] In either case, the speaker assumes that both the nucleus and the satellite are true and should become part of the common ground – despite the 'indirect' conflict that exists. As before, we assume that highlighting the conflict and marking the nucleus as uncontroversial increases the hearer's acceptance of the nucleus, that is the EDU denoting the proposition that is central to the speaker's line of argument.

(12) [1] Ich habe noch in Erinnerung, wie es 1982 war, als
        I   have still in memory   how it 1982 was when
        Sie vom   Verrat der Freien Demokraten sprachen.
        you from.the betrayal the Free Democrats spoke
    [2] In Wirklichkeit haben doch Sie selbst Helmut Schmidt gestürzt
        in reality   have DOCH you self   Helmut Schmidt overthrown
    [3] und niemand sonst.
        and no-one else
        '[1] I still remember how it was in 1982 when you were talking of the betrayal by the Free Democrats. [2] In reality, it was you who overthrew Helmut Schmidt [3] and no one else.' (Speech #14, 63475)

Although *doch* occurs most frequently in the nucleus of the two mononuclear discourse relations at issue, there are a number of examples in the corpus where *doch* occurs in the satellite. Consider (13), an ANTITHESIS relation. Like in example (9) in Section 3.1 and like in all corpus examples with *doch* in the satellite, [2] in (13) contains a negation. We propose that in these cases, *doch* is used to indicate that it is known and therefore uncontroversial that what the satellite rejects should indeed be rejected, and it highlights the contrast between the two discourse units.

(13) [1] Wir sind doch nicht in der Abteilung Wahrsagerei,
        We are DOCH not   in the section   fortune.telling
    [2] sondern im   Deutschen Bundestag.
        but   in.the German   parliament
        '[1] We are not in the department of fortune-telling [2] but in the German parliament.' (Speech #16, 75067)

---

[14] This issue needs closer scrutiny in future research because the assumption that there must be a 'genuine' conflict in an ANTITHESIS relation (Mann & Thompson 1988) is not very restrictive if the conflict can be 'just anywhere'. It is unclear at the moment if this is a problem or not.

Overall we suggest that no matter whether *doch* occurs in the nucleus or in the satellite of the mononuclear contrastive discourse relations it fulfils the function of marking the respective EDU$_{MP}$ as already being in the common ground and thus as uncontroversial, and the function of highlighting an indirect conflict. The latter plausibly has the effect of pre-empting potential counterarguments against the nucleus. The former should lead to a quicker acceptance of the respective EDU$_{MP}$.

Let us next turn to the discourse relations for which we had not formulated predictions with respect to *doch* but which the corpus analysis revealed to be relevant for the distribution of the particle. Of these, EVIDENCE, INTERPRETATION, JUSTIFY, and MOTIVATION occurred more frequently than expected. For the EVIDENCE relation we propose that *doch* here essentially has the same function as *ja*, that is, that of marking the evidence that is presented in the satellite as uncontroversial, thereby enhancing the chance that the proposition denoted by the nucleus is more easily accepted. Furthermore, *doch* – by indicating that there is a conflict – indicates that another, inconsistent proposition in the context must be removed from the discourse commitments of the addressee, which should also have the effect of increasing the addressee's inclination to accept the nucleus.

INTERPRETATION is a relation where the satellite offers a judgment on the situation expressed in the nucleus. The judgment can be an explanation, a comparison or some other kind of subjective perspective on or understanding of the state of affairs presented in the nucleus. Consider (14), where the speaker interprets the interest of his Japanese colleague as a sign of appreciation of the success of the reforms. By the use of *doch* the speaker in (14) marks the interpretation of the nucleus given in the satellite as uncontroversial, which we assume is intended to increase the chance that this interpretation gets accepted. The meaning component of conflict that *doch* expresses is directed at a proposition outside the INTERPRETATION relation.

(14) [1] Mein japanischer Kollege Hashimoto hat mich gebeten, Experten aus unserem Land nach Japan zu schicken […], um dort zu erläutern, wie die Deutschen vorgegangen sind.
[2] Das ist doch ein Zeichen dafür, dass diese Reform
this is DOCH a sign for.this that this reform
großartig gelungen ist.
excellently succeeded is
'[1] My Japanese colleague Hashimoto has asked me to send experts from our country to Japan to explain how the Germans proceeded.
[2] This shows clearly that this reform is a great success.' (Speech #14, 69498)

JUSTIFY is a causal relation on the pragmatic level. In the satellite the speaker justifies the utterance of the nucleus, that is, explains why s/he uttered the nucleus. For instance, in (15) the speaker says that s/he wishes to be honest. JUSTIFY often involves meta-discursive utterances. We propose that in (15) *doch* serves to contrast the speaker's decision to put the proposition(s) denoted by the nucleus on the Table with the decision of the audience to remain silent. The reminder/retrieval function of *doch* here does not serve its literal function but is applied in what we may call a manipulative way. For examples like (15) it is implausible to assume that the proposition that the speaker should make a statement that s/he just made, is already in the common ground. The addressee would have to be quite clairvoyant to already have been committed to this proposition. Still, the speaker in (15) uses *doch*. We assume that s/he does so in order to mark the discourse move that is justified in (15[2]), i.e., (15[1]), as undebatable and self-evident. We will come back to the manipulative uses of modal particles in the general discussion.

(15) [1] Da ist es nicht nur eine Frage des Geldes, sondern auch des guten Willens oder andernfalls des totalen Versagens.
 [2] Das muss man doch einmal klar und deutlich sagen.
 That must one DOCH part clearly and distinctly say
 '[1] It is not only a question of money but also of good will or else of complete failure. [2] We should say this very clearly.' (Speech #16, 76760)

The last relation where *doch* occurred more frequently than expected is the MOTIVATION relation. The nucleus in a MOTIVATION is a request by the speaker, and the satellite provides information which is supposed to increase the addressee's wish to perform the requested action. As with the mononuclear contrastive relations discussed above, *doch* occurs in the Motivation relation more often in the nucleus than in the satellite. Eighty percent of these nuclei are imperatives. (16) is a typical example.

(16) [1] Hören Sie doch überhaupt mal zu!
 listen you DOCH at.all part verb.part
 [2] Es hat keinen Sinn, dass Sie hier im Saal sitzen und sich einfach nach dem Muster verhalten: Weil der das sagt, ist es falsch
 '[1] You should actually listen to me! [2] It does not make sense if you sit in this room and simply behave like: it is him that says these things, so they have to be wrong.' (Speech #5, 22919)

When a speaker orders or advises an addressee to do something s/he usually does this in situations when the addressee was not going to perform the action anyway. It has been argued that this latter condition on the use of imperatives is a presupposition (cf. Kaufmann 2012). We may assume that similarly to the JUSTIFY case *doch* occurs as marking the contrast between performing an action and not performing an action. Due to the nature of the structure of the discourse relation, this contrast concerns the nucleus of the relation. The occurrences of *doch* in the satellite of MOTIVATION (not illustrated), again can be explained as a manipulative use by the speaker who marks information that is supposed to motivate the hearer to do something, as undebatable.

Let us finally turn to the CIRCUMSTANCE relation, where *doch* – just as in ELABORATION, CONDITION, and LIST, which were already discussed above – occurred less frequently than expected. In the CIRCUMSTANCE relation the satellite delivers the 'framework' for the interpretation of the nucleus, for instance, it may mention the time and place of an event that is reported in the nucleus. From a discourse point of view, it is not evident why *doch* (or *ja*) should not occur in CIRCUMSTANCE. We propose that the reason is a formal one. In the reference corpus, 90% of the satellites in the CIRCUMSTANCE relation are embedded temporal clauses (e.g., introduced by *wenn* and *als* ('when')). These cannot occur with modal particles (cf. Coniglio 2011 for a discussion of modal particles in embedded clauses).

This concludes our discussion of the occurrence of *ja* and *doch* in individual discourse relations in a corpus of political speeches. In the next section we present our experimental study.

5 Experiment: The choice of modal particles in BACKGROUND and JUSTIFY

In the experiment we tested if speakers, when faced with an explicit choice between particles for a target utterance, show sensitivity to the discourse relation that the target utterance has with the previous discourse unit. Thus, we expand our investigation of the interplay of modal particles and discourse relations from one speaker (Helmut Kohl) to many speakers, and we test – for a small subset of discourse relations – whether the findings of the corpus analysis can be corroborated by evidence gathered with a quantitative method where naive speakers have to make conscious decisions.

The two discourse relations that we tested in the experiment were BACKGROUND and JUSTIFY. There were two reasons for this choice. First, the corpus study revealed these two relations to be among the discourse relations that are most highly correlated with the use of *ja* and *doch*, respectively. Thus, we expect speakers to choose *ja* in discourses with a BACKGROUND relation, and *doch* in discourses with a JUSTIFY relation.[15] The second reason is a methodological one. For BACKGROUND and JUSTIFY it is relatively easy to construct a large number of minimal pairs that can be used as conditions in an experiment such that naive listeners can identify the intended discourse relation in a fairly consistent way. We comment more on this methodological issue further below.

5.1 Method

Participants. Forty-eight German native speakers (mean age: 29.7 years, range: 19–54 years, 16 male) living in the Berlin/Brandenburg region in Germany participated in this experiment after giving informed consent. They were paid 7 Euros.

Stimuli and design. The design of the experiment was a one-factorial design where the factor DISCOURSE RELATION (DR) had the two levels BACKGROUND and JUSTIFY. The experimental material consisted of 32 three-sentence discourses each of which presented a view on an aspect of one of two issues that are very likely to be considered controversial in a German context: the many ways of providing adequate schooling for children (e.g., all-day schools and home schooling) and the pro and cons of wind farms. In the first sentence of each discourse, a claim was made for which the second sentence either provided background information or a justification, and in the third sentence another claim was made, see (17) for a set of sample items. The factor DR was manipulated by inserting different sentences as the second sentence in the discourses so that the relation between the first and the second sentence varied between BACKGROUND and JUSTIFY. The BACKGROUND relation was implemented by the second sentence conveying obvious and uncontroversial information that is generally known. The JUSTIFY relation was implemented by using meta-discursive utterances where the speaker defends his/her previous speech act. In (17) sentence [2B] states that the generators in wind turbines are very big and therefore very noisy, which is something most people would take to be uncontroversial and non-new. So [2B] provides background information for the claim made in sentence [1]. Sentence [2J] conveys that the speaker considers the claim made in the previous sentence as important because it concerns an aspect that cannot be ignored. So [2J] defends and justifies the previous speech act.

---

[15] Recall, however, that *doch* also occurs in BACKGROUND relations so it is certainly not excluded from this relation. The same holds for *ja* in JUSTIFY relations.

The second sentence always contained a gap, which is indicated by the underscore in (17) [2B] and [2J]. The position of the gap is the position where a modal particle occurs if there is one. In the experiment, participants filled the gap with one out of three modal particles they were offered in a forced lexical choice task: *ja, doch,* SCHON ('admittedly'). The choice of particle was the dependent variable.

(17) [1] Für Anwohner im näheren Umkreis von Windkraftanlagen könnte auch der Geräuschpegel ein Problem werden.
'For people living near wind farms the noise could also become a problem.'
[2B] BACKGROUND
Die Motoren   in den Anlagen sind _ riesig   und
the generators in the turbines are   _ enormous   and
verursachen entsprechend Lärm
cause   respective   noise
[2J] JUSTIFY
Das können wir _ nicht einfach als lächerlich abtun.
that can   we   _ not   simply   as   ridiculous dismiss
'We can't just dismiss this as absurd.'
[3] Die Häuser müssen also eventuell mit Lärmschutzfenstern ausgerüstet werden.
'So possibly soundproof windows must be fitted in the homes.'

Note that the gap was always in the sentence that changed with the experimental conditions. This methodological choice, that is, manipulating the sentence containing the gap and keeping the context constant, rather than manipulating the context and keeping the sentence with the gap constant, was motivated by the intention to have a clear criterion for distinguishing the discourse relations that we tested. Using a meta-discursive move as an implementation for the JUSTIFY relation left little room for a misinterpretation of the discourse relation by the participants in the JUSTIFY condition. Furthermore, the meta-discursive moves that we used cannot be interpreted as expressing a BACKGROUND relation so that the chance that participants interpreted the two discourses as containing different discourse relations was very high. Of course, this choice of implementation also limits the scope of the findings to the particular instantiation of the JUSTIFY relation but given that discourse relations other than the easy-to-identify CAUSE and SEQUENCE relations have not been tested extensively in experimental research, even findings with limited scope for BACKGROUND and for JUSTIFY are welcome.

The particles of interest in the experiment were *ja* and *doch*. The stressed modal particle SCHON ('admittedly') was added to the range of choices to serve as a distractor.[16] SCHON was chosen because the corpus analysis in Döring (2016) showed that it occurred in different relations than *ja* and *doch*.

The 32 experimental items were distributed over two lists in a Latin square design so that each participant would see each discourse in only one version. In addition to the experimental items, there were 40 filler discourses, which contained discourse relations like EVALUATION, where according to the corpus analysis in Döring (2016) SCHON often occurs, and ELABORATION. The order in each list was pseudo-randomized.

Procedure. Participants were seated in front of a computer screen in a quiet room. They saw one discourse at a time, presented with MS Excel. The second sentence of each discourse contained a drop-down menu at the gap site. Participants were told to choose the MP which they thought would fit the discourse most naturally. They were informed that *schon* would occur in capitalized form to indicate that it was stressed. There was no time limit.

5.2 Results

The data of all participants were included in the analysis. Table 2 gives the mean proportions averaged over participants for the choice among the three particles in the two discourse relations. The box-and-whiskers plot in Figure 6 illustrates the overall distribution of the choice between all three particles over the two discourse relations – the data for SCHON are added for illustrative purposes.

Table 2: Mean proportion of particle choice for each discourse relation and for the entire set of discourses. Averaged over participants, standard deviation in brackets.

Particle	Background	Justify	All discourse relations
ja	.652 (0.165)	.296 (0.150)	.474 (0.238)
doch	.233 (0.157)	.457 (0.160)	.345 (0.193)
SCHON	.115 (0.085)	.247 (0.125)	.181 (0.125)

---

[16] *Schon* also exists in an unstressed variant as a modal particle, but this variant is homophonous with the temporal adverb *schon* ('already'). We wished to avoid this ambiguity. The temporal adverb can only be stressed in (metalinguistic) corrections, which are not licensed by the contexts in the experimental items.

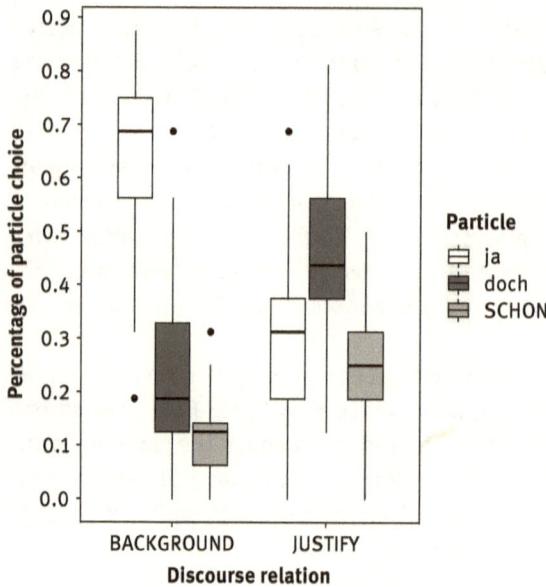

Figure 6: Proportion of particle choice per discourse relation (averaged over participants).

For the statistical analysis only the data for *ja* and *doch*, the two critical items, were considered. We applied general linear mixed effect models with a binomial logit function (R package lme4, Version 1.0–4, Bates, Bolker, Maechler & Walker 2013), and tested the use of *ja* and *doch* dependent on the fixed factor DR. Participant and item were random factors. The simplest best model – determined via model comparisons – included intercepts for participants and items, and random slopes for items for DR. The model parameters are given in Table 3. The analysis revealed that the factor DR had a highly significant effect on the choice of *ja* and *doch*: *ja* was chosen more often in the BACKGROUND relation than in the JUSTIFY relation, *doch* was chosen more often in the JUSTIFY relation than in the BACKGROUND relation.

Table 3: Parameter estimates and standard errors for fixed effects.

	Estimate	Se	z-value
Intercept	1.3086	0.2202	5.944
Discourse relation (BACKGROUND-JUSTIFY)	−1.8202	0.2697	−6.750

5.3 Discussion

The experiment showed that when given a choice of modal particles, naive speakers choose the particle depending on the discourse relation that EDU$_{MP}$ has with another EDU. The predictions that we had developed on the basis of the corpus analysis were confirmed: *ja* is preferred in the satellite of the BACKGROUND relation, and *doch* is preferred in the satellite of the JUSTIFY relation.

6 General discussion and conclusion

Both the corpus study and the experimental investigation that we presented showed that the occurrence of the modal particles *ja* and *doch* systematically varies with the type of discourse relation that the EDU$_{MP}$ entertains with other discourse units. These findings can be explained by our assumptions developed in Sections 2 and 3, namely that the systematic variation is a consequence of the modal particles' common ground managing function: modal particles create or enhance coherence in discourses and help the speaker achieve his/her communicative goal to increase the common ground without getting entangled in conversational crises. The meaning of *ja* and *doch* is well-suited for the avoidance and resolution of conversational crises. By pointing out that a proposition is already in the common ground (*ja*, *doch*), and by pointing out that there is a conflict in the set of beliefs of the addressee (*doch*), the speaker will reduce the chance of an objection of his/her discourse move by the addressee and/or enhance the chance that the addressee readily retracts a discourse commitment, which the speaker considers to be inconsistent with the common ground.

For the reminder/retrieval function of *ja* and *doch*, we proposed that a proposition p, which is already in the common ground, is placed on the Table even though it is not new. The speaker marks it as not new by the use of *ja* or *doch*. Although the presentation of a non-new proposition p does not actually increase shared knowledge, it has an effect on the discourse structure. The corresponding discourse unit is placed in a position in the discourse structure where it enters a discourse relation with another discourse unit, often as the satellite of that relation. Since p is (signalled to be) already in the common ground it is uncontroversial. This status makes p particularly suitable for enhancing the effect the satellite has on the nucleus in the given discourse relation. We argued that this is exactly what *ja* does in the satellite of the BACKGROUND relation, where the satellite helps the addressee to understand what is conveyed in the nucleus. The uncontroversial satellite increases the chance that the addressee understands and thus accepts more easily what is conveyed in the nucleus. So the desired effect of the use of *ja* is the pre-emption of a conversational crisis, that is, an objection.

For *doch*, the corpus investigation showed that the particle does not often occur in the satellite of a BACKGROUND relation even though it shares one of its meaning components with *ja*. This finding could be corroborated in the experimental investigation: Speakers prefer *ja* over *doch* and *schon* in BACKGROUND relations. This suggests that BACKGROUND is not easily compatible with the contrastive meaning component of *doch*. Arguably, if there is contrast the discourse relation changes. Interestingly, in the EVIDENCE relation, both *ja* and *doch* are used. We may assume that the reminding/retrieval function of the particles is used by the speaker to mark the evidence that the satellite presents as uncontroversial, which plausibly strengthens the argument made in the nucleus. The contrastive meaning component of *doch* plausibly is used in discourses where arguments are used to dismiss counterarguments and respective evidence: *doch* points at such conflicts.

We also suggested that speakers may use especially the particle *doch* in discourse situations where it is quite clear that the conditions on its use are not met. Recall the frequent use of *doch* in the satellite of the JUSTIFY relation, where the addressee certainly cannot have known that the speaker was going to make a certain utterance, which *doch* seems to indicate. We called these uses *manipulative uses*. The speaker *pretends* that something is undebatable and tries to 'win the argument' that way. It is important to highlight here that *ja* unlike *doch* did not occur often in JUSTIFY in the corpus, and that the experimental results clearly show that *doch* is preferred over *ja* in discourses with a JUSTIFY relation. So in the JUSTIFY relation, the contrastive meaning component of *doch* seems to be crucial. We propose that the goal of a speaker placing *doch* in the satellite of a JUSTIFY relation is to avoid a protest of the addressee about the previous speech act by dismissing (potentially) conflicting assumptions.

Of course, there might also be situations where the speaker does not actually *know* what the addressee's knowledge about the status of the common ground is. Still, s/he might just try his/her luck, as it were, by pretending that the proposition is uncontroversial. The addressee will perform an accommodation, as in other cases of presupposition accommodation. Note that the addressee him/herself might not be sure whether or not the respective proposition was in the common ground. The speaker's intention in such trial-and-error scenarios is the same as in the default non-manipulative case: to improve discourse coherence, for example, by pre-empting a conversational crisis. It is clear that our ideas about such uses of modal particles at the moment are hypotheses that need to be tested in future research: we cannot verify the intentions of a speaker or his/her assumptions about the common ground in a corpus study. Similarly, for the experiment we do not know whether the participants, when they chose *ja* for the satellite in the BACKGROUND relations, accommodated the common ground status of the proposition denoted by the satellite. Still, we think that what we sketched here is a plausible way of conceiving of speaker-hearer interactions with respect to common ground management.

An important finding of the corpus study is that even though there seem to be manipulative uses of the particles we certainly cannot place particles *ad libitum* in any position in the discourse. The manipulative use must be meaningful in the context of the particular discourse relation, that is, it must support the effect that the speaker intends the satellite to have on the nucleus of the relation. Indeed, in discourse relations where the satellite ideally conveys new information (ELABORATION), or must be non-factive content (CONDITION), *ja* and *doch* occur infrequently (ELABORATION) or not at all (CONDITION).

Although we argued that *ja* and *doch* have a particular function in the satellite of a discourse relation – namely that of enhancing the satellite's effect on the nucleus, we also found that in some relations *doch* preferably is placed in the nucleus of the relation. This was the case in the mononuclear contrastive relations CONCESSION and ANTITHESIS, and in the MOTIVATION relation. For the former we proposed that the effect of placing *doch* in the nucleus on the one hand enhances the contrastivity of the relation and on the other hand highlights the uncontroversiality of the nucleus. Both of these effects are likely to increase the chance that the nucleus gets accepted and that the satellite gets dismissed. In a MOTIVATION, *doch* in the nucleus highlights the contrast with the non-performance of the action requested in the nucleus.

A final interesting outcome of the corpus study is the observation that neither *doch* nor *ja* frequently occurs in multinuclear, that is, symmetric, relations, for example, in LIST or CONTRAST. We proposed that using the particles tends to make a relation asymmetric. We suspect that the reminding function of the two particles is responsible for this effect. This function renders the EDU_{MP} different from the other EDU in the discourse relation: the proposition denoted by EDU_{MP} is assumed to be known, the one denoted by the other EDU is not. Supporting evidence for this assumption comes from a close comparison of *doch* with the conjunction *aber* ('but'), see Repp (2013) for details. The two elements have the same contrast-indicating function and differ only in the reminding function of *doch*. The conjunction *but* is a hallmark of the CONTRAST relation in all discourse theories (see Section 3), whereas *doch* – as we saw – hardly ever occurs in CONTRAST. The precise mechanisms of this effect need to be explored in future research.

Overall our investigation of the interplay of *ja* and *doch* with discourse structure has shown that the particles systematically interact with discourse structure in that they either enhance the function of a satellite in relation to that satellite's nucleus, or mark the nucleus, which is the more important unit in a discourse relation, as uncontroversial. Both functions serve the creation of coherence of the discourse in the sense that conversational crises can be avoided or quickly resolved. We have provided a detailed discussion of how the particles fulfil their function in individual discourse relations and have illustrated how they perform their common ground managing function.

References

Asher, N. & A. Lascarides. 2003. Logics of conversation. Cambridge: Cambridge University Press.
Asher, N., L. Prévot & L. Vieu. 2007. Setting the background in discourse. Discours 1: 1–29.
Bates, D., M. Bolker, B. Maechler & S. Walker. 2013. Linear mixed-effects models using Eigen and S4. lme4, version 1.0-4. CRAN repository. https://cran.r-project.org/
Carlson, L. & D. Marcu. 2001. Discourse Tagging Reference Manual. Ms.
Coniglio, M. 2011. Die Syntax der deutschen Modalpartikeln: Ihre Distribution und Lizenzierung in Haupt- und Nebensätzen. Berlin: Akademie-Verlag.
Döring, S. 2016. Modal Particles, Discourse Structure and Common Ground Management. Theoretical and Empirical Aspects. Dissertation. Humboldt-Universität zu Berlin.
Egg, M. 2013. Discourse particles, common ground, and felicity conditions. In: (D. Gutzmann & H.-M. Gärtner, eds) Beyond Expressives – Explorations in Use-conditional Meaning, 125–149. Leiden: Brill.
Egg, M. & M. Zimmermann. 2012. Stressed out! Accented discourse particles – the case of DOCH. In: (A. Aguilar, A. Chernilovskaya & R. Nouwen, eds) Proceedings of Sinn und Bedeutung 16: Volume 1, MIT Working Papers in Linguistics, 225–238.
Farkas, D. & K. Bruce. 2010. On reacting to assertions and polar questions. Journal of Semantics 27(1): 81–118.
Franck, D. 1980. Grammatik und Konversation. Königstein/Ts.: Scriptor.
Ginzburg, J. 1995. Resolving questions, I & II. Linguistics and Philosophy 18 (6):459–527, 567–609.
Grosz, B. & C. Sidner. 1986. Attention, intentions, and the structure of discourse. Journal of Computational Linguistics 12(3): 175–204.
Gutzmann, D. 2009. Hybrid semantics for modal particles. Sprache und Datenverarbeitung 33(1–2): 45–59.
Hobbs, J.R. 1985. On the coherence and structure of discourse. Technical Report CSLI-85-37.
Horn, L. R. 1989. A Natural History of Negation. Chicago: The University of Chicago Press.
Jacobs, J. 1991. On the semantics of modal particles. In: (W. Abraham, ed) Discourse Particles. Descriptive and Theoretical Investigations on the Logical, Syntactic and Pragmatic Properties of Discourse Particles in German and English, 141–162. Amsterdam: Benjamins.
Karagjosova, E. 2004. The Meaning and Function of German Modal Particles. Deutsches Forschungszentrum für Künstliche Intelligenz, DKFI; Saarland University, Dept. of Computational Linguistics and Phonetics.
Kaufmann, M. 2012. Interpreting Imperatives. Dordrecht. Springer.
Kehler, A. 2002. Coherence, Reference, and the Theory of Grammar. Stanford. CSLI Publications.
König. E. & S. Recquart 1991. A relevance-theoretic approach to the analysis of modal particles in German. Multilingua 10–12, 63–77.
Lindner, K. 1991. 'Wir sind ja doch alte Bekannte'. The use of German ja and doch as modal particles. In: (A. Werner, ed) Discourse Particles. Descriptive and Theoretical Investigations

on the Logical, Syntactic and Pragmatic Properties of Discourse Particles in German and English, 163–201. Amsterdam: Benjamins.

Mann, W. & M. Taboada. 2005–2015. RST website. http://www.sfu.ca/rst/

Mann, W. & S. Thompson. 1988. Rhetorical Structure Theory: A theory of text organization. Text 8(3): 243–281.

Mann, W. & S. Thompson. 1992. Relational discourse structure: A comparison of approaches to structuring text by 'contrast'. In: (S.J.J. Hwang & W.R. Merrifield, eds) Language in Context: Essays for Robert E. Longacre. The Summer Institute of Linguistics and the University of Texas at Arlington, 19–45. Summer Institute of Linguistics.

Menzel, U. 2013. Exact Multinomial Test: Goodness-of-Fit Test for Discrete Multivariate data. EMT, version 1.1. CRAN repository. https://cran.r-project.org/

Repp, S. 2013. Common ground management: Modal particles, illocutionary negation and verum. In: (D. Gutzmann & H.-M. Gärtner, eds) Beyond Expressives – Explorations in Use-conditional Meaning, 231–274. Leiden: Brill.

Rojas-Esponda, T. 2014. A QUD account of German doch. In: (U. Etxeberria, A. Fălăuş, A. Irurtzun & B. Leferman, eds) Proceedings of Sinn und Bedeutung 18: 359–376.

Sanders, T., W. Spooren & L. Noordman. 1992. Towards a taxonomy of coherence relations. Discourse Processes 15(1): 1–35.

Schiller, A., S. Teufel, C. Stöckert & C. Thielen. 1999: Guidelines für das Tagging deutscher Textcorpora mit STTS. Technical Report, Institut für maschinelle Sprachverarbeitung, Stuttgart.

Schmid, H. 1994. Probabilistic part-of-speech tagging using decision trees. In: Proceedings of the Conference on New Methods in Language Processing. Manchester, UK.

Searle, J.R. 1969. Speech Acts: An Essay in the Philosophy of Language. Cambridge: Cambridge University Press.

Stalnaker, R.C. 1978. Assertion. In: (P. Cole, ed) Pragmatics, 315–332.

Thurmair, M. 1989. Modalpartikeln und ihre Kombinationen. Tübingen: Niemeyer.

van der Sandt, R. 1991. Denial. Papers from CLS, 272. The parasession on negation. 331–344.

Waltereit, R. 2001. Modal particles and their functional equivalents: A speech-act-theoretic approach. Journal of Pragmatics 33(9): 1391–1417.

Zimmermann, M. 2004. Zum wohl: Diskurspartikeln als Satztypmodifikatoren. Linguistische Berichte 199, 253–286.

Zimmermann, M. 2012. Discourse particles. In: (P. Portner, C. Maienborn & K. von Heusinger, eds) Semantics. An international handbook of natural language meaning; Volume 3, (HSK 33.3), 2011–2038. Berlin, New York: Mouton de Gruyter.

Appendix: List of RST discourse relations annotated in the corpus

Relation Name	Nucleus	Satellite
Mononuclear Relations		
Antithesis	ideas favoured by the author	ideas disfavoured by the author
	The salaries have to be raised.	*You only want to increase the taxes.*
Background	text whose understanding is being facilitated	text for facilitating understanding
	We have to discuss the reform of the health insurance system.	*The reform was proposed by the government last month.*
Cause	a situation	another situation which causes that one
	The unemployment rate increases	*because companies have to cut jobs.*
Circumstance	text expressing the events or ideas occurring in the interpretive context	an interpretive context of situation or time
	We discussed this topic at length	*when the President of the United States was here last week.*
Concession	situation affirmed by author	situation which is apparently inconsistent but also affirmed by author
	The voters let you down	*although you overwhelm them with promises.*
Condition	action or situation whose occurrence results from the occurrence of the conditioning situation	conditioning situation
	We will agree to the draft	*if it includes the clause for minimal wages.*
Elaboration	basic information	additional information
	The election will be in two months.	*In two states, there are also regional elections.*
Evidence	a claim	information intended to increase the reader's belief in the claim
	The government's campaigns failed.	*The unemployment rates increased further.*
Interpretation	a situation	an interpretation of the situation
	You want to address families now.	*This is a new tactic.*
Justify	text	information supporting the writer's right to express the text
	The government failed to solve the problem.	*We have to be clear about that.*

Relation Name	Nucleus	Satellite
Mononuclear Relations		
MOTIVATION	an action	information intended to increase the reader's desire to perform the action
	Please explain your position on this point!	*It will help us to find a solution.*
RESULT	a situation	another situation which is caused by that one
	Economy remains weak	*therefore, the number of unemployed increases.*
Multinuclear Relations		
CONTRAST	one alternate	the other alternate
	One group wants to reform the law on minimal wages,	*the other group wants to abolish it.*
LIST	an item	a next item
	We want to raise the pensions,	*we will invest in the education of young people.*
SEQUENCE	an item	a next item
	We will decide on this proposal.	*Afterwards we will discuss the realization.*

Kordula De Kuthy and Britta Stolterfoht
Focus projection revisited: Pitch accent perception in German

1 Introduction

One of the important insights of the recent intensive study of information structure is that for intonation languages like English and German, there is a close relation between focus and prosodic prominence. More specifically, it is now widely accepted as a fact that in such languages focus is signaled by pitch accents. But one issue that is still much discussed is the nature of pitch accent placement in the focussed part of an utterance: is it determined by syntactic, pragmatic, or purely metrical factors or a combination of these? One line of research has established that there are syntactic rules that determine accent placement in focus structures, with the F-marking approach of Selkirk (1995) and the SAAR (Sentence Accent Assignment Rule) of Gussenhoven (1983) serving as prominent foundations. One prediction of these approaches is that certain accent patterns are ambiguous with respect to the possible focus domain: a pitch accent in a certain position can signal focus just on one word (narrow focus) or on a larger constituent (broad focus). The empirical question that arises from this claim is: is there any evidence that these accent patterns are really perceived as ambiguous between different focus interpretations by listeners?

In this chapter, we report on a perception experiment for German in which we tested whether listeners judge certain accent patterns as equally acceptable in different focus structure contexts. The results of the study will give an indication whether listeners perceive pitch accents in certain positions as ambiguous with respect to the possible information structuring of an utterance.

2 Focus projection and previous experimental results

Focus as part of the information structure has been characterized in a variety of ways as the 'most important' information of an utterance (cf. Krifka 2008) and can be defined to be the part of an answer that corresponds to the *wh*-part of a question.[1] As a simple example, the question–answer pairs in (1) illustrate different possible focus structures for a single sentence.

(1) a. What did John rent? John rented [a BICYCLE]$_F$ (narrow, NP focus)
    b. What did John do? John [rented a BICYCLE]$_F$ (broad, VP focus)
    c. What happened yesterday? [John rented a BICYCLE]$_F$ (broad, S focus)

The answers in (1) provide the element asked for, the focus in brackets. The word *bicycle* is always shown in small caps to indicate that it contains a syllable bearing a nuclear pitch accent. In all three sentences, the focused material thus is marked by a single pitch accent: in (1a), the pitch accent on the noun *bicycle* signals narrow NP focus on the object NP, in (1b) it signals broad VP focus on the VP *rented a bicycle*, and in (1c), the single accent signals broad focus of the entire sentence. A single pitch accent on a noun in object position thus seems to be ambiguous with respect to the focus domain it can occur in: it can signal narrow NP focus, broad VP focus or even broad sentence focus. This relation between pitch accent placement and focus interpretation as illustrated in (1) is referred to as *focus projection* when the relation is assumed to be mediated by syntax, and a number of lexical and syntactic conditions have been formulated in the literature to define when focus can project in this way (e.g., Gussenhoven 1983; Selkirk 1995; von Stechow & Uhmann 1986; Jacobs 1993). One much-discussed approach spelling out such syntactic conditions for accent placement is the focus projection rules formulated in Selkirk (1995), which determines the focus projection potential of a pitch accent depending on the syntactic structure of an utterance:

(2) F-marking:
    An accented word is F-marked.
    Vertical Focus Projection:
        F-marking of head of phrase licenses F-marking of phrase.
    Horizontal Focus Projection:
        F-marking of internal argument licenses F-marking of head.

This approach assumes that an accented word is syntactically F-marked. The horizontal focus projection rule determines under which conditions F-marking of one daughter in a phrase can license F-marking of another daughter, while the vertical focus projection rule determines when F-marking can be passed onto the

---

[1] We only use the term focus in this formal pragmatic sense to avoid confusion with the prosodic notion, which we only refer to as focus exponent or pitch accent.

mother of a phrase. The resulting F-Structure for the example (1c) is illustrated in (3), where starting from the F-marked noun *bicycle*, F-marking projects via the NP and VP up to the entire sentence. Additional focus interpretation rules then ensure that the highest node that is not dominated by another F-marked node in the structure is interpreted as the focus of the utterance, which in our example (3) is the entire sentence.

(3) What happened yesterday? [John$_F$ [rented$_F$ [a$_F$ BICYCLE$_F$]$_F$]$_F$]$_F$]

To explore whether there is empirical evidence for the prediction that certain accent patterns are ambiguous with respect to the possible focus domain they can occur in, several experimental studies have been conducted in which the perception of accent patterns in broad and narrow focus structures has been studied. These studies mostly investigate whether there is really only one single accent in the broad focus cases or whether additional accents on the verb improve the acceptability of the broad focus structure. Gussenhoven (1983) investigated the hypothesis that a single accent on an argument is sufficient for a VP to be focused. The experiment thus directly addresses the empirical grounding of a particular subcase of focus projection: whether and when focus projection over an unaccented verbal head is possible.

The perception experiment conducted by Gussenhoven to test his hypothesis is a context-retrievability experiment: participants in the experiment judge whether a question and an answer are from the same dialogue or whether the answer was given in response to another question. The experiment included two types of questions and two types of answers as illustrated in (4) and (5):

(4) a. What do you do? (broad, VP focus)
 b. What do you teach? (narrow, NP focus)

(5) a. I TEACH LINGUISTICS. (accents on verb and NP)
 b. I teach LINGUISTICS. (accent on NP only)

Gussenhoven hypothesizes that in a sentence with an accent on the argument such as (5b) the entire VP can be the focus, just like for (5a) where both words in the VP are marked by an accent. For the experiment, he thus predicts that listeners should not be able to tell any difference between the answers in (5a) and (5b) to the broad focus question in (4a).

This prediction was confirmed by the results of the experiment: listeners performed no better than chance in judging whether questions asking for wide or narrow focus and answers with a single accent on the argument were matched.

This finding supports the existence of focus projection: to focus the VP, it is sufficient to accent the object NP.

Birch & Clifton (1995) revisited the issues of Gussenhoven (1983) and also investigated broad focus structures with two accent patterns, one condition with only a single accent on the object NP, and one with an additional accent on the verb. They employed two experimental tasks: a *make-sense judgment task* asking about the appropriateness of a dialogue in which the time to make a yes/no judgment is measured, and a *linguistic judgment task* in which subjects rate prosodic appropriateness on a five-point scale. The examples in (4) show the types of question and answers used in dialogues in the experiments:

(6)   Isn't Kerry pretty smart?
    a. Yes, she TEACHES MATH.   (accents on V and NP)
    b. Yes, she teaches MATH.   (accent on NP only)

For the make-sense judgment task, Birch and Clifton report the same reaction times for answers with accents on both V and NP (6a) as for answers in which only the NP is accented (6b). This would support the hypothesis that focus can project from a pitch accented argument. For the linguistic judgment task, however, subjects showed a small but significant preference for answers with accents on both V and NP over an accent only on the NP which contradicts the results of the first task.

In a more recent study, Breen et al. (2010) investigate accent placement in narrow versus broad focus structures in a combined production and perception study. In the production study, speakers produced answers to given questions with broad and narrow focus structures. In the perception study, participants had to choose a matching question to the produced answer. The experimental setup included seven types of questions with varying broad and narrow focus structures, among them a broad focus question as in (7a) and a narrow focus question as in (7b).

(7) a. What happened this morning?   (broad focus)
    b. What did Damon fry this morning?   (narrow, NP focus)

(8)   Damon fried an OMELET this morning.

The results of their perception study show that for simple subject–verb–object sentences with a single accent on the object NP, as in (8), listeners correctly identified (noncontrastive) narrow object focus 57% of the time, interpreting it as wide focus only 13% of the time. Breen et al. (2010) interpret this as showing that a single accent on an object NP is not ambiguous between narrow and broad focus in English and conclude that this result is incompatible with an approach to focus projection like the one of Selkirk (1995).

In one of the few perception experiments for German, Féry (1993) tests the hypothesis that the same early nuclear pitch accent can signal narrow focus or broad focus. Minimal pairs of intransitive sentences with a pitch accent on the subject were recorded, as in (10), once as the answer to a question inducing narrow focus as in (9a) and one as the answer to a question inducing broad focus as in (9b).

(9) a. Wer ist verhaftet worden?   (narrow, object NP focus)
       who has arrested been
       'Who has been arrested?'

   b. Hast Du heute die Nachrichten gehört?   (broad focus)
      have you today the news heard
      'Did you hear today's news?'

(10) GORBATSCHOV ist verhaftet worden.
     Gorbachev has arrested been
     'Gorbachev has been arrested.'

The two recorded questions then were randomly paired with the realizations of the answer and the participants in the experiment had to judge whether a question and an answer were from the same or a different dialogue. Féry (1993) reports that listeners decided at random whether the realization of the answer was an answer to the question inducing narrow focus or to the one inducing broad focus. She thus concludes that there is no difference in tonal realization between a narrow and a wide focus answer, that is, the same pitch accent on the subject signals broad or narrow focus.

In another study related to focus projection in German, Féry & Stoel (2006) investigated the hypothesis that there is something like an unmarked prosodic structure, which is not only adequate in broad focus contexts, but also in other, narrow focus inducing contexts. They recorded transitive sentences in a topic-focus inducing context, that served as the unmarked prosodic structure with a rising pitch accent on the subject and a falling pitch accent on the object NP as in (11a).[2]

---

2 Féry & Stoel (2006) assume that this intonation contour with a rising accent on the subject and a falling accent on the focused word is the same as would be produced in a true broad focus

As a narrow focus structure they recorded sentences in a context inducing narrow corrective focus on the object NP as illustrated in (11b).

(11) a. My neighbor often throws big parties, and therefore she also gets lots of presents.
Movie directors give her movies, writers give her books, and ...
MALER	bringen	immer	BILDER	mit.	(topic focus)
painters	bring	always	pictures	along	

'Painters always bring pictures.'

b. It is said that painters always bring books to our neighbor. But this is not true:
Maler	bringen	immer	BILDER	mit.	(narrow focus)

'Painters always bring pictures.'

For the perception experiment, the sentences were cross-spliced and the participants were asked to judge the acceptability of the intonation of the target sentences occurring either in the matching context or in the nonmatching context. The results showed that the topic–focus intonation contour as in (11a) was judged almost as acceptable in the nonmatching narrow focus context as in the matching broad focus context, whereas the narrow focus sentences were judged as less acceptable in the nonmatching broad focus context. Féry and Stoel interpret this as supporting their hypothesis that there is an unmarked prosodic structure in German that is acceptable independent of a particular information structuring of the utterance. This result also partially supports a focus projection account like the one of Selkirk, since the pitch accent on the object NP in examples as in (11a) seems to be ambiguous between a narrow focus and a broad focus realization. The acceptability results obtained for a pitch accent produced on an object NP in a narrow focus context as in (11b), however, do not support a focus projection account, since such a pitch accent cannot ambiguously occur in a narrow or a broad focus setting.

In a recent study investigating the contours of nuclear falling accents in German, Kügler & Gollrad (2015) conducted a perception experiment investigating whether listeners can distinguish pitch accents on objects produced as a contrastive focus (12a) from accents produced in a broad focus sentence (12b).

---

inducing context. They are thus confident that this pattern would get similar high acceptability ratings in a broad focus context.

(12) a. Hat Martin den Frosch gesehen? (contrastive focus)
    'Has Martin seen the frog?'
    Nein, Martin hat den WAL gesehen.
    'No, Martin has seen the whale.'

   b. Erzähl mir bitte, was passiert ist? (broad focus)
    'Did you hear today's news?'
    Martin hat den WAL gesehen.
    'Martin has seen the whale.'

The perception experiment consisted of question–answer pairs, in which the intonation of the answer either matched (contrastive focus question and answer, broad focus question and answer) or did not match (contrastive focus question and broad focus answer and vice versa) the focus of the question. Participants of the experiment were asked to evaluate the intonation of the answer sentence as congruent or incongruent with respect to the question. The results revealed that listeners rated the matching question–answer pairs significantly more often as congruent compared to the nonmatching question–answer pairs. This result indicates that there is a difference in the tonal realization of a pitch accent produced in a contrastive environment and one produced in a broad focus environment that listeners are aware of. Since both studies on German comparing broad versus narrow focus on the object NP used contrastive focus, the interesting question arises whether listeners will also distinguish pitch accents produced in noncontrastive narrow focus contexts from those produced in broad focus contexts. Such a result would give a first indication that a pitch accent on an object NP is not necessarily perceived as ambiguous between narrow and broad focus.

3 An experimental study on German

The reported studies revealed rather mixed results. Some of the studies found that an utterance with a single pitch accent on the object NP was accepted as an answer to a broad focus question, as predicted under a focus projection approach. Other studies found that utterances produced in a narrow focus inducing context with a single accent on the object NP were much less acceptable in broad focus contexts. It thus remains an open issue whether a single accent on an object NP is really ambiguous between a narrow focus on the object NP and a wide VP focus as is predicted by the focus projection rules of Selkirk (1995) or the SAAR of Gussenhoven (1983). In particular, the question whether an utterance produced in the context of a wide focus question is ambiguous between a wide and narrow focus on the direct object has not been investigated so far. We therefore conducted a perception experiment in which listeners were asked to judge the acceptability of question–answer pairs.

3.1 The experiment

Our study investigates whether an utterance produced in a narrow object NP context is also acceptable in a wide VP context and, vice versa, whether an utterance produced in a wide VP context is also acceptable in a narrow object NP context. In contrast to the studies exploring accent patterns in German described above, we used sentences in which all verbal arguments remain in the middle field and exhibit the assumed base order for German, SOV (Subject > Object > Verb).

Question–answer pairs like the examples in (13) and (14) were used.

(13) a. Wen hat der Stier verletzt?   (narrow, object NP focus)
         who has the bull   injured
         'Who did the bull injure?'

     b. Maria hat verkündet, dass der Stier [den HÄNDler]$_F$ verletzt hat.
         Maria has announced that the bull the trader injured has
         'Maria announced that the bull injured the trader.'

(14) a. Was hat der Stier gemacht?   (broad, VP focus)
         what has the bull   done
         'What did the bull do?'

     b. Maria hat verkündet, dass der Stier [den HÄNDler verletzt hat]$_F$.
         Maria has announced that the bull the trader injured has
         'Maria announced that the bull injured the trader.'

We used these question–answer pairs as the two matching conditions and interchanged the questions and answers to create the two mismatching conditions.

Given the mixed results in previous studies, we can derive three competing predictions for our acceptability rating study:

<u>Hypothesis 1</u>
If a single accent on the object is ambiguous, and therefore can project focus independent of the context in which it was produced, ratings should not differ between match and mismatch conditions.

Hypothesis 2
If a single accent on the object produced in a broad VP focus or a narrow object focus context can be differentiated by listeners, significant rating differences between match and mismatch conditions should be found.

Hypothesis 3
If a single accent on the object produced in a broad VP focus is ambiguous, and one produced in a narrow object focus context is not ambiguous, a significant rating difference between match and mismatch conditions should only be found for answers produced in a narrow object focus context.

3.1.1 Method

3.1.1.1 Participants
Thirty-six undergraduate students of the University of Tübingen paid for their participation. All were native speakers of German.

3.1.1.2 Materials
Two female speakers read 40 question–answer pairs like the examples in (13) and (14). Thirty-six of them were used in the Experiment. We used the recorded question–answer pairs as the two matching conditions and interchanged the questions and answers to create the two mismatching conditions. Furthermore, we included two control conditions. As the match condition, we used the question–answer pair in (15), with a narrow focus on the subject NP. The mismatch condition was created by pairing the answer in (15) with a narrow object question as in (13).

(15) a. Wer hat den Händler verletzt?   (narrow, subject NP focus)
      who has the trader injured
      'Who did injure the trader?'

   b. Maria hat verkündet, dass [der STIER]$_F$ den Händler verletzt hat.
      Maria has announced that the bull   the trader injured has
      'Maria announced that the bull injured the trader.'

Thus, the independent variables were QUESTION TYPE (match vs. mismatch) and ANSWER TYPE [broad (VP) vs. narrow (object NP) vs. narrow (subject NP)].

All our question–answer pairs contained transitive verbs like 'verletzen' (to injure) and the answer sentences were produced as embedded clauses always exhibiting the word order subject–object–verb with a pitch accent on the object NP.

We analyzed the F0 values of the acoustic stimuli for the two critical answer sentences [broad (VP) vs. narrow(object NP)) as well as participants' ratings (see Figure 1). For the acoustic analyses, PRAAT (Boersma & Weenink 2001) and ProsodyPro (Xu 2006) were used. The mean F0 values for each word were submitted to an ANOVA with an error term that was based on item variability. The analyses revealed highly significant differences with regard to F0 values from the beginning of the embedded sentence until the object, with higher F0 values for broad (VP) up to the object determiner, and higher F0 values for narrow (NP) on the object NP. F0 values on the participle and auxiliary showed no significant differences: matrix subject $[F(1,39) = 15.68, p = .003]$; matrix auxiliary $[F(1,39) = 15.68, p < .001]$; matrix verb $[F(1,39) = 9.58, p = .004]$; complementizer $[F(1,39) = 31.52, p < .001]$; determiner $[F(1,39) = 5.38, p = .03]$; subject NP $[F(1,39) = 9.14, p = .004]$; determiner $[F(1,39) = 9.86, p = .003]$; object NP $[F(1,39) = 46.34, p < .001]$; verb $[F(1,39) = .05, p = .83]$; auxiliary $[F(1,39) = 1.63, p = .21]$.

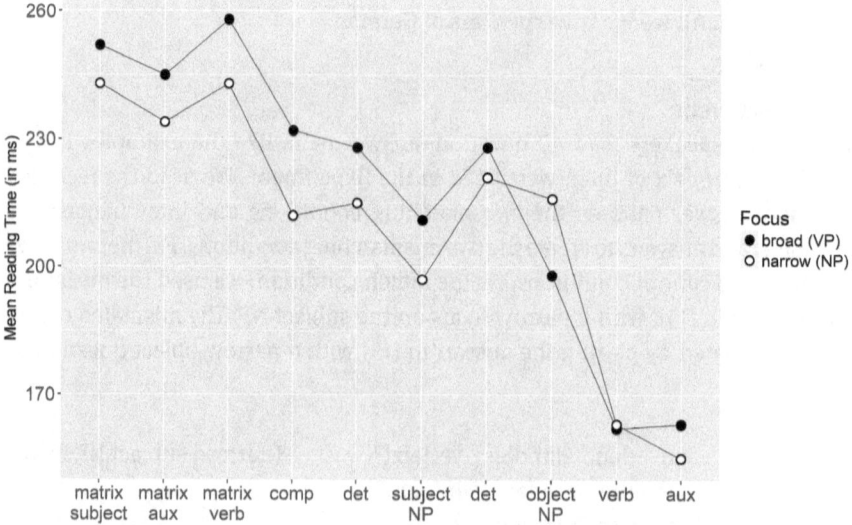

Figure 1: Mean F0 values (in Hz) for the two critical target sentences: broad (VP) and narrow (object NP) focus.

3.1.1.3 Procedure

The experiment was run on two PCs using E-Prime software (Psychology Software Tools, Inc.). Participants were seated in front of a computer screen and listened to the question–answer pairs via headphones. After listening, participants were asked to rate the question–answer pairs. The following question appeared on the screen:

Wie gut passt die Antwort zur Frage? ('How does the answer match the question?'), together with a five-point scale (5 = very good, 1 = very bad). Participants answered by pressing the corresponding numbers on the keyboard in front of them.

3.1.1.4 Data analysis
Participants' ratings were submitted to two separate ANOVAs – one with an error term that was based on participant variability (*F*1) and one with an error term that was based on item variability (*F*2). The ANOVAs we conducted were 2 [match (=congruent question–answer pairs) vs. mismatch (=incongruent question–answer pairs)] × 3 [broad (VP) vs. narrow (object NP) vs. narrow (subject NP)] ANOVAs with repeated measurement on the two factors in both the participant analysis and the item analysis.

3.2 Results

3.2.1 Rating data

Analyses of the rating data (Figure 2) revealed highly significant main effects of QUESTION TYPE [F_1 (1,35) = 105.20, p_1 < .001; F_2 (1,35) = 326.02, p_2 < .001] with lower ratings for the mismatch conditions compared to the match conditions (3.7 vs. 4.6), ANSWER TYPE [F_1 (2,70) = 93.29, p_1 < .001; F_2 (2,70) = 169.38, p_2 < .001] with

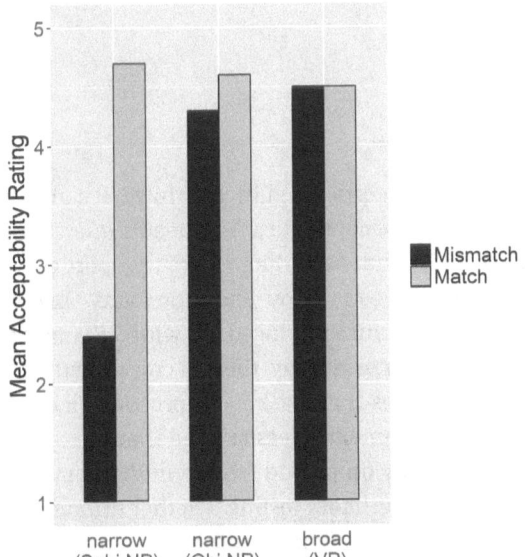

Figure 2: Mean acceptability ratings (scale 5-1) for the six experimental question–answer pairs.

lower rating for narrow (subject NP) compared to the other two conditions, narrow (object NP) and broad (VP) (3.6 vs. 4.5 and 4.5), and a highly significant interaction of the two factors [F_1 (2,70) = 65.15.20, p_1 < .001; F_2 (2,70) = 235.05, p_2 < .001].

Single comparisons (*match* vs. *mismatch*) for the three answer types showed decreased acceptability ratings for the control conditions with a narrow subject (NP) focus [F_1 = (1,35) = 102.09, p_1 < .001; F_2 (1,35) = 496.31; p_2 < .001] as well as for narrow object (NP) focus [F_1 (1,35) = 10.77, p_1 = .002; F_2 (1,35) = 22.30, p_2 < .001]. No significant acceptability difference was found for the broad (VP) focus [F_1 = (1,35) = .31, p_1 = .58; F_2 (1,35) = .51, p_2 = .48].

3.3 Discussion

The two main effects show decreased ratings for the mismatch conditions as well as for the control conditions with narrow focus (subject NP). More interestingly, we found a highly significant interaction of the two factors, driven by the different behaviors of the mismatch conditions for the three answer types. As expected, we see very low ratings for the control condition with narrow (subject NP) focus, significantly lower ratings for narrow (object NP) focus, but no decrease in ratings for broad (VP) focus. This pattern of results reveals evidence for Hypothesis 3. A single accent on the object produced in a broad VP focus seems to be ambiguous, whereas the one produced in a narrow object focus is not, shown by a significant difference between match and mismatch conditions only for answers produced in a narrow object focus context.

4 General discussion

All in all, our results show that an utterance produced in a narrow NP context paired with a wide VP context decreases acceptability. This result questions the assumption that a pitch accent, independent of the prosodic properties of the utterance as a whole, is ambiguous between narrow and wide focus. On the other hand, according to our results, an utterance produced in a wide VP context is also acceptable in a narrow NP context. Interestingly, there is cross-linguistic evidence that also in other language families that mark focus prosodically the accent pattern produced in a broad focus context is less marked than that produced on a narrow focus context: in a study on prosodic focus in Vietnamese, Jannedy (2007) conducted a perception experiment testing whether utterances produced as answers to certain wh-focus questions could be matched back to that question, which was presented as one of five possible question types. The results of the perception experiment showed that overall prosody in Vietnamese helped to disambiguate the context: for example listeners matched an utterance produced in a narrow NP context with the narrow focus question in 52.22% of the cases. For utterances produced in a broad VP context, however, the results were less clear: listeners matched the VP focus utterance with the corresponding VP question only in 25.56% of the cases, while matching it with an NP focus question in 18.89% of the cases and matching it with a broad sentence focus question in 32.78% of the cases. These data again show that a pitch accent on an object NP is not always ambiguous between a narrow and a broad focus as would be predicted by several syntactic focus projection accounts.

Based on the findings for different Germanic languages that focus generally boosts accents (Eady et al. 1986; Baumann et al. 2006) it has been observed that for German a narrow focus raises the $F0$ value of a pitch accent independent of the syntactic position in which the focused constituent occurs (cf. Féry & Kügler 2008). The results of our experiment give a first indication that this is not only a production phenomenon, but that this raising of pitch accents in certain focus structures is actually perceived by listeners: the raised pitch accent on the narrow focus is more or less only acceptable in that narrow focus structure and is less acceptable in a broad focus context. The intonation pattern used in a broad focus structure including a pitch accent on the NP object is less specific and is thus also acceptable in a narrow focus context. Our results also fit well with an observation by Hartmann (this volume) that for copular clauses in a null context wide focus is less marked than narrow focus. It is thus not generally the case that a single pitch accent on an object NP is ambiguous between a narrow focus and a broad VP focus.

As the acoustic analysis of our stimuli showed, the sentences produced with a narrow object NP focus and a broad VP focus differ not only with regard to the accent on the object NP, but also on the constituents preceding the object. In a follow-up study with cross-spliced materials, we will further investigate what are the exact properties of the intonation pattern that the listeners in our study perceived as (non-)ambiguous between narrow and broad focus.

References

Baumann, S., M. Grice & S. Steindamm. 2006. Prosodic Marking of Focus Domains – Categorical or Gradient? In: Proceedings SpeechProsody 2006. Dresden, Germany, 301–304.
Birch, S. & C. Clifton, Jr. 1995. Focus, Accent, and Argument Structure: Effects on Language Comprehension. Language and Speech 38(4): 365–391.

Boersma, P. & D. Weenink. 2001. Praat, a system for doing phonetics by computer. Glot International 5(9/10): 341–345.
Breen, M., E. Fedorenko, M. Wagner & E. Gibson. 2010. Acoustic correlates of information structure. Language and Cognitive Processes 25(7/8/9): 1044–1098.
Eady, S. J., W. Cooper, G. Klouda, P. Mueller & D. W. Lotts. 1986. Acoustical characteristics of sentential focus: Narrow vs. broad and single vs. dual focus environments. Language and Speech 29(3): 233–251.
Féry, C. 1993. German Intonational Patterns. Tübingen: Max Niemeyer Verlag.
Féry, C. & F. Kügler. 2008. Pitch accent scaling on given, new and focused constituents in German. Journal of Phonetics 36(4): 680–703.
Féry, C. & R. Stoel. 2006. Gradient perception of intonation. In: (G. Fanselow, ed) Gradience in Grammar: Generative Perspectives, 145–166. Oxford University Press, Oxford.
Gussenhoven, C. 1983. Testing the reality of focus domains. Language and Speech 26(1): 61–80.
Jacobs, J. 1993. Integration. In: (M. Reis, ed) Wortstellung und Informations-struktur, 63–116. Tübingen: Niemeyer.
Jannedy, S. 2007. Prosodic focus in Vietnamese. Interdisciplinary studies on information structure 8: 209–230.
Krifka, M. 2008. Basic Notions of Information Structure. Acta Linguistica Hungarica 55: 243–276.
Kügler, F. & A. Gollrad. 2015. Production and perception of contrast: The case of the rise-fall contour in German. Frontiers in Psychology 6: 1254.
Selkirk, E. 1995. Sentence Prosody: Intonation, Stress, and Phrasing. In: (J.A. Goldsmith, ed) The Handbook of Phonological Theory, 550–569. Oxford: Basil Blackwell.
von Stechow, A. & S. Uhmann. 1986. Some Remarks on Focus Projection. In: (W. Abraham & S. de Meij, eds) Topic, Focus, and Configurationality, 295–320. Amsterdam/Philadelphia: John Benjamins Publishing Co.
Xu, Y. 2006. Principles of Tone Research. In: Proceedings of the Second International Symposium on Tonal Aspects of Languages, 3–13. La Rochelle, France.

Jutta M. Hartmann
Focus and prosody in nominal copular clauses

1 Introduction

In this chapter, I address the interaction of syntax and focus in nominal copular clauses in English. I want to defend the claim that specificational copular clauses (=SCCs) crucially differ from nominal predicative copular clauses (=PCCs) in their syntactic and informational structural properties: (i) SCCs are inversion structures and (ii) the post-copular noun phrase in SCCs has to be focused, while no such requirement holds of PCCs, as illustrated in the examples in (1) and (2).

(1) A: Who was the culprit? (John or Bill?)
     B': JOHN was the culprit.   [PCC]
     B'': The culprit was JOHN.   [SCC]
     (Heycock & Kroch, 2002, 148)

(2) A: What was John? (Was John the culprit or the victim?)
     B': John was the CULPRIT.   [PCC]
     B''. *The CULPRIT was John.   [SCC]
     (Heycock & Kroch, 2002, 149)

While inversion of SCCs has been subject to extensive discussion (see Heggie 1988; Moro 1991, 1997, 2006; Heycock 1992; Mikkelsen 2005; among others) the relevance of the information-structural properties has been less prominent. Even though the pattern in (1) and (2) has been observed repeatedly (see Heggie 1988; Heycock 1994; Williams 1997), there has been no empirical study to support this

Acknowledgments: I would like to thank Susanne Winkler, Andreas Konietzko, and Sam Featherston for extensive discussion on different versions of the talk and the paper, to Robin Hörnig for advice on the design of the experiments, to Petra Augurzky, Sophia Schopper, Nico Heizmann for help with the preparation and analysis of the soundfiles, to Nico Deichl, Ad Neeleman, and the administration at UCL for support in running the experiments, to the two native speakers for the recordings and to the participants in the studies. The manuscript profited a lot from the helpful comments of three reviewers. The chapter is based on the work supported by the German Research Foundation (Deutsche Forschungsgemeinschaft DFG) via the grant to project A7 'Focus constructions and Freezing' of the SFB 833, which I thankfully acknowledge.

https://doi.org/10.1515/9783110623093-004

observation. As this observation is a crucial argument for the inversion analyses, the main empirical goal of this chapter is to substantiate the pattern in (1) and (2). Therefore, I will present two rating studies with auditorily presented stimuli, which match (1) and (2) and show that SCCs have a restricted information structure, while PCCs are more flexible in context. I will argue that the differences result from different derivations of the two structures. While the derivation of SCCs is guided by information-structural needs, namely focus on the postcopular noun phrase, as formulated in the hypothesis in (3), there is no direct influence of information structure in PCCs. As the small clause contains two noun phrases (DPs), SCCs are similar to equative structures; however, in contrast to the standard analysis, which equates the reference of two DPs, SCCs contain one DP with a functional[1] interpretation. PCCs are inherently asymmetric with a DP subject and a nominal non-DP/referential predicate, that is, base generated as [be [DP Pr NumP]].

(3) Specification as Focus Inversion
SCCs are base-generated [be DP-Pr-DP] structures, in which the assignment of a focus-background structure results in syntactic inversion of the background and a functional interpretation of the inverted DP.

The chapter is structured as follows: In Section 2, I provide the background for the two experiments that are presented in Sections 3 and 4. Experiment 1 investigates the acceptability of SCCs and PCCs with different intonation without context. Experiment 2 adds context to the sentences, which licenses the focus properties of the sentences. Section 5 provides the analysis of SCCs. Section 6 concludes the chapter.

Two notes on terminology are necessary, in order to avoid confusion in the discussion. I use the descriptive terms of DP1 and DP2 to refer to the noun phrases in their surface order (note that I indicate where the syntactic difference between NP and DP is relevant). This is illustrated in (4).

(4) PCC John   is   the culprit
    SCC The culprit is   John
        DP1   cop DP2

---

[1] I use the term 'functional interpretation' here, as a term to describe that this DP is not referential and it is the function that can take the other DP as its argument. I remain agnostic with respect to the precise semantic analysis as a concealed question or possibly other nonreferential interpretations as individual concepts or the like.

Additionally, I distinguish between two different types of subjects, the underlying subject, which is the noun phrase in the specifier of PrP. The term (surface) subject is used for the noun phrase in Spec,TP. This is important as in the inversion analysis of SCCs; the two subject positions are occupied by two different noun phrases.

2 Background

2.1 Classification of nominal copular clauses

Higgins (1979) distinguishes four different classes of copular clauses: predicational, identity/equative sentences, specificational, and identificational copular clauses illustrated in (5).[2]

(5) a. Susan is a doctor.   [predicative]
    b. She is Susan.   [identity/equative]
    c. The winner is Susan.   [specificational]
    d. This is Susan.   [identificational]

In the predicative sentence in (5-a) *Susan* is assigned the property of being a doctor. Thus, the noun phrase *a doctor* does not introduce or refer back to a salient referent or individual in the discourse. Copular clauses with definite noun phrases can also fall into this class; see the examples from the British National Corpus in (6).[3]

(6) a. The Sea Life Centre is *the perfect venue for many a*   (BNC, BPC 59)
       special occasion
    b. Since Edinburgh is *the focus of this study*, the context   (BNC, EJV 14)
       will be a Scottish one: ...

---

2 This four-way classification is often reduced to the three-way distinction of predicative, equative, and specificational (see, e.g., Huber 2002; Mikkelsen 2004). Den Dikken (2006b) provides a detailed overview of different classifications. For a recent subclassification of predicational copular clauses, see Roy (2013).
3 Some data cited in this chapter have been extracted from the British National Corpus Online service, managed by Oxford University Computing Services on behalf of the BNC Consortium. All rights in the texts cited are reserved. For details on the BNCweb edition, see Hoffmann (2008).

In equative sentences, two referents are stated to be the same individual. The traditional examples used are given in (7).[4]

(7) a. The morning star is the evening star.
    b. Peter Parker is Superman.

SCCs are those sentences in which the initial noun phrase opens a list and the postcopular noun phrase specifies the element(s) on this list.

(8) a. Mary's husband is John.
    b. The best candidate was John.

SCCs differ from predicative and equative sentences in that the initial noun phrase does not refer to an individual and it does not serve as an aboutness topic (in the sense of Reinhart 1982). The postcopular noun phrase is typically referential. Thus, SCCs neither predicate a property of an individual – which makes them different from PCCs – nor do SCCs equate two individuals – which sets SCCs apart from DP-be-DP equatives. Instead the meaning can be described as in (9) (taken from Mikkelsen 2005, 1, who paraphrases Akmajian 1979):

(9) '[A] specificational clause does not tell us something **about** the referent of the [surface] subject NP instead it says **who** or **what** the referent is' [emphasis in original].

The fourth class, the identificational copular clauses, usually has a deictic expression as the first nominal and the second noun phrase provides a name/reference. While these sentences are interesting in their own right, I remain agnostic here whether they need to be considered a separate class as proposed in Higgins (1979), or whether this class is heterogeneous and either falls into the class of SCCs or equatives; see Mikkelsen (2005) for discussion.

---

[4] Equative sentences also subsume sentences in which two properties are equated as in (i). I leave these aside here.

(i) a. Happy is happy.
    b. Slow is slow.

2.2 The syntax of predication

Since the influential work on the syntax of predication in Bowers (1993, 2001), PCCs are assumed to include a separate syntactic projection of PrP in which subject and predicate are base generated. The copula is a raising verb (see Stowell 1978 and follow-up work), and the underlying subject of predication in Spec,PrP raises to Spec,TP in PCCs. This is illustrated in (10).[5]

(10) [TP [DP John] [T' . . . [vP be [PrP John Pr the culprit]]]]

Concentrating on the analysis of SCCs, there are basically three different approaches to be distinguished:
(i) Analyses that take SCCs to be a type of their own, with special properties, see among others Akmajian (1970), Higgins (1979), Rothstein (2001), and Romero (2005).
(ii) Analyses that suggest that SCCs (including specificational pseudoclefts) are a subtype of equative sentences, see among others Jacobson (1995), Sharvit (1999), den Dikken et al. (2000), and Heycock & Kroch (2002).
(iii) Predicate inversion analyses, which claim that SCCs are derived from predicative sentences; see Heggie (1988), Moro (1991), Heycock (1992), Moro (1997), Mikkelsen (2005), den Dikken (2006a), and references therein.

While the first two sets of proposals treat SCCs as syntactically independent from PCCs, the last set of approaches derives SCCs from PCCs via syntactic inversion, roughly along the lines in (11). I call the first two sets base generation approaches and the third group inversion approaches.

(11) a. John is the culprit. [PCC]
 b. [The culprit]$_i$ is John [the culprit]$_i$. [SCC]

Summarizing the discussion on inversion in SCCs very briefly, the picture is the following (for a detailed discussion see Hartmann 2016; Heycock 2012; den Dikken 2006b; Mikkelsen 2004, 2005). While there are clearly syntactic reflexes of inversion visible cross-linguistically (agreement and nonavailability of SCCs as

---

[5] I do not go into differences in the nature of the projection of PrP, as these are not decisive here. PrP can either be headed by a specific head *Pr* à la Bowers (1993), or by a class of elements that count as relators as in den Dikken (2006a); alternatively PrP has been analyzed as a headless small clause that requires one or the other element to move out in the spirit of Moro (2000) (see also Shlonsky & Rizzi 2018).

small clause complements, see Section 5.1 for details), the major problem results from the fact that the initial noun phrase does not behave like a referential DP (e.g., it can be pronominalized by *it* and it does not introduce a referential antecedent), yet, it does not behave like a true predicative noun phrase either (not all predicative noun phrases can invert; plural pronominalization of DP1 in SCC patterns with concealed question DPs, not with predicative noun phrases). In order to reconcile the different sets of facts, Heycock (2012) proposes that SCCs are inversion structures, but that the initial noun phrase is not a predicate.

In light of this discussion, I concentrate here on another argument in favor of inversion, namely its restricted information structure: the postcopular DP has to be focused[6] (see Heggie 1988; Heycock 1994; Williams 1997 for the observation), that is, it cannot be backgrounded and deaccented (though it can be given; for the distinction of newly given, vs. marked focus background, see Hartmann 2016; Rochemont 1986, 2013; Katz & Selkirk 2011; Selkirk 2002). This is illustrated in the examples in (12) and (13) (repeated from above).

(12) A: Who was the culprit? (John or Bill?)
    B': JOHN was the culprit. [PCC]
    B": The culprit was JOHN. [SCC]
    (Heycock & Kroch, 2002, 148)

(13) A: What was John?
    (Was John the culprit or the victim?)
    B': John was the CULPRIT. [PCC]
    B": *The CULPRIT was John. [SCC]
    (Heycock & Kroch, 2002, 149)

This requirement of the postcopular focus is typical for inversion structures in English and as such, the pattern in (13) also supports the inversion analysis.

Thus, there are three issues that arise. First, can the focus facts be empirically supported? Second, how do the focus facts relate to inversion in SCCs? And third, are SCCs related to PCCs, that is, are SCCs a subtype of predicate inversion, or rather a type of their own. These questions are addressed in this chapter, empirically as well as theoretically. I will provide empirical support for the observation in (12) versus (13). These focus facts support the analysis of SCCs as inversion structures, as I will show. Furthermore, I will provide an analysis that links

---

[6] By focus I mean both the information-structural interpretation and the accentuation pattern that comes with it.

syntactic inversion to the focus properties of the structure. However, following Heycock (2012), I assume SCCs not to be predicate inversion structures but a different type, and I spell this intuition out by providing different syntactic structures for PCCs and SCCs.

3 Experiment 1: Nominal copular clauses without context

3.1 Introduction

In Sections 3 and 4, I present and discuss the two rating experiments. The aim is to test the hypothesis that Specification is a type of Focus Inversion: if it is, we expect to confirm the restriction discussed in (2B) and formulated as H1:

H1: SCCs require the postcopular noun phrase to be focused, even when the context would license focus on the precopular DP only.

In order to make sure that this restriction holds generally, I tested the relevant sentences without context (Experiment 1) and in an appropriate context (Experiment 2), and compared them to PCCs as a control condition. This also allows for testing to what extent SCCs and PCCs behave similarly and differently in more detail. For PCCs we test the behavior as follows:

H2: PCCs allow for focus on the pre- and postcopular noun phrase, as long as focus is contextually licensed.

In the experiments presented below, the different information structures are expressed in the test sentences with different types of intonation contours. I used three contours for SCCs and PCCs: a narrow focus on DP1, a narrow focus on DP2, and a neutral contour. In the narrow focus contours, the sentence accent falls on the respective DP with other material being deaccented. In the neutral contour both DPs receive an accent, but the main sentence accent falls on DP2, as the default position of the sentence accent in English. Narrow focus is marked, that is, it can only occur in a specific licensing context; thus, the prediction is that narrow focus on either DP1 or DP2 is rated worse than the neutral contour that does not require such contextual licensing. In order to investigate this, the test sentences are presented without context in Experiment 1 and in context in Experiment 2.

3.2 Method

3.2.1 Participants

There were 30 self-reported native speakers of English, five per list, mostly students, but not exclusively. They were aged between 19 and 73 years with a mean age of 30 years; 57% of participants were female, 43% male. The majority of speakers have a language background in England, but there were a few exceptions from Scotland, New Zealand, and the United States. All participants were paid £3 for their participation.

3.2.2 Design

Experiment 1 contains the manipulation of two factors. The first one is the type of copular clause, comparing PCCs versus SCCs. The second factor concerns the type of focus and distinguishes three levels: a narrow focus on DP1 (NFpre); a narrow focus accent on DP2 (NFpost); and a rather neutral wide intonation (neutral) in which DP1 receives a topic accent and DP2 a regular focus accent. Crossing the two factors results in the six conditions illustrated in Table 1. Capital letters indicate prominence and underlining indicates topic accents (following Wells 2006, the topic accent is a nonfalling accent).

Table 1: Conditions Experiment 1 (without context)

Focus type		Copular clause		
		Predicational (PCC)		Specificational (SCC)
NFpre	1	Trevor BAILEY is the wittiest host.	4	The wittiest HOST is Trevor Bailey.
NFpost	2	Trevor Bailey is the wittiest HOST.	5	The wittiest host is Trevor BAILEY.
Neutral	3	Trevor Bailey is the wittiest HOST.	6	The wittiest host is Trevor BAILEY.

3.2.3 Material

Twenty-four different lexicalizations in all six conditions were used for testing. The lexical items consisted of a definite noun phrase with a superlative adjective and a proper name. The sentences were recorded in a quiet setting. Two native speakers of British English (London Area) – one male, one female – read the sentences in the context of the corresponding question to facilitate the production of the different types of intonation. Typical examples of the intonation contours for the six conditions are given in Figure 1.

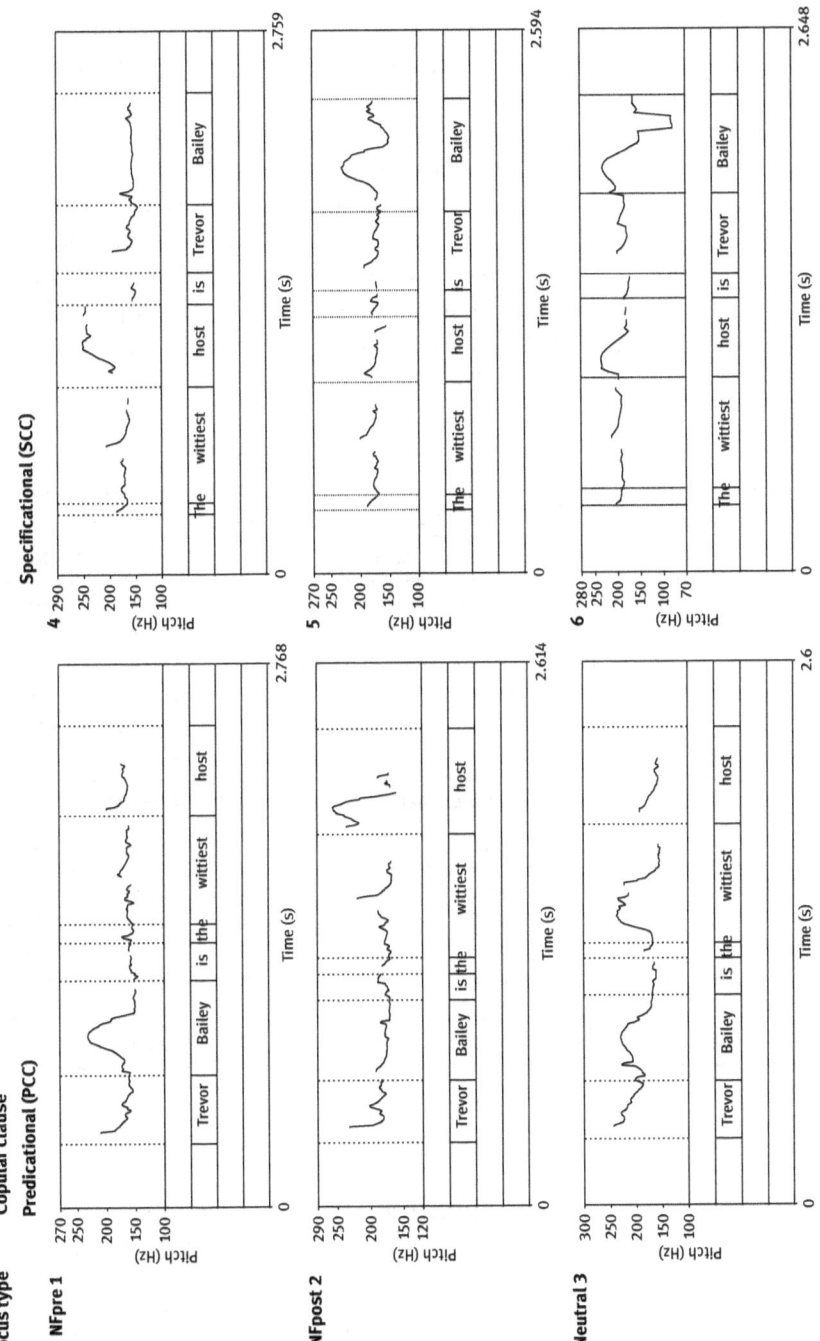

Figure 1: Intonation contours of material for Experiment 1.

The first contour had the main accent on the first noun phrase consisting of a first name and a last name, while the second noun phrase was deaccented. The second contour with the postcopular focus had the main accent on the noun of the postcopular phrase. In the third contour, the initial noun phrase got a topic accent (following Wells 2006, the topic accent is a nonfalling accent) followed by a boundary tone, while the second noun phrase still had the main accent. The contours in SCCs were basically the same, with the two noun phrases reversed. Table 2 provides more details about the phonetic properties of the materials per condition and speaker. We can see that the noun phrase in focus is longer and has a higher pitch when it is focused (note that the length is absolute, and thus, can only be compared in the columns between conditions), but not relative between DP1 and DP2.[7]

Table 2: Pitch range (Hz) and length (seconds) per speaker and condition for answers

PCC		DP1: Trevor Bailey			DP2: the wittiest host		
		Length	Pitch-min	Pitch-max	Length	Pitch-min	Pitch-max
i	Male	1.06	88.50	132.7	0.98	71	104
	Female	1.15	143.36	228.2	1.2	112.4	188.6
ii	Male	0.97	87.33	112.3	1.19	69.67	139.1
	Female	1.0	169.5	206.9	1.19	138.1	245.9
iii	Male	1.01	98.8	141.2	1.01	72.08	146.5
	Female	1.04	164.17	242	1.16	126.9	232.33
SCC		DP1: the wittiest host			DP2: Trevor Bailey		
		Length	Pitch-min	Pitch-max	Length	Pitch-min	Pitch-max
i	Male	1.37	73.5	182.5	.73	67.8	98.75
	Female	1.39	149.8	251.3	.83	141.1	174.8
ii	Male	1.25	81.3	120.6	.87	78.4	149.8
	Female	1.33	161.8	204.4	.93	125	226.25
iii	Male	1.26	86.7	182.8	.87	74.3	142.4
	Female	1.37	167.8	245.75	.86	126.33	226.7

3.2.4 Procedure

The recorded sound files were distributed across six lists in a Latin Square design. Additionally, 60 distractors were recorded and the test sentences were

---

[7] The measurements concern the whole DP as the boundaries of the DPs could be clearly marked. Additionally, there was some variation as to how the rising accent was distributed on noun and adjective, a variation that is not relevant for the question about DP1 and DP2 here.

randomized per participant. Each participant heard each lexical version once, all six conditions were tested four times per participant. The experiment was implemented in OnExp, and was run locally in a lab at UCL in London.

The task for the participants was to rate the naturalness of the sentence on a seven-point scale (1 = very unnatural to 7 = very natural). Before the experiment started, participants read the instructions on what they were to do for the experiment. They had to provide some further details about language background (mother tongue and dialect), profession and age. For each trial, participants had to click on an icon to have the stimulus played. Then, they provided a rating by selecting a value on a seven-point scale. By clicking on a button their rating was saved and they were moved on to the next trial. Participants were instructed to listen to the stimulus carefully and take into consideration, how the sentences are pronounced. The procedure was introduced in a practice stage with eight trials, so that participants were familiar with their task before they rated the experimental material.

3.3 Results and discussion

The individual ratings were collected and z-transformed including fillers. The overall results are given in Figure 2.

First, there is a main effect of (copular clause) TYPE $[F_1(1,29) = 7.16^*;$ $F_2(1,23) = 8.08^*]$.[8] On average, predicational sentences are more acceptable than specificational sentences. Second, there is a main effect of FOCUS $[F_1(2,58) = 19.48^{***}; F_2(2,46) = 25.62^{***}]$. Specified contrasts reveal that there is no difference between postcopular and precopular narrow focus $[F_1(1,29) = 1.6;$ $F_2(1,23) = 1.83]$, while neutral focus is more acceptable than precopular focus and postcopular focus $[F_1(1,29) = 39.87^{***}; F_2(1,23) = 20.00^{***}]$ as expected. Furthermore, there is a significant interaction between the two factors $[F_1(2,58) = 8.94^{***};$ $F_2(2,46) = 13.04^{***}]$. Precopular focus is more acceptable than postcopular focus in PCCs $[t_1 = 5.3^{***}, t_2 = 4.6^{***}]$. The opposite holds for SCCs though it is only marginally significant per subject $[t_1 = 1.55, p = 0.066; t_2 = 2.01, p = 0.028]$.

The results show three major points. First of all, participants are sensitive to different types of intonation in PCCs versus SCCs. Second, narrow focus out of context is marked, especially so for marked focus on the noun phrase that is not a proper name, that is, both DP2 focus in PCCs and DP1 focus in SCCs are rated

---

8 Significance levels are indicated as follows: *** for $p < .001$ ** for $p < .01$, and * for $p < .05$.

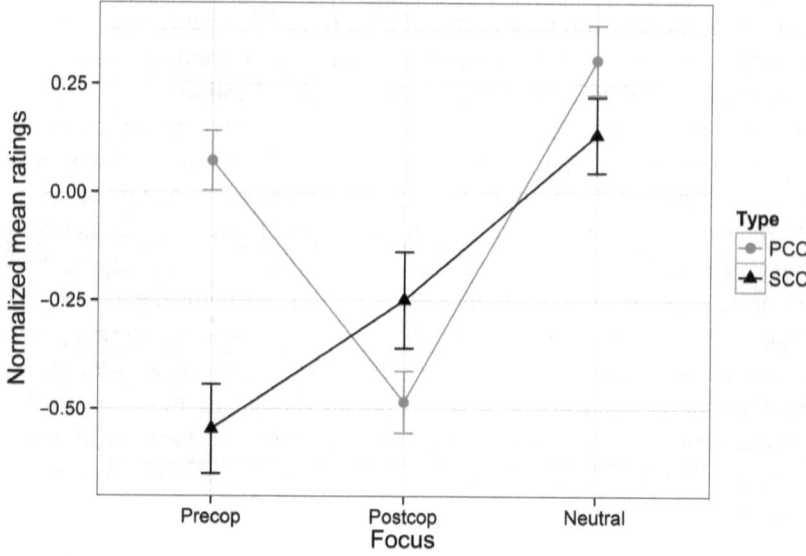

Figure 2: Experiment 1 w/o context: Average rating (z-score) per condition.

worst in their set.[9] Thus, it is not enough to look at specificational versus predicational copular clauses without context, as the shift of focus on the functional/nonreferential DP gives rise to lower acceptability to begin with. Therefore, it is necessary to look at the results in context, as will be done in Experiment 2.

4 Experiment 2: Nominal copular clauses in context

4.1 Introduction

In this section, I introduce the second experiment (Experiment 2). Here, the experimental sentences from Experiment 1 have been presented in a context that licenses the focus marking in the individual conditions. The comparison of Experiments 1 and 2 is necessary to figure out whether marked contours can be improved in

---

[9] The low rating of the postcopular focus as opposed to the higher rating of the precopular focus in PCCs might be due to the fact that it is easier to accommodate appropriate alternatives to proper names than alternatives to functional noun phrases.

context, and if that is the case, if narrow focus on DP1 is indeed problematic in SCCs as opposed to PCCs. If this is indeed the case, we expect the narrow focus condition on the predicate in PCCs to be improved with context, while this is not to be expected for the low rating in SCCs when the narrow focus falls on DP1. Beyond the interest of the analysis of SCCs and PCCs, this experiment also allows for an evaluation of the role of context for the naturalness ratings and to what extent context can serve to improve ratings of marked structures. Additionally, Experiment 2 helps to provide support for the claim that SCCs require a postcopular focus.

4.2 Method

4.2.1 Participants

There were 36 self-reported native speakers of English participating in the study. The age ranged from 17 to 72 years, with a mean age of 33 years. There were 53% female participants and 47% males. The majority of speakers were from England, but there were also a few from Canada and the United States. As before participants were mostly, but not exclusively students. They were paid £3 for their participation, which took around 30 min.

4.2.2 Design and material

The design of Experiment 2 was the same as in Experiment 1 (see Table 1). The only difference was that the conditions were supplemented by appropriate context to support the intonational patterns of focus. Thus, context is not an additional factor in the design. For the narrow focus conditions, an alternative question of the form in (14) was provided:

(14) a. Do you think that DP is [DP or DP]?
      b. Do you think that [DP or DP] is DP?

The neutral focus question sets up a general *What happens?* type of question with an additional prepositional phrase that provides a context frame for the sentence to come. An example for the context questions in all four conditions is provided in (15) and (16).

(15) a. Do you think that Trevor Bailey or Henry Blofeld is the wittiest host?
      Trevor BAILEY is the wittiest host.   [NPpre]

b. Do you think that Trevor Bailey is the wittiest host or the wittiest actor?
      Trevor Bailey is the wittiest HOST. [NFpost]
   c. What's new on ITV?
      Trevor Bailey is the wittiest HOST. [neutral]

(16) a. Do you think that Trevor Bailey is the wittiest host or the wittiest actor?
        The wittiest HOST is Trevor Bailey. [NPpre]
     b. Do you think that Trevor Bailey or Henry Blofeld is the wittiest host?
        The wittiest host is Trevor BAILEY. [NFpost]
     c. What's new on ITV?
        The wittiest host is Trevor BAILEY. [neutral]

The material consisted of the same 24 lexicalizations as in Experiment 1 with the addition of the context question. The questions were recorded in a quiet setting in individual sessions per native speakers. The question–answer sequences then were combined such that the question was provided by a different voice than the answer. Speaker voice was balanced across conditions and lists.

4.2.3 Procedure

The recorded sound files were distributed across six lists in a Latin Square design. Additionally, 60 further question–answer pairs were used as fillers. The sentences were randomized per participant. Each participant heard each lexical version once, all six conditions were tested four times per participant. The experiment was implemented in OnExp, but run locally in a lab in London.

Participants were asked to rate the naturalness of the answer in the context of the question on a seven-point scale (1 = very unnatural to 7 = very natural). The procedure was exactly the same as in Experiment 1.

4.3 Results and discussion

Raw ratings were z-transformed per participant. Overall results are depicted in Figure 3.[10]

---

[10] The average z-scores in Experiment 2 are much higher than in Experiment 1. As can be seen from the raw ratings for both experiments (see table below), there is a general numerical

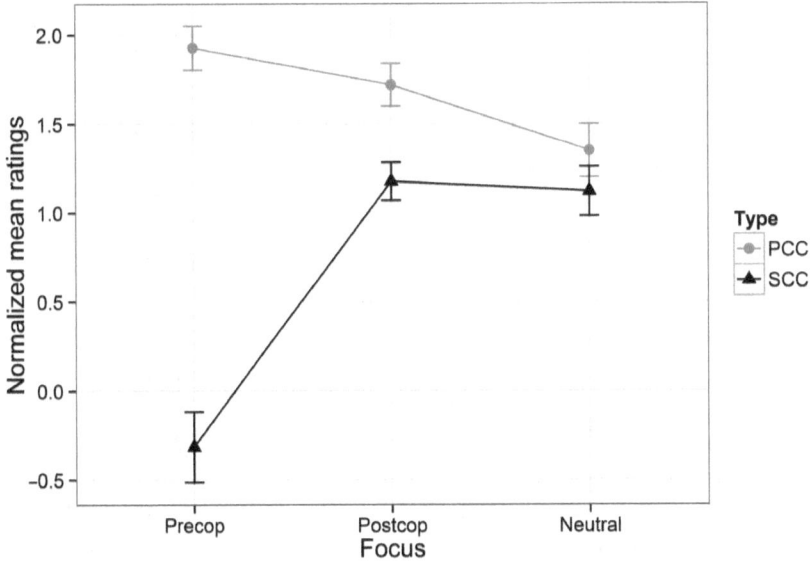

Figure 3: Experiment 2 with context: Average rating (z-score) per condition.

There is a main effect for (copular clause) TYPE [$F_1(1,35) = 64.88^{***}$; $F_2(1,23) = 93.29^{***}$]. On average, predicative sentences are rated more acceptable than specificational clauses. There is also a main effect of FOCUS [$F_1(2,70) = 6,88^*$; $F_2(2,46) = 3.11$, $p = .06$]; specified contrasts show that postcopular focus is significantly rated more acceptable than precopular focus across both constructions [$F_1(1,35) = 23,60^{***}$; $F_2(1,23) = 11.18^{***}$].

---

improvement of the marked conditions in PCCs and SCCs, while the context reduces acceptability in the neutral conditions and the worst condition in SCCs. It seems that this effect is strengthened as mean raw ratings for all fillers in Experiment 1 was slightly higher (4.74) than in Experiment 2 (4.61).

Mean ratings for Experiment 1 (without context) and Experiment 2 (with context)

Condition	Type	Focus	Rating Exp. 1	Rating Exp. 2
i.	PCC	Narrow focus on precopular	4.74	5.45
ii.	PCC	Narrow focus on postcopular	3.70	5.15
iii.	PCC	Neutral topic – focus	5.25	4.62
iv.	SCC	Narrow focus on precopular	3.60	2.80
v.	SCC	Narrow focus on postcopular	4.20	4.49
vi.	SCC	Neutral topic – focus	4.90	4.31

Finally, there is a significant interaction [$F_1(2,34) = 21.70^{***}$; $F_2(2,22) = 7.03^{***}$]. There is a clear and large difference between the narrow focus on DP1: This condition is rated highly in PCCs and it is the worst condition in SCCs.

What we can see in these results is that there is a clear difference between SCCs and PCCs. The former clearly do not allow a narrow focus on the initial DP, even if the context licenses such a prosodic focus marking. Additionally, narrow focus on DP1 and DP2 (proper name and nonreferential DP) can be licensed in context in PCCs, but not in SCCs. Thus, the observation reported in the theoretical literature on this phenomenon is clearly confirmed.

Additionally, the combinations of the two experiments show that the narrow focus contour needs contextual licensing, while the neutral contour does not: it is accepted even without context. This is similar to what is reported in De Kuthy & Stolterfoht (this volume), who find that a broad focus intonation is also licensed in a narrow focus context, but not vice versa. Note, however, that the relevant intonation in my study did not only vary with respect to the focus accent, but also with respect to the accentuation of the initial noun phrase, which is an important difference from their study.

5 A focus-based syntactic analysis of SCCs

The result of the preceding two experiments can be summarized as follows. SCCs require DP2 to be focused. A precopular focus in SCCs with a deaccented postcopular noun phrase cannot be improved by an appropriate question context. Thus, the observation in Heggie (1988), Heycock (1994), and Williams (1997) is clearly confirmed. The main question to be addressed here in this section is: why are SCCs restricted in this way, while PCCs are not?

The answer I want to defend here is that there is an intricate relationship between the syntax of these structures, their focus properties, and their interpretation. The syntactic derivation is affected by the information structure as phrased in the following hypothesis repeated from above.

(17) Specification as Focus Inversion
SCCs are base-generated DP-Pr-DP structures, in which the assignment of a focus-background structure results in a functional interpretation and syntactic inversion of the background.

As the specificational reading is a result of the focus assignment, which in turn gives rise to the inversion process in English, SCCs require DP2 to be focused – there are no SCCs without focus. No such relationship holds in PCCs; thus, they allow both a precopular and a postcopular focus.

In the following, I will first provide the main evidence for the syntactic inversion in SCCs, then I will provide an outline of the framework that allows for the implementation of (17) (see Hartmann 2016 for details), and then show how SCCs are derived.

5.1 SCCs as inversion structures

There are a number of arguments in favor of the inversion analysis, with respect to the syntax of SCCs and the interpretation of DP1 (see Heggie 1988, Heycock 1994, 173ff, and references therein for collections and the original sources, Mikkelsen 2005 for a more recent overview, Rothstein 2001 for a different perspective).

The first syntactic argument relies on subject–verb agreement. Moro (1997) shows that subject–verb agreement in Italian in SCCs is governed by the underlying subject, DP2.

(18) Il   colpevole   sono/*è   io/*me.
     the   culprit   am/*is   I/*me
     'The culprit is me.'

The same holds for German, see (19).[11]

---

[11] S. Löbner (p.c.) pointed out to me that agreement cannot be evidence for inversion as there are cases in German where agreement is with DP2, yet DP2 seems to be the predicate in the structure, see (i).

(i) Das   sind   gute   Freunde   von   mir /   zwei   schlaue   Frauen.   [pointing at two people]
     that   are   good   friends   of   mine /   two   smart   women
     'These are good friends of mine / two smart women.'

Note though, as Higgins (1979) pointed out, the pronoun *that* is a special case. It cannot be used with bare nouns as predicates even when pointing to the respective person. The same holds for German, see (iii).

(ii) a. That woman is Mayor of Cambridge.
      b. *That is Mayor of Cambridge.
      (Higgins, 1979, 239)

(iii) a. Peter ist Pianist / schlau.
         Peter is piano.player / smart.
      b. *Das ist Pianist / schlau.
         That is piano.player / smart

(19) a. Die   Ursache des   Feuers waren brennende Kerzen.
       the   Cause   the.GEN   fire   were   burning   candles

   b. dass die Ursache des   Feuers brennende Kerzen   waren.
      that the cause   the.Gen   fire   burning   candles were

If DP2, in fact, is the underlying subject, this agreement pattern can be explained more or less straightforwardly.[12]

Second, the order of SCCs does not occur in the complement of *consider*-type verbs without the copula, only the predicative order is possible. If both PCCs and SCCs are base generated from the same underlying small clause, this observation is expected. SCCs need a target position for inversion, which is not available in bare small clauses.[13]

(20) a. I consider John the real culprit.
   b. *I consider the real culprit John.
   (Heycock, 1994, 177)

Higgins (1979) concludes that copular clauses with deictic *that* in precopular position are all identificational. *That* seems to be only possible when the predicate nominal is a noun phrase that has enough syntactic structure to express number (adjectives and bare nouns are not possible). To my mind, this indicates that *that* needs to inherit number from the post-copular DP. The agreement pattern in these cases therefore does not question the argument based on agreement for SCCs.

12 For intricate patterns of intra- and interlanguage speaker variation with respect to agreement in SCCs, see Béjar & Kahnemuyipour (2017), Hartmann & Heycock (2014, 2017, 2018a,b).

13 Note that this argument needs to be taken with a grain of salt. The type of small clauses *consider* (and other verbs) selects is restricted in other ways, too, see Heycock (1994, 177ff). So there is potentially another semantic reason why the reverse order is ruled out.

(i) a. *I consider John off my ship.
   b. ?I consider John at the peak of his career.
   (Heycock, 1994, 85)

Additionally, Heycock & Kroch (1999) have argued that specificational small clauses do occur, see (ii):

(ii) But if what you say is true, that would make the real murderer John!

The restrictions are certainly intricate; however, *make* can select potentially larger, namely verbal, structures. Thus, the example (iii) is not a compelling counterexample.

(iii) Mary made Peter leave.

Third, the focus structure of SCCs is more restricted than of PCCs, as reported above. In an inversion analysis, this restriction is expected, as the focus on the noninverted DP is a characteristic feature of inversion structures (see Culicover & Winkler 2008).

Fourth, there is also an asymmetry with respect to extraction, which is not observed in PCCs. SCCs disallow extraction of, and subextraction from, the postverbal DP (see Moro 1997 among others), which again is a feature that is observed with other inversion structures (see, e.g., locative inversion, Bresnan 1994).

Finally, it has been argued that DP1 in SCCs is not a referential DP, but rather behaves as a predicate, with respect to the pronominalization with *it* and *that* (as anaphora for properties) (cf. Kuno 1972 cited in Mikkelsen 2005, see also Büring & Hartmann 1998). This can be observed with tag questions, as in (21), left dislocation as in (22), and anaphoric reference, see (23).

(21) a. The tallest girl in the class is Molly, isn't it?
 b. The tallest girl in the class is Swedish, isn't she/*it?
 (Mikkelsen, 2004, 64)

(22) a. The tallest girl in the class, {that/it}'s Molly.
 b. The tallest girl in the class, {she/*it/*that} 's Swedish.
 (Mikkelsen, 2004, 64)

(23) a. SCC
    Q: Who is the tallest girl in class?
    A: {That/It}'s Molly.
 b. PCC
    Q: What nationality is Molly?
    A: {She/*It/*That}'s Swedish.
 (Mikkelsen, 2004, 64)

These facts have led a number of researchers to propose that SCCs and PCCs are the regular and inverse order of the same underlying small clause (see Mikkelsen 2005; Moro 1997; Heycock 1994).

However, several observations suggest that the inversion in SCCs is not inversion of a predicate. First of all, not every PCC has an equivalent SCC variant; see (24).[14]

---

[14] Mikkelsen (2005) argues that this is an information-structural restriction. As soon as the initial noun phrase is more complex and allows a link to be made to the preceding discourse, indefinite noun phrases are possible, as in the initial noun phrase in (i).

(24) a. John is a doctor.
　　 b. *A doctor is John.
　　 (Heycock & Kroch, 1999)

Second, as Heycock (2012) points out, pronominalization shows that DP1 is a type of concealed question (along the lines of Romero 2005), rather than a predicative noun phrase. A concealed question means that a noun phrase as *the winners* in (25) does not refer to individuals, but rather expresses a question such as *who the winners are*. Heycock (2012) observes that concealed questions require a different pronoun, namely *they*, when used with a plural; see (25). True predicative NPs in plural still are pronominalized with *it*; see (26).[15]

(25) Plural concealed question.　　　　　　　　　　　　　*it: *; them:* OK
　　 We won't know the winners until they announce *it/them.
　　 (Heycock, 2012)

(26) Plural predicate.　　　　　　　　　　　　　　　　　*it:* OK; *them: *
　　 They are the winners, although they don't look it/*them.
　　 (Heycock, 2012)

In SCCs, the pronoun used for plurals matches the concealed question interpretation, not the pronoun *it* which is used for predicate nominals.

(i) A philosopher who seems to share Kiparsky's intuitions on some factive predicates is Unger (1972) ... (cited from Mikkelsen, 2005, 155)

Note, though, that the additional modification with a relative clause seems to make the indefinite specific. Thus, these NPs are not truly predicative and they differ in this respect from cases such as (24).

15 A reviewer pointed out that this test actually might give different results in German, see (i) where *das* can be used with the subject noun phrase in a PCC.

(i) Q: Glaubst Du, dass Trevor Bailey oder Henry Blofeld der geistreichste Moderator ist?
　　　 Do you think that T.B. or H.B. is the wittiest host?

　　 A: Trevor BAILEY, {der/das} ist der geistreichste Moderator.
　　　 T.B. {he/that} is the wittiest host.

Note though that this only shows that German *das* is not a good test case, especially in combination with left dislocation; as pointed out in Footnote 11, German *das* has a number of other properties that are not yet well understood. Additionally, (i) does not tell us much about the status of the other DP, namely *the wittiest host*, which is the crucial point here.

(27) Plural DP1 in specificational sentence.   *it*: *; *them*: OK
      The winners were Blanchett and Nyong'o, *wasn't it/weren't they?
      (Heycock, 2012)

What we see here then is that there is evidence for inversion in SCCs; however, this is not simply the flip version of a regular PCC. Bringing together these two observations, I follow Heycock (2012) in arguing that SCCs are inversion structures with the inverted noun phrase not being a predicative noun phrase, but a full-fledged DP that receives a functional, that is, nonreferential, interpretation. The structure is given in (28).

(28) My best friend is John

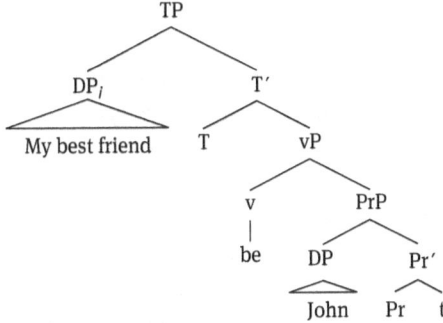

From a syntactic point of view, the inversion analysis gives rise to two fundamental questions.
– What allows the underlying subject in PrP to stay low?
– What makes the complement of PrP move instead?

My answer to these questions is that Focus-Background Mapping is responsible for both processes. I will illustrate in the following sections what I mean by that.

5.2 Focus assignment and inversion

The crucial proposal that I want to make here is that SCCs give rise to a specific Focus-Background Mapping already in the core predication, that is, in the Small Clause (=PrP). This is phrased as the Focus Mapping Hypothesis (FMH) in (29) and illustrated in (30).

(29) Focus Mapping Hypothesis
In specificational sentences with a DP subject and DP predicate, the predication phrase (PrP) is mapped onto a focus-background division.

(30) Mapping: Focus-Background

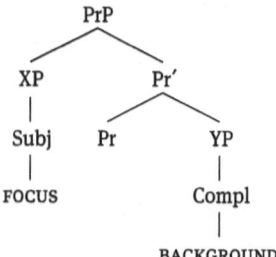

This mapping gives rise to the inversion process. In order to implement this, we need a model of grammar that allows for the interaction of syntax and information structure during the derivation. The model used here is the Phase-based Interface Model proposed in Hartmann (2016). In this model, information structure is a separate module (=InfS module) and it interacts with syntax at the phase level. The major task of the InfS module is to link phases to the discourse. It provides the interface between syntax, PF, and LF by assigning feature bundles to these constituents. These feature bundles consist of features that are readable to semantics (for example features that are relevant for focus interpretation), features readable to the PF component (such as those relevant for prominence or deaccentuation), and these bundles can contain syntactic features that drive further movement. Additionally, the information-structural module can assign mappings such as the one provided in (30). The mapping basically assigns sets of feature bundles to specifier and complement of the phase head.

In such a framework, the derivation of the SCC in (31) proceeds in the following steps. I use the following abbreviations in the illustration: D = discourse features, IS = information structural features, PF = phonological form; Foc = marked focus giving rise to the relevance of alternatives; FocProm = a feature that is interpreted at PF to provide focus prominence; EF = edge feature that drives movement in syntax; BG = background.

(31) What's new in the murder case?
The culprit is John.

The syntax generates the two DPs, which are sent to the InfS module independently. The phrase *the culprit* can be inferred from the setting of the murder case, and it is thus accessible (see Chafe 1994; Gundel 1996; Baumann & Grice 2006 for the relevant notion of accessibility).

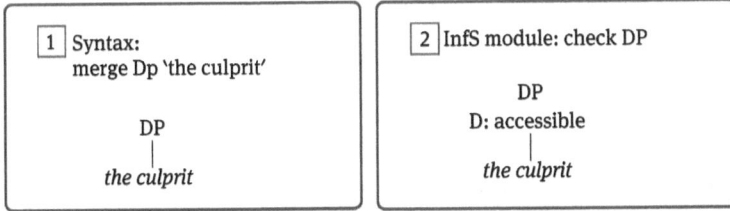

The DP phase 'John' is also generated in syntax and sent to the InfS module. As John has not been mentioned in the previous discourse, the DP is marked as discourse new.[16]

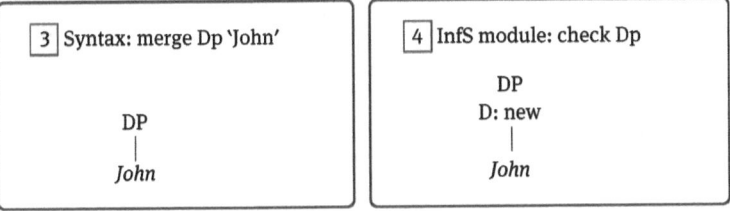

The next stage is to merge the next phase PrP in the syntax. I take PrP to be a phase (see den Dikken 2006a, 2007).

---

[16] In some analyses of definite DPs, including proper names, they cannot be entirely new, as they need to be identifiable. I take this notion of identifiability relevant for the common ground, not discourse, thus, this property of definite DPs is not part of the InfS module proper, as proposed here. Additionally, definite DPs do occur in *there*-sentences outside of the list reading (see Ward & Birner 1995; Hartmann 2008 for discussion), hence, definite noun phrases are not necessarily known (present in the common ground) or given (mentioned in the discourse).

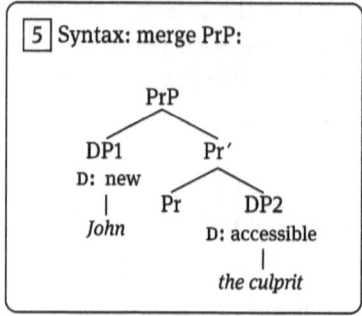

In the InfS module, the Focus-Background Mapping is applied according to the FMH. This is the crucial step. I take this mapping to be triggered by a type mismatch of two definite and referential DPs. The result of this mapping is a functional interpretation of the background (some type of a concealed question interpretation along the lines of Romero 2005). In English, this Focus-Background Mapping assigns a formal feature to the background, a feature that is readable to syntax. This feature, which I call edge feature (=EF) in line with current syntactic terminology, drives the DP *the culprit* to move. Thus, I crucially rely on a framework in which movement is triggered by a feature on the moved item (and not solely on the requirements of a probe).

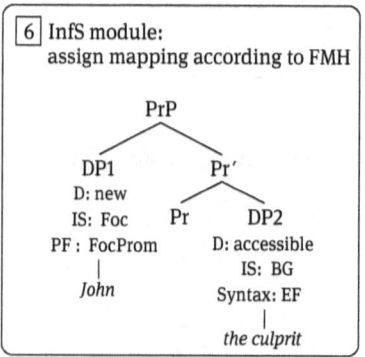

The structure is sent back to syntax. The formal feature on the background makes the background move to the edge. This results in low inversion of the DP; see Heycock (2012) on low inversion.

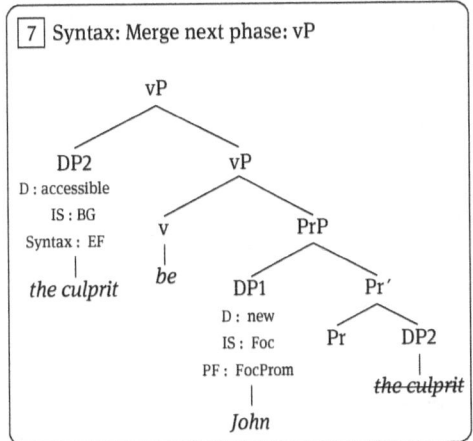

7 Syntax: Merge next phase: vP

Depending on the precise mechanism of movement, the Pr-head might move to the v-head, giving rise to phase extension, along the lines proposed in den Dikken (2007). The vP phase is sent to the InfS module, where nothing particularly relevant for the discussion here happens. After this step, the syntax builds the CP phase.

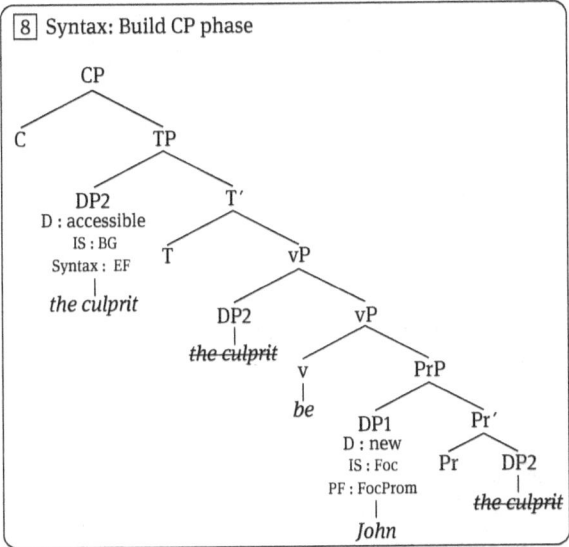

8 Syntax: Build CP phase

This phase is then sent to the InfS module, which sends the phase on to LF, where the structure is fully interpreted. The proposition is added to the common ground and discourse. At PF the prosody of the phase is determined on the basis of the phonetic features assigned in the InfS module and default rules.

The crucial step in this derivation is step 6, where Focus and Background are mapped onto the two DPs in PrP, which results in the inversion of the DP *the culprit* in the syntactic derivation. Thus, information structure can affect and interact with syntax during the derivation of individual sentences.

5.3 Subject focus assignment in PCCs is not specification

After having discussed focus assignment in SCCs, I want to briefly turn to focus assignment in PCCs and the differences to SCCs. As discussed above, SCCs have three interrelated properties: (i) focus on DP2, (ii) functional interpretation of DP1, and (iii) syntactic inversion. All three are related in the FMH provided in (29) above. Now given these three properties, the following questions are relevant with respect to PCCs: Why does focus on the underlying subject not result in inversion? Is focus assignment on the underlying subject enough for a specificational interpretation? The first question is partly a technical question, given that SCCs are not cases of predicate inversion. I assume that the syntactic structure of the non-referential noun phrase in SCCs and PCCs is different. For SCCs, I assume that the precopular noun phrase is a full-fledged DP, while the predicative noun phrase is lacking a proper DP layer and only projects lower projections, which I take to be NumP, but other labels might be equally appropriate (see Zamparelli 2000; Hartmann 2008 for discussion of the syntax of different types of noun phrases).

(32) a. [$_{DP}$ [$_D$ the] culprit] is John.
    b. John is [$_{NumP}$ the [$_{Num}$ ⌀] culprit].

As a result, Focus-Background Mapping can be defined for DP-Pr-DP structures as done in (29) and (30), and it does not apply to PCCs, which have the form DP-be-NumP. Focus mapping is not required and if it applies, it does not lead to inversion, because the conditions for (29) are not met.[17]

---

[17] I leave it to future research whether this means that Focus-Background Mapping does not apply in PCCs or whether it is a different mapping with different properties. In essence, this means that so far, the Focus-Background Mapping is a construction-specific mapping. I am currently investigating the hypothesis that Focus-Background Mapping is triggered by the semantic-type mismatch resulting from the interpretation of the two DPs (both definites of type < e >). This type mismatch can be resolved by assigning a functional meaning to the complement of Pr. This functional meaning is what the background expresses (for a different idea of how type shifting and focusing interact, see Ogihara 1987; Surányi 2011). Note that true equatives also have the underlying structure DP-Pr-DP; I assume that here Topic-Comment mapping takes place, and the comment becomes the functional interpretation. This idea is based on the observation in

The derivation of a PCC with a focus on the subject as in the experimental context, see (33), is therefore along the following lines:[18]

(33) a. Do you think that John or Bill is the wittiest actor?
      b. John is the wittiest actor.

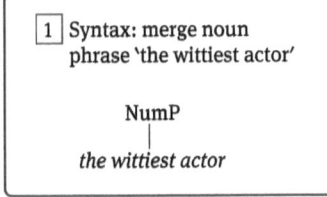

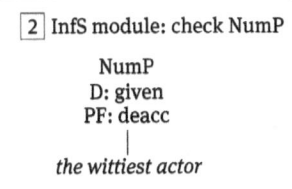

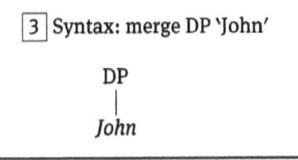

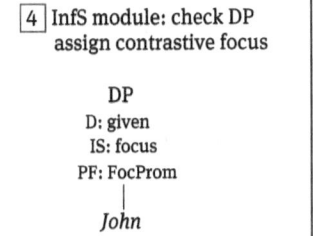

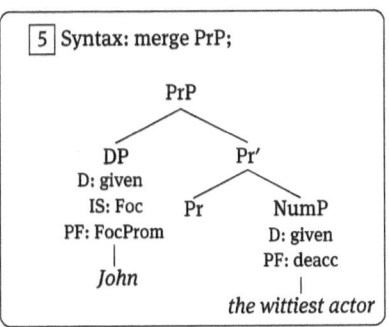

Hartmann & Hegedűs (2009) that in Hungarian, equatives do not show a neutral order: they either exhibit a topic comment, or a focus-background structure.

18 Note that there is a syntactic issue, whether a predicative noun phrase is a phase in itself. If it is not a phase, the InfS module assigns features at the PrP level. As this issue is not relevant for the main point of the discussion, I gloss over it here.

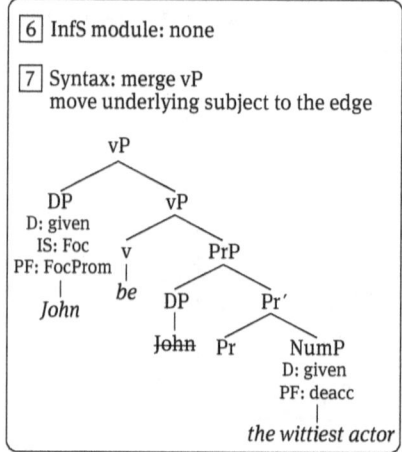

The derivation proceeds as with SCCs with the difference that here the highest noun phrase that moves to Spec,TP is the underlying subject.

The second question can be rephrased as: Can *JOHN is the culprit.* have a specificational interpretation? It might have two of the properties of SCCs, namely (i) focus on JOHN and (ii) a functional interpretation of *the culprit*. I think that this is not the case and that in English the specificational interpretation is tightly linked to inversion. First,[19] the DP *the culprit* has a different semantic (and syntactic) status in the PCC order than in the SCC order as evidenced from the differences in plural tags reported above in (25)–(27). The noun phrase *the winners* can be pronominalized with *it* (as expected under a predicational reading), but the pronominalization with *they* is out as expected under my analysis in which the PCC order does not have a specificational reading, see (34) versus (35):

(34) a. Who are the winners? Are Mary and Sally the winners?
 b. No, [John and Bill]F are the winners although they don't look it/*them.

Additionally, a concealed question DP cannot be the antecedent for an elided NP in the predicational order, see (35a), while the specificational order allows for such an antecedent (35b) using the pronoun *they*.

---

19 Thanks to Caroline Heycock for insightful discussion of this question.

(35) Did you guess the winners?
  a. #I thought John and Bill were, but in fact Mary and Sally were.
  b. I thought they were John and Bill, but in fact they were Mary and Sally.

Note that ellipsis is perfectly fine if the predicational noun phrase is overt in the question, while SCCs with a pronominal *they* in subject position are marked in this context[20]:

(36) Did you guess who were the winners?
  a. I thought John and Bill were, but in fact Mary and Sally were.
  b. ??I thought they were John and Bill, but in fact they were Mary and Sally.

Second, SCCs and PCCs exhibit differences with respect to focus interpretation. On the one hand, focus on the subject goes hand in hand with deaccenting the postcopular material in the PCC order. Nothing of this sort is required in SCCs, where the respective noun phrase, *the culprit*, can or cannot be deaccented. On the other hand, this difference can be shown when considering the availability of focus-sensitive additive particles like *also* or *too*. These particles cannot associate with the postcopular constituent in SCCs, see (37) (note that I exclude the possible reading in which *too* associates with the whole clause). Association is possible in PCCs; see (38).[21, 22]

(37) a. #Mary's brother is John, too.
  b. #Mary's brother is also John.

---

[20] For reasons that are unclear to me, it is not possible to have *it* in predicative position *John and Bill were it. in the context in (36). Note though that it is possible to refer back to the ellipsis site using *it* in the context of (35): *John and Bill were, even though they didn't look it.*
[21] Thanks to B. Surányi (p.c.) for pointing me to this set of data.
[22] The context of the BNC example discusses a comparison of the British versus US American political situation after Major has won the elections in Britain in 1992, and before US American elections with Clinton and Bush senior competing for presidency.
  (i) 1047 Just like Mr Major, Mr Bush succeeded a leader who very much knew what he/she thought, whose stamp of ideology was far clearer, who was a hero/heroine to a missionary movement. 1048 Like Mr Major, Mr Bush is frequently accused of being colorless and too pragmatic. 1049 The voters, it is said, 'do not know who he is or what he stands for'. 1050 He is slightly dull.

  1051 Just like Americans, many Britons, with the ideological and stylistic gap between the two parties narrowing, were said to be simply 'bored' with the Tories after 13 years.

(38) a. John, too, is Mary's brother.
b. Mr. Clinton, too, is the candidate of 'change' (BNC, AK9 1052)

The same point can be made with the Hungarian data. In Hungarian, a predicative noun phrase (including definite predicates like *the president*) occupies the preverbal position. When the subject of such a predicative structure is focused, association with *is* 'too' is possible; see (39). This is not the case, with specificational noun phrases; see (40).[23]

(39) Most már JÁNOS is kéne, Hogy az elnökünk
now already John also should.be that the president.POSS.2PL
legyen.
be.subjunctive
'It's time now for JOHN too to be our president.'
(PCC: *the president* is in preverbal predicative position)

(40) *Most már JÁNOS is kéne, hogy legyen az
now already John also should.be that be.subjunctive the
elnökünk.
president.POSS.2PL
'#The president should now be John, too.'
(SCC: *the president* not in preverbal predicative position)

Thus, I conclude that focus on DP1 in PCCs is not enough for a specificational interpretation. Instead there is tight relation between the three properties of (i) Focus, (ii) functional interpretation, and (iii) inversion, which is supported by the empirical data reported in Sections 3 and 4, and grasped in the analysis suggested in Hartmann (2016) in its slightly revised version as presented in this section.

6 Conclusion

In this chapter, I have provided the results of two experimental rating studies based on auditorily presented material. They show that a narrow focus on the precopular noun phrase is not possible in SCCs. This shift of accent cannot be licensed by an appropriate context. This is in stark contrast to predicational

---

[23] The example is an instance of long focus movement: the preverbal position is only occupied by the predicative phrase if there is no focus phrase in the same clause.

copular clauses in which a narrow focus is possible on both the initial and the postcopular noun phrase in an appropriate context. Thus, this observation by Heggie (1988), Heycock (1994), and Williams (1997) is clearly confirmed. I provided an analysis in which this restriction is due to the nature of SCCs: they are inversion structures and this inversion is a result of the focus assignment to the postcopular DP. Thus, the focus properties in SCCs are built into the syntactic structure. As a result, the focus structure is not flexible, but fixed and the postcopular DP has to be focused. Beyond the discussion of SCCs, this chapter also contributes to the study of marked structures in context: narrow focus structures with flanking deaccented material require licensing in context, while this is not true for neutral contours.

References

Akmajian, A. 1970. On deriving cleft sentences from pseudo-cleft sentences. Linguistic Inquiry 1(2): 149–168.
Akmajian, A. 1979. Aspects of the grammar of focus in English. New York: Garland.
Baumann, S. & M. Grice. 2006. The intonation of accessibility. Journal of Pragmatics 38(10): 1636–1657.
Béjar, S. & A. Kahnemuyipour. 2017. Non-canonical agreement in copular clauses. Journal of Linguistics 53(3): 463–499.
Béjar, S. & A. Kahnemuyipour. 2018. Not all phi-features are created equal: A reply to Hartmann & Heycock 2018. Journal of Linguistics 54(3): 629–635.
BNC. 2001. British National Corpus, Version 2 (world edition). http://www.natcorp.ox.ac.uk/
Bowers, J. 1993. The syntax of predication. Linguistic Inquiry 24(4): 591–656.
Bowers, J. 2001. Predication. In: (M. Baltin & C. Collins, eds) The handbook of contemporary syntactic theory, 299–333. Malden, MA/Oxford: Blackwell.
Bresnan, J.W. 1994. Locative inversion and the architecture of universal grammar. Language 70(1): 72–131.
Büring, D. & K. Hartmann. 1998. Asymmetrische Koordination. Linguistische Berichte 174: 172–201.
Chafe, W. L. 1994. Discourse, consciousness, and time. Chicago, IL / London: University of Chicago Press.
Culicover, P. & S. Winkler. 2008. English focus inversion. Journal of Linguistics 44(3): 625–658.
den Dikken, M. 2006a. Relators and linkers: The syntax of predication, predicate inversion, and copulas. Cambridge, MA: MIT Press.
den Dikken, M. 2006b. Specificational copular sentences and pseudoclefts. In: (M. Everaert & H. van Riemsdijk, eds) The Blackwell companion to syntax, Vol IV, 292–409. Malden, MA/Oxford: Blackwell.
den Dikken, M. 2007. Phase extension. Contours of a theory of the role of head movement in phrasal extraction. Theoretical Linguistics 33(3): 1–41.
den Dikken, M., A. Meinunger & C. Wilder. 2000. Pseudoclefts and ellipsis. Studia Linguistica 54(1): 41–89.

Gundel, J. 1996. Relevance Theory meets the givenness hierarchy. An account of inferrables. In: (T. Fretheim & J. Gundel, eds) Reference and referent accessibility, 141–153. Amsterdam: Benjamins.
Hartmann, J.M. 2008. Expletives in existentials: English *there* and German *da*. Utrecht: LOT Dissertation Series 181.
Hartmann, J.M. 2016. The syntax and focus structure of Specificational Copular Clauses and clefts. Tübingen: Habilitationsschrift.
Hartmann, J.M. & V. Hegedűs. 2009. Nominal copula clauses in English and Hungarian. Manuscript.
Hartmann, J.M. & C. Heycock. 2014. Agreement in copula clauses: Evidence for a dual mechanism of agreement. Talk given at GLOW Conference 2014, 4. April 2014, Brüssel.
Hartmann, J.M. & C. Heycock. 2017. Variation in copular agreement in Insular Scandinavian. In: (H. Thráinsson, C. Heycock, H. P. Petersen & Z. Svabo Hansen, eds) Syntactic variation in insular Scandinavian, 234–275. Amsterdam & Philadelphia: John Benjamins.
Hartmann, J.M. & C. Heycock. 2018a. A remark on Béjar & Kahnemuyipour 2017: Specificational subjects do have phi-features. Journal of Linguistics 54(3): 611–627.
Hartmann, J.M. & C. Heycock. 2018b. More on phi-features in and out of copular sentences: A reply to Béjar & Kahnemuyipour 2018. Journal of Linguistics 54(3): 637–646.
Heggie, L. 1988. The syntax of copular constructions. University of Southern California, Los Angeles, CA: USC doctoral dissertation.
Heycock, C. 1992. Layers of predication and the syntax of the copula. Belgian Journal of Linguistics 7(1): 95–123.
Heycock, C. 1994. The internal structure of small clauses. In: (J. Beckmann, ed) Proceedings of NELS 25, 223–238. Amherst, MA: University of Massachusetts, GLSA.
Heycock, C. 2012. Specification, equation, and agreement in copular sentences. Canadian Journal of Linguistics / Revue canadienne de linguistique 57(2): 209–240.
Heycock, C. & A. Kroch. 1999. Pseudocleft connectedness: Implications for the LF interface level. Linguistic Inquiry 30(3): 365–398.
Heycock, C. & A. Kroch. 2002. Topic, focus, and syntactic representation. In: (L. Mikkelsen & C. Potts, eds) Proceedings of WCCFL 21, 141–165. Somerville, MA: Cascadilla Press.
Higgins, R. 1979. The pseudo-cleft construction in English. New York, NY: Garland.
Hoffmann, S. 2008. Corpus linguistics with BNCweb: A practical guide (English corpus linguistics). Frankfurt a. M.: Peter Lang.
Huber, S. 2002. Es-Clefts und det-Clefts: Zur Syntax, Semantik und Informationsstruktur von Spaltsätzen im Deutschen und Schwedischen. Lund: Lund University doctoral dissertation.
Jacobson, P. 1995. On the quantificational force of English free relatives. In: (E. Bach, E. Jelinek, A. Kratzer & B. Partee, eds) Quantification in natural languages, 451–486. Dordrecht, NL: Kluwer.
Katz, J. & E. Selkirk. 2011. Contrastive focus vs. discourse-new: Evidence from phonetic prominence in English. Language 87(4): 771–816.
Kuno, S. 1972. Some properties of referential noun phrases. In: (R. Jacobson & S. Kawamoto, eds) Studies in general and oriental linguistics. Presented to S. Hattori on occasion of his 60th birthday, 348–373. Tokyo: TEC.
Mikkelsen, L. 2004. Specifying who: On the structure, meaning and use of specificational copula constructions. Santa Cruz, CA: University of California at Santa Cruz doctoral dissertation.

Mikkelsen, L. 2005. Copular clauses: Specification, predication and equation. Amsterdam/ Philadelphia: Benjamins.
Moro, A. 1991. The raising of predicates: Copula, expletives, and existence. In: (L. Cheng & H. Demirdache, eds) More papers on wh-movement, MIT Working Papers in Linguistics, 119–181. Cambridge, MA: MIT Press.
Moro, A. 1997. The raising of predicates: Predicative noun phrases and the theory of clause structure. Cambridge, MA / New York, NY: Cambridge University Press.
Moro, A. 2000. Dynamic antisymmetry. Cambridge, MA: MIT Press.
Moro, A. 2006. Copular sentences. In: (M. Everaert & H. van Riemsdijk, eds) The Blackwell Companion to Syntax, Vol 2, 1–23. Malden, MA/ Oxford: Blackwell.
Ogihara, T. 1987. 'Obligatory focus' in Japanese and type-shifting principles. In: (M. Crowhurst, ed) WCCFL 6: The Proceedings of the 6th West Coast Conference on Formal Linguistics, 213–227. Stanford, CA: CSLI Publications.
Reinhart, T. 1982. Pragmatics and linguistics: An analysis of sentence topics. Bloomington: Indiana University Linguistics Club.
Rochemont, M.S. 1986. Focus in generative grammar. Amsterdam/ Philadelphia: Benjamins.
Rochemont, M.S. 2013. Discourse new, F-marking, and normal stress. Lingua 136 [SI: Information Structure Triggers]: 38–62.
Romero, M. 2005. Concealed questions and specificational subjects. Linguistics and Philosophy 28(6): 687–737.
Rothstein, S.D. 2001. Predicates and their subjects. Dordrecht, Boston, London: Kluwer.
Roy, I. 2013. Nonverbal predication: Copular sentences at the syntax-semantics interface. Oxford: Oxford University Press.
Selkirk, E. 2002. Contrastive FOCUS vs. presentational focus: Prosodic Evidence from right node raising in English. In: (B. Bel & I. Marlin, eds) Speech Prosody 2002: Proceedings of the 1st International Prosody Conference, 643–646. Aix-en-Provence: Laboratoire Parole et Langage.
Sharvit, Y. 1999. Connectivity in specificational sentences. Natural Language Semantics 7(3): 299–339.
Shlonsky, U. & L. Rizzi. 2018. Criterial Freezing in small clauses and the cartography of copular constructions. In: (J. M. Hartmann, M. Jäger, A. Kehl, A. Konietzko & S. Winkler, eds) Freezing. Theoretical approaches and empirical domains, 29–65. Berlin, Boston: De Gruyter Mouton.
Stowell, T. 1978. What was there before there was there. In: (D. Farkas, ed) Proceedings of the 14th regional meeting of the Chicago Linguistics Society, 458–471. Chicago, IL: CLS.
Surányi, B. 2011. An interface account of identificational focus movement. In: (T. Laczkó & C.O. Ringen, eds) Approaches to Hungarian, Vol 12: Papers from the 2009 Debrecen conference, 163–208. Amsterdam, New York, NY: Benjamins.
Ward, G. & B. Birner. 1995. Definiteness and the English existential. Language 71(4): 722–742.
Wells, J.C. 2006. English Intonation: An Introduction. Cambridge: Cambridge University Press.
Williams, E. 1997. The asymmetry of predication. In: (R.C. Blight & M.J. Moosally, eds) Texas Linguistic Forum 38: The syntax and semantics of predication: 323–333. Austin: University of Texas at Austin, Department of Linguistics.
Zamparelli, R. 2000. Layers in the determiner phrase. New York, NY / London: Garland.

Andreas Konietzko, Janina Radó and Susanne Winkler
Focus constraints on relative clause antecedents in sluicing

1 Introduction

In this chapter, we investigate the effect of information structure on the accessibility of potential antecedents for sluiced *wh*-remnants. The question what linguistic components are involved in antecedent selection for ellipsis and what principles govern it has been a matter of much debate in the ellipsis literature. Although there are in-depth analyses of antecedent selection in elliptical constructions such as VP-ellipsis (Hardt & Romero 2004; Kehler 2000) and sluicing (Romero 1998; Remmele 2017), there is relatively little empirical work about the interaction of information structure and syntax in this field. In this chapter, we examine sluicing with a relative clause (RC) in the correlate clause, as given in (1). We will call such cases *complex sluicing*:

(1) a. Die Polizei hat einen Wiederholungstäter verhaftet, der
   the police has a$_{acc/masc}$ repeat offender arrested who
   ein Geschäft ausgeraubt hat, aber ich weiß nicht
   a$_{acc/neut}$ store robbed has but I know not
   welchen / welches.
   which$_{acc/masc}$ / which$_{acc/neut}$

   b. Die Polizei hat einen Wiederholungstäter, der ein
   the police has a$_{acc/masc}$ repeat offender who a$_{acc/neut}$
   Geschäft ausgeraubt hat, verhaftet, aber ich weiß nicht
   store robbed has arrested but I know not
   welchen / welches.
   which$_{acc/masc}$ / which$_{acc/neut}$

Previous analyses have established that antecedent selection in sluicing is determined by information structure. Romero (1998), for example, shows that

---

Acknowledgments: This chapter has benefited from the valuable comments of the editors of this volume and three anonymous reviewers. We are also grateful to Peter Culicover, Robin Hörnig, Jason Merchant, and Michael Rochemont for comments and feedback. This research is based upon work supported by the German Research Foundation (Deutsche Forschungsgemeinschaft) under the SFB 833 grant (Project A7 *Focus and Extraction in Complex Constructions and Islands*).

https://doi.org/10.1515/9783110623093-005

antecedent selection is not restricted by syntactic locality, contra assumptions made in Chung et al. (1995). Moreover, Romero argues in great detail that in sluicing the focused *wh*-remnant and its antecedent have to contrast (see Romero 1998: 28; cf. also Dröge, Fleischer & Bornkessel-Schlesewsky, this volume, for a different type of unmarked reference relation). A similar kind of parallelism is assumed by many authors for various elliptical constructions. Carlson (2002), Konietzko & Winkler (2010), and Winkler (2005, 2016) argue, for example, that focus parallelism is required for instances of contrastive ellipsis such as gapping and stripping. It is, however, still an open question to what extent the interpretation in complex sluicing is modulated by the syntactic structure of the correlate clause (see Weskott, Hörnig & Webelhuth, this volume, for the contextual licensing hypothesis for another type of marked syntactic structure).

In this chapter, we will show that the accessibility of antecedents in complex sluicing interacts with the focus assignment in the complex correlate clause. Two factors are relevant: first, whether the parallelism condition between the *wh*-remnant and the antecedent is obeyed; and second, the exact syntactic location of the antecedent in the correlate clause. We will provide evidence for the claim that the accessibility of an antecedent which is located inside an RC depends on the actual position of the RC. It is crucial for focusing reasons whether the antecedent occurs in an extraposed relative clause (ERC) as in (1a) or an in situ relative clause (IRC) as in (1b). We will argue that this effect is rooted in the information structural properties of ERCs versus IRCs. ERCs benefit from an additional focusing effect that facilitates accessibility of the antecedent (Büring 2013, Hartmann 2013, Poschmann & Wagner 2016). This focusing effect is absent in IRCs, which has the consequence that parallelism between the *wh*-remnant and the antecedent cannot be properly established in such cases. The assumption that the accessibility of the antecedent in sluicing is influenced by the syntactic position of the RC is independent of whether sluicing with RC antecedents constitutes an island violation or not. The hypotheses of this chapter are summarized in (2):

(2) (i) In complex sluicing parallel focus is preferred over nonparallel focus (Parallelism Condition).
    (ii) The syntactic position of the RC is information-structurally relevant; the main clause correlate is preferred over the RC correlate with IRCs but not with ERCs (contra Frazier & Clifton's prediction that matrix correlates are generally preferred over RC correlates).
    (iii) The RC position affects RC correlates but not main clause correlates.

The chapter is organized as follows: Section 1.1 introduces the phenomenon and describes the syntax of sluicing. Section 1.2 discusses the focus properties of

IRC and ERC. Section 1.3 discusses previous experimental research on sluicing. Section 1.4 lays out the main claim of the chapter and derives the predictions for two experimental studies, which are presented in Section 2. Section 3 contains the discussion of the main findings and the conclusion.

1.1 The phenomenon: Complex sluicing

Sluicing is a type of ellipsis where the sentential portion of a matrix or embedded question is elided, leaving only the *wh*-phrase. The *wh*-phrase (the remnant) typically has an explicit antecedent (the correlate) in the immediately preceding discourse (the correlate clause). The remnant and the correlate clause may appear in the same sentence as in (3a) or in separate sentences as in the dialogue in (3b):

(3) a. The police officer is looking for a repeat offender, do you know who?
 b. A: The police is looking for a repeat offender.
    B: Do you know who?

In complex sluicing the correlate clause contains an RC, which hosts an additional correlate. The potential ambiguity can be resolved by the morphology of the remnant, as in (4).

(4) The police officer arrested a repeat offender who robbed a store,
 a. do you know who?
 b. do you know which [one]?

In (4a), the remnant *who* refers to the object correlate DP *a repeat offender who robbed a store*. In (4b), the remnant *which (one)* refers to the object DP *a store* inside the RC. As RCs are islands to movement, the version of (4b) without ellipsis, given in (5), is ungrammatical. The extraction site is marked by underscore:

(5) *The police officer is looking for a repeat offender who robbed a store, do you know [CP [which store]$_i$ [the police officer is looking for a repeat offender [CP who robbed __$_i$]]

However, as already observed by Ross (1969), (4b) is considerably better than (5), although Ross originally didn't judge data as in (4b) as fully grammatical.

There have been three major approaches to sluicing: deletion theories, LF-copying theories and direct interpretation approaches. Deletion theories (Ross

1969; Sag 1976; Lasnik 2001; Merchant 2001, among others) assume that the input to the sluicing case in (3a) is (6):

(6) a. do you know [$_{CP}$ [$_{IP}$ the police officer is looking for who]]
　　b. do you know [$_{CP}$ who$_i$ [$_{IP}$ the police officer is looking for __$_i$]]
　　c. do you know [$_{CP}$ who$_i$ [$_{IP}$ e]]

In (6b), the *wh*-phrase in the constituent question undergoes movement to the front of the subordinate clause, and then the IP of the subordinate clause is deleted as in (6c). As the elided portion is semantically identical to the corresponding part in the main clause, interpretation is possible.

LF-copying or reconstruction approaches (e.g., Chung et al. 1995; Lobeck 1995; Williams 1977) assume that the remnant is base generated in Spec-CP and the ellipsis site is empty at S-Structure/Spell-Out. At logical form (LF), the representation of the correlate clause (the phrase marker) is copied into the ellipsis site, thereby allowing interpretation.

Since both deletion and reconstruction/LF-copying accounts assume the presence of structure at the ellipsis site (in the syntax and at LF, respectively), we will refer to them collectively as structural accounts: They contrast with the so-called direct interpretation approaches (Ginzburg & Sag 2000; Culicover & Jackendoff 2005; Sag & Nykiel 2011), which hold that there is no deleted or reconstructed structure in sluicing; the only element present in the syntactic representation is the *wh*-remnant, which functions as an anaphor that needs to find a discourse antecedent.

In the substantial literature on sluicing (cf. Chung et al. 1995; Merchant 2001, 2006, 2008; Sag & Nykiel 2011; van Craenenbroek & Merchant 2013; Barros 2014; Vicente 2018), various arguments have been put forth for the different approaches. Connectivity effects, that is, case matching between the remnant and the elided verb, as well as a parallelism between the possibilities of preposition stranding in sluicing and in *wh*-movement in general in a given language have been used to support structural accounts (but cf. Sag & Nykiel 2011 for counterarguments). On the other hand, cases where the correlate cannot be reused directly, for example, the interpretation of indexical pronouns and the Relational Opposites Puzzle (Hartman 2009) are more easily dealt with in direct interpretation accounts (but cf. Chung et al. 2011). We will not review this debate here. Instead we will concentrate on one particular case: complex sluicing, illustrated in (4) above.

Looking at complex sluicing in German, it is not clear whether the approaches discussed above can fully explain the observed effects. Winkler (2013: 464, ex. 2c), for instance, observes that sluicing with correlates inside IRCs is marginal in German:

(7) ??Sie wollen nur einen Linguisten, der eine Balkansprache
    they want only a linguist who a Balkan language
    spricht, einstellen, aber Ich weiß nicht welche.
    speaks hire but I know not which

By contrast, a corresponding sentence with a matrix correlate is fine (Winkler 2013: 464, ex. 2d):

(8) Sie wollen nur einen Linguisten, der eine Balkansprache
    they want only a linguist who a Balkan language
    spricht, einstellen, aber ich weiß nicht wen.
    speaks hire But I know not who$_{acc}$

The contrast between RC and main clause correlates is less severe when the RC is extraposed:

(9) ?Sie wollen nur einen Linguisten einstellen, der eine
    they want only a linguist hire who a
    Balkansprache spricht, aber ich weiß nicht welche.
    Balkan language Speaks but I know not which

(10) Sie wollen nur einen Linguisten einstellen, der eine
     they want only a linguist hire who a
     Balkansprache spricht, aber ich weiß nicht wen.
     Balkan language Speaks but I know not who$_{acc}$

The data suggest that the accessibility of correlates inside RCs in sluicing is dependent on whether the RC is extraposed or not. In the next section we will derive the observed difference from the focus properties of IRC versus ERC.

1.2 Focus in complex sluicing

In this section, we will describe the information structural properties of complex sluicing. We will argue that the accessibility of the correlate interacts with focus marking and the position of the RC. Let us first look at standard cases of sluicing as in (11). Here and in the rest of the chapter, the focus exponent is marked with capitalization and the focus phrase is marked with brackets:

(11) Context: I heard that the police arrested some offender. Do you know more about it?
The police officer arrested [a REPEAT offender]$_F$, but I don't know [WHICH]$_F$.

Under a deletion approach to sluicing, the derivation would be as in (12), where deletion is marked by strikethrough:

(12) The police officer arrested [a REPEAT offender]$_F$, but I don't know [WHICH]$_F$ ~~repeat offender the police officer arrested~~.

As discussed in Section 1.1, sluicing isolates a *wh*-remnant and deletes the rest of the clause which is contextually given. The *wh*-remnant (*which*) is obligatorily focused and contrasts with a salient antecedent in the correlate clause (*a repeat offender*), which also bears focal stress, as required by the parallelism condition. In the case of complex sluicing as in (13), the same information structural principles apply. However, the RC contains a further DP (*a store*), which could also function as a focus exponent such that, in principle, ambiguity may arise:

(13) Context: I heard that the police arrested some offender. Do you know more about it?
The police officer arrested a [REPEAT offender]$_F$ who robbed [a STORE]$_F$, but I don't know [WHICH]$_F$.

Under the assumption that there are several contextually salient *repeat offenders* and several contextually salient *stores* that both provide an equally plausible correlate for the elliptical clause, the *wh*-remnant may either take *repeat offender* or *store* as its correlate in (13). Although judgments are shaky in such cases, some speakers express a slight preference for the matrix correlate. This corresponds to Ross' (1969) original intuition that the RC correlate, which would require a parse where the *wh*-phrase in the elliptical clause is extracted out of an island, is not perfect.

Let us now turn to German. In German (as in English), RCs may be in situ or extraposed (cf. Büring 2013; Hartmann 2013; Poschmann & Wagner 2016). Consider the complex sluicing examples in (14) and (15) with matrix and RC correlates, respectively. In each case, a context is provided which requests information about the matrix correlate in (14) and the RC correlate in (15). The examples in (14a) and (15a) contain ERCs, those in (14b) and (15b) contain IRCs:

(14) Context: *Kannst du mir sagen, wen genau die Polizei verhaftet hat?*
 Can you me tell who exactly the police arrested?
 a. Die Polizei hat einen Wiederholungstäter verhaftet, der ein
 the Police has a repeat offender arrested who a
 Geschäft ausgeraubt hat, aber ich weiß nicht genau
 store robbed has but I know not exactly
 welchen.
 which$_{acc/masc}$

 b. Die Polizei hat einen Wiederholungstäter, der ein Geschäft
 the Police has a repeat offender who a store
 ausgeraubt hat, verhaftet, aber ich weiß nicht genau
 robbed has arrested but I know not exactly
 welchen.
 which$_{acc/masc}$

(15) Context: *Die Polizei hat wohl einen Wiederholungstäter verhaftet. Weißt Du, was er genau gemacht hat?*
 The police has possibly arrested a repeat offender. Do you know exactly what he has done?
 a. ?Die Polizei hat einen Wiederholungstäter verhaftet, der ein
 the Police has a repeat offender arrested who a
 Geschäft ausgeraubt hat, aber ich weiß nicht welches.
 store robbed has but I know not which$_{acc/neut}$

 b. ??Die Polizei hat einen Wiederholungstäter, der ein Geschäft
 the Police has a repeat offender who a store
 ausgeraubt hat, verhaftet, aber ich weiß nicht welches.
 robbed has arrested but I know not which$_{acc/neut}$

These examples show that the ERC and IRC in (14) are equally acceptable if the *wh*-remnant refers to the matrix clause correlates. The markedness contrast between (15a, b), however, shows that an correlate inside an RC is considerably more acceptable if the RC is extraposed, as in (15a). Clearly, the difference in acceptability between (15a vs. b) cannot be rooted in the island violation, which the data exhibit prior to deletion: Under the island repair theory proposed by Merchant (2008), the offending structure is deleted irrespective of whether the RC is extraposed or not. What we would like to propose instead is that the difference in acceptability stems from the parallelism condition, which requires that the *wh*-remnant and the correlate phrase are contrastively focused. The context provided in (15) suggests the focus marking in (16a, b). The focus on *Wiederholungstäter* is a default focus marking accent on the DP in the preverbal position in German. The focus accent on the DP *Geschäft* in the RC, and on the remnant *welches* are contrastive focus accents.

(16) a. ?Die Polizei hat [einen WiederHOLungstäter]_F verhaftet, der
the police has a repeat offender arrested who
[ein GESCHÄFT]_F ausgeraubt hat, aber ich weiß nicht [WELCHES]_F.
a store robbed has but I know not which_acc/neut

b. ??Die Polizei hat [einen WiederHOLungstäter]_F, der [ein GESCHÄFT]_F
the police has a repeat offender who a store
ausgeraubt hat, verHAFtet, aber ich weiß nicht [WELCHES]_F.
robbed has arrested but I know not which_acc/neut

The reason why it is easier to establish parallelism with ERCs as in (16a) is that extraposition adds extra prominence to the correlate (cf. Büring 2013; Hartmann 2013). ERCs in German function like other focus constructions in which a syntactic operation moves a constituent into focus (cf. Rochemont & Culicover 1990). Büring calls it *prosodic extraposition* for this reason. In (16a), the contrastive focus on the sluicing remnant operates over sets of alternatives introduced by the RC correlate *ein Geschäft* (a store). The IRC in (16b), however, does not show this extra focusing function. Rather the accent rules of German require a further accent on the verb *verhaftet* (arrested), which renders (16b) a prosodically marked structure that violates the prosodic requirement of the parallelism condition (cf. Winkler 2018).

As initial evidence that there is a correlation between the position of the RC and focus, let us compare cases where the RC contains new information and cases where the RC is discourse given. Consider (17), where the answer contains an RC that provides additional information about the *repeat offender*. By contrast, in (18), the context already contains the information that appears in B and B' in the RC and the question requests more specific information about the head noun that the RC modifies. The context is given in (A), ERCs in (B) and IRCs in (B'), respectively:

(17) A: Ich habe gehört, dass die Polizei einen Wiederholungstäter
I have heard that the police a repeat offender
verhaftet hat. Weißt du zufällig wen?
arrested has Know you accidentally who

B: Die Polizei hat einen Wiederholungstäter verhaftet, der
   the police has a   repeat offender   arrested who
   einen Laden ausgeraubt hat. Wen sie   genau   verhaftet
   a   store robbed   has who they precisely arrested
   haben, weiß ich aber   nicht.
   have   know I however not

B': #Die Polizei hat einen Wiederholungstäter, der   einen Laden
    the   police has a   repeat offender   who   a   store
    ausgeraubt hat, verhaftet. Wen sie   genau   verhaftet
    robbed   has arrested   who they   precisely arrested
    haben, weiß ich aber   nicht.
    have   know I however not

(18) A: Ich habe gehört, dass jemand einen Laden ausgeraubt hat.
        I   have heard   that someone a   store robbed   has
        Die Polizei hat wohl   schon   jemanden verhaftet. Weißt
        the police has arguably already someone   arrested   know
        du zufällig   wen?
        you accidentally who

  B: Die Polizei hat einen Wiederholungstäter verhaftet, der   den
     the police has a   repeat offender   arrested who   the
     Laden ausgeraubt hat. Wen Sie   genau   verhaftet
     store robbed   has who they   precisely arrested
     haben, weiß ich aber   nicht.
     have   know I however not

  B': #Die Polizei hat einen Wiederholungstäter, der   den Laden
      the   police has a   repeat offender   who the store
      ausgeraubt hat verhaftet. Wen Sie   genau   verhaftet
      robbed   has arrested   who they   precisely arrested
      haben, weiß ich aber   nicht.
      have   know I however not

The context in (17A) predicts that the RC contains new information. Therefore, the ERC in (17B) seems intuitively better than the in situ variant in (17B'). The observation that in situ constituents preferably contain given and therefore deaccented information also provides an explanation of why new information RCs are less felicitous *in situ* (cf. also Poschmann & Wagner 2016). The effect observed in (17) is even stronger if the head noun *Wiederholungstäter* is pronominalized, as (19) shows:

(19) A: Ich habe gehört, dass die Polizei einen Wiederholungstäter
I have heard that the police a repeat offender
verhaftet hat. Weißt du zufällig wen?
arrested has Know you accidentally who

B: Die Polizei hat den verhaftet, der einen Laden
the police has the one arrested who a store
ausgeraubt hat.
robbed has

B': #Die Polizei hat den, der einen Laden ausgeraubt
the police has the one who a store robbed
hat, verhaftet.
has arrested

In (18), by contrast, the RC with new information is equally felicitous in either position. We suspect that the reason for this is that extraposition may affect discourse new as well as discourse given material. The correlation between position and information status then seems to be a partial one. In situ constituents are typically given, while extraposed ones may host given as well as discourse new material. Thus, if the RC is discourse new, it prefers to extrapose.

1.3 Experimental studies on complex sluicing

Turning to psycholinguistic investigations of sluicing, the assumption has been that syntactic structure is present or reconstructed at the ellipsis site (cf. also Frazier & Clifton 1998; Poirier et al. 2010; Dickey & Bunger 2011). For instance, Frazier & Clifton (2005) argued that the elided structure influences processing on the basis of examples like (20) and two additional control conditions (their experiment 3). (20b) involves an adjunct island violation, whereas in (20d) the offending part of the structure is not overtly present. However, if the island violation is still 'visible' then (20d) should be less acceptable than (20c).

(20) a. What lecture was Sally impressed with?
b. What lecture was Sally impressed after?
c. Sally was impressed with some lecture, but I don't know what.
d. Sally was impressed after some lecture, but I don't know what.

In a speeded grammaticality study, Frazier & Clifton found a significant difference in acceptance rates between (20c) and (20d) although the difference was smaller than the one between the fully grammatical (20a) and the island-violating (20b). They conclude that this penalty is the result of an incomplete repair of the island violation by sluicing along the lines of Merchant's (2006) approach. In addition to the syntactic component, Frazier & Clifton (2000, 2005) and Carlson et al. (2009) argue that the interpretation of sluicing, and of ellipsis in general, also includes a discourse component that relates the remnant to the discourse representation that is being constructed. As a consequence, comprehenders typically interpret the elided material as relating to the most salient information in the correlate clause. For instance, the preferred reading of *did too* in the VP-ellipsis constructions in (21) depends on which clause expresses the main assertion (and not on linear order):

(21) a. Mary laughed after she made a joke about the supervisor. Then Tina did too.
b. After Mary laughed, she made a joke about the supervisor. Then Tina did too.

(Frazier & Clifton 2005, Experiment 6)

The preference to relate the elided material to salient information in discourse is also reflected in the finding that focus influences the choice of correlate in ellipsis. Carlson et al. (2009) presented evidence for the effect of default focus as well as syntactically marked (cleft construction) and prosodic focus (pitch accent) on the interpretation of the *wh*-remnant. We will take up this study in more detail in the discussion.

Frazier & Clifton (2005) also tested whether focus makes a correlate inside a syntactic island more available. They investigated complex sluicing sentences like (22) as well as their counterparts in (23). Participants were instructed to interpret the capitalized words as accented.

(22) a. They hired someone who won but I can't remember what.
b. They hired someone who won something but I can't remember what.
c. They hired someone who won SOMETHING but I can't remember what.

(23) a. Someone won but I can't remember what.
b. Someone won something but I can't remember what.
c. Someone won SOMETHING but I can't remember what.

In an offline questionnaire (their experiment 8a), (22c) was rated as significantly more acceptable than the same sentence without accent on the RC object (22b), which in turn was significantly better than the presumably ungrammatical (22a), where the elided material has to be reconstructed without an overt linguistic correlate ('sprouting', cf. Chung et al. 1995). However, in a speeded acceptability rating study (Frazier & Clifton's experiment 8b) conditions with the correlate inside an RC (22) were found to be significantly worse than those that do not involve an island violation (23). In this study, orthography apparently did not make a difference, neither in the RC nor in the matrix conditions. Frazier & Clifton emphasize that the observed focus effect in experiment 8a is all the more impressive since focus inside the RC presumably makes the RC more salient, which in turn should make the syntactic violation, if anything, more noticeable in the focus condition.

Thus, Frazier & Clifton's (2005) experiment on complex sluicing did not provide conclusive results either concerning the grammaticality status of remnants with correlates inside RCs, or with respect to the role of focus in complex sluicing. Under structural accounts, the deletion of the island-forming node in sluicing may ameliorate the island violation, but we may still expect correlates inside islands to be somewhat degraded, as Frazier & Clifton argue with respect to the results of their experiment (3) (cf. (20) and the discussion above). The results Frazier & Clifton (2005) present concerning the influence of focus are not conclusive, presumably because their focus manipulation via orthography was rather weak.

1.4 Hypotheses and predictions

We conducted two coherence rating studies: one with IRCs (Experiment 1) and another with ERCs (Experiment 2). The studies examined the acceptability of complex sluicing constructions concentrating on cases with an overt correlate; context was used to systematically manipulate focus on the correlate.

Based on the hypotheses in (2) above, we derived the predictions in (24):

(24) (i) a focus parallelism effect in both experiments regardless of the position of the RC;
 (ii) an effect of the correlate with IRCs (Experiment 1) but not with ERCs (Experiment 2);
 (iii) higher ratings for RC correlates in Experiment 2 than in Experiment 1 due to focus parallelism;
 (iv) no difference in the ratings for main clause correlates between Experiment 1 and Experiment 2, since the main clause correlate is always focused.

Note that predictions (i) and (iii) are in direct opposition to Frazier & Clifton's (2005) conjecture: If focus in the RC makes the perceiver aware of the fact that the RC correlate constitutes an island violation, then RC correlates should be generally worse than main clause correlates, and possibly even more so if RC is extraposed and thus receives extra focus.

2 Complex sluicing: Two coherence rating studies

In the experiments reported here, we manipulated the position of the correlate (main clause vs. inside an RC) and focus parallelism between the remnant and the correlate. There is ample evidence showing that focused elements are more salient than unfocused ones (Birch & Garnsey 1995; Birch & Rayner 1997; Foraker & McElree 2007). Referents in linguistically prominent positions (topic, information focus, contrastive focus) have been found to be good correlates for discourse anaphora (e.g., Almor 1999; Arnold 1998; Cowles, Walenski & Kluender 2007; Kaiser 2011). Assuming that the syntactic and the discourse processor operate in parallel, as proposed by Frazier & Clifton (2000, 2005), we may expect discourse factors, such as focus, to play a greater role when the syntactic processor encounters difficulties in interpreting a construction, for instance, because the intended interpretation involves a syntactic violation. On the other hand, as pointed out by Frazier & Clifton, focus on an offending constituent may have the effect of directing attention to the syntactic violation, making the construction less rather than more acceptable.

We used context to manipulate focus in the target sentences. The context consisted of two or three sentences and introduced a fairly typical situation, as well as some details about the situation. The target was a complex sentence with a restrictive RC modifying the main clause object. It described a similar situation as the context, but differed from it in one of two respects: either in the referent of the main clause object (main contrast, cf. (25)) or in the content of the RC (RC contrast, cf. (26)).

(25) Main contrast
      Context Wenn die Polizei wegen Diebstahls ermittelt, handelt es sich häufig um Ersttäter. Meist sind es Einbrüche in kleinere Geschäfte.
      '*When the police investigate a case of theft, the culprit is often a first offender. They usually break into small stores.*'
      Target   Die Polizei wird jetzt aber einen Wiederholungstäter, der ein Geschäft ausgeraubt hat, suchen.
      '*But now the police will look for a repeat offender that robbed a store.*'

(26) RC contrast
Context Wenn die Polizei wegen Diebstahls ermittelt, handelt es sich häufig um Wiederholungstäter. Meist sind es Einbrüche in Eigenheime.
'When the police investigate a case of theft, the culprit is often a repeat offender. They usually break into private households.
Target Die Polizei wird jetzt aber einen Wiederholungstäter, der ein Geschäft ausgeraubt hat, suchen.
'But now the police will look for a repeat offender that robbed a store.'

The target sentence is identical in (25) and (26). In (25) *first offender* in the context contrasts with *repeat offender*, and the main clause object in the target sentence. In (26) both the context and the target contain *a repeat offender*, but the content of the RC of the target sentence (*store*) contrasts with *private homes* mentioned in the context. In order to highlight the opposition with the context, in the target sentence we used the conjunction *aber* ('but'), which has been analyzed as focus sensitive (cf. Umbach 2005). Moreover, the target sentence always began with a temporal adverbial referring to a single specific event, which contrasted with the temporal or aspectual setting of the context (which often expressed generic statements). Apart from these elements and the contrastively focused constituent, the target sentence only repeated information already given in the context. In contrast to some previous experimental studies of sluicing, we used indefinite noun phrases rather than indefinite pronouns as matrix objects to make sure that they are informative and can easily bear focus/pitch accent. Finally, to minimize structural parallelism between the context and the target sentences, the context did not include an RC; the information that was repeated in the RC of the target sentence (as in (25)) or contrasted with the RC of the target sentence (as in (26)) was introduced in a separate main clause.

The context + target sentences were paired with one of the *wh*-remnants in (27).

(27) a. Main correlate
Weißt du auch wen?
'Do you know who$_{acc}$?'

b. RC correlate
Weißt du auch welches?
'Do you know which$_{AccSg}$?'

(25)–(27) together form the four conditions of an item. (25) (main contrast) followed by (27a) (remnant with main clause correlate) results in parallel focus between the remnant and the correlate, and so does (26) (RC contrast) followed by (27b) (remnant with RC correlate). Combining (25) with (27b) or (26) with (27a), however, leads to nonparallel focus between the remnant and its correlate.

To test whether the effect of focus and position of the remnant interact with the position of the RC, two separate studies were conducted. The items of the two studies were identical, except for the position of the RC. Experiment 1 contained IRCs (cf. the sample item in 25–27). In experiment 2, the equivalent sentences with ERCs were used.

2.1 Experiment 1: in situ relative clauses

2.1.1 Materials

Twenty-four items were constructed in the four conditions shown in (25)–(27). As described earlier, the context typically consisted of two or three sentences and did not use RCs. The target sentence included an initial temporal adverbial and used the conjunction *aber* (but); the matrix object of the target sentence was always an indefinite NP modified by a restrictive RC. The designated correlates in the main and the RC differed in their case + gender combination to make the *wh*-remnant unambiguous as to its correlate. Remnants always matched either the main or the RC correlate in *case + gender*. We used the appropriate form of *wer* (who) for main clause correlates, and *welcher* (which) for RC correlates. This differs from Frazier & Clifton's (2005) experiment 8a,b, where the correlate in the RC was an indefinite pronoun (*someone*), and the majority of the items contained the remnant *what*.

In addition to the 24 experimental items, 48 distractors were written, consisting of three declarative sentences followed by a question. The distractors exhibited various conjunctions and question types and ranged from fully coherent to rather incoherent.

2.1.2 Procedure

The 24 *context + target* sequences combined with the two (main vs. RC) remnant continuations yielded a 2 (main vs. RC correlate) × 2 (parallel vs. nonparallel focus) design as shown in (28):

(28) a. Main correlate – Parallel focus
 b. Main correlate – Nonparallel focus
 c. RC correlate – Parallel focus
 d. RC correlate – Nonparallel focus

In line with the discussion above, we hypothesized that focus parallelism between the remnant and the correlate is preferred. This led to the prediction that (28a) and (28c) should receive better ratings than (28b) and (28d). Moreover, if the interpretation of sluicing only involves semantics and discourse and has no structural component, then the factor *correlate* should not influence acceptability, whereas significantly lower ratings for the RC correlate conditions (28c–d) than for (28a–b) would support structural analyses of sluicing.

The 24 items were combined with 40 of the distractors and the resulting 64 discourses were distributed on four presentation lists according to a Latin square design. Each participant saw a target sentence only once, and across the experiment, each combination of context–target–remnant was tested equally often. Eight additional distractors were used as practice trials.

Participants were tested individually in a sound-attenuated room. The stimuli were presented on a computer screen using the E-Prime software. On each trial, the context and the target sentence were presented in a single display and participants were instructed to press a button when they had read and understood it. The button press initiated the presentation of the question (the remnant), which was displayed word-by-word using rapid serial visual presentation with a presentation rate of 280 ms + 20 ms/character. This presentation rate has been found to still allow comprehension while being fast enough to keep participants from reflecting on the stimuli (Bader & Schmid 2009). As soon as the last word disappeared, participants were prompted to rate the coherence of the context–target–question sequence on a scale of 1 (total nonsense) to 7 (fully coherent). To ensure that participants read the stimuli carefully, 30 of them (12 items, 18 fillers) were combined with recognition probes testing different parts of the texts. Half of the probe words required an *yes* response, the other half a *no* response. An experimental session lasted approximately 30 min. Thirty-six native German speakers (students at Tübingen University) received 5 euros for participation.

2.1.3 Results

Four participants were excluded from the data analysis due to a probe recognition accuracy below 80%. The overall probe recognition accuracy of the remaining 32 participants was 86% and did not differ across conditions.

The results are shown in Figure 1. Ratings were high in all conditions (lowest mean 4.73 on a seven point scale). Then 2 × 2 repeated measures ANOVAs with the within factors *correlate* (main vs. RC) and *parallelism* (parallel vs. nonparallel) were calculated using participants (F_1) and items (F_2) as random factors. There was a significant main effect of *parallelism* ($F_1(1,31) = 14.71$, $p < .01$, $F_2(1,23) = 19.29$, $p < 0.01$). The main effect of *correlate* was also significant by participants, but marginal by items ($F_1(1,31) = 8.03$, $p < .01$, $F_2(1,23) = 3.06$, $p < 0.9$). The interaction was not significant ($F_1(1,31) = 1.165$, $p > .20$, $F_2 < 1$).

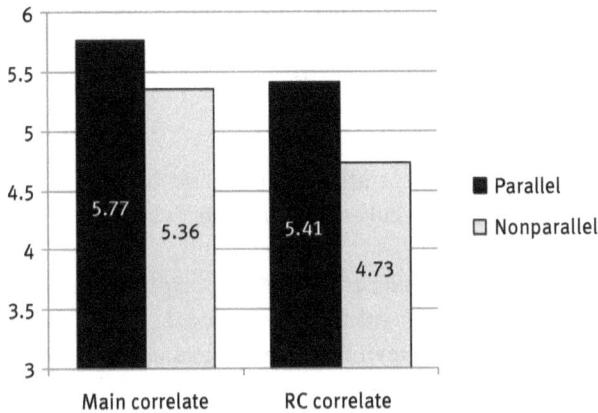

Figure 1: Coherence ratings for in situ relative clauses.

2.1.4 Discussion

The results of Experiment 1 show that focused correlates are considerably better than unfocused correlates. This is reflected in main effect of *parallelism*, that is, the fact that discourses with parallel focus receive higher ratings than their nonparallel counterparts. These results provide initial evidence for our hypothesis in (2i). Moreover, there is also a significant main effect of *correlate*, which shows that main clause correlates are judged better than RC correlates. In particular, the parallel condition with an RC correlate receives lower ratings than the main correlate–parallel condition (cf. 25 + 27a vs. 26 + 27b). This result partly replicates previous results by Frazier & Clifton (2005) on complex sluicing (cf. the discussion of the data in (20) above) and receives a straightforward explanation under the assumption that the island configuration is marked even under island repair, as originally observed by Ross (1969). In the nonparallel conditions (25 + 27b and 26 + 27a) the ratings are lower due to a violation of the focus parallelism condition in (2i). Note also that the position of the RC seems to interact with focus and affect the availability of correlates in IRCs. The interaction of RC position and focus on the correlate will therefore be further investigated in the second experiment, which tested ERCs.

2.2 Experiment 2: Extraposed relative clauses

2.2.1 Materials and procedure

This experiment tested the same materials as Experiment 1, except that this time the RC was extraposed. The context + target sequences are shown below; they were paired with the same remnants as in (27) above.

(29) Main contrast
      Context Wenn die Polizei wegen Diebstahl ermittelt, handelt es sich häufig um Ersttäter. Meist sind es Einbrüche in kleinere Geschäfte.
               'When the police investigate a case of theft, the culprit is often a first offender. They usually break into small stores.'
      Target   Die Polizei wird jetzt aber einen Wiederholungstäter suchen, der ein Geschäft ausgeraubt hat.
               'But now the police will look for a repeat offender that robbed a store.'

(30) RC contrast
      Context Wenn die Polizei wegen Diebstahl ermittelt, handelt es sich häufig um Wiederholungstäter. Meist sind es Einbrüche in Eigenheime.
               'When the police investigate a case of theft, the culprit is often a repeat offender. They usually break into private households.
      Target   Die Polizei wird jetzt aber einen Wiederholungstäter suchen, der ein Geschäft ausgeraubt hat.
               'But now the police will look for a repeat offender that robbed a store.'

In addition, the word order in some fillers was changed to make them more similar to the items. No other changes were made.

The procedure was the same as in Experiment 1. Thirty-three native German speakers participated in the experiment for 5 euros. None of them had taken part in Experiment 1.

2.2.2 Results

One participant had a probe recognition accuracy below 80% and was excluded from the data analysis. The overall probe recognition accuracy of the remaining 32 participants was 84% and did not differ across conditions.

The results are shown in Figure 2. Ratings were high in all conditions (lowest mean 5.3 on a seven-point scale). The data were subjected to 2 × 2 repeated measures ANOVAs with the within-factor *parallelism* (parallel vs. nonparallel) and *correlate* (main vs. RC), using participants (F_1) and items (F_2) as random factors. There was a significant main effect of *parallelism* ($F_1(1,31) = 5.65$, $p < .03$, $F_2(1,23) = 8.55$, $p < .01$); the main effect of *correlate* and the interaction of *parallelism* and *correlate* were not significant (all $Fs < 1$).

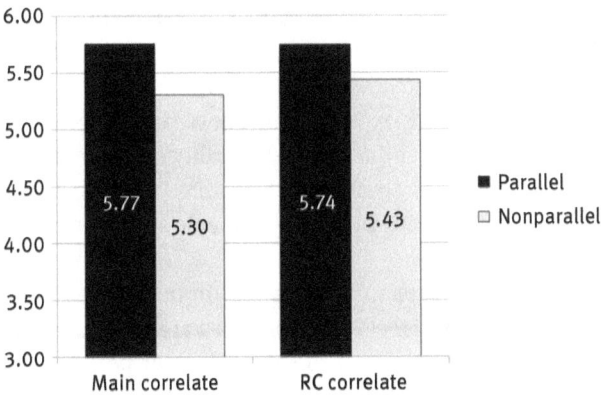

Figure 2: Coherence ratings for extraposed relative clauses.

2.2.3 Discussion

The results lend further support to the parallelism hypothesis in (2i). As expected, ratings were systematically higher when the context focused the grammatically compatible correlate than when the focus was on a different part of the target sentence. This is consistent with the findings of Carlson et al. (2009) and Frazier & Clifton (2005). Moreover, the lack of a main effect of *correlate* indicates that the conditions where the remnant had a correlate in the ERC were just as acceptable as the ones with a main clause correlate. This conflicts with Frazier & Clifton's results. The sentence final position is typically reserved for information that is new and focused, whereas given information tends to occur early in the sentence (cf., e.g., Arnold et al. 2000; Birner & Ward 1998; Chafe 1976; Clark & Haviland 1977, among others). Consequently, a final RC may easily be interpreted as bearing focus. Moreover, as Büring (2013) and Hartmann (2013) have argued, extraposition of RCs in German is governed by prosodic structure, which renders ERCs very often the unmarked case. Thus, the ERCs in our experiment seem to have invited a focused interpretation.

3 General discussion and conclusion

The aim of this study was to investigate the interpretation of the *wh*-remnant in complex sluicing. We have hypothesized that accessibility of the correlate in complex sluicing is influenced by focus parallelism, and by the position of the RC (IRC vs. ERC). Our results show that RC correlates, which putatively give rise to an island violation prior to deletion, are no worse than fully grammatical main clause correlates as long as the RC is extraposed. At the same time, we observed a penalty for IRC correlates. We have argued that these findings interact with the focus effect, which was observed in both experiments. These results receive a natural explanation under the assumption that the accessibility of the correlate in sluicing is subject to a parallelism condition, which requires that the correlate of the sluicing remnant also be focused. Our results provide support for this theory.

There are several interesting implications that follow from our results. If the right type of contrast can be established, RC correlates are as grammatical as main clause correlates. ERCs are moved to sentence final position for focus reasons. Contrastively focused constituents in ERCs, therefore, are readily accessible as correlates for the sluicing remnant. Thus, it appears that island repair phenomena need to be flanked by information structural components to be fully acceptable. This result partly confirms and partly contradicts Frazier & Clifton's results. First, it lends further support to the view that focus plays a crucial role in the acceptability of island repair constructions. However, our experiments also show that under certain conditions, that is, additional focusing in the case of ERC, there is no penalty for island repair. This suggests that the manipulation with capitalization used by Frazier & Clifton might have been weaker than our manipulation, which elicited data by providing context information. Taken together, our results do not only shed new light on island repair phenomena in sluicing and their interaction with information structure but also contribute to the current debate on the impact of information structure in the domain of RCs.

References

Almor, A. 1999. Noun-phrase anaphora and focus: The informational load hypothesis. Psychological Review 106(4): 748–765.

Arnold, J.E. 1998. Reference form and discourse patterns. Stanford, CA: Stanford University dissertation.

Arnold, J.E., T. Wasow, A. Losongco & R. Ginstrom. 2000. Heaviness vs. newness: The effects of structural complexity and discourse status on constituent ordering. Language 76(1): 28–55.

Bader, M. & T. Schmid. 2009. Verb clusters in colloquial German. The Journal of Comparative Germanic Linguistics 12(3): 175–228.

Barros, M. 2014. Sluicing and identity in ellipsis. New Brunswick, NJ: Rutgers University dissertation.

Birch, S.L. & K. Rayner. 1997. Linguistic focus affects eye movements during reading. Memory & Cognition 25(5): 653–660.

Birch, S.L. & S.M. Garnsey. 1995. The effect of focus on memory for words in sentences. Journal of Memory and Language 34(2): 232–267.

Birner, B.J. & G. Ward. 1998. Information status and noncanonical word order in English. Amsterdam/Philadelphia: John Benjamins.

Büring, D. 2013. Syntax, information structure, and prosody. In: (M. den Dikken, ed) The Cambridge Handbook of Generative Syntax, 860–895. Cambridge: Cambridge University Press.

Carlson, K. 2002. Parallelism and prosody in the processing of ellipsis sentences. Oxford: Routledge.

Carlson, K., M.W. Dickey, L. Frazier & C.E. Clifton. 2009. Information structure expectations in sentence comprehension. Quarterly Journal of Experimental Psychology 62(1): 114–139.

Chafe, W.L. 1976. Givenness, contrastiveness, subject, topic, and point of view. In: (C.N. Li, ed) Subject and topic, 27–55. New York, NY: Academic Press.

Chung, S., W. Ladusaw & J. McCloskey. 1995. Sluicing and logical form. Natural Language Semantics 3(3). 239–282.

Chung, S., W. Ladusaw & J. McCloskey. 2011. Sluicing(:) Between structure and inference. In: (R. Gutierrez-Bravo, L. Mikkelsen & E. Potsdam, eds) Representing language: Essays in honor of Judith Aissen, 31–50. California Digital Library eScholarship Repository. Linguistic Research Center, UCSC

Clark, H. & S.D. Haviland. 1977. Comprehension and the given new contract. In: (R.O. Freedle, ed) Discourse production and comprehension, 1–40. Norwood, NJ: Ablex.

Cowles, H.W., M. Walenski & R. Kluender. 2007. Linguistic and cognitive prominence in anaphor resolution: Topic, contrastive focus and pronouns. Topoi 26(1): 3–18.

Craenenbroeck, J. van, & J. Merchant. 2013. Ellipsis phenomena. In: (M. den Dikken, ed) The Cambridge Handbook of Generative Syntax, 701–745. Cambridge: Cambridge University Press.

Culicover, P.W. & R. Jackendoff. 2005. Simpler syntax. Oxford: Oxford University Press.

Dickey, M.W. & A. C. Bunger. 2011. Comprehension of elided structure: Evidence from sluicing. Language and Cognitive Processes 26(1): 63–78.

Foraker, S. & B. McElree. 2007. The role of prominence in pronoun resolution: Availability versus accessibility. Journal of Memory and Language 56(3): 357–383.

Frazier, L. & C.E. Clifton, Jr. 1998. Comprehension of sluiced sentences. Language and Cognitive Processes 13(4): 499–520.

Frazier, L. & C.E. Clifton, Jr. 2000. On bound variable interpretations: The LF-only hypothesis. Journal of Psycholinguistic Research 29(2): 125–139

Frazier, L. & C.E. Clifton, Jr. 2005. The syntax-discourse divide: Processing ellipsis. Syntax 8(2): 121–174.

Ginzburg, J. & I.A. Sag. 2000. Interrogative investigations. The form, meaning and use of English interrogatives. Stanford, CA: CSLI Publications. [Distributed by U. Chicago Press]

Hardt, D. & M. Romero. 2004. Ellipsis and discourse structure. Journal of Semantics 21(4): 375–414.

Hartman, J. 2009. When E-GIVENness over-predicts identity. Paper presented at the Fourth Brussels Conference on Generative Linguistics, Ellipsis Workshop. Hogeschool-Universiteit Brussel.

Hartmann, K. 2013. Prosodic constraints on extraposition in German. In: (M. Sailer, G. Webelhuth & H. Walker, eds) Rightward movement from a comparative perspective, 439–472. Amsterdam: John Benjamins.

Kaiser, E. 2011. Focusing on pronouns: Consequences of subjecthood, pronominalisation, and contrastive focus. Language and Cognitive Processes 26(10): 1625–1666.

Kehler, A. 2000. Coherence and the resolution of ellipsis. Linguistics and Philosophy 23(6): 533–575.

Konietzko, A. & S. Winkler. 2010. Contrastive ellipsis: Mapping between syntax and information structure. Lingua 120(6): 1436–1457.

Lasnik, H. 2001. When can you save a structure by destroying it? In: (K. Min-Joo & U. Strauss, eds) Proceedings of the North Eastern Linguistic Society 3, Vol. 2, 301–320. Amherst, MA: GLSA.

Lobeck, A. 1995. Ellipsis: Functional heads, licensing, and identification. Oxford: Oxford University Press.

Merchant, J. 2001. The syntax of silence: Sluicing, islands, and the theory of ellipsis. Oxford: Oxford University Press.

Merchant, J. 2006. Sluicing. In: (M. Everaert & H. van Riemsdijk, eds) The Blackwell Companion to Syntax 6, 271–291. Oxford: Blackwell.

Merchant, J. 2008. Variable island repair under ellipsis. In: (K. Johnson, ed) Topics in Ellipsis, 132–153. Cambridge: Cambridge University Press.

Poirier, J., K. Wolfinger, L. Spellman & L.P. Shapiro. 2010. The real-time processing of sluiced sentences. Journal of Psycholinguistic Research 39(5): 411–427.

Poschmann, C. & M. Wagner. 2016. Relative clause extraposition and prosody in German, Natural Language & Linguistic Theory 34(3): 1021–1066.

Remmele, B. 2017. The prosody of sluicing: Production studies on prosodic disambiguation. Tübingen: University of Tübingen dissertation.

Rochemont, M. & P. Culicover. 1990. English focus constructions and the theory of grammar. Cambridge: Cambridge University Press.

Romero, M. 1998. Focus and reconstruction effects in wh-phrases. Amherst, MA: University of Massachusetts at Amherst dissertation.

Ross, J.R. 1969. Guess who? In: (R. Binnick, A. Davison, G. Green & J.L. Morgan, eds) Papers from the Fifth Regional Meeting of the Chicago Linguistic Society, April 18–19, 1969, 252–286. Chicago: Chicago Linguistic Society. https://eric.ed.gov/?id=ED030865
Sag, I.A. 1976. A logical theory of verb phrase deletion. In: (S. Mufwene, C.A. Walker, & S.B. Steever, eds) Papers from the 12th Regional Meeting of the Chicago Linguistic Society, April 23–25, 1976. 533–542. Chicago: Chicago Linguistic Society.
Sag, I.A. & J. Nykiel. 2011. Remarks on sluicing. In: (S. Müller, ed) Proceedings of the HPSG11 Conference, Department of Linguistics, University of Washington, 188–208. Department of Linguistics, University of Washington: CSLI Publications.
Umbach, C. 2005. Contrast and information structure: A focus-based analysis of but. Linguistics 43(1): 207–232.
Vicente, L. 2018. Sluicing and its subtypes. In: (J. van Craenenbroeck & T. Temmerman, eds) The Oxford Handbook of Ellipsis, 479–503. Oxford: Oxford University Press.
Williams, E. 1977. Discourse and logical form. Linguistic Inquiry 8(1): 101–139.
Winkler, S. 2005. Ellipsis and focus in generative grammar. Berlin/New York: Mouton de Gruyter.
Winkler, S. 2013. Syntactic diagnostics for island sensitivity of contrastive focus in ellipsis. In: (L. Cheng & N. Corver, eds) Diagnosing syntax, 463–484. Oxford: Oxford University Press.
Winkler, S. 2016. Ellipsis and information structure. In: (C. Féry & S. Ishihara, eds) The Oxford handbook of information structure, 359–382. Oxford: Oxford University Press.
Winkler, S. 2018. Ellipsis and Prosody. In: (J. van Craenenbroeck & T. Temmerman, eds) The Oxford Handbook of Ellipsis, 357–386. Oxford: Oxford University Press.

Robin Hörnig and Caroline Féry
Markers of discourse status in descriptions of altered spatial layouts

1 Introduction

Beginning with Linde & Labov (1975), there have been several studies on how people describe static spatial layouts, with apartment descriptions as a paradigmatic example. For the most part, these studies concentrated on the macrostructure of this kind of discourse addressing, for instance, strategies that people use in linearizing spatial configurations into speech (see also Levelt 1982). In the present work, we examine the microstructure of German descriptions of changing layouts. We concentrate on these aspects that can be used to encode information structure, or, more specifically, discourse status (givenness) or newness (focus). As Arnold et al. (2013:403) put it, '[i]nformation structure helps explain why people say things in different ways. Speakers constantly make choices about how to phrase their utterances.' We assume that speakers in our study make choices in particular about the definiteness of the target expression, the constituent order of the linguistic localization of a target, and the tonal contour of the pitch accent carried by the target expression. We consider our work as a study on audience design[1] (Clark & Murphy 1982), assuming that speakers tailor their utterances to their listeners by taking account of the common ground, that is, mutual knowledge of speaker and (imaginary) listeners about entities, the arrangement of the entities, and changes in the arrangement of the entities. The speaker's evidence about the common ground is her utterances up to the utterance of the target localization.

Linguistic localizations are usually uttered to inform the addressee about the place of a *located object*, *LO*, a place currently unknown to her or him. The task of conveying the unknown place to the addressee requires the speaker to relate that place to something known to the addressee. In describing a layout this can be done by linguistically relating the place of the LO to the place of another entity, a

---
[1] We see commonalities between audience design and common ground management presented by Döring & Repp (this volume).

Acknowledgments: This research was supported by the Deutsche Forschungsgemeinschaft (SFB 632). We thank Franziska Koch, Laura Herbst, and Kristin Irsig for collecting the data, as well as Esther Sommerfeld and Kristin Irsig for their help in preparing the material. We also thank the anonymous reviewers and Thomas Weskott for helpful comments on a previous draft of this paper.

https://doi.org/10.1515/9783110623093-006

reference object RO, both of which – the entity and its place – are supposed to be known to the addressee. We call such localizations, which are frequently uttered in descriptions of altered layouts, *relational localizations*. A relational localization typically includes a *locative expression LX* of which RO forms a proper part, as in 28:4 below. Localizations are especially well suited for the study of effects of the discourse status on the form of the produced utterances because three of four properties are generally fixed while the fourth property can be experimentally manipulated: the reference object RO and its place should be known to the addressee, the place of the located object LO is unknown to the addressee, yet the LO itself may be known or unknown to the addressee.

In our experimental setting, participants described a linear layout of three, or sometimes two, toy animals to an imaginary addressee. A sentence from our corpus, 28:4, serves as an example (labeling is explained in what follows).

28:4 [Links   [vom Pferd]$_{RO}$]$_{LX}$ steht   jetzt   [ein Zebra]$_{LO}$
     '[To-the-left [of-the horse]$_{RO}$]$_{LX}$ stands   now   [a zebra]$_{LO}$'

The layout was repeatedly altered. In most instances, one of the animals was removed and a new one was added to the otherwise unchanged layout (*added target*). In other instances, one of three animals was removed and one of the two remaining animals was relocated (*relocated target*), see Figure 1 below for an overview of all layouts. These manipulations were intended to influence the discourse status of the LO and its place. This paper examines the linguistic reflexes of these influences. The experiment shows that speakers make reliable use of markers of discourse status, see below, yet not to the same extent.

1.1 Discourse status of the place of the target

In the following, a *target* is a toy animal that has been added to the layout, or one that has been relocated within the layout. Either way, once the instructor has placed the target, its place was new and unknown to the imaginary addressee. The task of the speaker was to inform the addressee about the place of the target. The speaker did so by means of a linguistic localization, called a *target localization*.

As the places of the other animals in the layout were unchanged and known to the addressee, the speaker could linguistically localize the target by spatially relating it to another animal in the layout, that is, by uttering a relational localization. If, for instance, a bear was added to the right of a horse, the speaker could naturally describe this change in the layout by uttering (1a).

(1) a. [A bear]₍ₗₒ₎ is [to the right of [the horse]₍ᵣₒ₎]₍ₗₓ₎.
    b. [The horse]₍ₗₒ₎ is [to the left of [a bear]₍ᵣₒ₎]₍ₗₓ₎.

Although (1a) and (1b) follow from each other and hence convey the same information,[2] it would sound odd if the speaker uttered (1b) under these circumstances. Relational localizations like (1a) and (1b) assign distinct semantic roles to the internal argument of the spatial preposition, the reference object RO, and to the external argument, the located object LO (figuring here as grammatical subject). The RO expression forms a proper part of the locative expression LX, which comprises the whole prepositional phrase. The locative expression LX denotes a place in the layout. A key feature of a relational localization is its use to spatially relate an object, the place of which is unknown to the addressee, relative to another object, the place of which is known to the addressee. In this account, speakers are expected to produce relational localizations with the target as located object and another object already known to the addressee as reference object. Early comprehension studies demonstrated strong effects of the role assignment in relational placement instructions on the ability of participants to act out these instructions by adding new objects relative to given objects with English learning children (Huttenlocher & Strauss 1968) and English speaking adults (Clark 1972; Harris 1975; see also Hörnig, Oberauer & Weidenfeld 2005, on German speaking adults). Listeners and readers are substantially faster and more often correct in adding a located object to a reference object than in adding a reference object to a located object.

Based on the linguistic analysis and the experimental evidence in support of it, we will restrict the analyses to relational target localizations in which the target constitutes the located object LO. This claim generalizes to non-relational localizations in which targets can only figure as LO. The place of the LO is thus new.

1.2 Discourse status of the target

While the place of the target is always new, the target itself can be new or given. Specifically, the target is new if it has been added to the layout, whereas it is given if it has been relocated within the layout. Important exceptions to this general

---

[2] We presuppose the *deictic* or *viewpoint-dependent reading* of spatial prepositions and disregard their *intrinsic reading*. That (1a) and (1b) follow from each other does not hold with an intrinsic reading.

correlation arise whenever the speaker mentions the target before she linguistically localizes it.

(2) A horse has been added. [*The horse*]~LO~ is [*to the left of* [the bear]~RO~]~LX~.

In instances like (2), the target has already been mentioned and is given when the localization is uttered. Since we are interested in how speakers linguistically encode the discourse status of the target, the target is classified as given whenever it is mentioned prior to its localization. In the following, three linguistic devices are considered that can be used to mark the discourse status of the target in German: the definiteness of the target expression, the constituent order of the localization, and the melodic contour of the pitch accent carried by the target expression.

1.2.1 Definiteness of the target expression

An obvious candidate for marking the discourse status of the target as new or given is the definiteness in the target expression. Definite DPs are referring expressions meant to enable the addressee to identify the referent the speaker has in mind. Accordingly, the speaker will not use a definite DP unless she has reasons to believe that the addressee is familiar with the intended referent. In our setting, this requires that the target is known to the addressee from previous descriptions of the altering layout or from mentioning the target in the current utterance prior to the target localization. If the addressee is unfamiliar with the target, the speaker should introduce the new target by means of an indefinite DP. With this distinction, we follow the *familiarity theory of definiteness* (cf. Heim 1983). An indefinite DP blocks a co-referential reading with an antecedent in connected discourse. It is impossible to interpret the second occurrence of the indefinite DP *ein Bär* 'a bear' in (3) as co-referential with the bear introduced by the first instance of the indefinite DP. Assuming such a co-referential reading, the brief discourse in (3) sounds odd.

(3) Ein Bär steht neben dem Pferd. Nun wurde [*ein Bär*]~LO~ weggenommen
 'A bear stands next to the horse. Now was [*a bear*]~LO~ removed'

The earliest demonstration of the interrelation between discourse status and definiteness was documented by Osgood (1971). He asked his students in a graduate seminar to close and re-open their eyes on demand. With their eyes open, he shortly showed something to them, which they briefly described immediately afterwards with their eyes closed. The first three times he did the following: #1 he placed an orange ring in the middle of the table in front of him, #2 he held a black ball in his hand, #3 he placed the black ball in the middle of the table. The critical comparison for our concerns addresses the definiteness of the expressions referring to the orange ring in #1, which is new to the students, and the black ball in #3, with which the students are familiar with from #2. Osgood (1971:497f) reports with respect to #1 that '[s]entences with definite articles [...] almost never occurred', whereas 'demonstration #3 did regularly yield sentences with the definite article [...].' In line with Osgood's observation we expect to find a reliable correlation of the discourse status of a target as new or given with the target expression being indefinite or definite, respectively.

1.2.2 Constituent order of the localization

Linguistic localizations have two obligatory parts, the LO expression, denoting the located object, and LX, the locative expression denoting the place of LO. The most general distinction that we draw is between the two possible orders of the LO expression and LX in the target localization: LO < LX versus LX < LO. The distinction applied to a relational localization is exemplified in (4) with the order LO < LX in (4a) and the order LX < LO in (4b).

(4) a. [Ein Bär]$_{LO}$ ist [rechts von   [dem Pferd]$_{RO}$]$_{LX}$.
       '[A bear]$_{LO}$ is [to-the-right of [the horse]$_{RO}$]$_{LX}$.'

     b. [Rechts von   [dem Pferd]$_{RO}$]$_{LX}$ ist [ein Bär]$_{LO}$.
       '[To-the-right of [the horse]$_{RO}$]$_{LX}$ is [a bear]$_{LO}$.'

The constituent order in German, compared, for example, to English, is relatively flexible, see Féry, Skopeteas & Hörnig (2010) for comparisons among several languages using comparable data to the ones presented in this chapter, and Weskott, Hörnig & Webelhuth (this volume). When the preverbal position of the verb-second main clause (the *prefield* of a V2 clause) harbors the grammatical subject, as in (4a), the constituent order is unmarked; with the prepositional phrase in the prefield, as in (4b), the constituent order is marked.[3] The German marked order,

---

[3] We consider the constituent orders in (4a) and (4b) unmarked and marked, respectively, because, as regards comprehensibility, the latter order is contextually more restricted than the former (cf. Hörnig & Weskott 2010). Unmarked constituent orders are read faster in neutral contexts in which LO and RO are both new; a marked constituent order is especially difficult to read in an inappropriate context in which the RO is new and the LO is given. However, a marked constituent

however, is less strongly marked than the corresponding English locative inversion in (4b) and it is not infrequent in German. Ullmer-Ehrich (1982) observed that the locative expression frequently precedes the LO expression in naturally elicited apartment descriptions in German. A similar observation is reported by Ehrich & Koster (1983) for Dutch in a more controlled setting. O'Brien & Féry (2015) compared English and German speakers, both in their L1 and in their L2 for similar data to those examined in the present chapter. German speakers uttered much more localizations with a marked constituent order than English speakers, and these both in English and in German. From comprehension studies (e.g., Hörnig et al. 2005) we know that a German relational localization with a marked constituent order is especially easy to comprehend as long as the reference object is given by the previous context, whereas the located object is new. However, with a definite determiner and in response to the question *Wo ist der Bär?* 'Where is the bear?', (4a), *Der Bär ist rechts von dem Pferd*, should be preferred over (4b), *Rechts von dem Pferd ist der Bär*, as the marked order variant sounds infelicitous after the located object has been prominently referred to in the question (cf. Hartsuiker et al. 1999, for acceptability of marked and unmarked constructions dependent on definiteness in Dutch; see also Ehrich & Koster 1983:184f; see also Chafe's 1970:215, comments on his example (5a), *The box is under the table*. In the context of the question (6a), *Where is the box?*).

Based on these intuitions and on the reported evidence, it can be expected that the constituent order of target localizations covaries with the discourse status of the target: when the speaker utters a target localization with a marked order LX < LO, she signals to the addressee that the target (LO) is new; a target localization with an unmarked order LO < LX, on the other hand, indicates a given target. Our hypothesis is most straightforward for relational target localizations. As argued by Hörnig et al. (2005), the marked constituent order facilitates comprehension through the given-before-new ordering established by putting the given reference object before the new located object (cf. Clark & Haviland 1977). Accordingly, we hypothesize that the constituent order is unmarked, LO < LX, unless the LO is new and follows LX with the given RO, thus LX < LO.

We anticipated that speakers would sometimes produce non-relational target localizations like $[Rechts]_{LX}$ *ist* $[ein\ Bär]_{LO}$ '[On-the-right]$_{LX}$ is [*a bear*]$_{LO}$.'

---

order is easiest to read if the context is appropriate, i.e., the LO is new and the RO is given. Reading an unmarked constituent order is much less sensitive to contextual properties. Hörnig & Weskott (2010) thus consider the particularly good comprehensibility of the marked order in an appropriate context an instance of a strong contextual licensing of a marked constituent order. Bader & Häussler (this volume) report on a similar observation for the *bekommen* passive in German. Weskott, Hörnig & Webelhuth (this volume) elaborate on markedness and contextual restrictions.

Since the preverbal constituent 'on the right' does not contain a given element, we need a generalization of our hypothesis on the constituent order of target localizations to account for non-relational target localizations. Hörnig, Weskott, Kliegl & Fanselow (2006) point out that, if a new LO is paired with a given RO, the preverbal PP of a relational localization refers to the place of the located object. This place is unknown to the addressee and thus new. However, the new place in question is easily accessible in the discourse model, be it by explicitly relating it to the given place of the given RO, as in a relational localization, or by implicitly relating it to some more abstract reference frame in the discourse model, as in a non-relational localization. The relevant reference frame for the interpretation of spatial adverbs in our setting is the array of toy animals in front of the speaker.

The binary given-new distinction can be replaced by a graded concept of givenness in terms of accessibility (e.g., Gundel, Hedberg & Zacharski 1993; Prince 1981; Baumann & Riester 2013; Röhr & Baumann 2011). In the spirit of such approaches, a new place is readily accessible in the discourse model, whereas a new target must be introduced into the model before it becomes accessible. According to Dryer (1996), a referent is 'accessible' if it bears a pragmatic relation to a locally prior reference. In our case, the location of toy animals render locations to their right or left accessible, whereas a not yet introduced referent is not accessible. To summarize, the following ordering on a givenness hierarchy is assumed: *given LO ≺ new place of LO ≺ new LO*.

With this modification in mind the hypothesis on the constituent order of target localizations can be formulated without referring to the reference object: the constituent order is unmarked, LO ≺ LX, unless the LO is new.

1.2.3 Pitch accent type carried by the target expression

As a third possible linguistic marker of discourse status we examined the contour of the pitch accents realized on the LO expressions. The question underlying this part of our study is whether we can find a correlation between the direction of pitch accents as rising (L*H in a tone-sequence notation, see Pierrehumbert 1980, for English, and Féry 1993, for German) or falling (H*L) and the discourse status of the constituent it is realized on. In line with an extensive literature on the subject, we assume that every pitch accent is the head of a prosodic phrase, called Φ-phrase. The prosodic features of German are organized around the pitch accents, which are often rightmost in their Φ-phrases, and which, as a result, often fall together with tonal boundaries. A coherent succession of syntactically driven Φ-phrases in a sentence is organized in an intonation phrase, called ι-phrase. Selkirk (1980, 1984) and Nespor & Vogel (1986) assume that the prosodic constituents are organized in a prosodic hierarchy, as illustrated in (5), and this view is still in use today. Each constituent preferably consists of constituents immediately below.

(5) Prosodic hierarchy
    ι-phrase   intonation phrase   (corresponds roughly to a clause)
    Φ-phrase   prosodic phrase   (corresponds roughly to a syntactic phrase)
    ω-word   prosodic word   (corresponds roughly to a grammatical word)

Pitch accents are associated with prominent elements in the sentence, thus focused or new ones, although pre-nuclear given elements also carry pitch accents. Only post-nuclear given elements are systematically deaccented. Pitch accents vary in two dimensions: the direction of the excursion as a bitonal rise or fall, and the intensity of the excursion. The latter dimension is not addressed in the result section of this chapter, because of the large number of speakers and the fact that they were using different grammatical means to express the localizations of interest. Instead we restricted the analysis to the first dimension, thus the distribution of rising and falling pitch accents.

The literature on pitch accents has introduced a relationship between discourse status (or information structure) and the kind of accents. Büring (1997), Féry (1993), Jackendoff (1972), Jacobs (1997), and Steedman (2000) establish a very direct relation between a falling accent (sometimes also called accent A) and focus on the one hand, and a fall-rise or a rise (accent B) and given constituents on the other hand, see Baumann (2006) and Hadelich & Baumann (2006) for psycholinguistic and perception experiments on the relationship between givenness and accentuation in German. Focus is an information structural category that we treat as equivalent to the concept of 'new referent' (new target) used in this chapter. It is predicted that given constituents are realized with a rising accent if they are pre-nuclear, that is, if they appear before the focus of the sentence, which carries the nuclear accent. If the given constituents are located in the post-nuclear position of the sentence, that is, after the focus, they are unaccented. To sum up, a new referent is focused and realized with a nuclear falling tone, and a given entity is part of the background, and as such is realized without any accent if post-nuclear or with a rising one, if pre-nuclear. We do not exclude that a given constituent can be a topic (see the Discussion section), in which case, it is pre-nuclear and carries a rising accent. Since the constituent order of LO and LX may vary as a function of the discourse status of the LO, it is a special concern of this chapter to examine the variation in the pitch accents as a function of constituent order. Constituent order has an important effect on pitch accents: a non-final accent is preferably rising, and a ι-phrase final accent is falling. Because of this correlation, we expect that a new target is preferably final and carries a falling accent, whereas a given referent is typically non-final and carries a rising pitch accent. This implies that the marked constituent order LX < LO may be preferred for this reason as well. Additionally, it supports the preference discussed above that a new target is mentioned after the locative expression. See the summary of our hypotheses in Section 2.1.3 below.

2 Production experiment

2.1 Method

2.1.1 Material and procedure

Ten plastic toy animals were used as stimuli, all of them approximately of the same size (about 8 cm in length). Participants were tested individually in a quiet room, seated at a table beside the instructor. They were asked to briefly describe the spatial layouts of the animals such that an imaginary addressee who does not know the layouts is able to reproduce the layouts with their own set of toy animals. Care was taken to avoid giving participants any example of an utterance. The instructor started the session by putting two toys, a crocodile and a gorilla, side by side on the table. Then she added a third one, in this case a horse (*horse* = target). The first task of the participants consisted in giving a brief oral description of this first layout L1. In a second step, the instructor removed the crocodile and added a lion (*lion* = target), creating in this way a second layout L2, altered minimally as compared to L1. Again, participants described the current layout of three animals. This procedure was repeated until the participants had described nine different layouts, L1 to L9, each consisting of three animals, two of them being part of the preceding layout and the third one, the target, being added to the layout. In addition, participants described two layouts L5R and L9R in which one of three animals was removed and one of the two remaining animals, the target, was relocated. Figure 1 gives an overview of the sequence of layouts, which was identical for all participants. Targets are set in italics.

L1	L2	L3	L4	L5	L5R	L6	L7	L8	L9	L9R
					B	B	B	*T*	*P*	
A G *H*	G H *L*	G H *B*	*Z* H B	H B *D*	D	D	D	D	T	*T* P
						G	*C*	C	D	

Figure 1: The 11 layouts L1–L5, L5R, L6–L9, and L9R; targets are set in italics (dark gray). Legend: Alligator · Bear · Cow · Dog · Gorilla · Horse · Lion · Pig · Tiger · Zebra.

2.1.2 Participants and recordings

Thirty students of the University of Potsdam, 28 women and 2 men, all in their twenties and native speakers of German, took part in the experiment. The participants' utterances were recorded on a DAT recorder (Sony T100). First, the recordings were transcribed into written files, subdivided according to the layouts L1 to L9, L5R, and L9R. In a second step, the recordings were analyzed using the acoustic speech analysis software Praat© (Boersma & Weenink 1994–2006). The sound waves were partly manually divided into labeled sub-strings with the help of spectrograms, and carefully inspected for their pitch accents.

2.1.3 Hypotheses

Before turning to the results, we summarize our hypotheses on information structural correlates of target localizations dependent on whether the target was new or given. We consider an added target 'new' as long as it is not mentioned in the utterance prior to the target localization, otherwise we call it 'given'. A relocated target has always been mentioned in a previous utterance and is thus given. Remember that the target figures as located object in all valid target localizations.

(i) Definiteness
   a. if target is new, the LO expression is indefinite
   b. if target is given, the LO expression is definite

(ii) Constituent Order
   a. if target is new, the constituent order of the target localization is LX ≺ LO
   b. if target is given, the constituent order of the target localization is LO ≺ LX

(iii) Pitch Accent
   a. if target is new, it is a focus and the LO expression carries a falling pitch accent (H*L).
   b. if target is given, it is a topic or part of the background. Then the LO expression carries a rising pitch accent (L*H) in case it is pre-nuclear or it is unaccented in case it is post-nuclear.

We consider definiteness, constituent order, and pitch accent as linguistic devices that respond directly to the discourse status of the target. As speakers may signal the discourse status by making use of more than one of the devices, responses from the different devices can correlate. Correlations, however, may in principle also result from interdependencies between the devices. It could be, for instance, that constituent order varies as a function of definiteness, in which case constituent order would signal definiteness rather than discourse status. Our statistical analysis reported below addresses this problem. The analysis answers the question whether our speakers' markings by definiteness, constituent order, and pitch accent all substantially contribute to a regression model predicting the discourse status of targets in a single blow. If constituent order in fact predicts definiteness, which in turn predicts discourse status, the joint predictive value of definiteness and constituent order should not exceed the predictive value of definiteness alone and the model would not identify constituent order as predictor for discourse status.

2.2 Data annotation and results

329 utterances were recorded altogether, 269 descriptions of the layouts L1 to L9 with an added target, and 60 descriptions of the layouts L5R and L9R with a relocated target. L6 of Participant 1 was inadvertently skipped by the instructor. For each utterance, the target localization, that is, the part of the utterance that conveyed the new place of the target, entered the analysis. The examples given below are labeled with regard to participant and layout, in this order. For example, utterance 2:9 is Participant 2, Layout L9 and 35:5R is Participant 35, Layout L5R. The LO expression, the locative expression (LX), and, if present, the RO expression of target localizations are enclosed in indexed brackets; target expressions are set in italics.

2.2.1 Categories of target localizations

We identified 279 valid target localizations in the 329 utterances (85%),[4] divided into three types: relational localizations (211), non-relational localizations (37), and mnemonic localizations (31).

Relational localizations overtly specify the place of the target with respect to at least one reference object. The vast majority of these localizations were realized by means of one of the spatial prepositions *neben* 'next to'/'beside', *vor* 'in

---

4 38 utterances contained no target localization, e.g. 'The gorilla was replaced by *a zebra*' (36:4) or '... from left to right: the gorilla, the horse, and *a bear*'. (32:3); 12 utterances were discarded because the added target was mentioned before it figured as RO in the target localization, e.g., 'In front of me is *the zebra*, [to the right of [*the zebra*]$_{RO}$]$_{LX}$ [the horse]$_{LO}$ ...' (18:4).

front of', *hinter* 'behind', *rechts von* 'to the right of', and *links von* 'to the left of', cf 28:4. The indeterminate preposition *neben* was usually qualified by *rechts* 'right' or *links* 'left', as in 33:9R. Some relational localizations were realized by a pronominal adverb like *dahinter* 'thereof-behind', as shown in 4:9.

28:4   [Links   [vom Pferd]$_{RO}$]$_{LX}$ steht   jetzt   [ein Zebra]$_{LO}$
       '[To-the-left [of-the horse]$_{RO}$]$_{LX}$ stands   now   [a zebra]$_{LO}$'

33:9R und [der Tiger]$_{LO}$ wird [links neben   [das Schwein]$_{RO}$]$_{LX}$ geschoben
       'and [the tiger]$_{LO}$ Is   [left next-to [the pig]$_{RO}$]$_{LX}$ pushed'

4:9   und [[da]$_{RO}$hinter]$_{LX}$ steht   [das Schwein]$_{LO}$
       'and [[there]$_{RO}$ behind]$_{LX}$ stands   [the pig]$_{LO}$'

29:4   Jetzt ist   [links außen]$_{LX}$ [das Zebra]$_{LO}$
       'Now   is   [on the far left]$_{LX}$ [the zebra]$_{LO}$'

15:5   In der Reihe   aus Pferd und Bär   befindet sich   [auf der rechten Seite]$_{LX}$
       'In the row   of horse and bear   is situated   [on the right side]$_{LX}$
       [ein Hund]$_{LO}$
       [a dog]$_{LOC}$'

17:4   Nun   steht   [da,   wo der Gorilla stand]$_{LX}$ [das Zebra]$_{LO}$
       'Now   stands [there, where the gorilla stood]$_{LX}$ [the zebra]$_{LO}$'

48:4   [An der Stelle des Gorillas]$_{LX}$ steht   nun   [ein Zebra]$_{LO}$
       '[At the place of-the gorilla]$_{LX}$ stands   now   [a zebra]$_{LO}$'

Non-relational localizations lack an overt reference object. These localizations often make use of a spatial adverb like *links* 'on the left' in 29:4. The spatial adverb implicitly refers to the row of animals as a reference frame, as becomes evident in the overt reference 15:5, where the row of horse and bear sets the reference frame.

Mnemonic localizations are specific instances of relational localizations in which the removed animal serves as a reference object to help the addressee identifying the place of the newly added target as the one from which the removed animal has been taken away (applies to L3, L4, L7, and L8). The examples 17:4 and 48:4 illustrate two possibilities how such a reference can be achieved.

To summarize, the analysis is based on 279 target localizations, classified as relational (76%), non-relational (13%), or mnemonic (11%).

2.2.2 Annotation of definiteness, constituent order, pitch accents, and discourse status

Definiteness of the target expression could be determined for almost all of the 279 target localizations by the determiner of the LO expression. The determiner was indefinite in 146 instances and definite in 126 instances. One of the 126 definite instances was a demonstrative determiner shown in 35:6. The demonstrative pronoun in 17:3 was classified as definite. Finally, the relative pronouns in six relative clauses exemplified in 2:1 below were also classified as definite.

35:6 Nun wurde *ein Gorilla* hinzugefügt und [*dieser Gorilla*]$_{LO}$
'Now was *a gorilla* added and [*this gorilla*]$_{LO}$
befindet sich nun [vor [dem Hund]$_{RO}$]$_{LX}$
is situated now [in-front-of [the dog]$_{RO}$]$_{LX}$.'

17:3 Nun wurde das Pferd durch *einen Bär* ersetzt, [*der*]$_{LO}$ steht jetzt
'now was the horse substituted for *a bear*, [*that-one*]$_{LO}$ stands now
[rechts]$_{LX}$.
[on-the-right]$_{LX}$.'

Above, marked constituent orders were distinguished from unmarked orders according to whether the grammatical subject (LO expression) precedes or follows the locative expression LX. Thus, we first briefly look at LO's grammatical function. LO figured as grammatical subject except for six target localizations, in which LO figured as direct object; in these cases, the subject was *wir* 'we' five times (e.g., 37:6) and an expletive subject of an existential construction once (42:5R).

37:6 [Vor [dem Hund]$_{RO}$]$_{LX}$ haben wir [*'n Gorilla*]$_{LO}$.
'[In-front-of [the dog]$_{RO}$]$_{LX}$ have we [*a gorilla*]$_{LO}$.'

42:5R Es gibt nur noch den Braunbären und [vor [ihm]$_{RO}$]$_{LX}$
'There is only the brown bear left and [in-front-of [him]$_{RO}$]$_{LX}$
[den Hund]$_{LO}$.
[*the dog*]$_{LO}$.'

Turning now to the constituent order of the 279 target localizations, it was 184 times LX ≺ LO (66%) and 95 times LO ≺ LX (33%). Among the 184 target localizations with the order LX ≺ LO, LX occupied the prefield (*Vorfeld*) of a verb second clause (German main clause) in 156 utterances. With the order LO ≺ LX the LO expression occupied the prefield in 64 instances. In the remaining localizations, the prefield was most often, 48 times, occupied by the temporal adverb *jetzt* or *nun* 'now'. One target localization came in the form of a verb final subordinate clause and six others as relative clauses subordinated to the LO, as in 2:1. Although the grammar requires that the LO expression in 2:1, that is, the relative pronoun, comes first in the relative clause, we accepted these six utterances for analysis.

2:1 Neu hinzugekommen ist   *das Pferd,*   [*das*]_LO
    'Newly added is   the horse,   [which]_LO
    [rechts neben [dem Affen]_RO]_LX   steht.
    [on-the-right next-to [the ape]_RO]_LX   stands.'

As for the pitch accents, they were strongly dependent on constituent order. The pitch accent on LO expressions of new targets was falling (H*L) in 66% of the cases. The falling contour was predictable when the target was mentioned last in the ɩ-phrase (74% of the cases). Since all sentences were declarative, the overall contour was usually falling, and the last falling accent was on the DP denoting the new target. The same is true when the only word following the LO expression of a new target was a participle. In those instances, the participle was unaccented, and the fall was realized entirely on the LO expression. One may wonder why an LO expression of a new target mentioned late in the sentence was realized 44 times with a rising accent (L*H). In most cases, the target was not mentioned last in the ɩ-phrase but subsequent accents were present, motivating a rising accent. For instance, a further localization was following the localization of the target in the same sentence. We call such a motivated rising accent at the end of a Φ-phrase a 'continuation rise'. The remaining cases came from so-called 'list intonations' at the end of an ɩ-phrase, where a fall is expected to signal finality. List intonations were realized when the participants adjusted their speech to the fact that the task was ongoing, in which case each layout was perceived as a subtask.

64 of the 81 given targets were realized with a rising tone. In 52 cases, this can be analyzed as resulting from constituent order, as the targets were not mentioned last in the ɩ-phrase. The remaining 12 occurrences were continuation rises or due to list intonation. Three of them were second mentions of added targets.

In sum, we find a high correlation between the shape of pitch accents and sentence position (i.e., constituent order), which is stronger than the association of newness with a falling accent predicted by Hypothesis (iii.a). For details of the pitch accent realizations and numerous illustrations, we refer the reader to Féry, Hörnig & Pahaut (2011).

The discourse status of added targets is new as long as the target is mentioned in the target localization for the first time in the utterance. This was frequently the case, as 198 of the 225 added targets were not mentioned prior to the target localization. In the remaining 27 utterances, the target was mentioned prior to the target localization and hence was given at the time when it was localized. The six localizations in relative clauses, cf. 2:1, belong to these instances. Another example was shown in 17:3 above. Alternatively this sentence is an instance of a V2 relative clause. As the discourse status of the 54 relocated targets is classified as given, the analysis is based on localizations of 198 new and 81 given targets.

2.2.3 Results

Table 1 gives an overview of the interdependency of the values of our variables, separately for localizations of new targets (left panel, all of them added animals) and given targets (right panel, 54 relocated and 27 added animals). In each panel the target localizations are first subdivided by whether the target expression was indefinite or definite; they are further subdivided by whether the target expression follows (LX < LO) or precedes the locative expression (LO < LX); the final subdivision distinguishes between falling and rising pitch accents on the target expression. Proportions indicate relative frequencies with respect to the previous level of subdivision.

The data shown in Table 1 were submitted to logistic regression analyses using the *glmer* function of the lme4 package in R. All analyses include the intercept of the random factor *participant*. First, we computed the full model with all three predictors: definiteness, constituent order, and pitch accent. As can be verified in Table 2, all three fixed factors reliably predict the discourse status of the target.

For each of the three predictors, we compared the full model against a model without the predictor. The full model proved to be superior in all three instances. It provided a reliably better fit of the data than the models without definiteness, $\chi^2(1) = 61.1^{***}$, without constituent order, $\chi^2(1) = 9.5^{**}$, and without pitch accent, $\chi^2(1) = 4.5^{*}$. Hence, each of the three devices has a predictive value beyond the predictive value of the other two.

We exemplify the relative independence of the predictors by comparing definiteness versus constituent order as markers of discourse status. As can be gathered from Table 1, the definiteness of the target expression is a highly valid signal if the expression is indefinite (138 of 143 indefinites if target is new: 97%), but it is a poor signal if the expression is definite (76 of 136 definites if target

Table 1: Target localizations of new and given targets, classified according to Definiteness of target expression, Constituent Order, and contour of Pitch Accent on target expression. Percentages are specified in terms of the immediately preceding level.

DISCOURSE STATUS of Target								
New				**Given**				
198				81				
71%				29%				

DEFINITENESS of Target Expression				DEFINITENESS of Target Expression				
Indefinite		Definite		Indefinite		Definite		
138		60		5		76		
70%		30%		6%		94%		

CONSTITUENT ORDER of Localization				CONSTITUENT ORDER of Localization				
LX < LO	LO < LX	LX < LO	LO < LX	LX < LO	LO < LX	LX < LO	LO < LX	
116	22	44	16	5	–	19	57	
84%	16%	73%	27%			25%	75%	

PITCH ACCENT on Target Expression						PITCH ACCENT on Target Expression					
Fall	Rise	Fall	Rise	Fall	Rise	Fall	Rise	Fall	Rise	Fall	Rise*
85	31	9	13	33	11	3	13	4	1	–	–	8	11	5	52
73%	27%	41%	59%	75%	25%	19%	81%			–	–	42%	58%	9%	91%

Note: The 52 rising accents in the rightmost column subsume two unaccented LO expressions

is given: 56%). Interestingly, since we have about the same number of new and given definite target expressions, we can look whether the constituent order of these target localizations is the same (if dependent on definiteness) or different (if dependent on discourse status). It turns out that the constituent order is not the same for new and given definite target expressions, as three quarters of the given instances have the constituent order LO < LX, whereas three quarters of the new instances have the reverse order, LX < LO.

Table 2: Outcome of the Logistic Regression Analysis with definiteness, constituent order, and pitch accent as predictors (fixed factors) for discourse status with participant as random factor (intercept). ***$p < .001$; **$p < .01$; *$p < .05$

Fixed factors	Coefficient	Standard error	z
Intercept	−4.717	0.681	−6.93***
Definiteness	−3.760	0.678	−5.55***
Constituent order	−1.493	0.501	−2.98***
Pitch accent	−1.112	0.510	−2.19***

2.3 An unexpected observation of apprehended relocation

We occasionally observed a phenomenon reminiscent of the Ternus display. Josef Ternus, a Gestalt psychologist, showed his participants a sequence of four point displays (Ternus 1926). Let's call the points *a*, *b*, *c*, and *d* from left to right. Each display showed *b* and *c*, while *a* and *d* showed up in alternation (cf. Figure 2, *a* visible at t_1, *d* visible at t_2). Ternus observed that this kind of stimulus can induce two different interpretations, *element motion* or *group motion*. With perceived element motion, participants distinguish four points: *b* and *c* are considered constant entities at fixed places ($b_1 = b_2$, $c_1 = c_2$), with *a* and *d* as additional entities, each one at a fixed place of its own. Hence, *a* and *d* are alternately added and new with respect to the previous display. With perceived group motion, participants distinguish three points that repeatedly move together from left (*a*, *b*, *c* are visible) to right (*b*, *c*, *d* are visible) and back ($a_1 = b_2$, $b_1 = c_2$, $c_1 = d_2$). *a*, *b*, and *c* are repeatedly relocated and always perceived as given from the preceding layout.

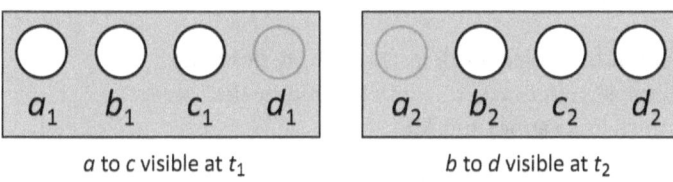

a to *c* visible at t_1 *b* to *d* visible at t_2

Figure 2: Ternus display with two alternative states.

Now, let A, B, C, and D be toy animals on a table instead of points on a display: A is a zebra, B a horse, C a bear, and D is a dog. If the zebra disappears and the dog shows up, we have the transition from L4 (ZHB) to L5 (HBD). The perceived identity of entities is not ambiguous because the toy animals can be easily distinguished. Apprehended group motion due to an added target is nevertheless possible. A speaker S, who produces non-relational localizations, will answer the question *Where is the horse?* differently for L4 and L5 although the horse was not actually moved: *The horse is in the middle* is an adequate answer for L4, but *The horse is on the left* is apt for L5. This is what we observe in 29:4 and 29:5. Participant 29 localizes the horse in the middle of L4 (29:4); in doing so, she uses the words *immer noch* 'still' to express that the horse was also placed in the middle of L3. In describing L5 shortly afterwards, she begins her utterance 29:5 by stating that the horse is now on the left, from which we recognize that she apprehends the horse as being moved from the middle to the left of the layout. Interestingly, Participant 29 begins her utterance 29:4 by localizing an added new target and her utterance 29:5 by localizing a 'relocated' given non-target. These two localizations bear the opposite constituent order in agreement with Hypothesis (ii). The very same happens in 29:2 and 29:3, which mirror 29:4 and 29:5. The LO expression precedes the locative expression if LO is given (29:2 and 29:5), but it follows the locative expression if LO is new (29:3 and 29:5). In addition, the utterance-final target localizations in 29:2 and 29:5 have the opposite constituent order of the utterance initial localizations of a 'relocated' non-target, again in agreement with Hypothesis (ii). However, localizations of non-targets in 29:2 to 29:5 do not consistently signal the givenness of the LO by the unmarked constituent order LO < LX. Even if we disregard the localizations of non-targets in 29:3 and 29:4 since the places of the non-targets are not new, the marked order of the bear's localization in 29:5 is not as predicted.

29:2 Jetzt ist der Affe links außen, das Pferd in der Mitte
'Now is the monkey leftmost, the horse in the middle,
und [rechts]$_{LX}$ [der Löwe]$_{LO}$.
and [on-the-right]$_{LX}$ [the lion]$_{LO}$.'

29:3 Nun ist [rechts außen]$_{LX}$ [ein Bär]$_{LO}$, in der Mitte das Pferd
'Now is [rightmost]$_{LX}$ [a bear]$_{LO}$, in the middle the horse,
und immer noch links außen der Affe.
and still leftmost the monkey.'

29:4 Jetzt ist [links außen]$_{LX}$ [das Zebra]$_{LO}$, in der Mitte immer noch das Pferd
'Now is [leftmost]$_{LX}$ [the zebra]$_{LO}$, in the middle still the horse,
und rechts außen immer noch der Bär.
and rightmost still the bear.'

29:5 Nun ist das Pferd links außen, in der Mitte der Bär
'Now is the horse leftmost, in the middle the bear,
und [rechts außen]$_{LX}$ [ein Hund]$_{LO}$.
and [rightmost]$_{LX}$ [a dog]$_{LO}$.'

The phenomenon is not peculiar to Participant 29. By inspecting the descriptions of the three layouts in which the target was placed at the opposite side of the removed animal, L2, L5, and L9, we found 13 further descriptions produced by eight participants that started with a non-relational localization expressing an apprehended relocation of a given non-target, all of them with an unmarked constituent order LO < LX. The subsequent target localizations of 11 of these 13 descriptions had the opposite constituent order, LX < LO, in agreement with

Hypothesis (ii). Although there is no strict correspondence between the constituent order of the localizations and the discourse status of LO, we consider these occasional observations as evidence in support of our Hypothesis (ii).

3 Discussion

This chapter reported on a production study in which German native speakers described a repeatedly changing layout of toy animals on a table. We were interested in how speakers mark the discourse status of a target, that is, an animal that appeared at a new place in the layout, either by being added to the layout or by being moved to a different place in the layout. In particular, the experiment tested how speakers make use of definiteness, constituent order, and the contour of pitch accents to mark the target as new or given. According to hypotheses (i) to (iii), a new target should be introduced by an indefinite DP, a marked constituent order LX < LO, and a falling pitch accent; a given target should come along with a definite DP, an unmarked constituent order LO < LX, and a rising pitch accent. Target localizations carrying all three markers of discourse status were indeed most frequent among localizations of new targets (85/198 = 43%) and given targets (49/81 = 60%). The statistical analysis confirmed that the three markers of discourse status reliably predict the discourse status of the target; the model fit significantly decreased if any one of the three predictors was excluded from the model, thus all three markers substantially contributed to the model's prediction.

The most reliable predictor in the model was the definiteness of the target expression. Target expressions were almost never indefinite when the target was given; hence, the indefinite determiner was a highly valid cue for the discourse status of the given target. This was expected if speakers were willing to provide a coherent discourse about the changing layout and the indefinite determiner blocked a co-referential interpretation. The definite determiner was a less valid cue as it was quite often used with a new target. However, the constituent order LX < LO signaled the newness of the target in almost three-fourths of these instances. It can thus be concluded that linguistic markers of discourse status were used here in a compensatory fashion.[5]

Compared to the indefinite determiner, the marked constituent order LX < LO is a less valid cue for the newness of the target, as it was more often

---

[5] A model with a specified interaction of constituent order and definiteness did not converge, because there is no localization of a given target with a marked constituent order and an indefinite target expression. A separate model with the interaction coded as a main effect yielded a marginal effect, $z = 1.75$, $p = .08$, providing some support for compensatory usage.

used with a given target. On the assumption that LX < LO is a marked order that must meet contextual constraints to be felicitously used, for example, LO is new, one would expect that localizations of given targets with a marked order are less frequent than localizations of new targets with an unmarked order. The counts in the small sample coincided with this prediction (24 vs. 38), but the moderate difference did not provide strong evidence for of a markedness difference, see 8:1 for a sample utterance from the present study with LX preceding a given target.

8:1 Drei Tiere nebeneinander, ein Krokodil, ein Gorilla und *ein Pferd*.
'Three animals side-by-side, a crocodile, a gorilla and *a horse*.
Der Gorilla steht in der Mitte,
The gorilla stands in the middle,
links davon steht das Krokodil und [rechts [da]$_{RO}$von]$_{LX}$ steht [*das Pferd*]$_{LO}$.
left thereof stands the crocodile and [right [thereof]$_{RO}$]$_{LX}$ stands [*the horse*]$_{LO}$.'

Speaker 8 starts her utterance with identifying a horizontal array, followed by an enumeration of the three animals that constitute the array. She continues with describing how the three animals are arranged. First, the gorilla is set as an anchor in the middle of the layout; here, LO precedes LX. The speaker proceeds by telling the addressee which place to the left and the right of the gorilla is harboring which animal; LO follows LX in both cases. We may assume with some certainty that the three animals do not differ much in discourse status. Even if givenness is in principle conceived of as graded, the gradation described in the literature does not apply to this case (see Prince 1981 and Baumann & Riester 2013 for gradation of givenness). It seems therefore impracticable to account for the different constituent orders in terms of discourse status.

Ullmer-Ehrich (1982) also reported numerous localizations with LX preceding a definite LO expression referring to pieces of furniture that had been mentioned before in an enumeration. Ehrich & Koster (1983:185), based on their own observations, considered dismissing the given/new explanation in favor of a topic/comment account based on Reinhardt's (1981) analysis of aboutness topics. Roughly, this means for 8:1 that the anchoring of the gorilla in the layout is a comment about the gorilla, which serves as the topic of the first localization: *Where is the gorilla?* The two subsequent localizations are then comments about the place to either side of the gorilla. These places each serve as a topic of a localization: *What is to the left/right of the gorilla?* We think that such an approach is on the right track, yet an elaboration is beyond the scope of this paper (see Büring 2003, 2016 for a view of topics as organizing the discourse). We emphasize, however, that constituent order showed a substantial relationship with the target's discourse status in our study. Aboutness topichood remains a potentially superior substitute for discourse status in our scenario.

The contour of the pitch accents on target expressions is the third possibility to mark the discourse status of targets. The statistical analyses showed that pitch accents reliably marked the discourse status of targets, though to a lesser extent than definiteness and constituent order, and that pitch accents were informative beyond the other two markers. Hence the contour of the pitch accents turns out to be more than a mere correlate of the constituent order, in spite of what we thought previously (see Féry, Hörnig & Pahaut 2011 for such a view): LO expressions carried a falling pitch accent if late in the sentence, but a rising or no accent if early in the sentence. Whether an LO expression came early or late in a sentence depended on whether it preceded or followed LX and hence on constituent order. Indeed, three-fourths of our target localizations redundantly marked the discourse status of the target by constituent order as well as contour of pitch accent, LX < LO together with a falling accent or LO < LX together with a rising accent. In the remaining fourth of our target localizations, constituent order and pitch accent conflicted with each other. In 24 instances, 9% of the whole sample, the pitch accent marked the discourse status of the target in line with our hypotheses and the constituent order did not: there were 12 new targets with LO < LX with a falling accent and 12 given targets with LX < LO with a rising accent, as a signal that the utterance was not yet ended, thus the rising accent indicated a continuation contour. Out of the 12 new targets, 11 were marked as new by an indefinite determiner, a highly valid cue for the newness of the target, as we saw above. Without challenging the informativeness of the pitch accent cue, we nevertheless attest this cue a considerable portion of redundancy.

If we compare our data on pitch accents with Baumann & Riester's (2013) results, a great deal of similarities becomes apparent. Baumann & Riester also examined a corpus of spontaneous speech for the prosodic realization of referential expressions with different levels of information status, 218 referents in total. They were especially interested in the relation between different levels of givenness and newness and the kind of pitch accents realizing them. They hypothesized that a new referent should be realized with a falling pitch accent and a given referent with a rising accent, a lower falling accent or no accent at all. Their results did not confirm these hypotheses. In the spontaneous monologues they recorded and analyzed, that is, the data with pseudo-spontaneous speech most similar to our data, they found that all information statuses are similarly realized with a falling nuclear accent. Five categories out of six have "H*" (a falling accent) between 47 and 51% of the times. They interpret their finding with the fact that, like ours, their speakers realized short intonation phrases, and that each intonation phrase needs a final falling nuclear accent. This need supersedes the relation between information status and accent shape. It must be noticed that the notation they use is difficult to interpret, especially in relation with the pitch track they show, and that the large number of categories they use renders the results difficult to assess. However, their main result is that word order is the main predictor of the kind of accent in spontaneous data, a result completely in line with ours.

To summarize, the production study demonstrated that speakers make use of definiteness, constituent order, and the contour of pitch accents to mark the discourse status of a target as new or given. The examples showed that the sample of target localizations was far from being a homogeneous set of uniform utterances. Although almost all combinations of the three markers occurred at least once in our sample, the discourse status was preferably simultaneously marked by all three devices. We found evidence for both redundant and compensatory marking of discourse status. Whether the marking actually signals newness and givenness or rather some related discourse status like topichood is left open in this chapter. What may be safely concluded is that the speakers behaved cooperatively in communicating more than just the new places of targets, a finding well in agreement with the idea of audience design.

References

Arnold, J. E., E. Kaiser, J. M. Kahn & L. K. Kim. 2013. Information structure: Linguistic, cognitive, and processing approaches. Wiley Interdisciplinary Reviews: Cognitive Science, 4(4): 403–413.
Baumann, S. 2006. The intonation of givenness. Evidence from German. Tübingen: Niemeyer.
Baumann, S., & A. Riester. 2013. Coreference, lexical givenness and prosody in German. Lingua 136: 1651137.
Boersma, P. & D. Weenink. 2006. Praat: Doing phonetics by computer (Version 4. 4.20) [Computer program]. Retrieved May 3, 2006, http:www.praat.org
Büring, D. 1997. The 49th bridge accent. Berlin: Mouton de Gruyter.
Büring, D. 2003. On D-trees, beans, and B-accents. Linguistics and Philosophy 26(5): 511–545.
Büring, D. 2016. (Contrastive) topic. In: (C. Féry & S. Ishihara, eds) The Oxford handbook of information structure, 64–85. Oxford: Oxford University Press.
Chafe, W.L. 1970. Meaning and the structure of language. Chicago: University of Chicago Press.
Clark, H.H. 1972. Difficulties people have in answering the question 'Where is it?' Journal of Verbal Learning and Verbal Behavior 11(3): 265–277.
Clark, H. H. & S. E. Haviland. 1977. Comprehension and the given-new contract. In: (R.O. Freedle, ed) Discourse processes: Advances in research and theory 1: Discourse production and comprehension, 1–40. Norwood, NJ: Ablex.
Clark, H. H. & G. L. Murphy. 1982. Audience design in meaning and reference. In: (J.-F. Le Ny & W. Kintsch, ed) Language and comprehension, 287–299. Amsterdam: North-Holland.
Dryer, M. 1996. Focus, pragmatic presupposition, and activated propositions. Journal of Pragmatics 26(4): 475–523.

Ehrich, V. & C. Koster. 1983. Discourse organization and sentence form: The structure of room descriptions in Dutch. Discourse Processes 6(2): 169–195.
Féry, C. 1993. German intonational patterns. Tübingen: Niemeyer.
Féry, C., R. Hörnig & S. Pahaut. 2011. Correlates of phrasing in French and German from an experiment with semi-spontaneous speech. In: (C. Gabriel & C. Lleó, eds) Intonational phrasing in Romance and Germanic, 11–41. Amsterdam: John Benjamins.
Féry, C., S. Skopeteas & R. Hörnig. 2010. Cross-linguistic comparison of prosody, syntax and information structure in a production experiment on localising expressions. Transactions of the Philological Society 108(3): 329–351.
Gundel, J.K., N. Hedberg & R. Zacharski. 1993. Cognitive status and the form of referring expressions in discourse. Language 69(2): 274–307.
Hadelich, K. & S. Baumann. 2006. Accent type and givenness in German scene descriptions: Evidence from multi-modal priming. Paper presented at 19th CUNY Conference on Human Sentence Processing, New York, USA.
Harris, L.J. 1975. Spatial direction and grammatical form of instructions affect the solution of spatial problems. Memory & Cognition 3(3): 329–334.
Hartsuiker, R.J., H.H.J. Kolk & P. Huiskamp. 1999. Priming word order in sentence production. The Quarterly Journal of Experimental Psychology 52A(1): 129–147.
Heim, I. 1983. File change semantic cs and the familiarity theory of definiteness. In: (R. Bäuerle, C. Schwarze, & A. v. Stechow, eds) Meaning, use, and interpretation of language, 164–189. Berlin: de Gruyter.
Hörnig, R., K. Oberauer & A. Weidenfeld. 2005. Two principles of premise integration in spatial reasoning. Memory & Cognition 33(1): 131–139.
Hörnig, R., T. Weskott, R. Kliegl & G. Fanselow. 2006. Word order variation in spatial descriptions with adverbs. Memory & Cognition 34(5): 1183–1192.
Hörnig, R. & T. Weskott. 2010. Given and new information in spatial statements. In: (M. Zimmermann & C. Féry, eds) Information structure: Theoretical, typological, and experimental perspectives, 354–374. Oxford: Oxford University Press.
Huttenlocher, J. & S. Strauss. 1968. Comprehension and a statement's relation to the situation it describes. Journal of Verbal Learning and Verbal Behavior 7(2): 527–530.
Jackendoff, R.S. 1972. Semantic interpretation in generative grammar. Cambridge, MA: MIT Press.
Jacobs, J. 1997. I-Topikalisierung. Linguistische Berichte 168: 91–133.
Levelt, W.J.M. 1982. Linearization in describing spatial networks. In: (S. Peters & E. Saarinen, eds) Processes, beliefs, and questions. Essays on formal semantics of natural language and natural language processing, 199–220. Dordrecht, NL: Reidel.
Linde, C. & W. Labov. 1975. Spatial networks as a site for the study of language and thought. Language 51(4): 924–939.
Nespor, M. & I. Vogel. 1986. Prosodic Phonology. Dordrecht: Foris.
O'Brien, M.G. & C. Féry. 2015. Dynamic localization in second language English and German. Bilingualism: Language and Cognition 18(3): 400–418.
Osgood, C.E. 1971. Where do sentences come from? In: (D.D. Steinberg & L.A. Jakobovits, eds) Semantics. An interdisciplinary reader in philosophy, linguistics and psychology, 497–529. Cambridge: Cambridge University Press.
Pierrehumbert, J.B. 1980. The phonology and phonetics of English intonation. Cambridge, MA: MIT PhD thesis.
Prince, E.F. 1981. Toward a taxonomy of given-new information. In: (P. Cole, ed) Radical pragmatics, 223–255. New York, NY: Academic Press.

Reinhart, T. 1981. Pragmatics and linguistics: An analysis of sentence topics. Philosophica 27(1): 53–94.
Röhr, C.T. & S. Baumann. 2011. Decoding information status by type and position of accent in German. Online Proceedings of the ICPhS XVII 2011, 1706–1709.
https://www.internationalphoneticassociation.org/icphs-proceedings/ICPhS2011/index.htm
Selkirk, E.O. 1980. The role of prosodic categories in English word stress. Linguistic Inquiry 11(3): 563–605.
Selkirk, E.O. 1984. Phonology and syntax: The relation between sound and structure. Cambridge, MA: MIT Press.
Steedman, M. 2000. Information structure and the syntax-phonology interface. Linguistic Inquiry 31(4): 649–689.
Ternus, J.S.J. 1926. Experimentelle Untersuchungen über phänomenale Identität. Psychologische Forschung 7, 81–136. Condensed and translated as 'The problem of phenomenal identity' In: (W.D. Ellis, ed, 1939), A source book of Gestalt psychology, 149–160. New York: Harcourt, Brace.
Ullmer-Ehrich, V. 1982. The structure of living room descriptions. In: (R.J. Jarvella & W. Klein, eds) Speech, place, and action. Studies in deixis and related topics, 219–249. Chichester: John Wiley & Sons.

Thomas Weskott, Robin Hörnig and Gert Webelhuth
On the contextual licensing of English locative inversion and topicalization

1 Introduction

Comparisons of English and German often mention one dimension along which the two languages quite obviously vary: word order. While German exhibits movement of the verbal head to the C position in main clauses (the 'V2 property'), but has verb final word order in most embedded clauses, English is often perceived as much more rigid. This difference has often been attributed to the difference in morphological case marking, which German shows, and English almost completely lacks. While this picture certainly has something going for it, it can be argued to be a bit coarse and oversimplifying in the way it paints the relation between (relative) word order freedom and the factors determining it. For one thing, it does not tell us anything about other factors—apart from (lack of) case marking—which might influence word order. If richness of the case system were the only driving force behind word order freedom, we might, for example, expect Finnish to exhibit a more liberal word order than Latin, because the former has a richer case system than the latter; but that's not what we see. A further point in which this line of thinking underestimates the complexity of factors involved in the interplay of word order and other linguistic and extralinguistic factors is that even English shows deviations from its preferred SVO sentence structure in some cases, and that it does so in a quite systematic fashion, that is, these deviating cases have some context-related properties in common.

In what follows, we want to have a closer look at two types of noncanonical word order in English, locative inversion ('LI' henceforth), and topicalization, and their respective contextual properties. Below, we will introduce these two constructions in more detail, and discuss some of their syntactic and information-structural properties. This will lead up to the core idea of our contribution, the *contextual licensing hypothesis*. In Section 2, we take results from German showing that the counterpart of LI in German shows a strong contextual licensing pattern as a backdrop for a comprehension and a production study on LI. Section 3 presents experimental data on topicalization from acceptability

---

Acknowledgments: The authors thank Cheryl Hodgkinson, who carried out the experiments on English topicalization, and Christoph Scheepers for providing them with the opportunity to carry out these experiments at the Department of Psychology at the University of Glasgow.

https://doi.org/10.1515/9783110623093-007

rating and self-paced reading experiments in German and English. Section 4 concludes the paper with a discussion of the problematic aspects of our data, of the possible merits and problems in using contextual licensing as a gauge to measure the relative word order freedom of a given language, and gives an outlook on the prospects for further research.

In comparisons of the syntactic properties of English and German, the degree of word order freedom plays a prominent role. Across a wide range of syntactic environments, English seems to be governed by constraints that the syntax of German either does not exhibit at all, or which German seems free to violate in certain marked constructions. This difference is probably most conspicuous in the case of *argument scrambling* (i.e., reversal of the order of verbal arguments, like reversing the basic order SOV to OSV in embedded sentences), which English does not exhibit at all, and whose admissibility in German can be traced back to the topological organization of German sentences; that is, ultimately, to verb finality, or right-headedness of the verbal projection (see Webelhuth 1988, 1990; Haider 1993; Haider & Rosengren 1998, 2003, for theoretical analyses; and Bader & Meng 1999, for an overview over the experimental results from the 1990s, and Stolterfoht 2004, for an in-depth experimental investigation of argument scrambling). A further case that has received quite a lot of attention from both theoretical and experimental linguists is *superiority*: while English places a ban on reversing the canonical order of subject and object in multiple wh-questions, German seems to be less restrictive in this respect, too. The exact theoretical locus of the superiority constraint in English has been a matter of debate in recent years (see Hofmeister & Sag 2010; Sprouse, Wagers & Phillips 2012, and the subsequent publications in the debate following these publications), but the evidence available seems to suggest that English has a *grammatical* constraint banning wh-objects to be placed before/above wh-subjects, while German only shows a *processing* penalty for superiority violations (see Häussler, Grant, Fanselow & Frazier 2015; but see also Featherston 2005, for a different view). Further examples of this difference abound, extending the pattern—English being more restrictive than German—beyond the relative position of arguments in the middle field of the German sentence, for example, topicalization, on which more below; so-called short scrambling across negation and adverbials (see Stolterfoht 2004); split-NP constructions (see Fanselow 1988; and Fanselow & Cavar 1992, and much subsequent work), and various other cases of deviation from canonical patterns.

Overall, the comparison between English and German word orders seems to indicate a higher degree of freedom for German than for English. A reason for this difference may be found in the different degrees of case-marking the two languages exhibit: while German uses the comparatively elaborate case system to mark syntactic functions like *subject-of*, or *direct object-of*, English, lacking overt case almost entirely, has to code these functions in terms of linear position. This line of reasoning can be traced back at least to Keenan's (1978) 'principle of covariation of functional equivalents', stating that '[...] the more we assign a language overt case marking the freer can be its basic order and conversely' (ibid., 120f). An explicit statement with respect to the two languages at hand can be found in Gast and König (2012):

> The basic intuition that German has a relatively free word order, whereas the order of elements in English is fixed, however, is only a partially correct summary of the relevant differences. Given the elaborate case system of German, it comes as no surprise that the order of arguments like subject and object is, on the whole, more flexible than in English, since case marking allows us to identify the grammatical relation of a constituent independently of its position in the sentence. (ibid., p. 188)

Assuming, furthermore, that the basic arrangement of object and verb is OV in German, while in English it is VO, and the observation that only OV languages allow for rearrangement of argument phrases in the verbal projection (see Haider, 1993, and much subsequent work), the differences observed in word order freedom between the two languages do, as Gast and König note, not come as a surprise.

If we were only interested in the difference in word order freedom between English and German, we might stop here. However, our interest in this contribution is focused on cases that, at first blush, seem to constitute exceptions to Keenan's principle, that is, cases where English shows word orders that deviate from its canonical SVO order and that have—at least superficially—similar counterparts in German. The first is English LI, which we will compare to fronting of locative prepositional phrases in German ("German locative PP fronting" for short); the second is English topicalization of direct objects, which will be compared to German direct object topicalization, or 'Vorfeldbesetzung'. We want to emphasize, however, that we do *not* want to claim that LI in English has the same syntactic properties as German PP fronting, nor that English and German topicalization are the same in syntactic respects. While the factors driving topicalization in German seem quite variegated, topicalization of, for example, direct objects in English has been argued to be dependent on a single factor: a contrastive relation to an element in the preceding discourse (see Ward 1988), or, as Frey (2005) puts it, that the designated element is linked (ibid., p. 120). Similarly, the syntactic properties of English LI (as described in Bresnan 1994) clearly differ from those of German PP fronting, which, as an anonymous reviewer has pointed out to us, may be seen as an instance of the run-of-the-mill fronting operation in German. This being said, we want to make clear at the outset that we do not assume that LI/PP fronting or topicalization have syntactic similarities in German and English. Rather, what we are interested in are the conditions under which the markedness effects associated with these noncanonical forms in the two languages can be ameliorated, or even be turned around. That is, we want to address the question of how contextual licensing interacts with the two construction types in the two languages, and we leave the task of spelling out how contextual properties interact with, for example, syntactic positions in the two languages to further research. Thus, we will not give a full-fledged overview over the syntax and information structure of these constructions; this has been done by other authors (see, e.g., Birner 2009; Birner & Ward 2011; Bresnan 1994; Breul 2007; Culicover & Winkler 2008; and Frey 2005). Here, we will confine ourselves to a description of the properties of LI and topicalization that allow us to derive the hypotheses we want to test in our experiments.

The core hypothesis about contextual licensing crucially involves reference to the relation between marked and unmarked forms on the one hand, and certain information-structural properties characterizing the context surrounding these forms on the other. Before turning to the specific instances of the hypothesis, let us state it here in a general form: in comparison to its unmarked counterpart, a marked form shows a stronger *contextual restriction*. By *contextual restriction* we mean a restriction on the types of context that the form may felicitously appear in. Note in passing that this claim mentions *types* of context, not specific instances of these types; note furthermore that we are not taking this to be an explication of the notion of markedness, but rather a mere working definition allowing us to talk about differences in markedness. If a certain context fulfills the restriction that the marked form imposes, we say that the marked form is *contextually licensed*. Our main aim in the current contribution is to look at the differences that the contextual requirements between marked and unmarked forms of certain constructions show in German and English, that is, we want to look, as it were, at differences between differences: differences in licensing strength. By taking this approach, we hope to learn more about the relation that certain marked word orders entertain to information-structural properties of their surrounding contexts.

2 Locative inversion

An example of this construction is exemplified in (1) as follows:

(1) a. The box is under the table.
    b. Under the table is the box.

The word order in (1.b) deviates from the canonical SVO in two ways: the prepositional object 'under the table', normally positioned after the verb, is placed preverbally; and the subject has been put after the verb, in this case the copula 'be'. Despite this rather drastic deviation from the canonical S-copula-PP order, the sentence in (1.b) is a well-formed, if somewhat marked, sentence of English.

The syntactic properties of English LI have been extensively discussed in Stowell (1981) and Bresnan (1994); for our present purposes, the details of the syntactic analysis of (1.b)—whether it involves movement of the PP, or whether the PP is base generated in some left peripheral position; and, respectively, for the copula verb and the subject DP—are of minor interest. What is important for our concerns here, however, is that spatial relational sentences with inverted order like the one in (1.b) are perceived as *marked* in comparison to their S-copula-PP variants exemplified by (1.a). What do we mean by 'marked'? First of all, the inverted sentences incur lower acceptability judgments than their noninverted variants when presented out of the blue; readers may easily verify this by themselves. We disregard the fact here that both DPs, the subject and the prepositional object, are definite, and as such necessitate accommodating their respective referents in a null context, since this holds for both word order variants; we hasten to acknowledge, however, that a pragmatic function of LI consists in presenting new referents relative to a location, and that in presentational uses of LI, the inverted subject is usually indefinite.

We take this difference in acceptability in the out-of-the-blue context to reflect a difference in the *contextual requirement* of the two variants. While the canonical S-copula-PP in (1.a) is acceptable in different types of context like (i) a null context or an out-of-the-blue context like 'What's going on?', and in wh-question contexts like (ii) 'Where's the box?' and (iii) 'What's under the table?', its noncanonical counterpart (1.b) is only acceptable in the last type of context (iii). Syntactic differences alone are most certainly not sufficient to explain this difference in contextual requirement—apparently, the syntactic deviation from the canonical form has a function here: it signals a more restricted connection between the sentence and its preceding context than the canonical S-cop-PP.[1] Looking at the context (iii), exemplified by a question like 'What's under the table?', more closely, we note that it features the referent of the DP 'the table'; thus, the referent of the DP 'the table' in (1) is *given* in that context, while the referent of the subject DP 'the box' is not. With Chafe (1970) we can argue that it is exactly this difference in discourse status that is responsible for the deviation from the canonical word order: the phrase containing the given discourse referent is the preferred '[...] starting

---

[1] Note that this function is bought at the cost of loosening the reliability of the covariation between position and syntactic function that English exploits in its canonical forms. In this case, this cost is relatively low, since the PP cannot be mistaken for a *bona fide* subject even if it is in preverbal position.

point [...] to which the new information can be related' (ibid., 211). The notion of 'starting point' has some intuitive plausibility to it: if, for example, a person consulting a printed city guide of Göttingen in order to find her way from the station to the main university campus in Göttingen, and finds herself to be confronted with the sentence pair 'The botanic garden is to the north of the old city wall. Behind the botanic garden is the main university campus', the usefulness of this instruction depends on that person's being in the know about the exact location of the botanic gardens; if she is not, the whole instruction is pointless, since the location of the main campus (the *locatum* referent) is described *in relation to* that of the botanic garden (the *relatum* referent). These two arguments of spatial relations have been argued to exhibit a number of interesting asymmetries (see Miller & Johnson-Laird 1976). For our purposes, the asymmetry in discourse status is the crucial one: while the locations of relatum referents in spatial relational sentences tend to be part of the common ground, the locations of locatum referents typically are discourse new (see Vandeloise 1986; Skopeteas, Hörnig & Weskott 2009). Let us call this the '*relatum = given* principle', which can be taken to explain why the marked form in (1.a) can only appear in a context in which the relatum (the table) is mentioned (i.e., in a type of context like (iii)): in order for LI to be contextually felicitous, the relatum has to be discourse given (see Bresnan 1994, a.o.). If one thinks of a spatial relational assertion of the type exemplified by (1) as an instruction to the hearer how to reach the place where the locatum (the box) is, the givenness constraint on the relatum makes immediate sense: its pragmatic function is to be a landmark from which a direction (in this case 'under' or 'below') has to be followed to reach the point where the locatum is. In fact, placement instructions combining a new locatum referent with a given relatum referent are easier to comprehend and act out than the reverse combinations, as has been shown by Huttenlocher & Strauss (1968) for children and by Clark (1972) and Harris (1975) for adults. Note, however, that this pragmatic function of providing a landmark is independent of word order and could be assumed by both the postverbal prepositional argument in (1.a) and the preverbal one in (1.b). The crucial reason why the word order variant in (1.b) seems only to be felicitous in contexts of type (iii) has been argued to reside in the fact that this order, given contexts like (iii), exhibits a *given-new* ordering: the given relatum is mentioned before the new locatum. Clark & Haviland (1977) took up Chafe's idea of a starting point in proposing their *given-new contract* account of processing, which has been shown to govern comprehension (but see Clifton & Frazier, 2004, for some counterevidence to the principle). Taken together, the felicity of an LI sentence like (1.b) depends on the constraints that the relatum referent is discourse given and the locatum referent is discourse new. In what follows, we will call types of context where this condition is fulfilled *licensing contexts*: in these contexts, a sentence with marked LI order such as (1.b) is not only as pragmatically felicitous as its unmarked counterpart (1.a); it can be argued to be even more felicitous because it adheres to the *given-new* ordering. And since the *given-new* contract of Clark & Haviland (1977) ultimately boils down to a hypothesis about the processing preferences for sentences containing discourse-new and discourse-given information, we might even assume that, given a licensing context, a marked word order like (1.b) may even be easier to process than its unmarked counterpart. Adopting the terminology of Weskott et al. (2011), we call this hypothesis the *strong contextual licensing hypothesis*. It states that, in a licensing context, the prototypical markedness effects on acceptability and processing difficulty are reversed: the marked order is more acceptable and easier to process than the unmarked one. The corresponding *weak contextual licensing hypothesis* claims that in a licensing context, the prototypical markedness effects mentioned above are leveled out, that is, there is no difference in acceptability or processing difficulty between marked and unmarked orders.

2.1 Hörnig et al. (2005) on German PP fronting

Although they did not name it that way, Hörnig et al. (2005) tested the contextual licensing hypothesis, and showed that both principles mentioned in the preceding section, *relatum = given* and *given-before-new*, are in force in the comprehension of German sentences exhibiting a word order comparable to that of English LI, that is, in German-locative PP fronting. They asked 22 participants to read 128 items consisting of two spatial premises (P1 and P2) like the ones in (2) in a sentence-wise self-paced fashion, and then to judge the truth of an arrangement of pictures given the two premises; the dependent variable of interest here was the reading time for the second premise. Constituents denoting given referents in P2 are printed in bold face; constituents denoting new referents are rendered in *italics*.

(2) a. Unmarked word order, new relatum, **given**-*new* ordering:
      (P1) *Der Bär* ist links *vom Esel*.
            'The bear is left of-the donkey.'
      (P2) **Der Esel** ist links *vom Hund*.
            '**The donkey** is left of-the dog.'

  b. Marked word order, new relatum, *new*-**given** ordering:
      (P1) Links *vom Esel* ist *der Bär*.
            'Left of-the donkey is the bear.'
      (P2) Links *vom Hund* ist **der Esel**.
            'Left of-the dog is **the donkey**.'

c. Unmarked word order, given relatum, *new*-**given** ordering:
(P1) *Der Bär* ist links **vom Esel**.
   'The bear is left **of-the donkey**.'
(P2) *Der Hund* ist rechts **vom Esel**.
   'The dog is right **of-the donkey**.'

d. Marked word order, given relatum, **given**-*new* ordering:
(P1) Links **vom Bär** ist *der Esel*.
   'Left **of-the bear** is the donkey.'
(P2) Links **vom Esel** ist *der Hund*.
   'Left **of-the donkey** is the dog.'

Hörnig et al. (2005) predicted that reading a second premise is easier and thus faster if the relatum is given and the locatum is new; and, in addition, there should be shorter reading times for marked word orders with a given new ordering, that is, a given-new advantage. Both predictions were borne out by the results: for unmarked second premises, comprehension times were about the same with a given relatum but a new-given order and with a given-new order but a new relatum. More importantly, comprehension times were strongly influenced by word order. With a given relatum, marked word order facilitated comprehension considerably compared to unmarked word order, but marked word order rendered comprehension especially difficult with a new relatum. Table 1 illustrates these findings from Hörnig et al. (2005).

Table 1: Reading times for second premises in milliseconds dependent on word order and discourse status of the PP object from Hörnig et al.'s (2005) study on German PP fronting (conditions (2a)–(2d)).

Discourse status of relatum	Word order	
	Unmarked (S-copula-PP)	Marked (PP-copula-S)
New	(2a) 4,625	(2b) 5,967
Given	(2c) 4,493	(2d) 3,787

The critical interaction between word order and discourse status of the relatum was statistically reliable. Hörnig et al. (2005) attribute the strong effect of discourse status on second premises with marked word order to the two principles mentioned earlier: a general preference for given new orderings, and a preference specific to spatial relational assertions that the relatum be given. In German, a marked word order in a spatial relational sentence as in (1.b) can be as easy to comprehend as its unmarked counterpart, and in fact be easier to comprehend and thus read faster, if the context renders the referent of the PP object given, because it adheres to both principles: in this context, given information precedes new information, and the relatum (the 'landmark') is given. The result pattern found by Hörnig et al. (2005) thus constitutes a piece of evidence—and, as far as we know, the first—in favour of the *strong contextual licensing hypothesis*: although there have been successful attempts to show that a marked word order of German can be judged to be as acceptable, and is read as fast as its unmarked counterpart (see Weskott et al., 2011 for an overview of the findings), there had been no evidence for strong licensing before the publication of Hörnig et al. (2005).

2.2 Experiment 1: Testing the strong contextual licensing hypothesis using LI

In the general discussion of Hörnig et al. (2005), the authors relate the previous failure to demonstrate a given new advantage in spatial relational assertions in English (Baguley & Payne 2000; Ehrlich & Johnson-Laird 1982) to the fact that only canonical orders were used in these experiments. Given this observation, as well as the claims on the discourse properties of LI mentioned in Section 2, it is compelling to ask whether LI in English can be strongly licensed in a context that renders its relatum argument (i.e., the referent of the prepositional object) discourse given. It is this hypothesis that the current experiment sets out to test. In order to do so, we translated the original materials of the Hörnig et al. study in the DP conditions (see footnote 2), while retaining their design and predictions.

2.2.1 Method

2.2.1.1 Participants
Twenty-four native speakers of American English (14 female) who participated in a student exchange between Göttingen University and UCLA in summer 2007 volunteered to take part in the experiment.

2.2.1.2 Materials
The stimuli consisted of a subset of 64 items of the three-term items of Hörnig et al. (2005). Each item consisted of three terms, which named animals, fruits or vegetables, vehicles, musical instruments, or other common objects of everyday life. These objects were depicted by 120 × 120 black-on-white pixel line drawings. Each item consisted (i) of two verbal premises describing the relative position of

three objects to each other (the first relating two, and the second relating one of them to the third object), and (ii) of an arrangement of two pictures that were not explicitly related to each other in the verbal premises (the conclusion to be verified). The relations described one-dimensional (one half of the items, horizontal or vertical) or two-dimensional layouts (other half of the items). The spatial prepositions 'left of', 'right of', 'above' and 'below' in the second premises were balanced and all DPs were definite. As exemplified in (3), each item was available in four conditions by manipulating the discourse status of the relatum (new in (3a/b), given in (3c/d)) and the word order (unmarked in (3a/c), marked in (3b/d)).[2] We adopt the marking of given and new referents from example (2).

(3) a. Unmarked word order, new relatum, **given**-*new* ordering:
 (P1) *The bear* is to the left of the donkey. (P2) **The donkey** is to the left of the dog.

 b. Marked word order, new relatum, *new*-**given** ordering:
 (P1) To the left of *the donkey* is the bear. (P2) To the left of *the dog* is **the donkey**.

 c. Unmarked word order, given relatum, *new*-**given** ordering:
 (P1) *The bear* is to the left of the donkey. (P2) *The dog* is to the right of **the donkey**.

 d. Marked word order, given relatum, **given**-*new* ordering:
 (P1) To the left of *the donkey* is the bear. (P2) To the right of **the donkey** is *the dog*.

In the case of (3), the arrangement to be verified consists of a picture of the bear and a picture of the dog, that is, of the two entities not explicitly located with respect to each other in the verbal premises. Half of the picture arrangements matched the premise pair, the other half did not. There were no fillers. The 24 premise picture sets were distributed across four lists according to a Latin square design. These four lists were assigned to participants randomly. The order of items was randomized for each participant separately.

---

2 The grammatical function of the antecedent in P1 was varied between items. In all four conditions it figured either as PP object (relatum), like the donkey in (3), or as grammatical subject (locatum).

2.2.1.3 Procedure
Participants were tested individually at a PC. They were instructed that they would read descriptions of layouts of three pictures each, hanging on a wall either beneath each other, beside each other, or a combination thereof, and that their task was to judge whether the pictorial conclusion conformed to the verbal premises. A trial consisted of a prompt to press the space bar to start the trial. After that, the first premise appeared. Participants were instructed to read the premise carefully and press the space bar as soon as they were able to imagine the layout described. When the participant pressed the space bar again, the first premise was replaced by the second one, and participants were asked to press the space bar once more as soon as they were able to imagine the spatial layout of the three objects as a whole. This yielded the dependent variable (comprehension times for second premises). With the pressing of the space bar, the participants were presented with the picture verification task, which we will not discuss here. Afterwards participants started the next trial by pressing the space bar again. The experiment lasted approximately 40 min.

2.2.1.4 Design and predictions
The design was a 2 (WORD ORDER of second premise, S-copula-PP vs. PP-copula-S) × 2 (GIVENNESS of relatum, given vs. new). Following Hörnig et al. (2005), we predicted a contextual licensing effect: that is, we predicted an interaction between WORD ORDER and GIVENNESS. Comprehension times for second premises for unmarked S-copula-PP word orders should be largely unaffected by GIVENNESS, whereas the comprehension of marked PP-copula-S orders should be facilitated and reading times should be shorter if the PP object (relatum) is given, while comprehension should be more difficult if WORD ORDER is marked and the PP object (relatum) is new.

In addition, we were interested in the strength of the licensing effect: if the word order of English is less sensitive to contextual properties, we would expect the licensing effect for English LI to be somewhat weaker than that for German PP fronting. Finding a similar pattern for English LI as Hörnig et al. (2005) found for German, however, would indicate that there are marked word orders in English that are susceptible to strong contextual licensing.

2.2.2 Results

All in all, participants had provided us with 1,536 cases of reading times of second premises. Reading times for second premises were manually screened for outliers (100 ms < RT < 15,000 ms); outliers were excluded (84 trials). The percentage of correct responses a participant had given in the verification task was computed (mean = 91%, ranging from 71% to 98%); one participant was excluded and replaced because s/he had a correctness score lower than 75%. Only trials in which participants had responded correctly to the verification question went into the analysis of the reading times; this exclusion affected a further 132 cases. The remaining 1,320 cases of second premise reading times were log-transformed, and observations beyond 3 standard deviations from the participant mean were removed, affecting only two trials. The descriptive data of the cleaned untransformed reading times for second premises are given in Table 2.

Table 2: Reading times for second premises in milliseconds (standard deviations in brackets) dependent on word order and discourse status of the PP object for Experiment 1 (conditions (3a)–(3d)).

Discourse status of PP object	Word order	
	Unmarked (S-copula-PP)	Marked (PP-copula-S)
New	(3a) 6,139 (3,034)	(3b) 7,103 (3,217)
Given	(3c) 5,451 (2,742)	(3d) 4,749 (2,527)

Using the *lmer* function of the *lme4* package (Bates, Maechler, Bolker & Walker, 2015, version 1.1-9) for the *R* software for statistical computing (version 3.1.1, R Core Team, 2014), we fitted a linear mixed effects model to the log-transformed reading times[3] for second premises with WORD ORDER and GIVENNESS as fixed factors and subjects and items as random factors, with both random intercepts and random slopes (cf. Barr, Levy, Scheepers & Tily 2013). Below, we show the output of the model specified as (log RT ~ (word_order*givenness) + (1 + (word_order*givenness) | subject) + (1 + (word_order*givenness) | item)) and the *p*-values derived from model comparisons using the likelihood-ratio chi-squared test.

Table 3: LMM parameters for the fixed effects worder (i.e., word order) and given (i.e., givenness) and their interaction.

	Estimate	Standard error	*t*-Value	$p_{LR}\chi^2$ (df = 1)
(Intercept)	10.85492	0.06996	155.16	
worder1	−0.01318	0.01267	−1.04	> .10
given1	0.14267	0.01373	10.39	< .001
worder1:given1	−0.07713	0.01170	−6.59	< .001

---

[3] Submitting the untransformed cleaned data to the model did not change the effects pattern.

As can be gleaned from Tables 2 and 3, WORD ORDER per se did not have a significant effect on reading times for second premises, while GIVENNESS did. More importantly, WORD ORDER and GIVENNESS interacted significantly in the predicted direction: while the unmarked orders showed only a moderate, though significant effect of GIVENNESS (688 ms slowdown for new given), comprehension times for the marked order were quite high when the referent of the sentence-initial PP object was discourse new, and particularly short for the condition where the PP object referent was discourse given (2354 ms difference). Apart from the fact that the unmarked word orders showed a difference in English, which was not the case in German, this pattern of results is in line with the findings for German.

2.2.3 Experiment 1: Discussion

Returning to the question put forward in Section 2.2 concerning the strong contextual licensibility of English LI, the answer is in the positive: LI can indeed be strongly licensed by contexts that render the referent of the PP object discourse given. This means that the marked word order, while being strongly dispreferred in a type of context where the referent of the PP object is discourse new (see condition (3.b) above), is easier and thus faster to comprehend in comparison to its unmarked counterpart when it appears in a licensing context. Given the strong parallelism between the findings for German PP fronting and English LI, we can safely assume that even in languages like English, the apparently rigid word order is susceptible to alternations that are licensed by information structural/discourse properties of the preceding context. This context sensitivity seems to be restricted to the marked word order: marked word orders are licensed only if they result in a given new ordering. This conclusion with respect to the given new preference is further supported by the finding that the first premises—that is, in the null context—in both the German (5,384 vs. 5,644 ms) and the English experiments (6,920 vs. 7,193 ms) showed a slowdown of processing in the marked PP-copula-S word order as compared to the unmarked S-copula-PP order; it should be noted, however, that this effect was significant in the Hörnig et al. study only, but failed to reach significance in our current Experiment 1. Taken together, these findings show—to our knowledge, for the first time—that English has marked word orders that can be strongly licensed by context. However, given the claim that word order is more rigid in English than in German, we need to independently establish the higher markedness status of English LI as compared to that of German PP fronting. This was the objective of Experiment 2.

2.3 Experiment 2: Elicited production of spatial relational assertions in German and English

In order to have independent evidence for the degree of contextual restriction of the marked variants—LI in English and PP fronting in German—in comparison to their unmarked counterparts, we conducted an elicited production study where participants were asked to describe spatial layouts of three geometrical shapes in written form. By coding the productions for instances of the critical marked word orders (LI and PP fronting) as well as the discourse status of the referents of the sentence initial PP objects, we hoped to get an answer to the question whether the PP-copula-subject order in English exhibits a *stronger* contextual restriction than its German equivalent. If it is indeed correct that German is more liberal with respect to deviations from canonical orders, this should be reflected in a higher proportion of marked word orders under certain context conditions as compared to the allegedly more rigid English.

2.3.1 Method

The two experiments were completely parallel for the two languages. Hence, we will report them together.

2.3.1.1 Participants
In the German experiment, we tested 188 first-year students of psychology at Potsdam University, all of them native speakers of German. In the English installment of the experiment, we tested 136 undergraduate students at UCLA, all of them native speakers of English. Participants were tested in groups.

2.3.1.2 Material and procedure
Both experiments consisted of one-item only. Participants were handed a sheet of paper with a short instruction asking them to describe a layout printed below the instruction, and to do so in a manner that would allow someone who is not familiar with the layout to draw it. Layouts consisted of an arrangement of three geometrical shapes: a circle, a triangle, and a square. They were arranged either in one (left-right, top-bottom) or two dimensions; number of dimensions and the ordering of shapes were counterbalanced across sheets. Participants wrote down their description and handed the sheets back in.

2.3.2 Results and discussion

Our dependent variable was the absolute frequency of occurrences of marked versus unmarked word orders; see Hörnig & Féry (this volume) and Bader & Häussler (this volume) for a similar methodology. The descriptions were coded with respect to word order (marked vs. unmarked); we coded only those descriptions in which two shapes were mentioned, and one of the shapes had been mentioned before in the written description of the participant, while the other shape was discourse new. Figure 1 gives an example of a layout with a complete description in English in (4). The two clauses that we coded and included into our analysis are rendered in *italics*.

Figure 1: Sample depiction of a layout.

(4) There is a circle and *to the right of it is a triangle. Above the triangle is a square.*

Not all descriptions made use of relational placements; other strategies of describing the layouts involved coordinate systems, the face of a watch, or other absolute orientation systems such as the location on the sheet (e.g., measured in inches or centimeters from the upper left corner) to describe the positions of the shapes. All in all, we got 171 valid descriptions for the German experiment, and 59 in the English one.[4] Table 4 gives the absolute numbers of relational descriptions containing a given and a new argument dependent on markedness:

---

[4] Note that in the German experiment, we coded only the last relational statements containing a given and a new argument, while all relational statements were coded in the English study (as the two in our example above) in order to attain sufficient statistical power. The number of participants producing at least one marked variant in the English experiment was 21.

Table 4: Absolute frequencies of unmarked and marked word orders in English and German (percentage of marked forms in parentheses).

	Unmarked	Marked	(% marked)
English	24	35	(59%)
German	18	153	(89%)

The first thing to note is that the percentage of marked forms (last column) is much higher in German than in English, thus lending credibility to the idea that speakers of English employ marked word orders more reluctantly than those of German: the *markedness status*, if you will, of English LI, is higher than that of German PP fronting. This assumption is further backed up by the statistical significance of the chi-square test on the absolute numbers of Table 4 (Pearson's $\chi^2_{df=1}$ (with Yates' correction for continuity) = 24.73, $p < .001$), indicating a reliable interaction of markedness and language. Still, speakers of both languages produced more marked than unmarked structures, although this effect was not statistically reliable for the English speakers. That is, in this context the marked form is used more frequently than the unmarked one, but this preference is reliable only in German ($\chi^2_{df=1} = 106.58$, $p < .001$), not in English ($\chi^2_{df=1} = 0.70$, $p > .10$). In sum, Experiment 2 provided us with an independent assessment of the markedness status of English LI and German PP fronting vis-à-vis their unmarked counterparts, suggesting that LI is more marked in English than PP fronting is in German.

2.4 Contextual licensing of English LI and German PP fronting: The story so far

Experiment 1 provided us with evidence for strong contextual licensing in comprehension: as its German equivalent, PP fronting, English LI is amenable to strong contextual licensing. Experiment 2 showed that there are differences in markedness status between LI and its German equivalent: in production, the former seems more marked than the latter. Even if this has to be taken with caution, given the relatively sparse production data from Experiment 2, we may conclude that LI, although it is highly marked in English, can still be strongly licensed in comprehension by a context that provides an antecedent of the preverbal PP. Following Hörnig et al. (2005), we might assume that two principles drive the strong licensing effect: *relatum = given* and *given-before-new*. However, as Hörnig & Weskott (2009) have argued, the reference to the discourse status of the sentence-initial (fronted or inverted) constituent as being *given* is misleading: a closer look at the sentence-initial constituents (the PPs) in cases like (2.d), (3.d), and the italicized clauses in (4) reveals that the referent of the PP as a whole is *not* given: it denotes the place at which the locatum has to be placed, and as such, it is discourse new, because this place has not been mentioned in the previous discourse; nor has it, as Hörnig et al. (2006) have argued, been added to the mental model at the point when it is encountered. This can be made explicit if we take a closer look at the first relational sentence of (4) again. The first (presentational) sentence 'There is [a circle]$_i$...' is followed by the relational assertion '... and [$_{PP}$ to the right of it$_i$] is a triangle'. Although it is certainly correct that the PP contains the discourse-given pronoun 'it' (=the circle), and that the ordering on the level of DPs used in the second clause is given new, the PP itself is not *given*, but rather introduces a *new* referent which is, as it were, built using the relational predicate 'to the right of __'. From this observation, Hörnig et al. (2006) have concluded that the preference for marked word order in spatial relational sentences, although aptly characterized by the *relatum = given* principle in Hörnig et al. (2005), is not correctly described as an instance of *given-new* ordering. Instead, Hörnig et al. (2006) propose a different principle, along and compatible with *relatum = given*, to be responsible for the strong contextual licensing effect found in Hörnig et al. (2005): *poset licensing*. The notion of *posets* has been introduced into the literature on English marked word orders in Hirschberg (1985), Ward (1988), and *poset* licensing has been proposed by Prince (1997, 1999) and states that the preverbal constituent in a marked word order sentence has to stand in a (salient) **partially ordered-set** relation to a referent in the preceding context (also see Speyer 2004, for an application of *poset* licensing to German 'Vorfeldbesetzung'). *Posets* are defined as being asymmetric, irreflexive, and transitive (or, in the weaker version comprising identity: antisymmetric, reflexive, and transitive). Typical instances of *poset* licensing include enumerations of set members, or of mereological parts of (complex) entities. Asymmetric spatial relations like 'to the right of' constitute a further instance of *poset* relations. Hörnig et al. (2006) directly compared the *given-new* and the *poset* account of strong contextual licensing of marked word order in spatial relation assertions by adding a minimal extension of the experimental materials of Hörnig et al. (2005), which allowed them to dissociate the effect of given-new licensing from that of poset licensing. They were able to show that comprehension is affected by both licensing principles: marked word orders profited from *given-new* orderings lacking the *poset* property; but, importantly, they found an additional effect for *poset* licensing on top of mere adherence to the *given-new* principle (see Hörnig et al. 2006; Hörnig & Weskott 2009, for details). Given this experimental evidence, as well as the corpus evidence on the licensing effect of *poset* relations in English topicalization constructions (see, e.g., Ward 1988; Prince 1997), one might wonder exactly which licensing force is behind the results we reported here for Experiment 1. Regrettably, the construction that Hörnig et al. (2006) employed to dissociate the two licensing mechanisms in German spatial relational assertions has no equivalent in English: 'From the circle is the triangle right.' is not a well-formed sentence of English, whereas 'Vom Kreis aus ist das Dreieck rechts.' is grammatical in German. Therefore, in order to test whether English shows strong contextual licensing effects in *poset* contexts, as German does, we had to resort to a different type of context and a different construction.

3 Licensing topicalization in English and German

The contexts that serve as the poster child of poset licensing are enumerations of sets of the type exemplified in (5), taken from Prince (1999).

(5) a. She had an idea for a project.
    b. She's going to use three groups of mice.
    c. One, she'll feed them mouse chow, just the regular stuff they make for mice.
    d. Another, she'll feed them veggies.
    e. And the third she'll feed junk food.

The sentences in (5.c) through (5.e) exhibit marked word orders: (5.c) and (5.d) are left-dislocation constructions, while (5.e) is an instance of topicalization. We will not be concerned with left-dislocation here, but refer the interested reader to Shaer et al. (2009). What makes (5.e) a felicitous utterance in the context of the discourse in (5) seems to be the fact that the discourse referent of the fronted constituent 'the third' elliptically denotes the third of the three groups of mice introduced in (5.b). The poset relation licensing the marked word order in (5.c–e) is the subset relation; see Hörnig & Weskott (2009), for a detailed discussion of this example. The mereological counterpart of the subset, or inclusion relation is the part-of relation. Accordingly, the poset licensing carries over to an example built in analogy to (5), but featuring part-of relations between referents instead of subset relations:

(6) a. He had an idea for a training plan.
    b. He would train the different parts of the team differently.
    c. The defenders, he would make them practice headers.
    d. The midfielders, he'll have them make sprints.
    e. And the forwards he'll feed steroids.

Apparently, the felicity of the topicalization in (5.e) and (6.e) is not affected by the difference in the poset relation (subset vs. part-of)—in both cases, the fronting of the direct object, although a highly marked syntactic operation in English, does not seem to induce infelicity, or unacceptability. What this example seems to imply is that poset relations between the referents of topicalized constituents and referents in the context are able to exert a quite strong licensing effect. Experiment 3 was designed to test this under controlled conditions.

3.1 Weskott et al. (2011) on whole-part licensing of German topicalization

There have been various attempts to experimentally induce licensing of German OVS structures (i.e., topicalization of direct objects) by means of embedding these structures into different contexts—anaphoric, contrastive, corrective, and so on; see Weskott et al. (2011) for an overview. However, none of these efforts yielded a strong licensing effect proper (some of them, as e.g. Bornkessel & Schlesewsky 2006, reporting strong effects, which, however are dependent on a parallel OVS structure in the context preceding the critical OVS sentence; see also Crocker 2002, and Weskott 2003, for parallel structure effects on OVS orders). Weskott et al. (2011) report on a series of experiments employing context–target pairs of the following type:

(7) a. Peter   hat   den   Wagen   gewaschen.
        Peter$_{NOM}$ has theAcc car   washed.

    b. Er   hat   den   Außenspiegel ausgelassen.
        He$_{NOM}$ has   the$_{ACC}$ side mirror left-out.

    b'. Den   Außenspiegel hat er   ausgelassen.
        The$_{ACC}$ side mirror has he$_{NOM}$ left-out.

Weskott et al. tested OVS sentences of the type exemplified in (7.b') and their unmarked SVO counterparts in (7.b) with and without a context like the one in (7.a). Note that this context provides a referent, the car, which stands in a whole part relation to the referent of the topicalized direct object; and whole part is, as the reader can easily verify, an instance of a poset relation.

The authors report strong licensing effects for both acceptability ratings and reading times from word-wise self-paced readings. For both dependent variables, there were statistically reliable interactions between the context factor (null context vs. whole-part context) and the word order factor. Table 5 summarizes their results.

Table 5: Means for seven-point scale acceptability judgments and for raw reading times for the sentence-final participles in ms (*sds* in brackets) from Weskott et al. (2011).

	SVO	OVS
Null context	5.78 (1.44)	5.61 (1.46)
	656 (99)	647 (132)
Whole-part context	5.93 (1.59)	6.33 (1.18)
	652 (171)	599 (86)

While SVO does not show any major effect of context, OVS reacts to the presence of the whole-part licensing context quite dramatically: ratings go up to a higher level than in any of the unmarked conditions, and reading times go down. Statistically, this amounts to an interaction of the factors WORD ORDER and CONTEXT, and—unsurprisingly—to a main effect of CONTEXT, but not to a main effect of WORD ORDER.

Taking these findings for German OVS structures as a backdrop, we wanted to know whether topicalization in English is susceptible to strong contextual licensing at all; and if so, whether it is susceptible to the same extent as German topicalization.

3.2 Acceptability rating and self-paced reading experiment on English topicalization

3.2.1 Method

In order to have maximum comparability between the German and the English variant of the experiment, the materials of the adversative condition of Weskott et al. (2011)—where in the context, a predicate applies to the whole, whereas in the critical sentence, the predicate is negated for the part—were translated into English (with a few minor changes). The experiment itself was carried out in Glasgow.

3.2.1.1 Participants
Thirty-two monolingual native speakers of English were tested in the acceptability experiment (16 for each context group; 25 of them female, mean age 21.3, age range 18–32 years). For the self-paced reading, we also tested 16 monolingual native speakers of English per context group (23 of them female, mean age 21.6,

age range 17–36 years). Each participant of the rating study was paid 1£; the participants of the self-paced reading study were paid 4£.

3.2.1.2 Materials

The experimental material consisted of 16 items in two word order variants: SVO versus OSV (within subject factor); see sample given in (8a) with SVO and (8b) with OSV.

(8) a. [Frank washed his car every Sunday.] He forgot the side mirror this week.
 b. [Frank washed his car every Sunday.] The side mirror, he forgot this week.

The temporal adverbial ('this week') was included to have lexically identical material in the sentence-final region, analogous to the verbal participle in the German experiment (cf. (7)). This was mandatory for the comparison of word order conditions in the self-paced reading experiment. Experimental items were equipped with a whole-part context, which featured a whole-part relation between the object in the context sentence and the object in the target sentence (car – side-mirror, house – window, etc.). Contexts were presented to participants or not, dependent on the context condition (between subject factor).

The filler materials consisted of another experimental set of 24 items (passives with locative adverbials), on which we will not report here, and 24 benchmarking items. The benchmarking items served as fillers with four groups of six sentences: one of fully acceptable sentences, one containing a semantic error, one containing a syntactic error and another group containing both of the latter (see Weskott & Fanselow 2009, for details of these items). These items were used to set a bar for the different levels on the acceptability scale but also as a means of checking the reliability of the subjects' answers. Those participants who did not show the predicted answer pattern on the benchmarking items were excluded and replaced for the analysis.

Items were assigned to lists according to a Latin square design (two lists for the −context group, and four for the whole-part context group due to the filler passives). The 16 experimental items were intermixed with the fillers and the benchmarking items, and the order of items was pseudorandomized. Lists were doubled by inverting them to check for possible effects of order of presentation; however, none of the datasets to be reported below showed significant effects of order of presentation. The items were the same in the rating and in the self-paced reading study.

3.2.1.3 Procedure

The rating was conducted in a pen and paper study. The participants were given written instructions at the beginning of the experiment to rate the items on the seven-point scale (1 = totally unacceptable; 7 = totally acceptable) presented below each item; participants in the −context group were asked to rate the target sentences according to their grammaticality; in the + context group, the task was to rate the target sentence according to its contextual felicity given the context sentence. For further demonstration, they were given one example for each extreme of the scale where the acceptable sentence featured two canonical SVO sentences and the less acceptable sentence contained severe ungrammaticality ('A man saw a dog. Run dog the towards he'). For the context group, another demonstration item featuring a context mismatch was presented ('Who likes dogs? Jane is eating an apple'). The participants were urged not to rely on normative standards in their assessment of the sentences but on their intuition as a native speaker. Participants were tested individually in a quiet university café. It took them approximately 12 min to complete the task.

For the self-paced reading study, participants were tested individually at a computer using the program LINGER version 2.94 (http://tedlab.mit.edu/~dr/Linger/). Before the experiment, the participants were given oral and written instructions on the task at hand and some practice items to familiarize themselves with the procedure. The sentences were all left-aligned and for the whole-part context condition, the sentence pairs were presented in two lines. The items were presented phrase-wise deviating from the presentation mode in Weskott et al. (2011), who presented their items word-wise. The different method of presentation was chosen because it was not seen as a disadvantage for the English SV structure to present the subject and the verb simultaneously. At the beginning of each trial, the sentences were masked and presented by underscores on the screen. By pressing the space bar, the participants could disclose the sentences phrase-wise and at their own pace. The presentation mode was non-cumulative, meaning that the succeeding phrase would be hidden with the revealing of the next. Therefore, the participants could not go back and forth in the sentence while reading. At the end of each trial, there was a *yes/no*-comprehension question. Following Weskott et al. (2011), the questions were designed to ask for the factuality of the event in the target sentences. The participants were only given feedback if they answered a question incorrectly. The experiment lasted between 15 and 25 min.

3.2.1.4 Design and predictions

For both the rating and the self-paced reading study, the design consisted of a two-level factor WORD ORDER (unmarked SVO vs. marked OSV) tested within participants and items. The two-level factor CONTEXT (null vs. whole-part) was tested between subjects and within items. We predicted that, if English topicalization is amenable to contextual licensing, there should be a significant interaction of WORD ORDER and CONTEXT to the effect that the unmarked word order SVO should show only a small or no effect of the CONTEXT manipulation, while the marked word order OSV should show higher acceptability ratings, and shorter reading times for the sentence-final adverbial in the whole-part condition as compared to the null condition.

3.2.2 Results

Table 6 shows the results for the acceptability rating (mean ratings per condition) along with the results of the self-paced reading time experiment (mean reading times for the sentence-final adverbial). For the statistical analysis, reading times were treated as in Experiment 1, that is, they were manually screened for outliers (100 ms < RT < 3,000 ms); observations 3 standard deviations beyond a participant's mean and trials with incorrect answers to the comprehension question were excluded (36 of 512 cases). The remaining reading times were log-transformed and corrected for the length of the sentence-final adverbial by means of a linear regression with segment length as predictor. The values given in Table 6 are the cleaned raw RTs.

Table 6: Means for seven-point scale acceptability judgments and for raw reading times for the sentence-final adverbials in ms (*sds* in brackets) for Experiment 3.

	SVO	OSV
Null context	6.02 (1.7)	3.73 (2.05)
	806 (377)	809 (418)
Whole-part context	6.07 (1.49)	5.05 (1.69)
	702 (512)	723 (423)

Let us look at the acceptability ratings first. As in the data of Weskott et al. (2011), the unmarked SVO order did not show a strong effect of context, while the marked OSV order proved to be sensitive to the contextual manipulation: ratings for OSV orders improved more than one scale point if presented in a whole-part context, whereas the ratings for SVO orders remain unaffected by context. Statistically, this data pattern supported an interaction of the two factors that was significant in a model comparison (see Section 2.2.2 for the details of the statistical procedure, which we adopted for Experiment 3; the model we fitted was specified as follows: rating ~ context * wo + (1 + wo | subject) + (1 + (context * wo) | item)).

The results of the inferential statistics are summarized in Table 7.

Table 7: LMM parameters for the fixed effects worder (i.e., word order) and context and their interaction for the acceptability ratings.

	Estimate	Standard error	t-Value	$p_{LR}\chi^2$ (df = 1)
(Intercept)	6.0339	0.19885	30.344	
Worder	−1.6836	0.20183	−8.342	< .001
Context	−0.0182	0.16361	−0.111	.43
Worder:context	−0.6055	0.17582	−3.444	.001

As Table 7 reveals, the WORD ORDER factor had a significant effect on ratings, while CONTEXT had no significant effect. Importantly, the interaction was statistically reliable, as in the German data, thus supporting the hypothesis that the acceptability of marked word orders is more sensitive to the influence of context than that of unmarked word orders. However, note that there is an important difference between the Weskott et al. (2011) acceptability data and those of Experiment 3: while in the case of German, the marked OVS order was rated to be *more* acceptable than its unmarked counterpart in the whole-part context (i.e., a strong licensing effect), the English OSV order even failed to reach the acceptability level of the unmarked orders. Pairwise comparison of the SVO/whole-part and the OSV/whole-part condition showed that this difference in acceptability between the two word orders was statistically reliable ($|t|$ = 4.42, $p_{LR}\chi^2$ (df = 1) < .001). This means that the factor CONTEXT failed to even weakly license the marked OSV word order in the sense of raising the acceptability of this order to the level to that of the unmarked SVO.

Concerning the reading times for the sentence-final adverbials, the exceedingly large variance in the data set (cf. the standard deviations in Table 6) apparently destroyed any possible effect of the manipulated factors: there were no significant main effects of WORD ORDER or CONTEXT, nor an interaction of the two, all $|t|$s < 1. An attempt to detect possible effects at the two earlier positions in the sentence, for which reading times residualized on the restricted cubic spline of the sentence position, was equally doomed to failure: there simply was too much noise in the data.

3.2.3 Discussion of Experiment 3

The data from the acceptability rating seem to indicate that, contrary to its German counterpart, topicalization in English cannot be licensed by a poset relation. Although the marked OSV word order showed context sensitivity (viz. the significant interaction), the marked word order in the whole-part context condition did not reach the acceptability level of the unmarked variant. Given our hypothesis, we have to conclude that poset is not among the contexts licensing—strongly, or at least weakly—the topicalization of direct objects in English. Regrettably, the reading time data were not fit to contribute to the picture for the sheer amount of noise in this data set did not allow us to establish any reliable effect.

4 General discussion

The overall aim of this chapter was to evaluate the hypothesis that although English has a comparably rigid word order, it still exhibits sensitivity to contextual properties for certain marked word orders, that is, that it exhibits contextual licensing. The results of Experiment 3, although providing some evidence for the context sensitivity of a highly marked structure as topicalization in English in the acceptability data, remain inconclusive given the vast amount of noise in the self-paced reading data. Thus, we have to leave open the question in which sense topicalization in English is less amenable to contextual licensing than German topicalization/Vorfeldbesetzung, which shows strong licensing. We could conclude that the markedness of English topicalization (i.e., ultimately, its syntactic properties) defy licensing; or that the whole part is too weak a licensor for this construction, and that a stronger licensor (e.g., contrast) is needed to license object topicalization in English. This latter conclusion raises the question whether different types of contextual licensing can have different effects in different languages (see, e.g., Doherty 2003, for an approach that seems to imply such a difference). The answers to these questions are of course an empirical matter, and the evidence available so far precludes a definitive answer. It is quite tempting to speculate that contextual licensing of English topicalization does not affect processing, but the null result in the reading time data provide no solid basis for this, and furthermore the result in the acceptability data blocks this line of reasoning. Further evidence on the processing of marked word orders such as topicalization in English is needed to delineate the exact degree of contextual licensibility of this type of structure.

Given the results from Experiments 1 and 2, we consider it safe to conclude that English LI can indeed be strongly licensed by contexts with properties of the right kind. For spatial relational assertions in English, like probably in many other languages (see Skopeteas, Hörnig & Weskott 2009, for some typological evidence), these contextual properties are: the discourse referent of the relatum argument has to be discourse given and the locatum has to be new. Taking these contextual properties and adding Clark & Haviland's (1977) given-new preference yields the prediction that Hörnig et al. (2005) showed to be true for German, and which the data from Experiment 1 showed to hold for English LI also, where the discourse status of the prepositional argument is given, the marked word order PP-copula-S is easier to process than the unmarked word order. Whether this case of strong contextual licensing should be attributed to the joint effect of the *relatum = given* and the *given-before-new* principle, or rather be taken as an instance of poset licensing, is of minor interest here (but see Hörnig & Weskott 2009, for discussion of this issue). Again, the null effect in the processing data of Experiment 3 hinders us in drawing any conclusions in that direction. What is important about the result from the experiments on LI is that, despite the higher markedness status of English LI as compared to German PP fronting that Experiment 2 has corroborated, English LI is still susceptible to strong contextual licensing. At the current point in our research, we are not able to answer the question why it is that LI exhibits strong contextual licensibility, while topicalization apparently does not. One possible reason might be that the copula figuring in our LI materials, being a very light verb imposing relatively low restrictions on its arguments, is less of an impediment for word order variation than the lexical verbs that we tested in our experiments on English topicalization.[5] This would be in line with the observation that other types of inversion, for example, stylistic inversion, and other marked word orders in English seem to be restricted to light verbs, too.[6] Furthermore, it might well be that spatial relational assertions are susceptible to inversion because inversion does not create syntactic function

---

[5] Although this might weaken the point made above, as one of the reviewers has correctly pointed out, we think that the copula in the type of sentences employed in Experiment 1 is predicational in nature, and as such is less symmetric than the copula in identity statements. We are aware that this presupposes that spatial relational assertions may quantify over locations. However, we assume that it does not matter for the issues discussed here whether these sentences state the identity of two locations, or predicate over one location that stands in such-and-such relation to another one.

[6] What we are thinking of here are cases like 'I had expected him to be tall, and tall indeed he was.'; 'So let's party, if party we must.' We are not aware of any literature giving a systematic account of these properties. The observation was brought to the attention of the first author by Peter Culicover (p.c.).

ambiguities, at least in languages that mark the thematic roles of these constructions unambiguously by means of prepositional objects denoting the relatum role—even languages like English which in the overwhelming majority of cases indicate thematic role by means of position, a violation of the correlation of position and thematic role might be tolerable if the thematic role of the relatum can be read off of its prepositional object status.

Looking at things from a more content-oriented point of view, it may well be that it is the *locational* nature of the content of this type of sentence that makes it susceptible to these contextual features. After all, it seems quite plausible that one prominent pragmatic function of spatial relational assertions—for example, in directions—is to communicate to the addressee how to get from a location known to him (e.g., his or her current location) to a place the exact location of which is unknown to him or her; see Webelhuth (2010) for an elaboration of an argument along these lines.

On a more general note, our results show that the degree of markedness of a given structure in a language can be assessed by implanting this configuration into a certain information structural configuration (i.e., a context rendering the relatum given and the locatum new), and using a combination of comprehension and production tasks to calibrate its sensitivity to the properties of this contextual configuration. We think that this idea of using contextual licensing as a gauge for relative word order freedom should be further pursued. Needless to say, we are aware that our attempt at an independent assessment of the markedness status of these forms is but a small first step. More evidence from both corpora and experiments is needed to get a clearer and more elaborate empirical picture of the conditions under which English allows marked word orders.

References

Bader, M. & M. Meng. 1999. Subject-object ambiguities in German embedded clauses: An across-the-board comparison. Journal of Psycholinguistic Research 28(2): 121–143.
Baguley, T. & S.J. Payne. 2000. Given-New versus New-Given? An analysis of comprehension times for spatial descriptions. In: (S. O'Nualláin, ed) Spatial cognition: Foundations and applications, 317–328. Amsterdam: Benjamins.
Barr, D.J., R. Levy, C. Scheepers & H.J. Tily. 2013. Random effects structure for confirmatory hypothesis testing: Keep it maximal. Journal of Memory and Language 68(3): 255–278.
Bates, D., M. Maechler, B. Bolker & S. Walker. 2015. Fitting linear mixed-effects models using lme4. Journal of Statistical Software 67(1): 1–48.
Birner, B. J. 2009. Noncanonical word order and the distribution of inferrable information in English. In: (B. Shaer, P. Cook, W. Frey & C. Maienborn, eds) Dislocated elements

in discourse. Syntactic, semantic, and pragmatic perspectives, 232–254. New York: Routledge.
Birner, B.J. & G. Ward. 2011. Discourse effects of word order variation. In: (K. von Heusinger, C. Maienborn & P. Portner, eds) Semantics: An international handbook of natural language meaning, Vol. 2, 1934–1963. Berlin/Boston: Mouton de Gruyter.
Bornkessel, I. & M. Schlesewsky. 2006. The role of contrast in the local licensing of scrambling in German: Evidence from online comprehension. Journal of Germanic Linguistics 18: 1–43.
Bresnan, J. 1994. Locative inversion and the architecture of universal grammar. Language 70(1): 72–131.
Breul, C. 2007. Focus structure, movement to spec-Foc, and syntactic processing. In: (K. Schwabe & S. Winkler, eds) On information structure, meaning and form. Generalizations across languages, 255–274. Amsterdam/Philadelphia: Benjamins.
Chafe, W.L. 1970. Meaning and the structure of language. Chicago: University of Chicago Press.
Clark, H.H. 1972. Difficulties people have in answering the question 'Where is it?' Journal of Verbal Learning and Verbal Behavior 11(3): 265–277.
Clark, H.H. & S.E. Haviland. 1977. Comprehension and the given-new contract. In: (R.O. Freedle, ed) Discourse production and comprehension, 1–40. Hillsdale, NJ: Erlbaum.
Clifton, C. & L. Frazier. 2004. Should given information come before new? Yes and no. Memory & Cognition 32(6): 886–895.
Crocker, M. W. 2002. Adopting dispreferred interpretations: Eye-movement evidence from on-line comprehension of OVS and SVO constructions. Paper presented at: Workshop on Gradedness, Potsdam, Germany, October 2002.
Culicover, P.W. & S. Winkler. 2008. English focus inversion. Journal of Linguistics 44(3): 625–658.
Doherty, M. 2003. Topikalisierungsstrategien aus Perspektive diskursadäquater Übersetzungen. Linguistische Berichte 194: 183–212.
Ehrlich, K. & P. N. Johnson-Laird. 1982. Spatial descriptions and referential continuity. Journal of Verbal Learning and Verbal Behavior 21. 296–306.
Fanselow, G. 1988. Aufspaltung von NPn und das Problem der 'freien' Wortstellung. Linguistische Berichte 114: 91–113.
Fanselow, G. & D. Cavar. 1992. Distributed deletion. In: (A. Alexiadou, ed) Theoretical approaches to universals, 65–107. Amsterdam, Philadelphia: Benjamins.
Featherston, S. 2005. Universals and grammaticality: wh-constraints in German and English. Linguistics 43(4): 667–711.
Frey, W. 2005. Pragmatic properties of certain German and English left peripheral constructions. Linguistics 43(1): 89–129.
Gast, V. & E. König. 2nd edn. 2009. Understanding English-German contrasts. Berlin: Erich Schmidt Verlag.
Haider, H. 1993. Deutsche Syntax – generativ. Tübingen: Narr.
Haider, H. & I. Rosengren. 1998. Scrambling. Sprache und Pragmatik, 49. Lund: Germanistisches Institut.
Haider, H. & I. Rosengren. 2003. Scrambling: Nontriggered chain formation in OV languages. Journal of Germanic Linguistics 15(3): 203–267.
Harris, L. J. 1975. Spatial direction and grammatical form of instructions affect the solution of spatial problems. Memory & Cognition 3(3): 329–334.
Häussler, J., M. Grant, G. Fanselow & L. Frazier. 2015. Superiority in English and German: Cross-language differences? Syntax 18(3): 235–265.

Hirschberg, J. 1985. A theory of scalar implicature. Philadelphia, PA: University of Pennsylvania dissertation.

Hörnig, R., K. Oberauer & A. Weidenfeld. 2005. Two principles of premise integration in spatial reasoning. Memory & Cognition 33(1): 131–139.

Hörnig, R., T. Weskott, R. Kliegl & G. Fanselow. 2006. Word order variation in spatial descriptions with adverbs. Memory & Cognition 34(5): 1183–1192.

Hörnig, R. & T. Weskott. 2009. Given and new information in spatial statements. In: (C. Féry & M. Zimmermann, eds) Information structure from different perspectives, 354–374. Oxford: Oxford University Press.

Hofmeister, P. & I.A. Sag. 2010. Cognitive constraints and island effects. Language 86(2): 366–415.

Huttenlocher, J. & S. Strauss. 1968. Comprehension and a statement's relation to the situation it describes. Journal of Verbal Learning and Verbal Behavior 7(2): 300–304.

Keenan, E. 1978. Language variation and the logical structure of universal grammar. In: (H. Seiler, ed) Language universals. Papers from the conference held at Gummersbach/Cologne,Germany, October 3–8, 1976, 89–123. Tübingen: Narr.

Miller, G.A. & P.N. Johnson-Laird. 1976. Language and perception. Cambridge, MA: Harvard University Press.

Prince, E.F. 1997. On the functions of left-dislocation in English discourse. In: (A. Kamio, ed) Directions in functional linguistics, 117–143. Amsterdam: Benjamins.

Prince, E.F. 1999. How not to mark topics. Topicalization in English and Yiddish. Texas Linguistic Forum. Austin: University of Texas. http://citeseerx.ist.psu.edu/viewdoc/summary?doi=10.1.1.18.927

R Core Team. 2014. R: A language and environment for statistical computing. R Foundation for Statistical Computing, Vienna, Austria. http://www.R-project.org/.

Shaer, B., P. Cook, W. Frey & C. Maienborn. 2009. Introduction. In: (B. Shaer, P. Cook, W. Frey & C. Maienborn, eds) Dislocated elements in discourse: Syntactic, semantic, and pragmatic perspectives, 1–27. New York, NY: Routledge.

Skopeteas, S., R. Hörnig & T. Weskott. 2008. Contextual versus inherent properties of entities in space. Linguistische Berichte 216: 431–454.

Speyer, A. 2004. Competing constraints on Vorfeldbesetzung in German. In: (B. Shaer, W. Frey, & C. Maienborn, eds) Proceedings of the Dislocated Elements Workshop. ZAS Papers in Linguistics 35(2). 519–541.

Sprouse, J., M. Wagers & C. Phillips. 2012. A test of the relation between working memory capacity and syntactic island effects. Language 88(1): 82–123.

Stolterfoht, B. 2004. Processing word order variations and ellipses: The interplay of syntax and information structure during sentence comprehension. Leipzig: Max Planck Institute for Human Cognitive and Brain Sciences.

Stowell, T. 1981. Origins of phrase structure. Cambridge, MA: MIT dissertation.

Vandeloise, C. 1986. L'espace en français: Sémantique des prépositions spatiales. Paris: Seuil.

Ward, G. 1988. The semantics and pragmatics of preposing. New York: Garland.

Webelhuth, G. 1988. A universal theory of scrambling. In: (V. Rosen, ed) Papers from the Tenth Scandinavian Conference of Linguistics, 284–298. Department of Linguistics and Phonetics, University of Bergen.

Webelhuth, G. 1990. Diagnostics for structure. In: (G. Grewendorf & W. Sternefeld, eds) Scrambling and barriers, 41–75. Amsterdam: Benjamins.

Webelhuth, G. 2010. Motivating non-canonicality in Construction Grammar: The case of locative inversion. Cognitive Linguistics 22(1): 81–105.

Weskott, T. 2003. Information structure as a processing guide: The left periphery of German verb-second sentences and its interpretation in context. Leipzig: University of Leipzig dissertation.

Weskott, T. & G. Fanselow. 2009. Scaling issues in the measurement of linguistic acceptability. In: (S. Featherston & S. Winkler, eds) The fruits of empirical linguistics, Vol. 1: Process, 231–245. Berlin: Mouton de Gruyter.

Weskott, T., R. Hörnig, G. Fanselow & R. Kliegl. 2011. Contextual licensing of marked OVS word order in German. Linguistische Berichte 225: 3–18.

Markus Bader and Jana Häussler
How to get from graded intuitions to binary decisions

1 Introduction

When producing language, most of us will feel obliged – at least to a large extent – to adhere to the rules of grammar. We typically do this unconsciously, but sometimes, especially in the case of written language, we may engage in a process of deliberate reasoning about whether we are entitled to produce a particular string of words. Although many gradient constraints may enter our decision process, ultimately we are facing a binary decision: shall we produce the word string under consideration, or shall we produce a different string instead?

Framing the task of language production in this way reveals an important commonality between language production and traditional grammaticality judgments – both require a binary decision at some point. Linguistic intuitions in the sense of "the internal evaluative state[s] toward a linguistic example" (Luka 2005: 480), in contrast, are gradient. As a growing body of experimental studies shows, speakers are able to assign fine grades of well-formedness to sentences (see overviews in Fanselow et al. 2006, and Schütze & Sprouse 2014).

How to refer to these fine grades of well-formedness is a controversial issue. Often, the terms "grammaticality" and "acceptability" are used interchangeably (e.g., Schütze 1996; Luka 2005). Another line of research follows the classical distinction between competence and performance and reserves the term acceptability for the perceived well-formedness of sentences (see Bard et al. 1996, for a succinct statement of this position). According to this approach, acceptability has to be sharply distinguished from grammaticality, which refers to a property assigned to sentences by the competence grammar. Grammaticality in this sense is not available for direct observation, but acceptability is neither, because both concepts refer to mental states. There is clearly a relationship between acceptability and grammaticality – the latter contributes to the former – but this does not mean that grammaticality necessarily shares the scaling properties of acceptability. While it is uncontroversial that acceptability is a gradient phenomenon, it depends on the particular syntactic framework whether grammaticality is binary or gradient. In the following, we will make the following terminological distinctions. With regard to the observable judgments given in experimental investigations, we will use the term "acceptability judgment" when participants have to rate sentences on a numerical scale (e.g., magnitude estimation, ratings on a Likert scale from 1 to 7) and "grammaticality judgment" when participants are told to judge sentences as either grammatical or ungrammatical. With regard to the mental states that are the ultimate causes of these judgments, we will use the terms "acceptability" for the evaluative intuition someone has concerning a particular sentence and "grammaticality" for the grammar's contribution to this intuition. We are thus basically following the terminology established in Bard et al. (1996).

The question addressed in this chapter is how gradient linguistic intuitions are related to binary decisions, either as part of the processes leading to binary grammaticality judgments or as part of the processes that lead to the selection of a particular syntactic structure during language production. Ultimately, answering this question presupposes a full-fledged model of linguistic behavior – a model that accounts for both production and comprehension as well as for metalinguistic behavior, including linguistic judgments of all sorts. A complete model would need to specify the relationship between grammar and processing, both with respect to language production and with respect to language comprehension. The model would also have to explain how linguistic intuitions emerge, how they are affected by linguistic and nonlinguistic factors (for an overview of relevant factors, see Schütze 1996), and how they enter metalinguistic behavior, which includes both gradient and binary judgments.

The chapter takes a modest step toward such a model by focusing on how gradient intuitions are mapped onto binary decisions – either in the form of binary judgments of grammaticality or in the form of binary decisions as part of the processes involved in language production – that is, decisions about whether to use or not to use a given structure for mapping a given meaning to a string of words. Decisions of this kind are ultimately responsible for how often a structure occurs in language use. The chapter therefore also contributes to the ongoing debate about the relationship between grade of grammaticality and frequency of usage. Our main point in this regard will be that grammaticality is among the factors determining frequency, and not the other way around.

The organization of this chapter is as follows. In Section 2, we discuss two current models of grammaticality judgments – the *Decathlon model* by Featherston (2005a) and the *Direct Mapping model* by Bader and Häussler (2010) – and propose the *Grammar First (GF) model*, which is a synthesis of these two models. In the remainder of the chapter, we discuss experimental and corpus evidence in favor of the GF model. The subject domain of the experiments is argument alternations involving ditransitive verbs in German. Based on prior experimental evidence that was obtained using either the method of magnitude estimation or binary grammaticality judgments, Section 3 discusses the relationship between gradient judgments, binary judgments, and frequency counts obtained in a corpus study. In order to test whether the choice between alternative structures during language production is governed by frequency, grammaticality, or both, Section 4 presents a new production experiment in which participants had to choose between two alternative argument realizations in one of two contexts. The chapter ends with a conclusion in Section 5.

2 Modeling linguistic intuitions

In his comprehensive review of grammaticality judgments, Schütze (1996: 171) states that "[a]lmost no work has been done by way of modeling the psychological representations and processes involved in making grammaticality judgments, despite the proliferation of models of other language behaviors, most notably sentence processing." The almost 20 years since the publication of Schütze (1996) have seen a steadily growing number of studies that have tried to put linguistic judgments onto a sound methodological basis (for a recent overview, see Schütze & Sprouse 2014). Despite this concern with linguistic judgments, attempts at modeling the mental processes responsible for judging the grammaticality of sentences are still rare.[1]

A first question to be answered by any model of linguistic intuitions concerns the source of gradience in acceptability and grammaticality judgments (for an overview of this issue, see Fanselow et al. 2006). The most direct answer to this question is provided by the framework of grammars with weighted constraints (cf. Pater 2009, for an overview). Such a grammar assigns a continuous harmony value to each sentence, which reflects the summed constraint violations of the sentence. Alternatively, the grammar might be of a more conventional form, as in the Minimalist Program, assigning only a small number of discrete grammaticality distinctions. In this case, gradient intuitions could result from gradient constraints being tied to conditions at the interfaces, or from the performance mechanisms that apply the grammar during language processing. These two sources of gradience do not exclude each other, of course. Furthermore, even if the grammar itself assigns continuous scores to sentences, as grammars with weighted constraints do, these scores are still subject to modification due to performance mechanisms (for concrete examples, see Kitagawa & Fodor 2006, and Fanselow & Frisch 2006).

---

[1] There have been a few important attempts at modeling linguistic judgments that we cannot discuss for reasons of space. These include Carroll et al. (1981), Bever & Carroll (1981), Gerken & Bever (1986), Luka (2005), and Sprouse (2007).

For our purposes it is sufficient to assume that each sentence is assigned a continuous evaluation score, which is a joint function of the mental representation of the grammar and the mental mechanisms responsible for language processing. Given this assumption, we are faced with the question of how gradient and binary judgments of well-formedness and choices during language production are related to continuous acceptability scores.

The *Decathlon model* of Featherston (2005a,b) provides an answer to these questions by specifying how grammaticality/acceptability judgments and language production are related to the competence grammar, which is conceived of as a set of weighted constraints. Figure 1 shows the major components of the Decathlon model. Each box in the figure represents a module. The first box can be roughly equated with the grammar though it also includes other factors affecting the well-formedness of a given string. This module applies syntactic constraints and assigns violation costs. The output is a continuous grammaticality score for each sentence. This score is mapped directly onto an overt rating when a gradient judgment is required. Scores assigned to alternative syntactic realizations of the sentence under consideration do not enter this process. Language production uses the same grammaticality scores but involves an additional competition between alternative ways of realizing a given input specification. Output selection happens in the second module (right box in Figure 1). Whether a particular syntactic structure is selected for production therefore depends not only on its degree of grammaticalness but also on the grammaticalness of its competitors.

By assuming that competition among syntactic structures is a feature of language production but not of sentence evaluation, the Decathlon model gives an elegant account of the finding that for a set of alternative syntactic structures corpus data are usually much more heavily skewed than gradient acceptability judgments. Thus, even when a structure S1 is judged as more acceptable than a competing structure S2 by only a moderate amount, the frequency of S1 is usually considerably greater than the frequency of S2. This follows when language production involves an additional competition process in which even a small lead in terms of grammaticality suffices to win the competition most of the time.

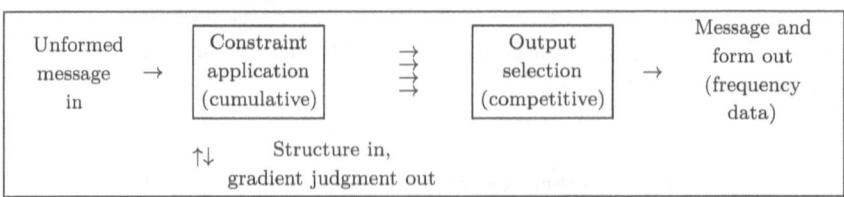

Figure 1: The Decathlon model (adapted from Featherston 2005a).

Judgments as included in Figure 1 of the Decathlon model are gradient judgments, obtained by methods like Magnitude Estimation. Binary judgments of grammaticality are not directly related to the grammaticality scores assigned by the grammar and are therefore not included in this figure. Instead, binary grammaticality judgments are assumed to be directly linked to processes of language production and only indirectly to gradient acceptability scores. The Decathlon model claims that binary grammaticality judgments are implicit judgments of whether the speaker has encountered the syntactic structure before or would use the structure in actual language production.

An involvement of processes of language production in rating sentence acceptability has also been considered by other researchers (e.g., Kempen & Harbusch 2008). However, as pointed out by Luka (2005: 488), the assumption of a strong link between linguistic judgments and language production is problematic because of discrepancies between the two. Speakers may rate a sentence as unacceptable and still use it in informal speech (Labov 1977; Schmidt & McCreary 1977). Part but not all of these inconsistencies may be attributed to the somewhat artificial situation of giving explicit judgments.[2] In a judgment situation, speakers might tend to use a more formal register and be more prone to prescriptive norms. Aphasia represents the reverse situation. Some aphasic patients are unable to produce or comprehend a sentence but still can give accurate acceptability judgments (Linebarger et al. 1983). Further evidence against a tight connection between binary judgments and usage frequencies comes from empirical data attesting consistent mismatches between corpus counts and judgment data (e.g., Arppe & Järvikivi 2007). This line of research shows that acceptable does not entail frequent nor does infrequent entail unacceptable.

The Decathlon model's claim that binary judgments derive from processes of language production and not from acceptability scores assigned by the grammar seems to stem from the assumption that gradient judgments provide a direct window onto graded acceptability, whereas binary judgments do not. Research following the publication of the Decathlon model has falsified this assumption. As a number of experimental studies show, binary judgments and gradient judgments correlate highly (Bader & Häussler 2010; Weskott & Fanselow 2011; Fukuda et al. 2012). Based on this observation, Bader & Häussler (2010) proposed the Direct Mapping model summarized in Figure 2. The first box is comparable to the Constraint Application module in the Decathlon model. Based on grammatical constraints, the parser

---

[2] Although note that judging the correctness of a sentence is not such an uncommon task. For instance, many people have some experience with proofreading texts. In addition, as pointed out to us by a reviewer, an even more common context for judging the well-formedness of sentences occurs in situations of first- and second-language learning.

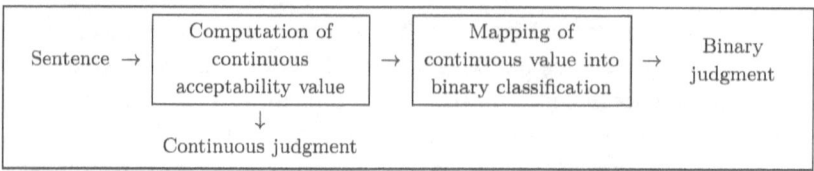

Figure 2: The Direct Mapping model (adapted from Bader & Häussler 2010).

computes a continuous acceptability value, which is then mapped to a continuous judgment. The Direct Mapping model is silent about language production, but it proposes a mapping mechanism for deriving binary judgments (right box in the figure).

The Direct Mapping model shares the Decathlon model's assumption that graded grammaticality is primary compared to binary judgments and independent from usage frequencies. The Direct Mapping model diverges from the Decathlon model by assuming that binary judgments of grammaticality are directly derived from graded acceptability scores, without a detour involving language production. More precisely, the Direct Mapping model claims that graded acceptability scores above a certain threshold are mapped onto the response 'grammatical' and acceptability scores below the threshold onto the response 'ungrammatical'. In this way, the Direct Mapping model captures the close correlation that has been observed for gradient and binary judgments of well-formedness.

The strength of the Decathlon model lies in its account of acceptability – frequency mismatches. The strength of the Direct Mapping model lies in its account of the relationship between gradient and binary judgments. To get the best of both models, we propose a new model that we call the *GF model*. This model is depicted in Figure 3. The first (upper left) box in this figure represents the grammar and the processor. As discussed earlier, we assume that grammar and processor jointly assign a continuous acceptability score to each sentence. These scores feed both into language production (horizontal path) and into judgment processes (vertical path). With regard to the former, we adopt the Decathlon model's assumption that language production involves a competitive element (output selection). With regard to judgment processes, we adopt the Direct Mapping model's assumption that acceptability scores are directly mapped onto linguistic judgments. This mapping happens in the two lower boxes shown in Figure 3.

How this mapping proceeds will depend on the particular task. One kind of mapping is needed to map internal acceptability scores to overt ratings on a numerical scale of sufficient granularity, that is, judgments using the magnitude estimation procedure or one of its variants (e.g., the thermometer method of Featherston 2009), but also – in an approximate way – judgments on a Likert

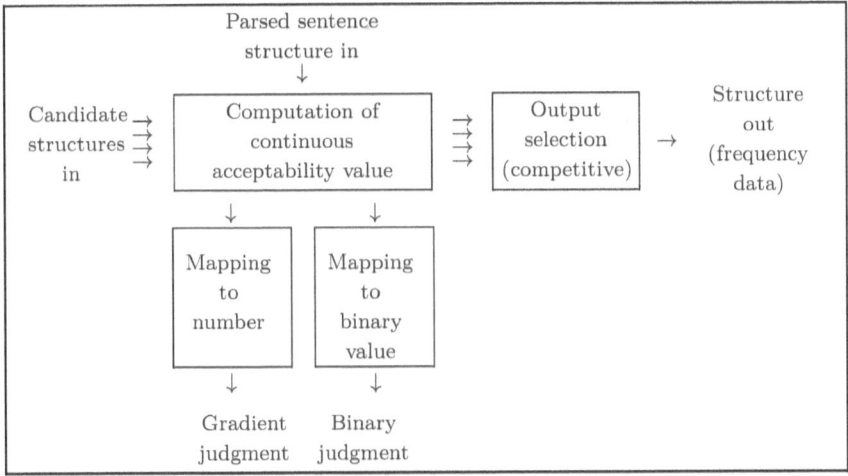

Figure 3: The Grammar First model.

scale with a sufficient number of distinct values. Neither the Decathlon model nor the Direct Mapping model has specified how this mapping proceeds. It seems clear that it involves more than simply attaching an overt number to an internal continuous state, but at this point we can do no more than refer the reader to the ongoing research investigating this mapping (e.g., Sprouse 2011; Hofmeister et al. 2014; Ellsiepen & Bader 2014).

A second kind of mapping is needed for giving binary judgments. As discussed above, the *Direct Mapping model* by Bader & Häussler (2010) implements this mapping by means of a threshold mechanism. Participants are assumed to adopt an internal threshold and to map acceptability scores above the threshold to the judgment "grammatical" and scores below the threshold to the judgment "ungrammatical".

In the GF model, the continuous acceptability scores assigned by the grammar and the processor are directly linked to gradient judgments of acceptability, binary judgments of grammaticality, and choices during language production. This claim makes two predictions. The first prediction concerns the relationship between gradient and binary judgments. Because both types of judgments involve a mapping from continuous acceptability scores onto overt responses, they should correlate highly with each other. The second prediction concerns the relationship between (gradient or binary) judgments and production frequencies. Correlations should only be found when considering sentences that are not fully acceptable. Otherwise, measures of acceptability and measures of frequency should not correlate with each other.

In the next section, we review data in support of the GF model. The data come from investigations of ditransitive verbs in German and draw on different types of evidence – graded acceptability ratings obtained with the magnitude estimation method, experimentally controlled binary grammaticality judgments, and corpus counts. Afterward, we present a new experiment that takes a closer look at the role of grammaticality and frequency for the purpose of language production.

3 Acceptability and frequency

The syntax of ditransitive verbs in German provides the subject area of the following explorations. A prototypical ditransitive verb has an agent argument which is mapped onto the syntactic function of subject, a recipient that is mapped onto the dative object, and a theme that is mapped onto the accusative object. An illustrating example is provided in (1).

(1) ... dass der Direktor dem Lehrer eine Medaille überreichte.
      that the principal the teacher a medal handed
   '... that the principal handed a medal to the teacher.'

Ditransitive verbs participate in several alternations that make them particularly suited for investigating the relationship between graded and binary grammaticality. The present study makes use of the alternation between active sentences and two types of passive sentences. First, ditransitive verbs can be put into the regular passive, which is formed with the auxiliary *werden* and the past participle of the lexical verb. The accusative object is promoted to subject, as illustrated in (2).

(2) ... dass dem Lehrer vom Direktor eine Medaille
      that the teacher by-the principal a medal
      überreicht wurde.
      handed was
   '... that a medal was handed to the teacher by the principal.'

A second type of passive is the so-called *bekommen* passive illustrated in (3).

(3) ... dass der Lehrer vom Direktor eine Medaille
      that the teacher by-the principal a medal
      überreicht bekam.
      handed got
   '... that the teacher was handed a medal by the principal.'

The *bekommen* passive differs from the regular passive with respect to the auxiliary (*bekommen* 'get' instead of *werden*) and with respect to the argument that is promoted to subject (dative versus accusative object). Though ditransitive verbs are the prototypical verb class for the *bekommen* passive, *bekommen* passive formation is not equally acceptable for all subclasses of ditransitive verbs (Leirbukt 1997; Bader & Häussler 2013). Previous work has shown that *bekommen* passive formation is not a categorical property but a gradient one (Lenz 2009; Bader 2012; Bader & Häussler 2013). For example, the status of certain verbs of negative transfer is rather doubtful. Sentences with verbs like *stehlen* or *klauen* (both meaning 'to steal') are judged as fully grammatical by some authors (e.g., Pittner & Berman 2013: 75), whereas others consider such sentences as deviant. Sentences of this type are produced from time to time, as in the following example from one of Germany's nationwide newspapers.

(4) Polizei: Zugreisendem 18.000 Euro gestohlen
Ein Mann macht sich mit 18.000 Euro per Zug auf den Weg zu seinem neuen Auto. Unterwegs bekommt er das Geld gestohlen.
'Police: 18,000 Euro stolen from a train traveler
A man traveling by the train carried 18,000 Euro with him on his way to buy a new car. Underway, he was stolen the money.'
(Frankfurter Rundschau, 2016/07/28,
www.fr-online.de/kriminalitaet/polizei-zugreisendem-18-000-euro-gestohlen,25733026,34559262.html)

When the applicability of the *bekommen* passive was investigated in a controlled way by means of judgment experiments and corpus analyses (Bader 2012; Bader & Häussler 2013), examples with verbs of negative transfer received mean acceptance rates of about 50%, indicating that these verbs are neither fully acceptable nor fully unacceptable in the *bekommen* passive. This conclusion was strengthened by corpus data showing that corpus examples with such verbs in the *bekommen* passive do occur, but with a frequency that is much lower than expected given the overall frequency of the verbs' lemmas.

In order to put this issue on a broader empirical basis, we examined 120 ditransitive verbs representing a wide variety of semantic classes (Häussler & Bader in preparation). For each verb, we constructed two sentences resulting in a total of 240 sentences. Each sentence occurred in the three constructions introduced above: in the *active voice* (1), in the *regular passive* (2), and in the *bekommen passive* (3).[3]

---

[3] The experiments included a second factor (number of arguments), which we do not discuss here for reasons of space.

One experiment used a standard magnitude estimation task (Bard et al. 1996; Cowart 1997). Three further experiments obtained binary grammaticality judgments. These experiments differed with regard to tense (past tense or present perfect) and with regard to whether judgments had to be given under time pressure or not. In order to have more stable estimates, we present the combined results from the binary judgment experiments. Magnitude estimation and binary judgments yielded comparable results, and in particular they both attest gradient effects with respect to voice alternations. While sentences in the active voice and the regular passive are highly acceptable for all verbs in the sample (88% and 90% acceptance rates in the binary judgment task, mean z-scores[4] of 0.37 and 0.27 in the magnitude estimation task), the *bekommen* passive exhibits a large amount of variation. Verb-specific acceptance rates span almost the complete range from consistent rejection to unanimous acceptance (ME ratings in terms of z-scores: mean of 0.07, range from −1.35 to 1.37; acceptance rates in the binary judgment task: mean of 77%, range from 11% to 94%). Apparently, *bekommen* passive formation is subject to constraints that do not apply to the regular passive.[5] For reasons of space, we cannot discuss these constraints here (but see Leirbukt 1997; Bader & Häussler 2013), and focus instead on the predictions made by the GF model.

The first prediction concerns the source of binary grammaticality judgments. As discussed in Section 2, the GF model integrates the Direct Mapping model's hypothesis that during sentence comprehension each sentence is assigned a graded acceptability score, which is mapped to a continuous judgment when the experimental task requires magnitude estimation from participants and to a binary judgment when the task requires binary grammaticality judgments. This predicts that the two kinds of judgments should correlate closely.

The second prediction concerns the relationship between (binary and gradient) judgments and usage frequencies. The GF model predicts correlations only for sentences that are not fully acceptable, because acceptability affects the competition between alternative structures only when structures vary with regard to acceptability. The less acceptable a sentence is, the less likely it is to be produced.

---

[4] z-Transformation normalizes the individual ratings of each participant by mapping it onto a scale with standard deviation as the basic unit. The standardized scale has a mean of zero and a standard deviation of 1. This is achieved by subtracting each individual score from the participant's mean score and dividing this difference by the participant's standard deviation.

[5] To give an example, verb semantics play a role. Verbs of negative transfer, that is, transfer away from the dative referent, are accepted in the *bekommen* passive only when the transfer is abstract as in *jemandem den Führerschein entziehen* ('to deprive somebody of his driving licence') but not when the transfer is concrete as in *jemandem den Wagen stehlen* ('to steal the car from somebody').

For candidate structures that are fully acceptable, acceptability has no influence on the competition. Such structures can accordingly be produced with frequencies of all sorts, depending on the linguistic and nonlinguistic context.

To evaluate these two predictions, we look at the 120 verb-specific mean values for the three sentence types examined in the experiments introduced above. Corpus counts were obtained from the *deWaC* corpus, which is a huge corpus of German and part of *Wacky*, a family of corpora built by web crawling (Baroni et al. 2009). From the raw frequencies, we computed for each verb the ratio with which the verb occurs in each of the three constructions. To this end, we divided the number of occurrences in the active voice by the total number of occurrences of the particular verb participle; likewise for the occurrences in the regular passive and in the *bekommen* passive. In addition, we computed log ratios by taking the natural logarithm of the computed ratio.

Figure 4 plots the three types of relations that are necessary to evaluate the predictions made above: (i) acceptance rates obtained by the binary judgment task against gradient acceptability ratings obtained by the magnitude estimation task (upper part); (ii) acceptance rates obtained by the binary judgment task against logarithmic frequency ratios (middle part); (iii) gradient acceptability ratings obtained by the magnitude estimation task against logarithmic frequency ratios (lower part). A first feature of the plots is that we find low acceptability ratings and low frequency counts only for the *bekommen* passive (note the difference in the scale across the three constructions).

The corresponding rank correlations (Kendall's tau) are given in Table 1.[6] This table also includes the rank correlations for all 360 data points resulting from putting 120 verbs into three voices. As shown, the correlation between binary and gradient judgments is higher than the correlations between either judgment type and frequency ratios. By itself, this is not surprising because the judgment data were obtained from the same materials. The question then is whether the higher correlation for the judgment data is just due to less variance or whether there are systematic reasons for this difference. That the latter is the case is revealed by a closer inspection of the correlations for each construction.

For the relationship between the two judgment types, we see significant correlations for all three constructions, with the strongest correlation for the *bekommen* passive. With regard to frequency, in contrast, we see significant correlations only for the *bekommen* passive, with one exception. There is a significant correlation

---

[6] A rank correlation quantifies how well two lists ordered according to some criterion agree with regard to their ranking. Like the better known Pearson correlation coefficient *r*, Kendall's tau ranges from –1 to 1. Pearson's *r* is not appropriate in our case because it presupposes that the values to be compared are normally distributed.

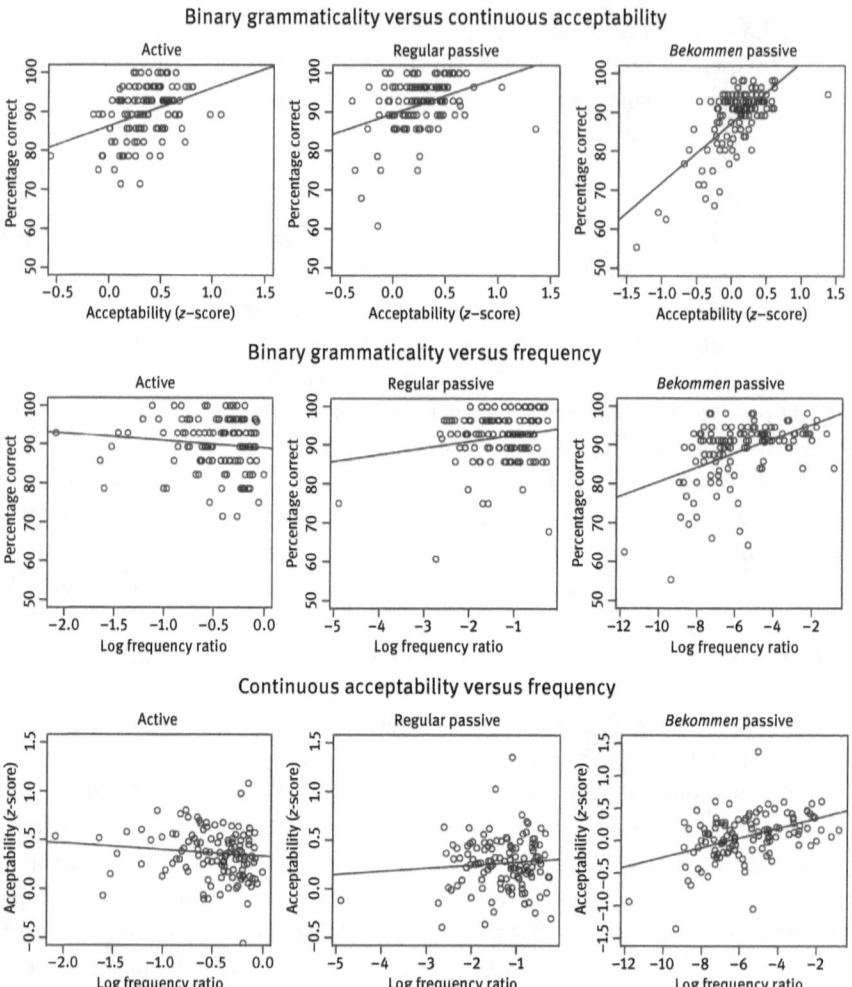

Figure 4: Upper part: Mean acceptance rates obtained by the binary judgment task plotted against mean ratings obtained by the magnitude estimation task. Middle part: Mean acceptance rates obtained by the binary judgment task plotted against corpus counts. Lower part: Mean ratings obtained by the magnitude estimation task plotted against corpus counts. In each plot, each data point represents one of the 120 verbs.

between the magnitude estimation data and the frequency ratios for the active forms. Since this correlation is rather small and in the wrong direction (acceptability seems to decrease with increasing frequency), we assume that it is a spurious effect, probably due to the higher mass in the upper frequency band and the few but acceptable verbs with comparatively low frequency in the active voice.

Table 1: Rank correlations (Kendall's tau) between binary grammaticality judgments, gradient acceptability judgments (magnitude estimation scores), and frequency ratios. Asterisks mark significance (* = $p < 0.05$, ** = $p < 0.01$).

	All	Active	Regular passive	*Bekommen* passive
Binary judgments – magnitude estimation	0.36**	0.29**	0.26**	0.39**
Binary judgments – frequency ratios	0.30**	−0.09	0.05	0.33**
Magnitude estimation – frequency ratios	0.24**	−0.12*	0.00	0.27**

Looking back to the plots in Figure 4, we can identify two configurations that are responsible for the lack of correlations between judgments and frequency: sentences with low frequency that reach nevertheless high acceptance rates and sentences with high acceptance rates that are nevertheless rare in the corpus. This observation adds to previous studies comparing experimentally elicited grammaticality/acceptability judgments with corpus-derived structural frequencies (e.g., Featherston 2005a; Kempen & Harbusch 2008; Arppe & Järvikivi 2007; Bader & Häussler 2010). All these studies revealed consistent mismatches between frequency counts and judgments: First, while degraded acceptability implies low frequency, full acceptability does not imply high frequency. Second, while high frequency implies high acceptability, low frequency does not imply degraded acceptability.

4 Experiment

The correlations presented in the preceding section provide initial evidence for the hypothesis that graded acceptability is a crucial factor for language production. We found consistent acceptability-frequency correlations only for the structure that is less acceptable for certain verbs. The other two structures (active and regular passive) were consistently judged to be highly acceptable, but nevertheless showed a large amount of variation with regard to frequency. As a consequence, frequency and acceptability did not correlate for them. In order to corroborate this finding, we ran an experiment that explicitly manipulated the factors that govern the selection of the syntactic form of an intended utterance. The experimental procedure of this experiment is the forced-choice selection paradigm that has been used repeatedly in research investigating the relationship between corpus frequencies and language production (Rosenbach 2005; Bresnan 2007; Bresnan & Ford 2010; Arppe & Järvikivi 2007).

In these studies, participants read a context from an original corpus passage and then have to choose between two alternative continuations. The selection task comes quite close to a production task. Instead of choosing whether to produce or not to produce a given string, participants choose this or that variant of a sentence. The version of the task Bresnan and colleagues used (Bresnan 2007; Bresnan & Ford 2010) also included a rating task. Participants had to distribute 100 points between the two alternatives. Since the ratings had to add to 100, they provide an estimate of relative production probabilities and not an estimate of acceptability because the task precludes a priori that two alternative structures both reach a rating value above 50 points. In fact, an explicit prediction task, in which participants had to guess which of two sentences occurred in the corpus, yielded similar results (Bresnan 2007). Participants quite reliably opted for the continuation that occurred in the actual example.

In the current experiment, we provided participants with a context question and had them choose between two possible answers expressing the same propositional content but differing in form. Under the assumption that grammaticality determines choices during production, participants should not select structures that are perceived as degraded. If frequency is the main determinant instead, participants should avoid infrequent structures even if they are fully grammatical. Since *bekommen* passive sentences are relatively rare, they provide a good test case for evaluating the two hypotheses.

In order to keep the experimental design manageable, we investigated only the choice between active voice and *bekommen* passive. The context question established either the agent or the recipient as topic. It was followed by two alternative answers, one in the active voice and the other one in the *bekommen* passive. Participants had to select the answer that they thought to fit the context question best. A complete example illustrating the experimental design is provided in (5) and (6).

(5) *Topic = Agent*
Was gibt es Neues von **Claudia**? ('What about Claudia?')
  a. *Active (Topic = subject)*
  Claudia hat unserem Enkel ein Märchen erzählt.
  C. has our grandson a fairy tale told
  'Claudia told a fairy tale to our grandson.'

  b. *Bekommen passive (Topic = by-phrase)*
  Von **Claudia** hat unser Enkel ein Märchen erzählt
  by C. has our grandson a fairy tale told
  bekommen.
  got
  'By Claudia, our grandson was told a fairy tale.'

(6) *Topic = Recipient*
Was gibt es Neues von **eurem Enkel**? ('What about your grandson?')
a. *Active (Topic = dative object)*
Unserem Enkel hat Claudia ein Märchen erzählt.
our grandson has C. a fairy tale told
'To our grandson, Claudia told a fairy tale.'

b. *Bekommen passive (Topic = subject)*
Unser Enkel hat von Claudia ein Märchen erzählt
our grandson has by C. a fairy tale told
bekommen.
got
'Our grandson was told a fairy tale by Claudia.'

In all four sentences used as answers in (5) and (6), the topic phrase is in a preferred position for a topic, namely the clause-initial position. The choice between the active voice answer and the *bekommen* passive answer thus boils down to a question of subject choice: is the agent realized as subject, as in the active voice, or is the recipient realized as subject, as in the *bekommen* passive? The literature concerned with argument realization has identified various prominence hierarchies that contribute to subject choice (see the overview in Aissen 1999). The three prominence hierarchies relevant in the current context are shown in (7).[7]

(7) a. Syntactic Function Hierarchy: Subject > Object
b. Semantic Role Hierarchy: Agent > Recipient
c. Discourse Hierarchy: Topic > ¬Topic

Table 2 shows how the four conditions of the experiment fare with regard to the constraints relevant for subject choice in the sentences under consideration. Since the subject itself is the most prominent element in the syntactic function hierarchy in (7-a), the most preferred configuration is one in which the subject is both an agent and a topic. As shown in the first row in Table 2, this holds when the context question establishes the agent as topic and the answer is formulated in the active voice. With the same question and thus the agent established as topic, the *bekommen* passive is a rather poor choice, as shown in the second row in Table 2. In this case, neither the agent nor the topic is realized as subject.

---

[7] The interplay of various prominence hierarchies can be formalized within OT by the method of harmonic alignment (Prince & Smolensky 1993/2004). See Aissen (1999) for a general outline and Bader (2012) for an application to subject choice in German.

Table 2: Constraint satisfaction profiles for the sentences investigated in the experiment.

			Subject =Agent	Subject =Topic	Compatibility with Bekommen Passive
(5-a)	Topic = Agent	Active	✓	✓	
(5-b)	Topic = Agent	Bekommen passive	*	*	(*)
(6-a)	Topic = Recipient	Active	✓	*	
(6-b)	Topic = Recipient	Bekommen passive	*	✓	(*)

In sum, when the preceding question establishes the agent as topic, a strong preference for active sentences is predicted.

A different pattern emerges when the recipient is established as topic. In this case, both candidates exhibit a conflict. With the recipient established as topic, the answer can adhere either to the semantic role hierarchy, as in the active voice (subject = agent), or to the discourse hierarchy, as in the *bekommen* passive (subject = topic), but not to both. The choice between active voice and *bekommen* passive thus depends on which of the two conflicting hierarchies is given more weight – the semantic role hierarchy or the discourse hierarchy. Establishing the relative weight given to the two hierarchies is the first aim of the current experiment.

The second aim of the experiment concerns the role played by the grammaticality of sentences in the *bekommen* passive. The judgment experiments discussed in the preceding sections have shown that the acceptability of individual verbs in the *bekommen* passive is not an all-or-nothing matter. While a large number of ditransitive verbs are fully acceptable in the *bekommen* passive, some verbs lead to reduced acceptability when used in the *bekommen* passive. As discussed earlier, there seems to be no single property that distinguishes verbs that can be used in the *bekommen* passive from verbs that cannot (see Leirbukt 1997 for extensive discussion). In Table 2, the constraint "Compatibility with *Bekommen* Passive" is used as shorthand for the various factors that contribute to the acceptability of a

Table 3: Judgment scores and frequencies for each of the three verb groups (Note that the labels ± gram and ± freq refer to the status of the verbs in the *bekommen* passive). ME, magnitude estimation; BGJ, binary grammaticality judgments.

	Active				Bekommen Passive			
	ME	BGJ	Ratio	Log ratio	ME	BGJ	Ratio	Log ratio
−gram, −freq	0.37	90	0.79	−0.25	−0.54	40	0.0007	−8.44
+ gram, −freq	0.49	94	0.72	−0.34	0.28	87	0.005	−5.90
+ gram, + freq	0.48	92	0.49	−0.83	0.32	92	0.09	−2.57

verb in the *bekommen* passive. Active sentences fulfill this constraint vacuously. *Bekommen* passive sentences can fulfill this constraint to various degrees, as indicated by putting a star in parentheses in the rows for the *bekommen* passive.

When the agent is established as topic, the constraint "Compatibility with *Bekommen* Passive" should not have any effect because sentences that may violate this constraint are already very low ranked because of violating the other two constraints. When the recipient is established as topic, in contrast, the constraint "Compatibility with *Bekommen* Passive" has a chance to influence the choice between active and *bekommen* passive form. In particular, the rate of choosing the *bekommen* passive form should be reduced even in case the constraint "Subject = Topic", which favors the use of the *bekommen* passive, is given priority over the constraint "Subject = Agent".

In sum, our experiment addresses two issues. The first one concerns the role of the two prominence hierarchies in (7) for the purposes of subject choice. The major question in this regard is how semantic role prominence and discourse prominence are weighted relative to each other in situations of conflict, as in the case when the recipient is established as topic. The second issue addressed by the experiment is whether the choice between active voice and *bekommen* passive is constrained by the compatibility between individual verbs and the *bekommen* passive. An additional question in this connection is whether effects of this kind are best captured in terms of frequency measures derived from corpus counts or in terms of grammaticality scores derived from judgment experiments.

4.1 Method

Participants. 48 students from the University of Konstanz participated either for course credit or for payment. All participants were native speakers of German and naive with respect to the purpose of the experiment.

Materials. The sentence material was constructed around a set of 24 ditransitive verbs that were selected on the basis of the data discussed above. First, we selected eight verbs that occur in the *bekommen* passive with some regularity and are highly acceptable in this construction. These verbs are listed in (8-a). Second, we selected eight verbs that occur only rarely in the *bekommen* passive but are nevertheless highly acceptable in this construction, cf. (8-b). Finally, we selected the eight verbs in (8-c), which also occur only rarely but are of degraded acceptability in the *bekommen* passive. Table 3 gives the mean frequency and mean acceptability scores for each of these three groups in the two relevant constructions (active voice and *bekommen* passive). Note that + frequent does not mean that the respective verbs occur very often in the *bekommen* passive. They simply occur at all in a noteworthy number of sentences, but still far less often than corresponding active sentences.

(8) a. verschreiben ('prescribe'), zustecken ('slip'), zurückbezahlen ('pay back'), zuspielen ('pass'), bewilligen ('concede'), spendieren ('stand sb. sth.'), zusenden ('send'), erstatten ('reimburse'),
b. hinterlegen ('deposit'), zeigen ('show'), absprechen ('deny'), zubereiten ('prepare (a meal)'), schildern ('describe'), erzählen ('tell'), vorlegen ('present'), vorsingen ('sing to sb.'),
c. geben ('give'), glauben ('believe'), stehlen ('steal'), klauen ('filch'), beschaffen ('purchase'), besorgen ('get'), kaufen ('buy'), ersparen ('spare')

For each verb, a sentence was created that appeared in one of the four versions shown in (5) and (6). Each context was paired with the two corresponding variants of the sentence so that participants could choose which one they would prefer as answer (see Table 4). In order to exclude the possibility that participants' choices were influenced by order of presentation, the order of the two answers was systematically varied by including *Order of Presentation* (active first or *bekommen* passive first) as a third factor that was fully crossed with the other two factors. The full experiment thus had a three-factorial design, with two within-item

Table 4: A stimulus for the experiment.

Topic = Agent	Was gibt es Neues von Stefan?
	what gives it new of Stefan
	'Anything new about Stefan?'
	○ Stefan hat unserem Deutschlehrer ein Buch geklaut.
	   Stefan has our German.teacher a book stolen
	   'Stefan stole a book from our German teacher.'
	○ Von Stefan hat unser Deutschlehrer ein Buch geklaut bekommen.
	   by Stefan has our German.teacher a book stolen got
	   'Our German teacher was stolen a book by Stefan.'

Topic = Recipient	Was gibt es Neues von eurem Deutschlehrer?
	what gives it new of your German.teacher
	'Anything new about your German teacher?'
	○ Unserem Deutschlehrer hat Stefan ein Buch geklaut.
	   our German.teacher has Stefan a book stolen
	   'Stefan stole a book from our German teacher.'
	○ Unser Deutschlehrer hat von Stefan ein Buch geklaut bekommen.
	   our German.teacher has by Stefan a book stolen got
	   'Our German teacher was stolen a book by Stefan.'

factors (context question and presentation order) and one between-item factor (verb class). The 24 sentences were distributed onto four lists according to a Latin square design with the two within-item factors.

Procedure. The experiment was administered as a questionnaire. For each sentence, the context question was followed by the two variants of the sentence, each on a separate line. Each of the four lists of 24 experimental sentences was combined with 24 filler sentences from an unrelated experiment.

Participants had to mark the structural variant they considered most appropriate given the context question by putting a cross into the small circle before the variant. The factor "Order of Presentation" is not shown.

When the context question established the agent as topic, the topic is the subject in an active sentence; when the context sentences established the recipient as topic, the topic is the subject in a *bekommen* passive sentence.

4.2 Results

For each participant and item, we recorded which alternative was chosen. Because the order in which the alternatives were presented below each context question had no significant effect, we dropped this factor from the experimental design. All statistical analyses reported in this chapter were computed using the statistics software R, version 2.14.2 (R Development Core Team 2012).

Table 5 shows the percentages of choosing the alternative in which the subject was the topic (active sentence for agent topics and *bekommen* passive for recipient topics). Responses were analyzed by means of logistic mixed-effects regression using the R-package *lme4* (Bates et al. 2015). Forward difference coding was used for the experimental factors. That is, they were coded in such a way that all contrasts tested whether the means of adjacent factor levels were different. We included participants and items as crossed random effects. Following the advice given in Barr et al. (2013), we first computed a model

Table 5: Percentages of choice 'topic = subject' for each of the three verb groups.

Context question	Grammaticality and frequency of bekommen passive		
	+grammatical, +frequent	+grammatical, −frequent	−grammatical, −frequent
Topic = Agent	95	96	97
Topic = Recipient	85	72	43

containing the full factorial design in the random slopes. Since this model did not converge, we dropped the interaction term from the random sentence factor, which resulted in a converging model. For each contrast, Table 6 shows the estimate, the standard error, the resulting z-value, and the corresponding p-value. The row labeled Verbtype-C1 gives the results for the first contrast within the factor Verbtype (second vs. third column in Table 5), the row Verbtype-C2 gives the results for the second contrast within that factor. Interactions are labeled accordingly.

Table 6: Mixed-effect model for the choice results of the experiment.

Contrast	Estimate	Std. error	z-Value	Pr(>|z|)
(Intercept)	2.9156	0.2656	10.980	<2e-16
Verbtype-C1	-0.5751	0.3880	-1.482	0.1383
Verbtype-C2	-0.7723	0.3974	-1.943	0.0520
Topic	-3.3300	0.4868	-6.840	7.9e-12
Verbtype-C1:Topic	-1.7151	0.7670	-2.236	0.0253
Verbtype-C2:Topic	-2.0522	0.9086	-2.259	0.0239

Table 5 shows a striking discrepancy between contexts establishing the agent as topic and contexts establishing the recipient as topic. When the agent was the topic, sentences in which the subject was the topic, that is active sentences, were chosen almost all of the time, without any difference between the three verb classes. When the recipient was the topic, we also see a preference for choosing the alternative in which the topic is the subject, which in this case is the *bekommen* passive sentence, but only with verbs that are fully acceptable in the *bekommen* passive. The *bekommen* passive alternative was chosen most often with verbs in the class [+grammatical, + frequent], but verbs in the class [+grammatical, – frequent] were chosen only slightly less often (85% versus 72%; $p < 0.05$). With verbs in the class [–grammatical, – frequent], however, there was no longer a preference for choosing the *bekommen* passive alternative; with 43%, there was even a small preference in favor of the active voice alternative in which the topic is realized as dative object.

4.3 Discussion

The current experiment has two major outcomes. First, when the context established the agent as topic, there was an almost categorical preference for sentences in the active voice. This was expected because in this case active sentences comply both with the syntactic function hierarchy and with the discourse hierarchy, whereas *bekommen* passive sentences violate both hierarchies. Second, when the context established the recipient as topic, participants' choices were affected by the compatibility of the verb with the *bekommen* passive. Consider first the conditions in which the verb was fully compatible with the *bekommen* passive. In this case, participants preferred the *bekommen* passive sentence over the active sentence, that is, the sentence with the subject as clause-initial topic phrase was chosen much more often than the sentence with the dative object as clause-initial topic phrase. This means that the constraint "Subject = Topic" is ranked higher than the constraint "Subject = Agent". In order to respect this ranking, participants made use of the *bekommen* passive, which allowed them to front the subject. Fronting of the object was thereby avoided. This is in line with independent evidence showing that speakers of German avoid object-before-subject sentences even when the object is the topic and use passive sentences instead (e.g., Skopeteas & Fanselow 2009; see Bader et al. 2017, for a recent overview). The switch to the noncanonical passive construction (*bekommen* passive) is furthermore compatible with the evidence for contextual licensing of marked structures (cf. Weskott et al. 2011 and Weskott et al. this volume).

When the verb was not compatible with the *bekommen* passive, the preference for the *bekommen* passive vanished. Instead, a preference for sentences in the active voice showed up, although not a strong one. This implies that the constraint "Compatibility with *Bekommen* Passive" is ranked as high as the constraint "Subject = Topic". Given that the preference for the active voice was small (43% vs. 57%), one possibility would be to postulate a tie between the two constraints, which would have the consequence that the grammar makes no determinate decision between the two competing alternatives.

Let us finally consider how the experimental results relate to the GF model proposed in this chapter (see Figure 3). Following earlier work, we conceive of the task used in this experiment as a production task in which the production system has to choose between two candidate structures for the message that has to be encoded. These candidate structures are input to the box labeled "Computation of continuous acceptability value". The results of our experiment suggest that the acceptability value is largely determined by grammaticality, although frequency also seems to have a minor effect. When the recipient was the topic, sentences with [+grammatical, + frequent] verbs differed from sentences with [+grammatical, −frequent] verbs by 13%. The difference between the conditions [+grammatical, − frequent] and [−grammatical, − frequent] was 29%, however. The structure with the higher acceptability value is then selected for output in the box labeled "Output selection".

It is clear that the GF model is just a first approximation to a more full-fledged model. One shortcoming of the model is that it does not take into account the incremental nature of language production and language comprehension. With regard to language production, Kempen & Harbusch (2008) argued against the Decathlon model because it seems to presuppose that complete candidate structures enter the competition for output selection. Since our model has taken over this part of the Decathlon model, the same criticism applies. We must leave it as a task for future research to integrate incremental processing into our model. Note, however, that word-by-word incrementality is surely not the only way for language production to proceed (cf. Ferreira & Engelhardt 2006). As long as the production mechanisms engage in a certain amount of preplanning, the necessary information to select candidate structure on the basis of syntactic constraints may be available.

5 Conclusion

According to the GF model, continuous acceptability scores are directly mapped onto either gradient or binary judgments. Gradient and binary judgments are therefore predicted to correlate closely. The experimental results reported here support this prediction, in line with previous results (Bader & Häussler 2010; Weskott & Fanselow 2011).

Continuous acceptability scores also play an important role during language production, although a less direct one. In a nutshell, a low acceptability score drives the production probability of a structure down, but a high acceptability score does not guarantee a high production probability. When two structures of high acceptability compete, other factors will decide the competition. The relationship between grammaticality/acceptability judgments and production frequencies is therefore hypothesized to be a loose one. In line with this prediction, we did not find judgment–frequency correlations across the board, neither for gradient nor for binary judgments. Correlations were only found for less acceptable structures, for example, when lexical restrictions were involved as in the case of the *bekommen* passive. This pattern has recurrently been found in the literature (e.g., Kempen & Harbusch 2008; Arppe & Järvikivi 2007).

The forced-choice experiment illustrates how factors other than grammaticality determine choice during production (for comparable findings with respect to discourse status, see Hörnig & Féry, this volume). This experiment also shows that frequency information may contribute to the probability of producing a structure, although to a lesser extent than grammaticality. More familiar structures are more likely to be produced (see also Luka 2005; Kempen & Harbusch 2008). However, frequency is only effective for less common structures. For very frequent structures like ditransitives in the active voice, frequency effects are no longer noticeable though they still might contribute to the competition.

To conclude, the data examined in this chapter show that the GF model, which is a synthesis of the Decathlon model (Featherston 2005a) and the Direct Mapping model (Bader & Häussler 2010), can explain more data than each of the two predecessor models alone. The GF model is thus a further step toward a complete model of the mental processes involved in linguistic decisions.

References

Aissen, J. 1999. Markedness and subject choice in Optimality Theory. Natural Language & Linguistic Theory 17. 673–711.
Arppe, A. & J. Järvikivi. 2007. Every method counts: Combining corpus-based and experimental evidence in the study of synonymy. Corpus Linguistics and Linguistic Theory 3(2). 131–159.
Bader, M. 2012. The German bekommen passive: A case study on frequency and grammaticality. Linguistische Berichte 231. 249–298.
Bader, M., E. Ellsiepen, V. Koukoulioti & Y. Portele. 2017. Filling the prefield: Findings and challenges. In: (C. Freitag, O. Bott & F. Schlotterbeck, eds.) Two perspectives on V2: The invited talks of the DGfS 2016 workshop "V2 in grammar and processing: Its causes and its consequences", 27–49. Konstanz: University of Konstanz.
Bader, M. & J. Häussler. 2010. Toward a model of grammaticality judgments. Journal of Linguistics 46(2): 273–330.
Bader, M. & J. Häussler. 2013. How much *bekommen* is there in the German *bekommen* passive? In: (A. Alexiadou & F. Schäfer, eds) Non-canonical passives, 115–139. Amsterdam: Benjamins.
Bard, E. G., D. Robertson & A. Sorace. 1996. Magnitude estimation of linguistic acceptability. Language 72(1): 32–68.
Baroni, M., S. Bernardini, A. Ferraresi & E. Zanchetta. 2009. The WaCky Wide Web: A collection of very large linguistically processed web-crawled corpora. Language Resources and Evaluation Journal 23(3): 209–226. 10.1007/s10579-009-9081-4.
Barr, D. J., R. Levy, C. Scheepers & H. J. Tily. 2013. Random effects structure for confirmatory hypothesis testing: Keep it maximal. Journal of Memory and Language 68: 255–278.
Bates, D., M. Mächler, B. Bolker & S. Walker. 2015. Fitting linear mixed-effects models using lme4. Journal of Statistical Software 67(1): 1–48. 10.18637/jss.v067.i01.
Bever, T. G. & J. M. Carroll. 1981. On some continuous properties in language. In: (T. Myers, J. Laver & J. Anderson, eds) The cognitive representation of speech, 225–233. Amsterdam: North-Holland.
Bresnan, J. 2007. Is syntactic knowledge probabilistic? Experiments with the English dative alternation. In (S. Featherston & W. Sternefeld, eds) Roots: Linguistics in search of its evidential base, 75–96. Berlin: Mouton de Gruyter.

Bresnan, J. & M. Ford. 2010. Predicting syntax: Processing dative constructions in American and Australian varieties of English. Language 86(1): 168–213.

Carroll, J. M., T. G. Bever & C. R. Pollack. 1981. The non-uniqueness of linguistic intuitions. Language 57: 368–383.

Cowart, W. 1997. Experimental syntax: Applying objective methods to sentence judgments. Thousand Oaks, CA: Sage Publications.

Ellsiepen, E. & M. Bader. 2014. The under-additive effect of multiple constraint violations. Cognitive Processing 15(Suppl 1): S100–S102.

Fanselow, G. & S. Frisch. 2006. Effects of processing difficulty on judgements of acceptability. In (G. Fanselow, C. Féry, R. Vogel & M. Schlesewsky, eds) Gradience in grammar: Generative perspectives, 291–316. New York: Oxford University Press.

Fanselow, G., C. Féry, R. Vogel & M. Schlesewsky (eds). 2006. Gradience in grammar: Generative perspectives. New York: Oxford University Press.

Featherston, S. 2005a. The Decathlon model of empirical syntax. In (M. Reis & S. Kepser, eds) Linguistic evidence. Empirical, theoretical and computational perspectives, 187–208. Berlin: de Gruyter.

Featherston, S. 2005b. Universals and grammaticality: Wh-constraints in German and English. Linguistics 43(4): 667–711.

Featherston, S. 2009. A scale for measuring well-formedness: Why syntax needs boiling and freezing points. In (S. Featherston & S. Winkler, eds) The fruits of empirical linguistics. Vol. 1: Process, 47–74. Berlin: de Gruyter.

Ferreira, F. & P. E. Engelhardt. 2006. Syntax and production. In (M. Traxler & M. A. Gernsbacher, eds) Handbook of Psycholinguistics, 61–91. New York: Academic Press 2nd edn.

Fukuda, S., G. Goodall, D. Michel & H. Beecher. 2012. Is Magnitude Estimation worth the trouble. In: (J. Choi, E. A. Hogue, J. Punske, D. Tat, J. Schertz & A. Trueman, eds) Proceedings of the 29th West Coast Conference on formal linguistics, 328–336. Somerville, MA: Cascadilla Proceedings Project.

Gerken, L. & T. G. Bever. 1986. Linguistic intuitions are the result of interactions between perceptual processes and linguistic universals. Cognitive Science 10. 457–476.

Hofmeister, P., L. Staum Casasanto & I. A. Sag. 2014. Processing effects in linguistic judgment data:(super-) additivity and reading span scores. Language and Cognition 6(1): 111–145.

Häussler, J. & M. Bader. in preparation. From graded to binary grammaticality. Manuscript in preparation, University of Wuppertal and Goethe University Frankfurt.

Kempen, G. & K. Harbusch. 2008. Comparing linguistic judgments and corpus frequencies as windows on grammatical competence: A study of argument linearization in German clauses. In (A. Steube, ed) The discourse potential of underspecified structures, 179–192. Berlin: de Gruyter.

Kitagawa, Y. & J. D. Fodor. 2006. Prosodic influence on syntactic judgements. In (G. Fanselow, C. Féry, R. Vogel & M. Schlesewsky, eds) Gradience in grammar: Generative perspectives, 336–358. New York: Oxford University Press.

Labov, W. 1977. Empirical foundations of linguistic theory. In (R. Austerlitz, ed) Papers of The First Golden Anniversary Symposium of the Linguistic Society of America – The scope of American linguistics, 77–133. Lisse: Peter de Ridder.

Leirbukt, O. 1997. Untersuchungen zum "bekommen"-Passiv im heutigen Deutsch. Tübingen: Niemeyer.

Lenz, A. N. 2009. On the perspectivization of a recipient role – cross-linguistic results from a speech production experiment on GET-passives in German, Dutch and Luxembourgish. Groninger Arbeiten zur Germanistischen Linguistik 49: 125–144.

Linebarger, M. C., M. F. Schwartz & E. M. Saffran. 1983. Sensitivity to grammatical structure in so-called agrammatism. Cognition 13: 361–392.

Luka, B. J. 2005. A cognitively plausible model of linguistic intuitions. In: (S.S. Mufwene, E. Francis & R. Wheeler, eds) Polymorphous Linguistics: Jim McCawley's legacy, 479–502. Cambridge, MA: MIT Press.

Pater, J. 2009. Weighted constraints in generative linguistics. Cognitive Science 33: 999–1035.

Pittner, K. & J. Berman. 2013. Deutsche Syntax: Ein Arbeitsbuch. Tübingen: Gunter Narr Verlag 5th edn.

Prince, A. & P. Smolensky. 1993/2004. Optimality theory. Constraint interaction in generative grammar. Oxford: Blackwell.

R Development Core Team. 2012. R: A Language and Environment for Statistical Computing. R Foundation for Statistical Computing Vienna, Austria. http://www.Rproject.org/.

Rosenbach, A. 2005. Animacy versus weight as determinants of grammatical variation in English. Language 81: 613–644.

Schmidt, R. W. & C. F. McCreary. 1977. Standard and super-standard English: Recognition and use of prescriptive rules by native and non-native speakers. TESOL Quarterly 11: 415–429.

Schütze, C. T. 1996. The empirical base of linguistics. Chicago: Chicago University Press.

Schütze, C. T. & J. Sprouse. 2014. Judgment data. In (R. J. Podesva & D. Sharma, eds) Research methods in linguistics, 27–50. Cambridge: Cambridge University Press.

Skopeteas, S. & G. Fanselow. 2009. Effects of givenness and constraints on free word order. In (M. Zimmermann & C. Féry, eds) Information structure: Theoretical, Typological, and Experimental Perspectives, 307–331. Oxford: Oxford University Press.

Sprouse, J. 2007. Continuous acceptability, categorical grammaticality, and experimental syntax. Biolinguistics 1: 123–134.

Sprouse, J. 2011. A test of the cognitive assumptions of magnitude estimation: Commutativity does not hold for acceptability judgments. Language 87(2): 274–288.

Weskott, T. & G. Fanselow. 2011. On the informativity of different measures of linguistic acceptability. Language 87(2): 249–273.

Weskott, T., R. Hörnig, G. Fanselow & R. Kliegl. 2011. Contextual licensing of marked OVS word order in German. Linguistische Berichte 225. 3–18.

Alexander Dröge, Jürg Fleischer and Ina Bornkessel-Schlesewsky
Scrambled Wackernagel! Neural responses to noncanonical pronoun serializations in German

1 Introduction

This chapter is concerned with the neurocognitive mechanisms involved in the processing of pronouns in different serializations. Before turning to pronouns, we will begin with a look at the order of nonpronominal DPs to examine relevant syntactic differences and similarities.[1] Some languages, such as English, show a rigid word order that is subject to specific syntactic conditions, whereas other languages, like German or Japanese, allow constituents to be positioned rather freely leading to multiple possible serializations of nominative-marked (NOM) subjects, accusative-marked (ACC) direct objects (DOs), and dative-marked (DAT) indirect objects (IOs). This seemingly free permutation of DPs is known as "scrambling" (Ross 1967). The sentences in (1a) and (1b) illustrate two well-formed serializations in German that both yield the same proposition. Of course, this syntactic freedom is not unconstrained, but a number of factors from other linguistic domains influence the serialization in a given sentence, such as focus, definiteness, and animacy (e.g., Lenerz 1977; Uszkoreit 1987; Müller 1999; Struckmeier 2014). (1a) shows the canonical word order with an unmarked information structure: the animate recipient ('the CEO') preceding the inanimate theme ('the coffee'). By comparison, (1b) may be appropriate only in certain contexts with a focus on the dative object, for example, a question asking to whom the assistant brought the coffee.

(1) a. Gestern   hat   der Assistent   dem Geschäftsführer
       yesterday has   [the assistant].NOM   [the CEO].DAT
       den Kaffee   gebracht.
       [the coffee].ACC   brought
       'Yesterday, the assistant brought the coffee to the CEO.'

---

[1] There is syntactic evidence to analyze (nonclitic) pronouns in German as maximal projections (e.g., Lenerz 1993, 1994; Cardinaletti & Starke 1996). However, for reasons of readability, we will henceforth refer to pronominal DPs (e.g., *er* 'he') simply as pronouns, and to DPs headed by a noun (e.g., *der Lehrer* 'the teacher') as nonpronominal or full DPs.

b. Gestern hat der Assistent den Kaffee
yesterday has [the assistant].NOM [the coffee].ACC
dem Geschäftsführer gebracht.
[the CEO].DAT brought
'Yesterday, the assistant brought the coffee to the CEO.'
c. *Gestern hat der Assistent gebracht dem Geschäftsführer
yesterday has [the assistant].NOM brought [the CEO].DAT
den Kaffee.
[the coffee].ACC

We understand "scrambling" as a mechanism of reordering arguments in the sense of Haider & Rosengren (1998, 2003). Other movement operations like object shift or movement of an argument across an adjunct are not considered scrambling. In German, the domain of scrambling in a sentence is the so-called middlefield, which is the region following the complementizer in a verb-final subordinate clause or the finite verb in a verb second configuration (e.g., *hat* 'has' in (1)), and preceding the nonfinite part of the predicate (e.g., *gebracht* 'brought' in (1)). Haider (2010) proposes that an underlying object–verb (OV) structure is a necessary (yet not sufficient) condition to license scrambling, even though not all OV languages show the same degree of word order freedom. While scrambling produces grammatical sentences, other permutations may result in syntactic violations. For example, (1c), where the verb is placed between the arguments in the middlefield, would be considered an ungrammatical structure.

The following discussion on canonical and noncanonical word orders will not be concerned with technical details of any particular syntactic framework. When we speak of a "canonical" serialization, we refer to an information-structurally neutral word order which can be the base order, but certain other serializations may also be considered canonical, as will be discussed later in this chapter. A "noncanonical" serialization (a serialization that violates canonicity principles) is a marked word order which may even be perceived as unacceptable without supporting context. As was shown in the examples, a structure that deviates from the canonical word order can be grammatical like the scrambled sentence (1b) or ungrammatical in case of the syntactic violation in (1c). Grammaticality, of course, is a construct defined by grammar theory and cannot be measured directly in psycholinguistic experiments, but event-related brain potential (ERP) data and acceptability judgments provide the empirical basis for testing hypotheses of theoretical accounts of German syntax.

1.1 Pronoun placement in the middlefield

Unstressed personal pronouns are subject to several syntactic conditions, and placement of such pronouns deviates drastically from the word order freedom of stressed pronouns or nonpronominal DPs (see, e.g., Lenerz 1993, 1994; Cardinaletti & Starke 1996; Müller 2002). In the following, we will describe the most important distributional properties of unstressed personal pronouns in the German middlefield (henceforth referred to simply as "pronouns").

Pronouns cannot stay in their base argument positions, but have to move to the left edge of the middlefield, the so-called Wackernagel position.[2] The phenomenon of pronoun movement is not uncommon, and not confined to German or other scrambling languages. It rather seems to be a general characteristic that can also be observed in verb–object (VO) languages such as English, where pronouns also have to surface in derived positions (Basilico 1999). Different hypotheses to account for pronoun movement to the Wackernagel position have been proposed in the literature. For example, Lenerz (1993) suggests that unstressed pronouns are thematic elements, and pronoun fronting is motivated by their referential properties (see also Haider & Rosengren 1998), while Müller (1999, 2007) assumes that pronoun movement is triggered by a functional projection specific for pronouns.

While the NOM > DAT > ACC order in (1a) is perfectly natural with nonpronominal DPs, the same serialization becomes ill-formed when the DO is realized as an unstressed personal pronoun, as illustrated in (2a), because it has not been moved to the Wackernagel position. The Wackernagel position can be understood as the position to the right of C^0 (which hosts the complementizer or the finite verb), but in fact unstressed object pronouns may alternatively occupy the position to the right of a nonpronominal subject or a stressed pronominal subject (see Lenerz 1993). Therefore, both (2b) with the pronoun following the finite verb as well as (2c) with the pronoun following the nonpronominal subject are well-formed sentences.

---

[2] It is interesting to note that the syntactic position named after Jacob Wackernagel originally referred to the second position in a clause occupied by certain clitic elements (see Wackernagel 1892), but in the literature on German syntax the term Wackernagel position is usually understood as the landing site of unstressed pronouns in the middlefield.

(2) a. *Gestern hat der Assistent dem Geschäftsführer es gebracht.
　　　　yesterday has [the assistant].NOM [the CEO].DAT it.ACC brought
　　b. Gestern hat es der Assistent dem Geschäftsführer gebracht.
　　　　yesterday has it.ACC [the assistant].NOM [the CEO].DAT brought
　　c. Gestern hat der Assistent es dem Geschäftsführer
　　　　yesterday has [the assistant].NOM it.ACC [the CEO].DAT
　　　　gebracht.
　　　　brought
　　　　'Yesterday, the assistant brought it to the CEO.'

When the subject, the DO, and the IO are realized as unstressed personal pronouns, their canonical order is NOM > ACC > DAT (see, e.g., Lenerz 1993; Haider & Rosengren 1998; Müller 1999). It is not possible for pronouns to undergo scrambling; instead, pronoun serialization seems to be rigid, at least in Standard German (but see the next section for a discussion of variation in pronoun order).

If the subject and the object are pronouns and fronted to the Wackernagel position, scrambling the object over the subject would result in an unacceptable sequence in Standard German, illustrated by the contrast between (3a) and (3b).³

(3) a. Gestern hat er es dem Geschäftsführer gebracht.
　　　　yesterday has he.NOM it.ACC [the CEO].DAT brought
　　b. ?Gestern hat es er dem Geschäftsführer gebracht.
　　　　yesterday has it.ACC he.NOM [the CEO].DAT brought
　　　　'Yesterday, he brought it to the CEO.'

If both objects in a ditransitive construction are pronouns, they occur in the order accusative-before-dative (ACC > DAT). This is particularly interesting because this serialization is the opposite of the base order of nonpronominal objects, which appear in the order dative-before-accusative (DAT > ACC) in an unmarked sentence.⁴ This ordering constraint on the serialization of object pronouns seems to hold for both German and Dutch, in spite of the fact that these two languages differ considerably with respect to scrambling of full DPs (see Zwart 1996; Neeleman & Weerman 1999; Haider & Rosengren 1998, 2003).

---

3 But see Weiß (2015, 2017) and the discussion in Section 4.5.
4 Note that there are certain verbs that require a base order of ACC > DAT for nonpronominal DPs, so-called low dative verbs (Haider & Rosengren 2003; Cook 2006).

The serialization in (4a) is canonical because the two object pronouns are fronted to the Wackernagel position and appear in the relative order ACC > DAT, which is the canonical order for unstressed pronouns. As we have seen in (2c), object pronouns may alternatively follow the subject-DP in the middlefield, so (4b) is also a canonical serialization. However, unlike full DPs that can be scrambled, pronoun order is considered to be rigid and deviations from the canonical serialization are unacceptable in Standard German, illustrated by the DAT > ACC order in (4c) and (4d). The reversed order of the two object pronouns in (4c) and (4d) is often treated as ungrammatical in the theoretical literature (e.g., Haider & Rosengren 1998; Müller 1999), but in the following we will argue that such an inversion of object pronouns is possible and yields a noncanonical but grammatical structure despite decreased acceptability.

(4) a. Gestern hat es ihm der Assistent gebracht.
yesterday has it.ACC him.DAT [the assistant].NOM brought
b. Gestern hat der Assistent es ihm gebracht.
yesterday has [the assistant].NOM it.ACC him.DAT brought
c. ?Gestern hat ihm es der Assistent gebracht.
yesterday has him.DAT it.ACC [the assistant].NOM brought
d. ?Gestern hat der Assistent ihm es gebracht.
yesterday has [the assistant].NOM him.DAT it.ACC brought
'Yesterday, the assistant brought it to him.'

1.2 Variation in pronoun serializations

An inversion of object pronouns results in a noticeable decrease in acceptability. Featherston (2009) reports an acceptability judgment study, where the relative order of dative and accusative object pronouns was manipulated (along with other conditions including light and heavy DPs). Results for pronouns showed that DAT > ACC sentences received significantly lower acceptability judgments compared to ACC > DAT sentences. Kempen & Harbusch (2004, 2005) analyzed serializations of pronominal and nonpronominal DPs in corpora of written and spoken German and found almost no occurrences of DAT > ACC orders with pronouns, which seems to support the assumption of a rigid pronoun order. However, the claim that two object pronouns always have to appear in the sequence ACC > DAT does not seem to hold for all combinations of object pronouns. Haider & Rosengren (1998) suggest that the ACC > DAT order is a strong preference for most pronoun combinations, but it is only obligatory for the third-person singular accusative neuter pronoun *es* ('it'), possibly because *es* is a reduced pronoun that can never bear stress. Taking a closer look, however, even this assumption cannot be maintained as there exist examples of an acceptable inverse order of two object pronouns including the reduced pronoun *es* if it is realized as the clitic variant *'s* (Lenerz 1993). The examples given in (5a) and (5b) (=(52c) and (52d) from Lenerz 1993, p. 142; English translation by the authors) are both acceptable, thus illustrating that it is possible for the clitic pronoun *'s* to appear in either ACC > DAT or DAT > ACC orders, respectively.

(5) a. weil   er's   mir   ja   gezeigt hat
       because he.NOM-it.ACC me.DAT PRT shown   has
    b. weil   er   mir's   ja   gezeigt hat
       because he.NOM   me.DAT-it.ACC PRT shown   has
    '...because he showed it to me.'

Clitic realizations of pronouns are typically found in dialectal varieties of German, and the DAT > ACC order indeed occurs in many regions. For example, a recent investigation of syntactic phenomena in dialects spoken in the German State of Hesse attests that DAT > ACC is a possible pronoun serialization there (Fleischer, Kasper & Lenz 2012; Fleischer 2013a, 2017). However, the DAT > ACC order is not found in all German dialects. Areal differences seem to systematically predict if object pronouns occur in DAT > ACC or ACC > DAT orders. Fleischer (2010a, 2011, 2012) found a diatopic distribution of pronoun order preferences in dialectal varieties of German: the ACC > DAT (=DO > IO) order is attested in the northern part of Germany where Low German dialects are spoken, whereas the DAT > ACC (=IO > DO) order predominates in Upper German dialects in southern and southwestern regions of the German-speaking area, and in certain Low German areas such as East Frisia.[5] Interestingly, Central German dialects, which are geographically situated between Upper and Low German areas, display both orders. Similar distributional patterns of pronoun serializations with the DAT > ACC order occurring in High German dialects but not in Low German dialects can also be observed for older stages of German (Fleischer 2005, 2010b, 2013b).

One further aspect that seems to systematically affect pronoun order in some dialectal varieties deserves attention. In the Central German dialects where both DAT > ACC and ACC > DAT orders are found, the accusative pronoun seems more likely to follow dative pronouns of the first- or second-person singular. For instance, in many locations in Hesse DAT > ACC is the preferred serialization with

---

[5] It should be noted that we consequently use the labels ACC and DAT to refer to the relative order of DO and IO, respectively, even though there are a number of German (especially Low German) dialects with case syncretism, where dative and accusative forms are no longer morphologically distinguishable.

a first-person singular dative pronoun, but ACC > DAT prevails with a third-person dative pronoun (Fleischer 2013a). Fleischer (2010a) suggests an explanation of these data from Central German dialects in terms of a split along the Person Hierarchy (see Silverstein 1976; Siewierska 1988). Dative pronouns of the first- and second-person singular favor a DAT > ACC order, whereas the third-person dative pronouns call for an ACC > DAT order.[6]

These empirical findings from German dialects seem difficult to reconcile with the theoretical conjecture that the reduced pronoun *es* strictly needs to appear in ACC > DAT order. However, if the type of text is rather formal such as in newspaper articles, object pronouns occur almost exclusively in the canonical ACC > DAT order, as was shown in corpora based on the Frankfurter Rundschau, a newspaper from Germany (Kempen & Harbusch 2004, 2005) as well as in a corpus study using primarily newspaper corpora from different parts of the German-speaking area, including Austria and Switzerland (Fleischer 2010a). This suggests that the ACC > DAT order is the canonical serialization in present-day Standard German, and there seems to be an awareness of this standard serialization among language users despite the great amount of regional variation.

---

6 There is another restriction of the combination of object pronouns in German that seems to be subject to dialectal variation. Anagnostopoulou (2008, 2017) argues that the so-called Person Case Constraint (PCC) described for clitics in many languages also applies for weak pronouns in German, but only in a specific syntactic configuration and only for a certain group of speakers. According to the PCC in its weak version, if there is a third person in a combination of a DO and an IO, it has to be the DO (Bonet 1991: 182). Anagnostopoulou (2008) suggests that the weak version of the PCC applies in German when the two object pronouns are followed by the subject, but not if they are preceded by the subject. So, (i) would violate the PCC and lead to an ungrammatical sentence because the subject follows the pronouns, but (ii) where the subject precedes the pronouns would be grammatical despite the violation of the PCC (examples from Anagnostopoulou 2008: 26).

(i) *weil   dich   ihm   irgendwer   vorgestellt   hat.
     because you.ACC   him.DAT someone.NOM   introduced   has

(ii) weil   sie   dich   ihm   vorgestellt   hat.
     because she.NOM   you.ACC him.DAT   introduced   has

Interestingly, Anagnostopoulou (2008) points out that the PCC only applies for those speakers who do not accept the noncanonical DAT > ACC order with object pronouns, whereas speakers who accept this order can also accept pronoun combinations that would violate the PCC. Even though this is an interesting finding, we will not discuss possible PCC effects in German here because all critical stimuli in our experiment used a third-person accusative pronoun; hence, the PCC would never be violated.

1.3 Neurocognitive approaches to word order variations

Having discussed the contrast between the canonical order of object pronouns in Standard German and the variation found in colloquial speech and in many dialects, the question arises how the language processing system handles noncanonical pronoun orders in real time. To investigate the temporal dynamics of online sentence comprehension in the brain, we conducted an ERP study (see Luck 2014, for an introduction to the ERP technique). Building on the aforementioned characteristics of the reduced accusative pronoun *es* ('it'), we aimed at testing how pronoun serializations that are noncanonical in Standard German are processed in light of the variation of pronoun orders found in dialects and colloquial speech.

To date, most psycholinguistic and neurolinguistic studies investigating word order in German have focused on nonpronominal DPs. For scrambled word orders in the middlefield, previous ERP studies have revealed a "scrambling negativity", a broadly distributed, sometimes left-lateralized, negative ERP response between ~300 and ~500 ms after stimulus onset. The scrambling negativity has been found for initial, noncanonically positioned DPs at the left edge of the middlefield: for an accusative object preceding the subject (Rösler, Pechmann, Streb, Röder & Hennighausen 1998; Bornkessel, Schlesewsky & Friederici 2002, 2003a; Schlesewsky, Bornkessel & Frisch 2003; Dröge, Fleischer, Schlesewsky & Bornkessel-Schlesewsky 2016), for a dative object preceding the subject (Rösler et al. 1998; Schlesewsky et al. 2003), and for an accusative object preceding the dative object but following the subject (Rösler et al. 1998). It could further be shown that the global acceptability of a noncanonical object-before-subject order was increased if the sentence was preceded by a licensing context, but even a contextually licensed scrambling order gave rise to a local scrambling negativity in the ERP (Bornkessel et al. 2003a; Bornkessel & Schlesewsky 2006a).

Schlesewsky et al. (2003) included pronouns along with nonpronominal DPs in their experiments and reported scrambling negativities for nonpronominal accusative and dative DPs at the first position in the middlefield, but found no such ERP effects for accusative or dative pronouns preceding the subject-DP. The scrambling negativity was interpreted as an index of a violation of canonicity principles: the scrambled object-DPs led to a noncanonical word order and gave rise to a scrambling negativity, whereas the fronted object pronouns appeared in their canonical Wackernagel position and did not elicit a scrambling negativity. Importantly, however, Schlesewsky et al. (2003) did not manipulate the relative order of two object pronouns in their study. Thus, it remains an open question whether the noncanonical order of two object pronouns might elicit effects similar to the scrambling negativity reported for full DPs.

To fill this gap, the relative order of accusative and dative pronouns was manipulated in the present study, and ERPs for each object pronoun within a sentence were analyzed in order to investigate neurophysiological effects to different pronoun serializations. In addition, we conducted an acceptability judgment task to gather information about the global acceptabilities of the sentences. We expected ACC > DAT to instantiate the canonical order and DAT > ACC the deviant order. However, the existing variation in pronoun serializations in colloquial speech and in many dialects might have an effect on the processing of the noncanonical DAT > ACC order even in the standard language. Although the experimental material consists of sentences in Standard German and all participants are competent in Standard German, participants may also be competent in one or more dialects that allow different pronoun orders or at least have been exposed to some degree of variability of pronoun order in colloquial conversations. The interesting question is whether the prescriptive bias of a rigid pronoun order in the standard language is strong enough to elicit effects of an outright syntactic violation when processing the DAT > ACC order. If, however, the DAT > ACC order is processed similarly to scrambling of full DPs, that is, as a marked but grammatical serialization, we would expect to observe a scrambling negativity. Using first-person singular (DAT.1SG; *mir* 'me') as well as third-person singular masculine and feminine (DAT.3SG; *ihm* 'him' and *ihr* 'her') dative pronouns, we created a further dimension for the analysis. Person might have an effect on the acceptability of the noncanonical DAT > ACC pronoun order as this order has a wider regional distribution with the dative in the first person than in the third person (see Fleischer 2010a, 2013a). Examples for each experimental condition are given in Table 1.[7]

Each combination of object pronouns appeared either in the canonical ACC > DAT order or the noncanonical DAT > ACC order. The dative object pronoun was either a first-person singular pronoun (DAT.1SG) or a third-person singular pronoun (DAT.3SG) that agreed in gender to one of the referents in the matrix clause. The critical positions are underlined for clarity here. English translations are only given for the canonical orders, but are equivalent for the respective noncanonical orders.

---

[7] Note that there are a number of morphologically identical forms in the inflectional paradigm of personal pronouns in German due to case syncretism. For example, *er* ('he') must always be nominative masculine singular, but *es* ('it') could be either nominative or accusative neuter singular. In principle, this aspect can be important for incremental processing, but in the current design we do not expect this to be an issue because the parser would not expect a second nominative form after the initial nominative pronoun *er*.

Table 1: Example stimuli of the four experimental conditions illustrating a sentence with a male proper name (above) and with a female proper name (below) in each row. The critical positions are underlined for clarity here. English translations are only given for the canonical orders, but are equivalent for the respective non-canonical orders.

Order	Person	Example stimuli
ACC > DAT	DAT.1SG	Felix berichtet Carsten, dass er es mir kostenlos reparieren kann. ('Felix tells Carsten that he can repair it for me at no charge.') Timo sagt Sophie, dass er es mir später vorspielen könnte. ('Timo tells Sophie that he could play it to me later.')
ACC > DAT	DAT.3SG	Felix berichtet Carsten, dass er es ihm kostenlos reparieren kann. ('Felix tells Carsten that he can repair it for him at no charge.') Timo sagt Sophie, dass er es ihr später vorspielen könnte. ('Timo tells Sophie that he could play it to her later.')
DAT > ACC	DAT.1SG	Felix berichtet Carsten, dass er mir es kostenlos reparieren kann. Timo sagt Sophie, dass er mir es später vorspielen könnte.
DAT > ACC	DAT.3SG	Felix berichtet Carsten, dass er ihm es kostenlos reparieren kann. Timo sagt Sophie, dass er ihr es später vorspielen könnte.

2 Method

2.1 Participants

Twenty-six individuals participated in the experiment, most of them undergraduate students at the University of Marburg. All participants took part voluntarily, gave informed written consent before the experiment, and were paid for their participation. Prior to the recording of the electroencephalogram (EEG), all participants filled in a screening questionnaire. The participants were all native speakers of German, right-handed (assessed with an adapted German version of the Edinburgh Handedness Inventory; Oldfield 1971), with normal or corrected-to-normal visual acuity. Participants were not specifically controlled for their places of birth and their dialect competences; various places in southern, central, and northern parts of Germany as well as self-reported dialect competences ranging from very low to very high were represented. Twenty participants entered the final data analysis (all monolingual; 10 males; mean age 22.9 years; age range 20–28 years). Four participants had to be excluded due to excessive EEG artifacts or insufficient accuracy in the word-recognition task. Despite a good EEG signal and good performance, we decided to exclude two further participants from analysis: one who was raised bilingually in Czech and German (see Cook, Iarossi, Stellakis & Tokumaru 2003, on effects of the L2 on L1 syntax processing), and one who reported to be a converted left-hander (see Klöppel, Vongerichten, van Eimeren, Frackowiak & Siebner 2007; Klöppel, Mangin, Vongerichten, Frackowiak & Siebner 2010, on neural differences between right-handers and converted left-handers).

2.2 Materials

The ERP technique allowed us to use the pronouns as critical events in the experiment. Our stimuli consisted of verb-final subordinate clauses containing the critical pronoun combinations, embedded in a neutral matrix clause that introduced two referents. The subordinate clauses always began with the complementizer *dass* ('that') and the nominative pronoun *er* ('he'), followed by the two object pronouns as the critical positions. The third-person dative pronouns (*ihm* 'him' or *ihr* 'her') agreed in gender with one of the referents in the matrix clause to establish possible reference relations. We varied between masculine and feminine to avoid gender-related confounds, and to provide some variation in the critical stimuli to prevent participants from adopting a strategy when processing too many lexically identical items. After the critical positions, we added varying lexical materials such as PPs and adverbs, and the verb at the end of the subordinate clauses. Thirty-six lexically different sentences were constructed (18 with a female proper name in the matrix clause; see Table 1 for examples). Each sentence had two slots for object pronouns and appeared in four versions (with ACC > DAT or DAT > ACC orders, and containing a first- or third-person dative pronoun), yielding a 2 × 2 experimental design with a total of 144 critical stimulus sentences (36 sentences per experimental condition).[8]

We added filler sentences to the material that were similar in structure (a matrix clause and a subordinate clause). A set of 72 filler sentences was grammatical, but contained either one or two pronouns in the embedded clauses to prevent participants from expecting a three-pronoun combination in all stimuli. Another set of 168 filler sentences that was designed for a different experiment contained two full DPs in the subordinate clauses (and no pronouns at all). Half of these sentences were constructed as semantically plausible, and the other half as completely implausible.

---

[8] As pointed out by an anonymous reviewer, some dative pronouns in our stimuli were free datives, that is, not selected by the verb of the subordinate clause. However, the syntactic status whether the dative was an argument or a free dative could only be processed at the final verb, but not at the position of the dative pronoun itself because of the incremental nature of sentence comprehension. Thus, this issue could not have affected the incremental interpretation of pronoun order in our study.

In the experimental sessions, each participant was assigned one of four lists that each contained the total set of 384 sentences in different pseudo-randomized orders.

2.3 Behavioral tasks

Two behavioral tasks followed each of the experimental stimulus sentences in the experiment. In an acceptability judgment task, participants were asked to rate the acceptability of each sentence on a four-point scale. With such a scale it was possible to capture not only the extremes, but also gradual differences in acceptability, yet the scale was simple enough for fast responses in a timed experiment (a greater number of acceptability choices would have increased reaction times; see Hick-Hyman law, Hick 1952; Hyman 1953). Participants were instructed that their judgments should reflect not only grammatical correctness but also whether a sentence sounded "normal" or "odd" in their personal opinion.[9] The instructions provided labels of the points of the four-point scale both in words and as a percentage scale, as shown in (6) (English translations have been added here).

(6) *absolut akzeptabel* 'absolutely acceptable' 100%
    ziemlich akzeptabel 'quite acceptable' 66%
    wenig akzeptabel 'not very acceptable' 33%
    gar nicht akzeptabel 'not acceptable at all' 0%

Responses of acceptability judgments were given by pressing one of four keys ("D", "F", "J", "K") on a computer keyboard using left and right index fingers and middle fingers, with the button configuration counterbalanced among participants between left-to-right and right-to-left (i.e., left middle finger on key "D" meaning "absolutely acceptable" in one configuration, and "not acceptable at all" in the other configuration).

---

[9] The exact wording of the acceptability judgment task in the instructions (bold print for emphasis as written in the instructions):

In dieser EEG-Studie werden Ihnen zahlreiche Sätze am Bildschirm gezeigt, welche Sie hinsichtlich ihrer **Akzeptabilität** *bewerten sollen. Damit ist gemeint, ob der Satz für Sie* **gut oder schlecht** *klingt. Es geht hierbei nicht nur darum, ob der Satz grammatisch korrekt formuliert ist, sondern auch, ob er „normal" oder „merkwürdig" klingt. Wir möchten Ihre persönliche Meinung erfahren; Sie können dabei nichts falsch machen!*

(Translation: In this EEG study, you will be presented with a number of sentences, which you should rate according to their **acceptability**. This refers to whether a sentence sounds **good or bad** to you. This not only means if a sentence is grammatically correct, but also if it sounds "normal" or "odd". We would like to hear your personal opinion; there are no incorrect answers!)

In a subsequent word-recognition task, participants had to decide whether a certain probe word was contained in the sentence they had read before in order to control for their attention. The word-recognition task was a binary choice of "word was contained" or "word was not contained". Over all critical and filler sentences, 50% of the probe words were actually contained in sentences. For the word-recognition task, only the two keys "D" and "K" were to be pressed with the respective middle fingers; button configuration of this task corresponded to the configuration of the acceptability judgment. Participants were encouraged to rest their fingers on the keys for the whole time so that they were able to respond quickly and intuitively without the need for searching for the keys on the keyboard during the experiment.

2.4 Procedure

Participants were comfortably seated in front of a 17-inch computer screen. Stimuli were visually presented phrase-by-phrase using the software Presentation (Neurobehavioral Systems, Inc., Berkeley, CA, USA). Each trial began with an asterisk (*) as a fixation target in the center of the screen displayed for 300 ms, followed by a blank screen of 200 ms. The stimulus sentence was then presented phrase-by-phrase. One-word phrases were shown for exactly 450 ms, phrases of more than one word (e.g., prepositional phrases) were presented for 500 ms. It should be noted that all of the phrases preceding the critical positions and the critical positions themselves (viz. the object pronouns) were one-word phrases in all sentences; therefore, the difference in phrase presentation time would not affect processing of the critical region. Each phrase was followed by a blank screen of 100 ms. After each stimulus sentence, a blank screen of 500 ms was shown, followed by a question mark (?), indicating the acceptability judgment task. Participants could give their rating within 2,000 ms. Following the acceptability rating and separated by another 500 ms blank screen, the probe word of the word-recognition task was presented for a maximum duration of 2,500 ms. After the word-recognition task and before the focus asterisk of the next stimulus, a blank screen was displayed for 1,000 ms.

Participants were instructed to sit still and avoid eye blinks during the presentation of the sentences, but eye blinks were allowed when responding to the tasks after a sentence. The procedure started with a training session of ten sentences that had a structure analogous to the stimuli in the experiment itself; the experimental session followed the training session and was divided into eight blocks with short pauses between them. The duration of the whole experiment including instructions, preparation of the EEG recording, training session, experimental session, and pauses was about 3 h per participant.

2.5 EEG recording

Twenty-four Ag/AgCl sintered electrodes were applied to the scalps of the participants by means of an elastic cap to record the EEG. The left mastoid was used for the reference electrode (EEG was re-referenced off-line to linked mastoid). Four electrodes were applied above and beneath the left eye and at the outer canthi of the eyes to record the electrooculogram (EOG). AFZ served as ground. Electrode impedances were kept below 5 kΩ. The EEG was recorded using a BrainAmp EEG amplifier and BrainVision Recorder software (Brain Products GmbH, Gilching, Germany) with a sampling rate of 500 Hz. The EEG was filtered off-line with a 0.3–20.0 Hz band-pass filter. After computing the statistical analysis, an additional 8.5 Hz low-pass filter was applied to smoothen the plots for display.

2.6 Data analysis

The respective sentences with female and male nouns were combined in each condition to yield a lexically balanced 2 × 2 experimental design with 36 items per condition for the statistical analyses of the acceptability judgments and ERP data. For the analysis of the acceptability judgments, repeated-measures analyses of variance (ANOVAs) were computed with the within-factor ORDER of object pronouns (canonical ACC > DAT vs. noncanonical DAT > ACC) and PERSON of the dative pronoun (first-person singular DAT.1SG vs. third-person singular DAT.3SG) by participants (F_1) and by items (F_2). Sentences with an incorrectly answered word-recognition task, and sentences with a button press time-out in either of the two behavioral tasks were excluded from analysis.

For the analysis of the ERP data, single-participant averages were calculated for each condition in the time window 200 ms before onset of the critical word to 1,200 ms after onset. This time window was also used for EEG artifact rejections (the EOG rejection criterion was 40 µV). Subsequently, grand averages were computed over all participants. For statistical analysis, time windows were chosen on the basis of findings from previous studies on scrambling and visual inspection of the data. Comparisons of the first critical object pronouns and comparisons of the second critical object pronouns were calculated in separate statistical analyses. Repeated-measures ANOVAs involving the within-participant factors ORDER of the object pronouns (canonical ACC > DAT vs. noncanonical DAT > ACC), PERSON of the dative pronoun (first-person singular DAT.1SG vs. third-person singular DAT.3SG), and topographical region of interest (ROI) were computed for mean amplitude values per time window. Analyses were calculated separately for lateral ROIs (left-anterior: F7, F3, FC5, FC1; right-anterior: F8, F4, FC6, FC2;

left-posterior: CP1, CP5, P3, P7; right-posterior: CP2, CP6, P4, P8) and midline ROIs (one electrode per ROI: FZ; FCZ; CZ; CPZ; PZ; POZ). The correction of Huynh & Feldt (1970) was applied whenever there was more than one degree of freedom in the numerator, and Mauchly's sphericity test (Mauchly 1940) had reached significance. Trials with EEG artifacts (e.g., eye blinks) at the critical positions, and sentences with incorrect answers or button press time-outs in the word-recognition task were excluded from statistical analysis.

3 Results

3.1 Word-recognition task

The word-recognition task was designed to assess whether participants read the sentences attentively. About 89.59% of all critical sentences were correctly answered, 9.89% incorrectly, and 0.52% with a button press time-out. Sentences in this experiment were relatively long, and probe words could occur at any position in order to draw participants' attention away from the critical positions in the subordinate clause. However, this made the task more demanding, which may explain the relatively high error rate.

The first half of the experiment, and in particular, the first experimental block showed a slightly higher error rate (results of first block: 82.01% correct; 16.52% incorrect; 1.47% time-outs). The reason might be that the training session was not sufficient for some participants to familiarize themselves with the tasks. Accuracy increased in the course of the experiment, and correctly answered word-recognition tasks in the critical conditions exceeded 90% in every experimental block of the second half of the experiment. The increase in accuracy indicates that difficulty or length of the experiment did not negatively affect participants' attention over the period of the experimental run.

3.2 Acceptability judgment task

All sentences had to be rated for their acceptability on a given four-point scale. As expected, sentences with the canonical ACC > DAT order were rated more acceptable than their counterparts in DAT > ACC order. However, noncanonical sentences containing a first-person singular dative pronoun were rated even less acceptable than those with a third-person singular dative pronoun. This is rather surprising considering that the DAT > ACC order containing a first-person singular dative pronoun should be more acceptable, at least in dialects that allow both serializations (see Fleischer 2010a, 2013a). A possible explanation is discussed in Section 4.4. Means of acceptability judgments are given in Figure 1.

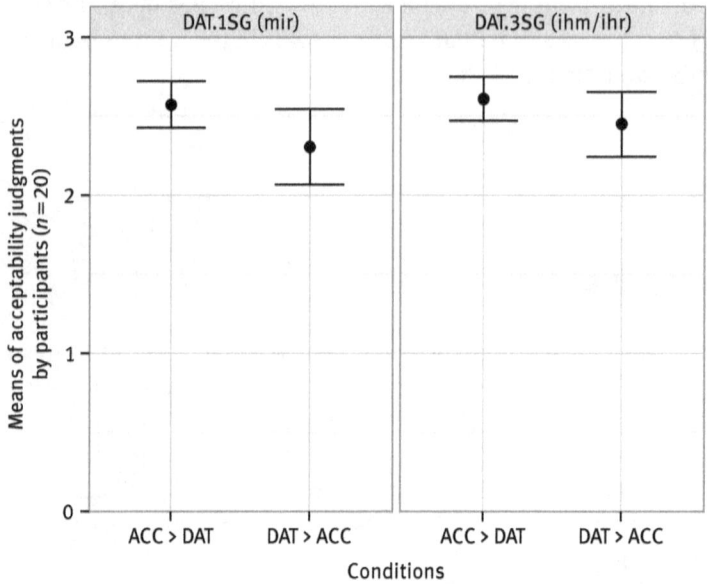

Figure 1: Means of acceptability judgments by participants (*n* = 20). On the given four-point scale, 3.0 is the highest rating ("absolutely acceptable"), 0 is the lowest rating ("not acceptable at all"). Error bars give 95% confidence intervals. The left column shows conditions containing a first-person singular dative pronoun (DAT.1SG), the right column shows conditions containing a third-person singular dative pronoun (DAT.3SG).

The ANOVA confirms significant main effects of ORDER ($F_1(1,19)$ = 5.44, $p < 0.05$; $F_2(1,35)$ = 48.07, $p < 0.001$) and PERSON ($F_1(1,19)$ = 12.95, $p < 0.01$; $F_2(1,35)$ = 13.55, $p < 0.001$), as well as an interaction ORDER × PERSON ($F_1(1,19)$ = 5.17, $p < 0.05$; $F_2(1,35)$ = 5.73, $p < 0.05$). Resolving this interaction for word order, we find a significant effect of PERSON in the noncanonical order ($F_1(1,19)$ = 18.98, $p < 0.001$; $F_2(1,35)$ = 13.19, $p < 0.001$), but no significant effect in the canonical order ($F_1(1,19)$ = 1.00, $p = 0.3$; $F_2(1,35)$ = 3.67, $p = 0.06$).

The DAT > ACC conditions received significantly lower acceptability judgments compared to the ACC > DAT conditions. Interestingly, however, noncanonical pronoun orders with an F_1 mean of 2.38 (SD: 0.5) seem to be relatively high in acceptability compared to a set of semantically implausible filler sentences (e.g., *Kilian erklärt Juliane, dass der Anwender den Computer trinkt* 'Kilian explains to

Juliane that the user is drinking the computer') that received an F_1 mean of 0.43 (SD: 0.51). The low rating of the unacceptable filler sentences indicates that participants made use of the full range of possible judgments on the four-point scale. Even though it is not trivial to compare acceptability ratings for semantic and syntactic manipulations, we may still infer that DAT > ACC pronoun orders can be considered less preferred but grammatical. Otherwise, if DAT > ACC orders were outright grammatical violations, these sentences should have received ratings at the lower end of the scale similarly to the implausible fillers.

Exploring acceptability judgments for each participant separately reveals some interindividual variation. While one group of participants rated sentences with ACC > DAT order as more acceptable than those with DAT > ACC order, another group of participants gave similar ratings to both serializations, in a few cases even with a slight advantage for the DAT > ACC order, which lends further support to the assumption that noncanonical pronoun serializations are grammatical structures. Such variability is not surprising considering the variation of pronoun orders between dialects and the standard language discussed in the introduction. Participants in the former group predominantly came from northern and central regions, whereas participants in the latter group were mostly from central and southern regions. However, due to the limited number of participants, further statistical analyses of these interindividual differences in our data set are not feasible. A systematic investigation of possible effects seems to be an interesting topic for future research.

3.3 ERP results

Our critical sentences contained two positions relevant for ERP analysis: the first and second object pronouns, for example: *dass er es mir* ... ('that he it.ACC me.DAT ...') and *dass er mir es* ... ('that he me.DAT it.ACC ...'). We will refer to the first object pronoun as the first critical position, and to the second object pronoun as the second critical position. In the following, no main effects of ROI will be reported. Visual inspection of the grand average ERPs, illustrated in Figure 2, reveals a negativity between 300 and 500 ms after pronoun onset in the DAT > ACC conditions at the second critical position, but not at the first critical position. Thus, this ERP effect seems to be a direct brain response to noncanonical pronoun orders.

The statistical analysis for the time window 300–500 ms confirms these impressions. At the first critical position (Figure 2, Panels (a) and (b)), there are no significant effects in midline ROIs. For lateral ROIs, we find an interaction ORDER × ROI ($F(3,57) = 5.28$, $p < 0.01$), and resolving this interaction for ROI, we find an effect of ORDER only in the left-posterior ROI ($F(1,19) = 6.03$, $p < 0.05$), which may be a confound caused by the earlier positivity discussed below.

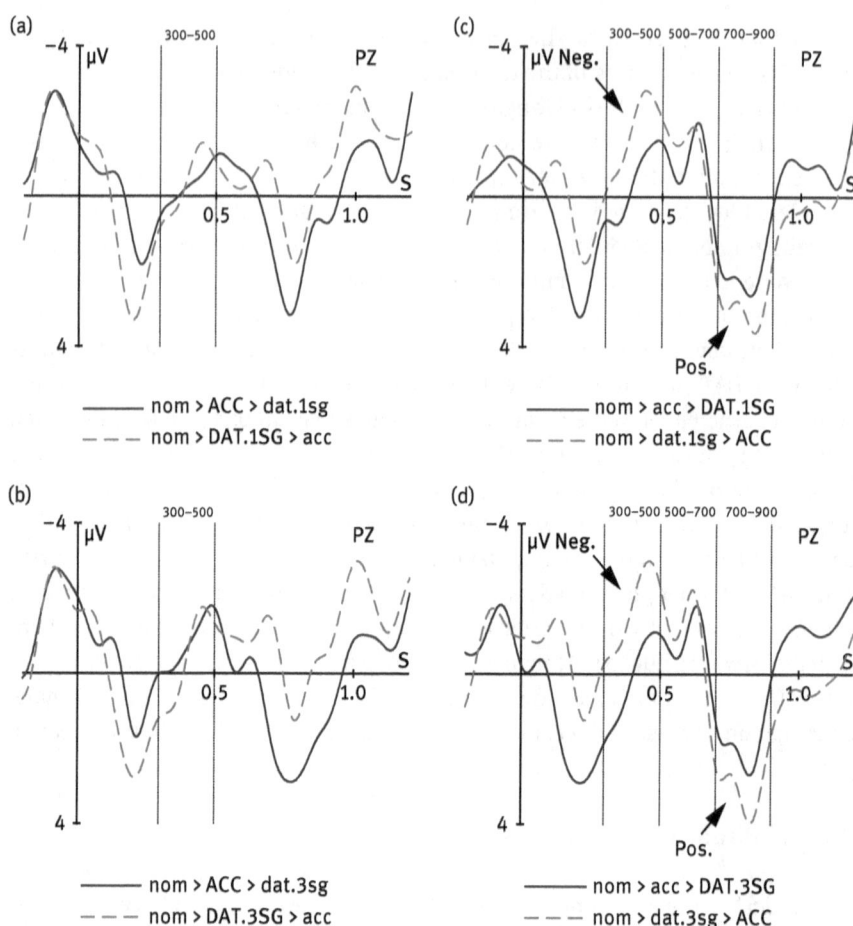

Figure 2: Grand average (*n* = 20) ERPs at the electrode site PZ. Panel (a) shows the conditions including a first-person singular dative pronoun (DAT.1SG) at the first critical position. Panel (b) shows the conditions including a third-person singular dative pronoun (DAT.3SG) at the first critical position. Panel (c) shows the conditions including a first-person singular dative pronoun (DAT.1SG) at the second critical position. Panel (d) shows the conditions including a third-person singular dative pronoun (DAT.3SG) at the second critical position. The critical positions are set in capitals in the legend (e.g., nom > ACC > dat.1sg). The solid lines indicate canonical orders and the dashed lines noncanonical orders. Negativity is plotted upward.

At the second critical position (Figure 2, Panels (c) and (d)), we find a clear main effect of ORDER in midline ROIs ($F(1,19) = 25.30$, $p < 0.001$) and lateral ROIs ($F(1,19) = 27.78$, $p < 0.001$), as well as an interaction of PERSON × ROI (midline ROIs: $F(5,95) = 7.80$, $p < 0.01$; lateral ROIs: $F(3,57) = 6.26$, $p < 0.01$). In lateral

ROIs, we also find an interaction of ORDER × ROI ($F(3,57) = 9.88, p < 0.001$) and ORDER × PERSON × ROI ($F(3,57) = 3.51, p < 0.05$). Resolving the interactions by ROI reveals significant ORDER effects in all lateral ROIs ($F_{max} = 50.93$ in the left-posterior ROI, $F_{min} = 7.90$ in the right-anterior ROI; $p < 0.05$ in the right-anterior ROI, all other $ps < 0.001$), but no PERSON effects or interactions of ORDER × PERSON (all $ps > 0.1$).

The broadly distributed negativity observed at the second position seems to be affected only by the factor word order. If the choice of person of the dative pronouns had elicited an effect, we would have expected an interaction of word order with person at the second critical position in the DAT > ACC order. However, in contrast to the person effect reported for the acceptability judgment task, grand average ERPs do not show a corresponding neurophysiological effect. Therefore, we will combine first- and third-person conditions in Figures 3, 4, and 5 for reasons of clarity and comprehensibility.

The ERPs in Figure 2 show an early positivity between 100 and 300 ms after pronoun onset for the dative pronouns at both the first and second critical positions. In language studies with visual word presentation, ERP effects in this early time window may be caused, for example, by differences in word length (Van Petten & Kutas 1990; Osterhout, Bersick & McKinnon 1997; Osterhout, Allen &

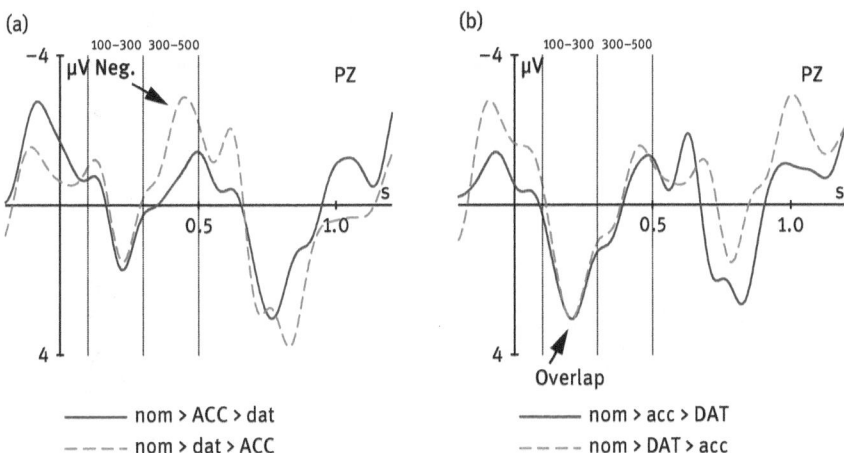

Figure 3: Grand average ($n = 20$) ERPs at the electrode site PZ. Panel (a) shows a comparison of the accusative pronouns at the first and second critical positions. Panel (b) shows a comparison of the dative pronouns at the first and second critical positions. The critical positions are set in capitals in the legend (e.g., nom > ACC > dat). First- and third-person conditions have been combined. The solid lines indicate canonical orders and the dashed lines noncanonical orders. Negativity is plotted upward.

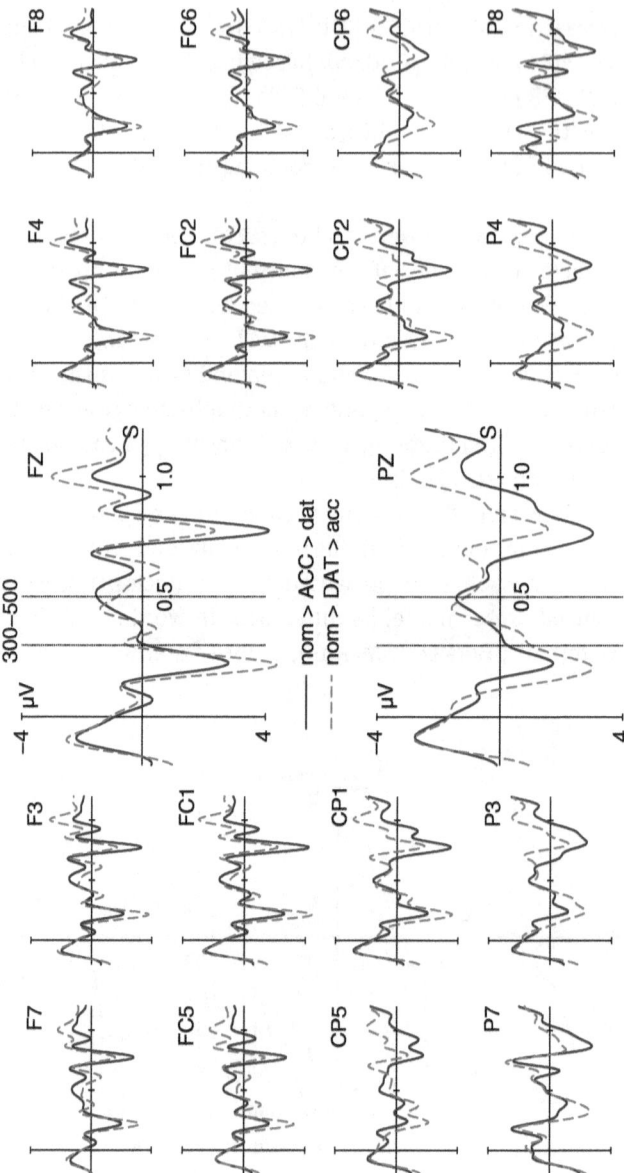

Figure 4: Grand average (*n* = 20) ERPs at selected electrode sites. Contrast of canonical ACC > DAT order and noncanonical DAT > ACC order is shown at the first critical position. The critical positions are set in capitals in the legend (e.g., nom > ACC > dat). First- and third-person conditions have been combined. The solid lines indicate canonical orders and the dashed lines noncanonical orders. Negativity is plotted upward.

Scrambled Wackernagel! Neural responses to pronoun serializations — 229

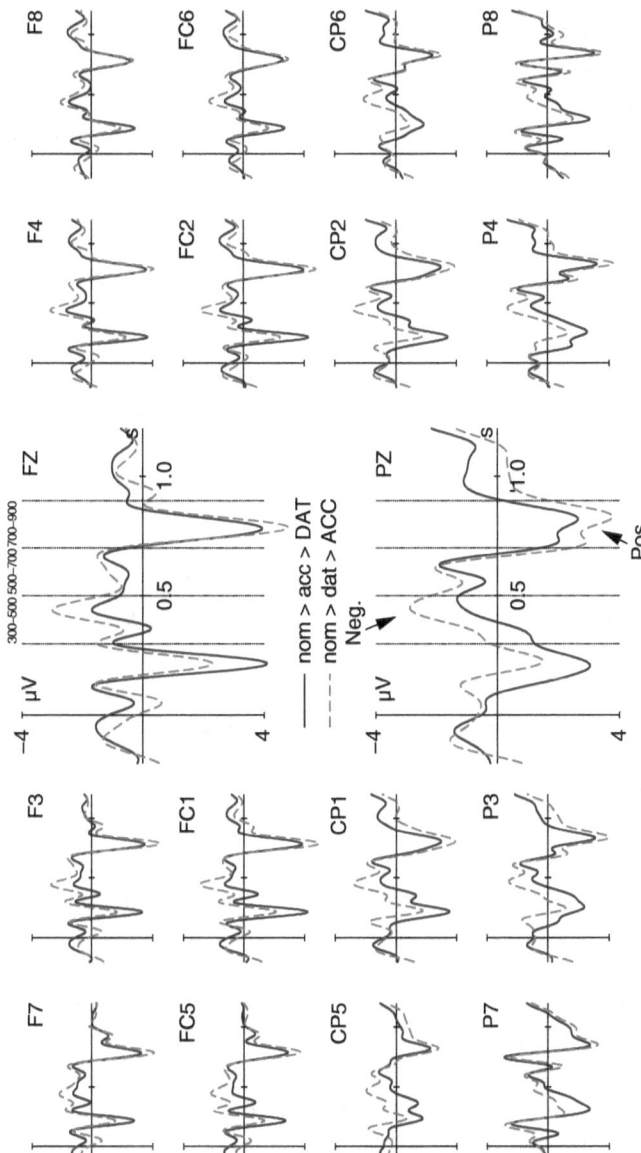

Figure 5: Grand average (*n* = 20) ERPs at selected electrode sites. Contrast of canonical ACC > DAT order and noncanonical DAT > ACC order is shown at the second critical position. The critical positions are set in capitals in the legend (e.g., nom > acc > DAT). First- and third-person conditions have been combined. The solid lines indicate canonical orders and the dashed lines noncanonical orders. Negativity is plotted upward.

McLaughlin 2002; Hauk & Pulvermüller 2004). And indeed, the early effect completely vanishes in visual inspection when plotting the identical pronoun forms to cancel out the difference in word length. Figure 3 shows the comparisons of the two accusative pronouns (e.g., *dass er es mir* ... vs. *dass er mir es* ...), and the two dative pronouns (e.g., *dass er es mir* ... vs. *dass er mir es* ...), respectively. Importantly, however, the word order effect in the 300–500 ms time window is still observable (see Figure 3, Panel (a)), which shows that this effect is indeed elicited by the noncanonical order and is not a confound induced by word length differences or other lexical effects.

This being said, we will not interpret any later ERP effects (later than 500 ms after pronoun onset) at the first critical position (see Figure 4) because these are confounded by the overlapping early effects of the immediately following second critical position, due to the fast word presentation rate (in other words, it is difficult to dissociate a late positivity at the first critical position from an early positivity at the second critical position). We do, however, consider later ERP effects at the second critical position because this position is always followed by the same lexical material irrespective of pronoun order (e.g., *letzte Woche* 'last week' in *dass er es mir letzte Woche* ... vs. *dass er mir es letzte Woche* ...). We can thus rule out a confounding lexical effect of the following word on the late ERP components at the second critical position.

At the second critical position, we also examined two later time windows: 500–700 and 700–900 ms. Grand average ERPs for selected electrodes are shown in Figure 5, with first and third person conditions combined. In the time window between 500 and 700 ms after pronoun onset, we observed a small negative deflection in the noncanonical order, which is most probably a continuation of the negativity reported for the time window 300–500 ms above. ANOVAs reveal a main effect of ORDER in lateral ROIs ($F(1,19) = 6.06$, $p < 0.05$), and an interaction of ORDER × PERSON × ROI in midline ROIs ($F(5,95) = 4.07$, $p < 0.05$), but no interaction of ORDER × PERSON for any of the midline electrodes when resolving the interaction by ROI (all $ps > 0.09$).

The last time window between 700 and 900 ms after pronoun onset gives the impression of a more positive deflection in the noncanonical order. ANOVAs confirm a main effect of ORDER (midline ROIs: $F(1,19) = 11.36$, $p < 0.01$; lateral ROIs: $F(1,19) = 8.01$, $p < 0.05$) and an interaction of ORDER × ROI (midline ROIs: $F(5,95) = 4.69$, $p < 0.05$; lateral ROIs: $F(3,57) = 4.00$, $p < 0.05$), but again no effect of PERSON or interaction of ORDER × PERSON. Resolving the interactions by ROI, we find significant ORDER effects in all midline ROIs ($F_{max} = 11.62$ at PZ, $F_{min} = 6.06$ at FZ; $p < 0.05$ at FZ, all other $ps < 0.01$), and in all lateral ROIs except for the right-anterior ROI (left-anterior ROI: $F(1,19) = 17.07$, $p < 0.001$; left-posterior ROI: $F(1,19) = 8.67$, $p < 0.01$; right-posterior ROI: $F(1,19) = 5.34$, $p < 0.05$).

4 Discussion

In the present ERP study, we sought to investigate neurocognitive signatures of different serializations of unstressed personal pronouns in the German middlefield. The pronoun sequence DAT > ACC was rated less acceptable in the acceptability judgments, and the ERPs showed a broadly distributed negativity (within a time window of 300–500 ms after pronoun onset) followed by a late positivity (700–900 ms) at the position of the deviant accusative neuter pronoun *es* ('it') in DAT > ACC sentences. At a first glance, these findings seem to corroborate accounts in the theoretical literature claiming that DAT > ACC is an ungrammatical structure, and it is obligatory for pronouns to occur in the canonical ACC > DAT order. However, there are good reasons to argue in favor of an analysis that DAT > ACC is a less preferred yet grammatical structure, similar to scrambling of full DPs. First, the acceptability ratings, though lower for the noncanonical serialization, are still relatively high on the given four-point scale, whereas implausible filler sentences were rated drastically lower, suggesting that the DAT > ACC order of pronouns was processed as a less acceptable but well-formed structure. Second, the negativity in the ERP resembles the "scrambling negativity" effect that was reported for full DPs in noncanonical but grammatical word orders in previous scrambling studies (e.g., Bornkessel et al. 2002; Schlesewsky et al. 2003). A syntactic violation typically engenders a late positivity (P600) in the ERP (e.g., Osterhout & Holcomb 1992; Hagoort, Brown & Groothusen 1993) – particularly in conjunction with a judgment task. We observed a late positivity in the noncanonical pronoun orders, but we will show that this late ERP effect is not identical in its latency and amplitude to the P600 effects that are often observed for ungrammatical or deeply implausible sentences (see Van de Meerendonk, Kolk, Vissers & Chwilla 2010). Therefore, an interpretation of a more general well-formedness evaluation may be better suited (see Bornkessel & Schlesewsky 2006b).

4.1 The scrambling negativity as a reflex to syntactic template updating

Previous studies on scrambling have reported a scrambling negativity for scrambled DPs (e.g., Bornkessel et al. 2002; Schlesewsky et al. 2003). Schlesewsky et al. (2003) suggested that the scrambling negativity should be interpreted as a neural response to a violation of canonicity principles (for converging findings from a functional MRI study, see Grewe et al. 2005). We would like to adopt this functional interpretation of the scrambling negativity as a general index of a canonicity violation in order to explain the negativity observed in the noncanonical pronoun order in our experiment. However, while the scrambling negativity is typically elicited at the position of the scrambled DP, we observed the negativity at the last pronoun. In this section we will present an explanation for this difference in light of predictive processes during online language comprehension.

A sentence unfolds over time and is processed incrementally, that is, the parser makes rapid use of incoming words and integrates syntactic, semantic, and phonological information (Marslen-Wilson 1975). One suggestion as to why this process can be so rapid is that it makes use of syntactic templates, that is, phrase structure representations stored in long-term memory (for various approaches making this assumption, though they differ in many other respects, see, e.g., Frazier 1989; Vosse & Kempen 2000, 2008; Townsend & Bever 2001; Bornkessel & Schlesewsky 2006b, 2006c; Van Valin 2006; Hagoort 2005, 2013; Arbib & Lee 2008; Bornkessel-Schlesewsky & Schlesewsky 2013; Barrès & Lee 2014). The key assumption of template-based approaches is that, during the parsing process, those templates are activated that are compatible with the incoming input and with the predictions on the upcoming structure. In the following, we will propose a processing account of word order variation in German that uses very basic syntactic templates describing the linear order of constituents (see also Konietzko & Lidzba, this volume, for another application of templates in psycholinguistic research on noncanonical word orders). It should thus be compatible with various strands of syntactic theories and sentence comprehension models. We will make use of templates mostly to illustrate how incremental processing leads to ERP responses at different positions in a sentence. Crucially, we understand the notion of syntactic templates in a psychological rather than a neurobiological way for the purposes of the chapter, and while this concept is very useful for a model of sentence parsing, we do not assume that syntactic templates (trees, constructions) correspond to actual neural circuits in the brain (see Bornkessel-Schlesewsky & Schlesewsky 2015). Thus, when we speak of "activating" or "updating" templates in this chapter, we refer to cognitive processes, but we do not attempt to explicate how these are neurobiologically grounded. Furthermore, we would like to emphasize that we do not intend to develop a syntactic theory based on templates. The templates used in the following represent the linear order of constituents, and we limit the syntactic and semantic information included in the templates to the minimum necessary for our purposes.

A canonical German sentence like *Gestern hat der Lehrer dem Schüler das Buch ausgeliehen* (lit.: yesterday has [the teacher].NOM [the student].DAT [the book].ACC lent 'Yesterday the teacher lent the student the book') may be represented mentally by the syntactic template (7a). A scrambled sentence like *Gestern hat dem Schüler der Lehrer das Buch ausgeliehen* (lit.: yesterday has [the student].DAT [the teacher].NOM [the book].ACC lent) may have the mental representation of the template (7b). Both sentences use the same basic template with three arguments and a ditransitive verb, but in (7a) the first argument slot is associated with the NOM subject, whereas in (7b) it is filled with the DAT IO.[10]

(7) a. ADV+AUX+ARG$_{[NOM]}$+ARG$_{[DAT]}$+ARG$_{[ACC]}$+VERB$_{[DITRANS]}$
    b. ADV+AUX+ARG$_{[DAT]}$+ARG$_{[NOM]}$+ARG$_{[ACC]}$+VERB$_{[DITRANS]}$

Templates such as those in (7) represent complete sentences, but do not take into account the dynamic nature of sentence processing. An initially activated syntactic template will likely need to be changed or updated during the comprehension process. For economy reasons, it seems undesirable to assume that *all* possible templates are activated simultaneously. It appears more likely that the parser only activates those templates that represent canonical continuations and require the fewest additional assumptions, as proposed by the "minimality principle" (Bornkessel & Schlesewsky 2006b; Bornkessel-Schlesewsky & Schlesewsky 2009). At the beginning of a sentence with no further information available to the parser, an intransitive construction as the minimal canonical structure is predicted and the respective template is activated. At each new word during incremental processing, the parser evaluates the template that has been activated and tries to integrate the word. If a word does not match the predicted template, the parser will update the existing template to accommodate the new input. Depending on the type of mismatch, specific ERP responses such as the scrambling negativity will be elicited.

As a notational convention for all templates in the following examples, the position currently available to the parser during incremental processing will be underlined, and all subsequent positions will be set in italic font. The italicized positions are predicted on grounds of previously processed information, but actual lexical items filling the positions are yet unknown. It has been suggested that languages with a flexible word order, like German, make use of bare templates without grammatical functions or other relational information (e.g., Bornkessel & Schlesewsky 2006b; Van Valin 2006). However, the syntactic templates in the following will not only contain categorial information but also include the possible case of each argument and transitivity of the final verb according to the predictions built up at the current position.

---

10 Abbreviations used in templates: ACC (accusative case), ACC|DAT (accusative case or dative case), ADV (adverb), ARG (argument), AUX (auxiliary verb), COMP (complementizer), DAT (dative case), DAT-INTRANS (intransitive verb selecting a dative object), DITRANS (ditransitive verb), INTRANS (intransitive verb), NOM (nominative case), NON-PRO (non-pronominal), PRO (pronominal), TRANS (transitive verb).

In the following we will discuss previous studies on scrambling as well as our results on pronoun order to show how template parsing based on the prediction of a canonical serialization respecting minimality can explain the presence or absence of a scrambling negativity during sentence comprehension. Schlesewsky et al. (2003) contrasted the processing of object-before-subject orders in the German middlefield including either a nonpronominal or a pronominal object. They found that an initial nonpronominal object (e.g., *Gestern hat den Schnuller der Vater* ... , lit.: yesterday has [the pacifier].ACC [the father].NOM ...) gave rise to a scrambling negativity, whereas an initial pronominal object (e.g., *Gestern hat ihn der Vater* ... , lit: yesterday has it.ACC [the father].NOM ...) did not engender such an ERP effect. The latter construction, even though being object-before-subject, is perfectly natural in German because of the fronting of unstressed pronouns to the Wackernagel position and does not violate canonicity principles.

The canonicity violation causing the scrambling negativity reported in Schlesewsky et al. (2003) can be better understood when we consider the canonical templates that are predicted immediately before the first argument is processed. At the position of the finite auxiliary (e.g. *hat* 'has'), which indicates the beginning of the middlefield, we posit that three canonical templates are activated, which are given in (8). Template (8a) is activated because of a general subject-first preference that is found across languages (e.g., Frazier 1987; Bader & Meng 1999; see also, e.g., Haupt et al. 2008, for neurophysiological evidence). Templates (8b) and (8c) are activated because of the language-specific Wackernagel position and the high occurrence frequency of pronominal constituents. Template (8b) is minimally complex including only one single argument: the subject pronoun. Template (8c) represents an object pronoun followed by a nonpronominal subject but is still a canonical continuation (see also Bornkessel-Schlesewsky & Schlesewsky 2009). Alternatively, (8b) and (8c) could be combined into one single template containing an auxiliary followed by a pronoun in the Wackernagel position with case unspecified. Since all templates in (8) can be considered canonical, no scrambling negativity is expected at an initial nonpronominal subject or any initial pronoun irrespective of case marking, as was shown in Schlesewsky et al. (2003).[11]

---

[11] Note that in German, the verb *haben* ('have') can be used as an auxiliary for the perfect tense and as a full verb (similar to English: "he has worked a lot" and "he has a good job"). In the templates given in (8), we propose that the parser analyzes the verb *hat* ('has') as an auxiliary because it is preceded by an adverb like *gestern* ('yesterday'), suggesting a past event. Formally, at the position of *hat* the parser could also opt for an interpretation of *hat* as a full verb, indicating a possession relation. This would not affect the expectation of the immediately following phrase because that phrase would still be either a subject-DP or a pronoun. But the interpretation as a full verb might have an effect on the overall template because *hat* as a full verb is transitive

(8) Canonical templates for *Gestern hat...*, lit.: yesterday has...
   a. ADV+AUX[PERFECT]+*ARG*[NON-PRO, NOM]+*VERB*[INTRANS]
      (e.g., *Gestern hat der Lehrer gelacht*, lit.: yesterday has the teacher laughed)
   b. ADV+AUX[PERFECT]+*ARG*[PRO, NOM]+*VERB*[INTRANS]
      (e.g., *Gestern hat er gelacht*, lit.: yesterday has he laughed)
   c. ADV+AUX[PERFECT]+*ARG*[PRO, ACC|DAT]+*ARG*[NON-PRO, NOM]+*VERB*[TRANS]
      (e.g., *Gestern hat ihn der Schüler gegrüßt*, lit.: yesterday has him.ACC [the student].NOM greeted)

Further support in favor of a dynamic activation of templates comes from scrambling studies with initial nonpronominal dative objects. If a dative object was preceded by a finite auxiliary in a verb-second main clause (e.g., *Gestern hat dem Sohn der Vater ...* , lit.: yesterday has [the son].DAT [the father].NOM ...), the DAT > NOM order gave rise to a scrambling negativity at the initial dative object (Schlesewsky et al. 2003). Interestingly, however, if the dative object occurred in a subordinate clause and was preceded by a complementizer (e.g., *dass* 'that'), no scrambling negativity was observed (Bornkessel et al. 2002). This difference can be accounted for if we assume that the parser activates the four canonical continuations in (9) when encountering the complementizer *dass* introducing a subordinate clause. Templates (9a–c) correspond to the templates (8a–c) for verb-second clauses, respectively. Template (9d), though dative-initial, is a canonical German subordinate clause; hence, no scrambling negativity is engendered. However, such a continuation will be barred if the dative object is preceded by the finite auxiliary *hat* instead of a complementizer (see Bornkessel et al. 2002; see also Kretzschmar 2010, for converging support from a combined EEG and eye-tracking study). When encountering the finite auxiliary in second position, only the main clause templates in (8) are possible, but an initial dative object results in a scrambling negativity because there is no compatible canonical template available (e.g., **Gestern hat dem Schüler geholfen wird*, lit: yesterday has the student helped is). The only exception would be a dative object experiencer verb (e.g., *Offensichtlich hat dem Schüler der Roman gefallen*, lit.: obviously has [the student].DAT [the novel].NOM appealed-to 'Obviously, the student found the novel appealing'). Such verbs require a different thematic ordering and hence allow an unmarked object-before-subject order (see, e.g., Bornkessel, Schlesewsky & Friederici 2003b, for a discussion). Interestingly, however, the legitimization of

---

(e.g., *Heute hat der Lehrer keine Zeit*, lit.: today has the teacher no time), and thus intransitive templates such as (8a) or (8b) would be ruled out.

the object-initial order due to a possibly upcoming object experiencer verb does not seem to be strong enough to prevent a scrambling negativity at the DAT DP following the auxiliary *hat* (see also Schlesewsky & Bornkessel 2006).

(9) Canonical templates for *Franz sagte Xaver, dass...*, lit.: Franz told Xaver that...
    a. COMP+*ARG*$_{[\text{NON-PRO, NOM}]}$+*VERB*$_{[\text{INTRANS}]}$
       (e.g., *...dass der Lehrer gelacht hat*, lit.: that the teacher laughed has)
    b. COMP+*ARG*$_{[\text{PRO, NOM}]}$+*VERB*$_{[\text{INTRANS}]}$
       (e.g., *...dass er gelacht hat*, lit.: that he laughed has)
    c. COMP+*ARG*$_{[\text{PRO, ACC|DAT}]}$+*ARG*$_{[\text{NON-PRO, NOM}]}$+*VERB*$_{[\text{TRANS}]}$
       (e.g., *...dass ihn der Schüler gegrüßt hat,* lit.: that him.ACC [the student]. NOM greeted has)
    d. COMP+*ARG*$_{[\text{NON-PRO, DAT}]}$+*VERB*$_{[\text{DAT-INTRANS, PASSIVE}]}$
       (e.g., *...dass dem Schüler geholfen wird,* lit. that [the student].DAT helped is)

In order to account for the scrambling negativity in our data, we must discuss which syntactic templates match the structural predictions at the different positions in the sentence. If we follow the interpretation of the scrambling negativity as indicating a canonicity violation, then why was the negativity in our experiment observed only at the position of the last pronoun (i.e., the second object pronoun) in the deviant order (e.g., ... *er ihm es* ... 'he.NOM him.DAT it.ACC'), but not before? Upon closer consideration, this is not surprising. At each word, the parser expects a canonical sequence to unfold, and as long as canonicity principles are not violated, no scrambling negativity will be engendered. At the position of the dative pronoun in the DAT > ACC order, the sentence might well have a canonical continuation because the following words, especially the verb of the subordinate clause providing the subcategorization frame, have not been processed yet. Possible templates that are activated at the dative pronoun are illustrated in (10). A minimal canonical continuation would include an intransitive verb requiring a dative object such as *helfen* ('help'), yielding a perfectly well-formed sentence like (10a). An alternative canonical but more complex completion would involve a nonpronominal accusative object and a ditransitive verb like (10b).[12] Importantly, the parser can detect a noncanonical pronoun order only at the second object pronoun in DAT > ACC order.

---

12 Note that under experimental conditions, some participants may develop confounding processing strategies when structurally similar sentences are presented repeatedly. Thus, we included different constructions as filler sentences so that participants were not trained to always anticipate a three-pronoun combination in the experiment (see also Section 2).

(10) Canonical templates for *Franz sagte Xaver, dass er ihm...,* lit: Franz told Xaver that he him...
   a. COMP+ARG[PRO, NOM]+<u>ARG[PRO, DAT]</u>+*VERB*[DAT-INTRANS]
      (e.g., *...dass er ihm geholfen hat,* lit.: that he him.DAT helped has)
   b. COMP+ARG[PRO, NOM]+<u>ARG[PRO, DAT]</u>+*ARG*[NON-PRO, ACC]+*VERB*[DITRANS]
      (e.g., *...dass er ihm das Buch ausgeliehen hat,* lit.: that he him.DAT [the book].ACC lent has)

The order ACC > DAT is the canonical order, and indeed this serialization did not engender a scrambling negativity at the second object pronoun. However, if we assume minimality, it might seem unclear why the parser in our experiment should activate the template (11a) with a ditransitive verb after processing the accusative pronoun. It could be argued that this complex structure violates minimality because there is still the simpler canonical template (11b) available: a transitive construction without an additional dative argument.

(11) Canonical templates for *Franz sagte Xaver, dass er es...,* lit.: Franz told Xaver that he it...
   a. COMP+ARG[PRO, NOM]+<u>ARG[PRO, ACC]</u>+*ARG*[PRO, DAT]+*VERB*[DITRANS]
      (e.g., *...dass er es ihm ausgeliehen hat,* lit.: that he it.ACC him.DAT lent has)
   b. COMP+ARG[PRO, NOM]+<u>ARG[PRO, ACC]</u>+*VERB*[TRANS]
      (e.g., *...dass er es gekauft hat,* lit.: that he it.ACC bought has)

One possibility is that even more complex templates are activated in addition to the minimal templates, as long as they are canonical and motivated by the sentence fragment processed so far. Following this reasoning, the three-pronoun template (11a) is quite likely to be activated because the constituent order is canonical, and two human referents have been introduced in the matrix clause, which suggests that a dative pronoun referring to one of the two human referents is highly probable to occur, even though this would not be the minimally complex structure.

It is reasonable to assume that a scrambling negativity is elicited when the input does not match the predicted canonical templates. Taking together the results from previous scrambling studies and this study, scrambling negativities occurred at different positions for nonpronominal and pronominal constituents, but a unifying trigger for this effect seems to be the detection of a canonicity violation that requires an updating of the activated template. This detection is possible at the scrambled DP in scrambling studies with nonpronominal DPs, but only later in pronoun studies because of the specific constraints of pronoun order. Although not the minimal structure, the ACC > DAT pronoun order as the canonical serialization is still activated and thus does not require a costly updating of the template. By contrast, the DAT > ACC pronoun order is indeed noncanonical and not motivated by any previous input or structural predictions, and thus completely unexpected; therefore, neither of the canonical templates that have been activated match the input, and the template therefore needs to be updated resulting in a scrambling negativity at the last pronoun. Thus, the scrambling negativity can be viewed as a neurophysiological reflex whenever the previous syntactic prediction of a canonical sequence must be revised and changed into a noncanonical yet grammatical continuation. Interestingly, even unexpected *canonical* continuations may result in a negativity, which was shown for an accusative object following the subject in an embedded wh-clause when the parser predicted an intransitive construction due to minimality (Bornkessel, Fiebach & Friederici 2004). Further parallels between such negativities will be discussed in the next section.

4.2 Parallels between the scrambling negativity and the N400

We have seen that syntactic templates representing minimal canonical continuations are predicted, and a prediction mismatch results in a scrambling negativity. Such predictions are not only relevant in the context of the scrambling negativity. There is ample evidence that the processing system builds up predictions what word to expect next in a sentence (Kamide 2008). Similar mechanisms of prediction may be involved in both sentence production and comprehension (Pickering & Garrod 2007, 2013), and beyond language (Friston 2005, 2010). A well-studied ERP correlate indicating the violation of a semantic expectation is the N400, a negative deflection between ~300 and ~500 ms after stimulus onset, often with a centroparietal scalp topography (Kutas & Hillyard 1984; see Federmeier 2007; Kutas, DeLong & Smith 2011, for reviews). Interestingly, the scrambling negativity occurs within the same time window as the N400, and it could be argued that both ERP components reflect some sort of prediction violation (Dröge et al. 2016). The N400 is engendered when an incoming element does not match the semantic prediction; the scrambling negativity is engendered when the structural prediction is not fulfilled and the currently activated syntactic template needs to be updated. The difference in topography (the scrambling negativity is broadly distributed) may not indicate two functionally distinct ERP components, but rather partially different sets of neural generators that are involved in the different kinds of predictions.

Indeed, parallels between negative ERP components in the time window 300–500 ms have recently been suggested by some authors. Molinaro, Barber and Carreiras (2011) propose that the so-called left-anterior negativity observed for agreement violations could be viewed as an expectancy violation to morphosyntactic cues, comparable to the N400 as an expectancy violation to semantic cues. Another ERP component, the ELAN, that is typically engendered by certain phrase structure violations may be interpreted as a mismatch to an expected syntactic structure (Lau et al. 2006; Hagoort 2009; Kaan 2009; see also Dikker, Rabagliati & Pylkkänen 2009; Dikker, Rabagliati, Farmer & Pylkkänen 2010).

The idea of predictions during online sentence comprehension seems compatible with predictive coding in the brain (see Friston 2005, 2010). Predictions may be considered part of an internal model that is built up during language processing. Bornkessel-Schlesewsky & Schlesewsky (2015) suggest a neurobiological model with a unifying account of negative ERP components as reflexes to prediction mismatches, which was extended with a recent neurocomputational approach by Alday (2015). The canonical ACC > DAT order for pronouns appears to be a strong component of such an internal model. Thus, an unexpected DAT > ACC order requires an updating of the internal model, which seems associated with the elicitation of the scrambling negativity.

4.3 The late positivity indicating an evaluation of well-formedness

In addition to the scrambling negativity, the noncanonical pronoun order elicited a late positivity in the time window between 700 and 900 ms after pronoun onset. At a first glance, this effect may well be interpreted as a P600 (Osterhout & Holcomb 1992) or Syntactic Positive Shift (SPS) (Hagoort et al. 1993). The P600 was initially interpreted as a reflex to syntactic anomalies, and it could be argued that the reversed pronoun order in the present study triggers some sort of syntactic reanalysis. However, P600 effects are also found for strong orthographic or semantic violations (Münte, Heinze, Matzke, Wieringa & Johannes 1998; Van de Meerendonk et al. 2010). The P600 might thus be better understood as a more general neural response to a detection of an anomaly as an improbable event, which is compatible with the hypothesis that the P600 is a member of the P300 component family. The P300 is an ERP component that is sensitive to stimulus probability and saliency, and typically found in auditory or visual oddball paradigms (see Donchin 1981; Polich 2007, for reviews). A number of studies have pointed out parallels between the P300 and P600, showing a similar influence of probability and saliency on the P600 during sentence comprehension (Gunter, Stowe & Mulder 1997; Coulson, King & Kutas 1998; Hahne & Friederici 1999). Furthermore, both the P300 and the P600 show categorization-related effects (Kretzschmar 2010; Bornkessel-Schlesewsky et al. 2011; Sassenhagen, Schlesewsky & Bornkessel-Schlesewsky 2014; Sassenhagen & Bornkessel-Schlesewsky 2015; Dröge et al. 2016). In the following, we will take a closer look at the late positivity in our data and discuss several reasons why an interpretation in terms of a reflex to a syntactic violation seems unlikely. As an alternative explanation, we will advance an account suggesting a more general evaluation of well-formedness, which is not syntax-specific.

First, a P600 is not always engendered after a scrambling negativity. Indeed, most scrambling studies have not reported P600 effects[13] (Rösler et al. 1998; Bornkessel et al. 2002, 2003a; Schlesewsky et al. 2003; Bornkessel & Schlesewsky 2006a). Dröge et al. (2016) found a late positivity following the scrambling negativity, which they ascribe to a strong binary categorization effect due to a contextually induced expectation mismatch. Considering the absence of typical P600 effects in most previous scrambling studies, it seems questionable why a noncanonical pronoun order eliciting a scrambling negativity should give rise to such a P600 effect.

Second, the late positivity in the current study differs in latency from previous P600 effects to syntactic anomalies. Most P600 effects start about 500 ms after stimulus onset (e.g., Hagoort et al. 1993), whereas our effect only begins after 700 ms. Note that the latency difference cannot be explained by the complexity of the lexical items because pronouns are extremely short closed-class words that should lead to shorter rather than longer latencies. In fact, it has been suggested that we should distinguish an earlier and a later subcomponent of the P600 (Hagoort & Brown 2000; Kaan, Harris, Gibson & Holcomb 2000; Friederici, Mecklinger, Spencer, Steinhauer & Donchin 2001; Barber & Carreiras 2005; Molinaro et al. 2011). Interpretations of those P600 subcomponents in the literature differ to some extent. For example, Kaan et al. (2000) discuss an earlier stage of the P600 between 500 and 700 ms and a later stage between 700 and 900 ms. One of the possible explanations suggested is that "the positivity between 700–900 ms may be an index of the energy needed to (re)activate an alternative representation in order to integrate the current input with it" (Kaan et al. 2000: 190). This seems to match our assumption that an unexpected syntactic template needs to be activated in the noncanonical conditions; however, we would rather consider the scrambling negativity to reflect such an activation of an alternative representation, and the late positivity to instantiate an evaluation of the well-formedness of the structure. Bornkessel & Schlesewsky (2006b) differentiate two functionally different late positive components: if a grammatical function needs to be reanalyzed, a P600 effect is engendered, whereas an ill-formed structure gives rise to

---

[13] Note that some studies (Bornkessel et al. 2003a; Bornkessel & Schlesewsky 2006a) report an earlier "focus positivity", which is different from the later P600 to syntactic anomalies. However, it might be the case that both positivities are related to the P300 component if we pursue an interpretation in terms of more general processing mechanisms (but see some counterarguments in Bornkessel et al. 2003a).

a late positivity during a processing phase of well-formedness evaluation and repair.[14] The positivity in our study seems to be very well compatible with such an interpretation in terms of a well-formedness evaluation.

Third, the late positivity in our study does not only have a late effect onset, it also seems relatively small in amplitude compared to other studies reporting very pronounced positive deflections to syntactic anomalies. Previous studies showed that P600 amplitude is dependent on the saliency of the syntactic violations (see also Coulson et al. 1998), and that P600 effects to syntactic violations were larger than P600 effects to grammatical but dispreferred structures (Osterhout, Holcomb & Swinney 1994; Kaan & Swaab 2003). Considering the relatively high acceptability ratings of our noncanonical conditions, it seems unreasonable to interpret the late positivity as a reflex to an outright syntactic violation. If we take the DAT > ACC order to be a dispreferred yet grammatical structure, this might explain the rather small effect amplitude.

Summing up, the late effect onset and relatively small amplitude point toward an interpretation of the late positivity as a well-formedness evaluation of a dispreferred but grammatical structure. Such an explanation is also compatible with the absence of a P600 in previous scrambling studies, and with the hypothesis that the P600 may be a member of the P300 component family, that is, an index of more general cognitive processes.

4.4 An unexpected person effect?

The ERP data did not show any reliable person effects, but somewhat surprisingly the acceptability ratings showed that noncanonical sentences with a first-person singular dative pronoun were rated even less acceptable than those with a third-person singular dative pronoun. Recall that data from Central German dialects suggested a bias toward a DAT > ACC order for first-person singular dative pronouns (Fleischer 2010a, 2013a; Fleischer et al. 2012). Thus, if person had an influence on the acceptability in the standard language at all, we would expect the first-person conditions to be more acceptable than the third-person conditions, which is contrary to what we found. A possible explanation of the behavioral data could be a parsing advantage of the third-person dative pronouns because the matrix clause always provided a possible human referent for these pronouns. By contrast, first-person pronouns are indexical referring to the speaker of an

---

[14] Note that Bornkessel & Schlesewsky (2006b) emphasize that their model-theoretic distinction of the two late positivities does not implicate whether these two ERP components differ in latencies.

utterance, and they do not need an antecedent in the sentence to establish an anaphoric reference. However, since two possible antecedents were introduced in the matrix clause, but the "speaker" had to be imagined by the participants in the experiment, third-person pronouns may have indeed been preferred under these experimental conditions. Note that in the ACC > DAT sequences, we did not find a person difference in the acceptability judgments suggesting that integration of the first-person dative pronoun was facilitated if pronoun order was canonical.

4.5 How can psycholinguistic findings inform syntactic theory building?

Experiments provide an important basis for linguistic research (see also Gerbrich, Schreier & Featherston, this volume). Psycholinguistic and neurolinguistic methods not only allow valuable insights into the cognition of language but can also inform theoretical approaches to German syntax. Even though we cannot measure "grammaticality" directly, experimental data provide the empirical foundation for theories of grammar. When an experimental condition is rated acceptable in a controlled experiment and this condition even produces cognitive responses comparable to those elicited by grammatical sentences, it seems reasonable to conclude that the tested condition would also be part of the internal grammar.

As discussed in the introduction, the combination of a dative pronoun followed by the (nonclitic) third-person singular accusative neuter pronoun, for example, *ihm es* (him.DAT it.ACC) is often considered ill-formed in Standard German. This combination is almost absent from newspaper corpora (Kempen & Harbusch 2004, 2005; Fleischer 2010a) and even treated as ungrammatical in some generative accounts of German syntax (e.g., Haider & Rosengren 1998; Müller 1999). We tested exactly this combination of pronouns in this study. The ERP data and acceptability judgments show that the alleged rigidity of pronoun order should rather be viewed as a preference, and that the reversed order of accusative and dative object pronouns does not seem to create an ungrammatical structure even in Standard German. Furthermore, our study reveals striking parallels between the inversion of object pronouns and scrambling of full DPs with respect to their processing effects. The parser seems to build a model of canonical serializations during online sentence comprehension, which is updated whenever new input requires activation of an unexpected syntactic template. While some authors consider the possibility that the reordering of pronouns is similar to the scrambling of nonpronominal DPs (e.g., Lenerz 1993; Gärtner & Steinbach 2003), others separate scrambling from pronoun movement (e.g., Haider & Rosengren 1998). We cannot elaborate a syntactic theory of scrambling and pronoun placement in this chapter, but we hope that our results will serve as useful data in future research for both experimental as well as theoretical linguists.

From a psycholinguistic perspective, inversion of accusative and dative objects seems to be processed very similarly for pronominal and nonpronominal DPs. However, some questions remain. In the introduction we discussed that serializations that are noncanonical in Standard German may well occur in certain dialects, and our results point to the conclusion that even in an experimental design using Standard German the noncanonical order is rather acceptable with a subset of participants even accepting both serializations equally well. Thus, it would be interesting to systematically test processing effects between speakers of different dialects.

Furthermore, it seems promising to explore not only the relative order of object pronouns, but also the effects when subject and object pronouns are reordered. A sentence like (12a) that requires movement of a pronominal object across a pronominal subject seems impossible compared to the respective scrambled sentence with nonpronominal DPs in (12b) which is marked but fully acceptable.

(12) a. ?Gestern hat es er gekauft.
Yesterday has it.ACC he.NOM bought
'Yesterday he bought it.'
b. Gestern hat das Buch der Lehrer gekauft.
Yesterday has [the book].ACC [the teacher].NOM bought
'Yesterday the teacher bought the book.'

Interestingly, however, taking a look at regional variation, it seems that personal pronouns appear in an object-before-subject order in some German dialects (Weiß 2015, 2017). Thus, even though (12a) seems particularly bad in Standard German, it might be an acceptable structure for speakers of some varieties. For further research, it therefore seems desirable to investigate possible processing differences of the DAT > ACC pronoun order in German dialects, as well as ACC > NOM and DAT > NOM pronoun orders.

Acknowledgments: The research reported here was part of the LOEWE program "Fundierung linguistischer Basiskategorien" (TP6: "Der Zusammenhang der Kasusmarkierung, Serialisierungsfixierung und Belebtheitshierarchie in den deutschen Regionalsprachen") funded by the German State of Hesse. Ina Bornkessel-Schlesewsky is supported by an Australian Research Council Future Fellowship (FT160100437). We are grateful for the fruitful discussion at Linguistic Evidence 2014 conference in Tübingen, and in particular we would like to thank Sam Featherston and Sebastian Löbner for their insightful comments and suggestions. Furthermore, we are thankful to Phillip Alday, Simon Kasper, Franziska Kretzschmar, Oliver Schallert, and Fiona Weiß for their helpful comments. We would also like to thank all the helping hands in the lab, and especially Fritzi Milde for her invaluable help with stimulus construction and EEG recordings. We would also like to thank the anonymous reviewers for their helpful comments on the manuscript.

References

Alday, P.M. 2015. Quantity and quality: Not a zero-sum game. A computational and neurocognitive examination of human language processing. Marburg: Philipps-Universität doctoral dissertation.

Anagnostopoulou, E. 2008. Notes on the Person Case Constraint in Germanic (with special reference to German). In: (R. D'Alessandro, S. Fischer & G. H. Hrafnbjargarson, eds.), Agreement Restrictions, 15–47. Berlin/New York: De Gruyter.

Anagnostopoulou, E. 2017. The Person Case Constraint. In: (M. Everaert & H. van Riemsdijk, eds.), The Wiley Blackwell Companion to Syntax, 2nd edn. Oxford: Wiley-Blackwell.

Arbib, M.A. & J. Lee. 2008. Describing visual scenes: Towards a neurolinguistics based on construction grammar. Brain Research 1225: 146–162.

Bader, M. & M. Meng. 1999. Subject-object ambiguities in German embedded clauses: An across-the-board comparison. Journal of Psycholinguistic Research 28(2): 121–143.

Barber, H. & M. Carreiras. 2005. Grammatical gender and number agreement in Spanish: An ERP comparison. Journal of Cognitive Neuroscience 17(1): 137–153.

Barrès, V. & J. Lee. 2014. Template Construction Grammar: From visual scene description to language comprehension and agrammatism. Neuroinformatics 12(1): 181–208.

Basilico, D. 1999. Pronoun positioning. Lingua 109(3): 155–181.

Bonet, E. 1991. Morphology after Syntax: Pronominal Clitics in Romance Languages. Cambridge, MA: MIT doctoral dissertation.

Bornkessel, I., C. Fiebach & A. D. Friederici. 2004. On the cost of syntactic ambiguity in human language comprehension: an individual differences approach. Cognitive Brain Research 21(1): 11–21.

Bornkessel, I. & M. Schlesewsky. 2006a. The role of contrast in the local licensing of scrambling in German: Evidence from online comprehension. Journal of Germanic Linguistics 18(1): 1–43.

Bornkessel, I. & M. Schlesewsky. 2006b. The extended Argument Dependency Model: A neurocognitive approach to sentence comprehension across languages. Psychological Review 113(4): 787–821.

Bornkessel, I. & M. Schlesewsky. 2006c. Generalised semantic roles and syntactic templates: A new framework for language comprehension. In: (I. Bornkessel, M. Schlesewsky, A. D. Friederici & B. Comrie, eds) Semantic role universals and argument linking: Theoretical, typological and psycholinguistic perspectives, 327–353. Berlin: de Gruyter.

Bornkessel, I., M. Schlesewsky & A.D. Friederici. 2002. Grammar overrides frequency: Evidence from the online processing of flexible word order. Cognition 85(2): B21–B30.

Bornkessel, I., M. Schlesewsky & A.D. Friederici. 2003a. Contextual information modulates initial processes of syntactic integration: The role of inter- versus intrasentential

predictions. Journal of Experimental Psychology: Learning, Memory, and Cognition 29(5): 871–882.
Bornkessel, I., M. Schlesewsky & A.D. Friederici. 2003b. Eliciting thematic reanalysis effects: The role of syntax-independent information during parsing. Language and Cognitive Processes 18(3): 269–298.
Bornkessel-Schlesewsky, I., F. Kretzschmar, S. Tune, L. Wang, S. Genç, M. Philipp, D. Roehm & M. Schlesewsky. 2011. Think globally: Cross-linguistic variation in electrophysiological activity during sentence comprehension. Brain and Language 117(3): 133–152.
Bornkessel-Schlesewsky, I. & M. Schlesewsky. 2009. Minimality as vacuous distinctness: Evidence from cross-linguistic sentence comprehension. Lingua 119(10): 1541–1559.
Bornkessel-Schlesewsky, I. & M. Schlesewsky. 2013. Reconciling time, space and function: A new dorsal–ventral stream model of sentence comprehension. Brain and Language 125(1): 60–76.
Bornkessel-Schlesewsky, I. & M. Schlesewsky. 2015. The Argument Dependency Model. In: (G. Hickok & S. L. Small, eds) Neurobiology of language, 357–369. Amsterdam: Academic Press.
Cardinaletti, A. & M. Starke. 1996. Deficient pronouns: A view from Germanic. A study in the unified description of Germanic and Romance. In: (H. Thráinsson, S. D. Epstein & S. Peter, eds) Studies in comparative Germanic syntax, Vol. 2, 21–65. Dordrecht: Kluwer.
Cook, P. 2006. The datives that aren't born equal: Beneficiaries and the dative passive. In: (D. Hole, A. Meinunger & W. Abraham, eds), Datives and other cases. Between argument structure and event structure, 141–184. Amsterdam/Philadelphia: John Benjamins.
Cook, V., E. Iarossi, N. Stellakis & Y. Tokumaru. 2003. Effects of the L2 on the syntactic processing of the L1. In: (V. Cook, ed.), Effects of the second language on the first, 193–213. Clevedon: Multilingual Matters.
Coulson, S., J.W. King & M. Kutas. 1998. Expect the unexpected: Event-related brain response to morphosyntactic violations. Language and Cognitive Processes 13(1): 21–58.
Dikker, S., H. Rabagliati, T.A. Farmer & L. Pylkkänen. 2010. Early occipital sensitivity to syntactic category is based on form typicality. Psychological Science 21(5): 629–634.
Dikker, S., H. Rabagliati & L. Pylkkänen. 2009. Sensitivity to syntax in visual cortex. Cognition 110(3): 293–321.
Donchin, E. 1981. Surprise! ... Surprise?. Psychophysiology 18(5): 493–513.
Dröge, A., J. Fleischer, M. Schlesewsky & I. Bornkessel-Schlesewsky. 2016. Neural mechanisms of sentence comprehension based on predictive processes and decision certainty: Electrophysiological evidence from non-canonical linearizations in a flexible word order language. Brain Research 1633: 149–166.
Featherston, S. 2009. A scale for measuring well-formedness: Why syntax needs boiling and freezing points. In: (S. Featherston & S. Winkler, eds), The fruits of empirical linguistics, Vol. I, 47–74. Berlin: De Gruyter.
Federmeier, K.D. 2007. Thinking ahead: The role and roots of prediction in language comprehension. Psychophysiology 44(4). 491–505.
Fleischer, J. 2005. Zur Abfolge akkusativischer und dativischer Personalpronomen im Althochdeutschen und Altniederdeutschen (8./9. Jahrhundert). In: (F. Simmler in co-operation with C. Wich-Reif & Y. Desportes, eds.) Syntax Althochdeutsch – Mittelhochdeutsch: eine Gegenüberstellung von Metrik und Prosa (Berliner Sprachwissenschaftliche Studien 7), 9–48. Berlin: Weidler.
Fleischer, J. 2010a. Norm and variation in the relative order of accusative and dative personal pronouns in German: evidence from corpora (18th–21st century). In: (A.N. Lenz &

A. Plewnia, eds.) Grammar between norm and variation (VarioLingua 40), 145–166. Frankfurt/Main: Lang.

Fleischer, J. 2010b. Zur Abfolge akkusativischer und dativischer Personalpronomen im Prosalancelot (Lancelot I). In: (A. Ziegler (in co-operation with C. Braun), ed.) Historische Textgrammatik und Historische Syntax des Deutschen: Traditionen, Innovationen, Perspektiven, 511–536. Berlin: De Gruyter.

Fleischer, J. 2011. ... und habe es ihr gesagt: zur dialektalen Abfolge pronominaler Objekte (eine Auswertung von Wenkersatz 9). In: (E. Glaser, J.E. Schmidt & N. Frey, eds.) Dynamik des Dialekts – Wandel und Variation (Akten des 3. Kongresses der Internationalen Gesellschaft für Dialektologie des Deutschen (IGDD), Zeitschrift für Dialektologie und Linguistik Beihefte 144), 77–100. Stuttgart: Steiner.

Fleischer, J. 2012. Pronominalsyntax im nordwestlichen Niederdeutsch: eine Auswertung des Wenker-Materials (mit Einbezug der friesischen und dänischen Formulare). Niederdeutsches Jahrbuch 135: 59–80.

Fleischer, J. 2013a. Hessische Pronominalsyntax: Ergebnisse einer Pilotstudie des Forschungsprojekts "Syntax hessischer Dialekte" (SyHD). In: (F. Grucza, ed.) Vielheit und Einheit der Germanistik weltweit, Akten des XII. Internationalen Germanistenkongresses, Warschau 2010, Vol. 17, 351–360. Frankfurt am Main: Peter Lang.

Fleischer, J. 2013b. Frühneuhochdeutsche und mittelniederdeutsche Syntax im Kontrast: die Abfolge des akkusativischen und dativischen Personalpronomens in der ältesten Luther- und Bugenhagen-Bibel. Zeitschrift für deutsche Philologie 132(1): 49–72.

Fleischer, J., S. Kasper & A.N. Lenz. 2012. Die Erhebung syntaktischer Phänomene durch die indirekte Methode: Ergebnisse und Erfahrungen aus dem Forschungsprojekt 'Syntax hessischer Dialekte' (SyHD). Zeitschrift für Dialektologie und Linguistik 79(1): 2–42.

Fleischer, J. 2017. Pronomenabfolge: direktes und indirektes Objekt. In: (J. Fleischer, A.N. Lenz & H. Weiß, eds.) SyHD-atlas, 490–509. Konzipiert von L. M. Breuer. Unter Mitarbeit von K. Kuhmichel, S. Leser-Cronau, J. Schwalm und T. Strobel. Marburg/Wien/Frankfurt am Main. DOI: dx.doi.org/10.17192/es2017.0003

Frazier, L. 1987. Syntactic processing: Evidence from Dutch. Natural Language and Linguistic Theory 5(4): 519–559.

Frazier, L. 1989. Against lexical generation of syntax. In: (W. Marslen-Wilson, ed.) Lexical representation and process, 505–528. Cambridge, MA: MIT Press.

Friederici, A.D., A. Mecklinger, K.M. Spencer, K. Steinhauer & E. Donchin. 2001. Syntactic parsing preferences and their on-line revisions: a spatio-temporal analysis of event-related brain potentials. Cognitive Brain Research 11(2): 305–323.

Friston, K. 2005. A theory of cortical responses. Philosophical Transactions of The Royal Society B 360(1456): 815–836.

Friston, K. 2010. The free-energy principle: A unified brain theory? Nature Reviews Neuroscience 11: 127–138.

Gärtner, H.-M. & M. Steinbach. 2003. What do reduced pronominals reveal about the syntax of Dutch and German? Part 1: Clause-internal positions. Linguistische Berichte 195: 257–294.

Grewe, T., I. Bornkessel, S. Zysset, R. Wiese, D.Y. von Cramon & M. Schlesewsky. 2005. The emergence of the unmarked: A new perspective on the language-specific function of Broca's area. Human Brain Mapping 26(3): 178–190.

Gunter, T.C., L.A. Stowe & G. Mulder. 1997. When syntax meets semantics. Psychophysiology 34(6): 660–676.

Hagoort, P. 2005. On Broca, brain, and binding: A new framework. TRENDS in Cognitive Sciences 9(9): 416–423.
Hagoort, P. 2009. Reflections on the neurobiology of syntax. In: (D. Bickerton & E. Szathmáry, eds.) Biological foundations and origin of syntax, 279–296. Cambridge, MA: MIT Press.
Hagoort, P. 2013. MUC (Memory, Unification, Control) and beyond. Frontiers in Psychology 4: 1–13.
Hagoort, P. & C. Brown. 2000. ERP effects of listening to speech compared to reading: The P600/SPS to syntactic violations in spoken sentences and rapid serial visual presentation. Neuropsychologia 38(11): 1531–1549.
Hagoort, P., C. Brown & J. Groothusen. 1993. The Syntactic Positive Shift (SPS) as an ERP measure of syntactic processing. Language and Cognitive Processes 8: 439–483.
Hahne, A. & A.D. Friederici. 1999. Electrophysiological evidence for two steps in syntactic analysis: Early automatic and late controlled processes. Journal of Cognitive Neuroscience 11(2): 194–205.
Haider, H. 2010. The syntax of German. Cambridge: Cambridge University Press.
Haider, H. & I. Rosengren. 1998. Scrambling (Sprache und Pragmatik 49). Lund: University of Lund.
Haider, H. & I. Rosengren. 2003. Scrambling: Nontriggered chain formation in OV languages. Journal of Germanic Linguistics 15(3): 203–267.
Hauk, O. & F. Pulvermüller. 2004. Effects of word length and frequency on the human event-related potential. Clinical Neurophysiology 115(5): 1090–1103.
Haupt, F. S., M. Schlesewsky, D. Roehm, A.D. Friederici & I. Bornkessel-Schlesewsky. 2008. The status of subject–object reanalyses in the language comprehension architecture. Journal of Memory and Language 59(1): 54–96.
Hick, W. E. 1952. On the rate of gain of information. Quarterly Journal of Experimental Psychology 4(1). 11–26.
Huynh, H. & L.S. Feldt. 1970. Conditions under which the mean square ratios in repeated measurement designs have exact F-distributions. Journal of the American Statistical Association 65(332): 1582–1589.
Hyman, R. 1953. Stimulus information as a determinant of reaction time. Journal of Experimental Psychology 45(3). 188–196.
Kaan, E. 2009. Fundamental syntactic phenomena and their putative relation to the brain. In: (D. Bickerton & E. Szathmáry, eds.) Biological foundations and origin of syntax, 117–134. Cambridge, MA: MIT Press.
Kaan, E., A. Harris, E. Gibson & P. Holcomb. 2000. The P600 as an index of syntactic integration difficulty. Language and Cognitive Processes 15(2): 159–201.
Kaan, E. & T.Y. Swaab. 2003. Repair, revision, and complexity in syntactic analysis: An electrophysiological differentiation. Journal of Cognitive Neuroscience 15(1): 98–110.
Kamide, Y. 2008. Anticipatory processes in sentence processing. Language and Linguistics Compass 2(4): 647–670.
Klöppel, S., J.-F. Mangin, A. Vongerichten, R.S.J. Frackowiak & H.R. Siebner. 2010. Nurture versus nature: Long-term impact of forced right-handedness on structure of pericentral cortex and basal ganglia. The Journal of Neuroscience 30(9): 3271–3275.
Kempen, G. & K. Harbusch. 2004. How flexible is constituent order in the midfield of German subordinate clauses? A corpus study revealing unexpected rigidity. In: Proceedings of the Linguistic Evidence Conference, Tübingen, Univ. of Tübingen.
Kempen, G. & K. Harbusch. 2005. The relationship between grammaticality ratings and corpus frequencies: A case study into word order variability in the midfield of German clauses. In:

(S. Kepser & M. Reis, eds.) Linguistic Evidence: Empirical, Theoretical and Computational Perspectives, 329–349. Berlin: De Gruyter.

Klöppel, S., A. Vongerichten, T. van Eimeren, R.S.J. Frackowiak & H.R. Siebner. 2007. Can left-handedness be switched? Insights from an early switch of handwriting. The Journal of Neuroscience 27(29): 7847–7853.

Kretzschmar, F. 2010. The electrophysiological reality of parafoveal processing: On the validity of language-related ERPs in natural reading. Marburg: Philipps-Universität doctoral dissertation.

Kutas, M., K.A. DeLong & N.J. Smith. 2011. A look around at what lies ahead: Prediction and predictability in language processing. In: (M. Bar, ed.) Predictions in the brain: Using our past to generate a future, 190–207. New York: Oxford University Press.

Kutas, M. & S.A. Hillyard. 1984. Brain potentials during reading reflect word expectancy and semantic association. Nature 307(5947): 161–163.

Lau, E., C. Stroud, S. Plesch & C. Phillips. 2006. The role of structural prediction in rapid syntactic analysis. Brain and Language 98: 74–88.

Lenerz, J. 1977. Zur Abfolge nominaler Satzglieder im Deutschen (Studien zur deutschen Grammatik 5). Tübingen: Niemeyer.

Lenerz, J. 1993. Zu Syntax und Semantik deutscher Personalpronomina. In: (M. Reis, ed.) Wortstellung und Informationsstruktur, 117–153. Tübingen: Niemeyer.

Lenerz, J. 1994. Pronomenprobleme. In: (B. Haftka, ed.) Was determiniert Wortstellungsvariation? Studien zu einem Interaktionsfeld von Grammatik, Pragmatik und Sprachtypologie, 161–173. Opladen: Westdeutscher Verlag.

Luck, S.J. 2014. An introduction to the event-related potential technique, 2nd edn. Cambridge, MA: MIT Press.

Marslen-Wilson, W.D. 1975. Sentence perception as an interactive parallel process. Science 189(4198): 226–228.

Mauchly, J.W. 1940. Significance test for sphericity of a normal n-variate distribution. The Annals of Mathematical Statistics 11(2): 204–209.

Molinaro, N., H.A. Barber & M. Carreiras. 2011. Grammatical agreement processing in reading: ERP findings and future directions. Cortex 47(8): 908–930.

Müller, G. 1999. Optimality, markedness, and word order in German. Linguistics 34: 777–818.

Müller, G. 2002. Harmonic alignment and the hierarchy of pronouns in German. In: (H. Simon & H. Wiese, eds.) Pronouns: Grammar and representation, 205–232. Amsterdam: Benjamins.

Müller, G. 2007. Towards a relativized concept of cyclic linearization. In: (U. Sauerland & H.-M. Gärtner, eds.) Interfaces + Recursion = Language?, 61–114. Berlin: de Gruyter.

Münte, T.F., H.-J. Heinze, M. Matzke, B.M. Wieringa & S. Johannes. 1998. Brain potentials and syntactic violations revisited: no evidence for specificity of the syntactic positive shift. Neuropsychologia 36(3): 217–226.

Neeleman, A. & F. Weerman. 1999. Flexible syntax: A theory of case and arguments (Studies in Natural Language and Linguistic Theory 47). Dordrecht: Kluwer.

Oldfield, R.C. 1971. The assessment and analysis of handedness: The Edinburgh Inventory. Neuropsychologia 9(1): 97–113.

Osterhout, L., M. Allen & J. McLaughlin. 2002. Words in the brain: lexical determinants of word-induced brain activity. Journal of Neurolinguistics 15(3–5): 171–187.

Osterhout, L., M. Bersick & R. McKinnon. 1997. Brain potentials elicited by words: word length and frequency predict the latency of an early negativity. Biological Psychology 46(2): 143–168.

Osterhout, L. & P.J. Holcomb. 1992. Event-related brain potentials elicited by syntactic anomaly. Journal of Memory and Language 31(6): 785–806.

Osterhout, L., P.J. Holcomb & D.A. Swinney. 1994. Brain potentials elicited by garden-path sentences: Evidence of the application of verb information during parsing. Journal of Experimental Psychology: Learning, Memory, and Cognition 20(4): 786–803.

Pickering, M.J. & S. Garrod. 2007. Do people use language production to make predictions during comprehension? TRENDS in Cognitive Sciences 11(3): 105–110.

Pickering, M.J. & S. Garrod. 2013. An integrated theory of language production and comprehension. Behavioral and Brain Sciences 36(4): 329–347.

Polich, J. 2007. Updating P300: An integrative theory of P3a and P3b. Clinical Neurophysiology 118(10): 2128–2148.

Ross, J. 1967. Constraints on variables in syntax. Cambridge, MA: Massachusetts Institute of Technology doctoral dissertation.

Rösler, F., T. Pechmann, J. Streb, B. Röder & E. Hennighausen. 1998. Parsing of sentences in a language with varying word order: word-by-word variations of processing demands are revealed by event-related brain potentials. Journal of Memory and Language 38(2): 150–176.

Sassenhagen, J. & I. Bornkessel-Schlesewsky. 2015. The P600 as a correlate of ventral attention network reorientation. Cortex 66: A3–A20.

Sassenhagen, J., M. Schlesewsky & I. Bornkessel-Schlesewsky. 2014. The P600-as-P3 hypothesis revisited: Single-trial analyses reveal that the late EEG positivity following linguistically deviant material is reaction time aligned. Brain and Language 137: 29–39.

Schlesewsky, M. & I. Bornkessel. 2006. Context-sensitive neural responses to conflict resolution: Electrophysiological evidence from subject–object ambiguities in language comprehension. Brain Research 1098: 139–152.

Schlesewsky, M., I. Bornkessel & S. Frisch. 2003. The neurophysiological basis of word order variations in German. Brain and Language 86(1): 116–128.

Siewierska, A. 1988. Word order rules. London, New York & Sidney: Croom Helm.

Silverstein, M. 1976. Hierarchy of features an ergativity. In: (R.M.W. Dixon, ed.) Grammatical categories in Australian languages, 112–171. Canberra: Australian Institute of Aboriginal Studies.

Struckmeier, V. 2014. Scrambling ohne Informationsstruktur? Prosodische, semantische und syntaktische Faktoren der deutschen Wortstellung (Studia Grammatica 77). Berlin/Boston: De Gruyter.

Townsend, D.J. & T.G. Bever. 2001. Sentence comprehension: The integration of habits and rules. Cambridge, MA: MIT Press.

Uszkoreit, H. 1987. Word order and constituent structure in German (CSLI Lecture Notes 8). Stanford: Stanford University.

Van de Meerendonk, N., H.H.J. Kolk, C.Th.W.M. Vissers & D.J. Chwilla. 2010. Monitoring in language perception: Mild and strong conflicts elicit different ERP patterns. Journal of Cognitive Neuroscience 22(1): 67–82.

Van Petten, C. & M. Kutas. 1990. Interactions between sentence context and word frequency in event-related brain potentials. Memory and Cognition 18(4). 380–393.

Van Valin, R.D., Jr. 2006. Semantic macroroles and language processing. In: (I. Bornkessel, M. Schlesewsky, A.D. Friederici & B. Comrie, eds.) Semantic role universals and argument linking: Theoretical, typological and psycholinguistic perspectives, 263–302. Berlin: De Gruyter.

Vosse, T. & G. Kempen. 2000. Syntactic structure assembly in human parsing: A computational model based on competitive inhibition and a lexicalist grammar. Cognition 75(2): 105–143.

Vosse, T. & G. Kempen. 2008. Parsing verb-final clauses in German: Garden-path and ERP effects modeled by a parallel dynamic parser. In: (B. Love, K. McRae & V. Sloutsky, eds) Proceedings of the 30th Annual Conference on the Cognitive Science Society, 261–266. Washington D.C.: Cognitive Science Society.

Wackernagel, J. 1892. Über ein Gesetz der indogermanischen Wortstellung. Indogermanische Forschungen 1: 333–436.

Weiß, H. 2015. When the subject follows the object. On a curiosity in the syntax of personal pronouns in some German dialects. The Journal of Comparative Germanic Linguistics 18(1): 65–92.

Weiß, H. 2017. Pronomenabfolge: Subjekt, Objekt. In: (J. Fleischer, A.N. Lenz & H. Weiß, eds.) SyHD-atlas, 481–489. Konzipiert von L.M. Breuer. Unter Mitarbeit von K. Kuhmichel, S. Leser-Cronau, J. Schwalm und T. Strobel. Marburg/Wien/Frankfurt am Main. DOI: dx.doi.org/10.17192/es2017.0003

Zwart, J.-W. 1996. Clitics, scrambling, and head movement in Dutch. In: (A. L. Halpern & A.M. Zwicky, eds) Approaching second: Second position clitics and related phenomena, 579–611. Stanford: CSLI.

Balázs Surányi and István Fekete
Logical and pragmatic meaning in the interpretation of disjunction: Contextual relevance and scalar implicatures

1 Defaultist and contextualist approaches to scalar implicatures

According to one prevailing view, endorsed by some prominent work pursuing a neo-Gricean approach (e.g., Levinson 2000; Landman 2000; Chierchia 2004; Magri 2009, 2011), scalar implicatures such as "but not both" in the exclusive interpretation of the conjunction *or* (="A or B but not both", see (1)) are generated automatically by default (though they may subsequently be canceled).

(1) a. I will invite John or Mary.
 b. *Scalar implicature in the exclusive interpretation of disjunction in (1a):*
 It's not the case that I will invite John and Mary.

One may distinguish between a strong version of defaultism, according to which implicatures are not effortful at all (e.g., Levinson 2000) and a weak version, according to which, while implicatures arise by default (even when a licensing context is lacking), they nevertheless (may) incur extra processing cost. On another, equally influential view, scalar implicatures only arise when required by the context (e.g., Sauerland 2004; Van Rooij & Schulz 2004; Noveck & Sperber 2007; Geurts 2011). The latter, contextualist view is advocated by Relevance Theory, according to which scalar implicatures are generated only in contexts in which they are relevant in the technical sense that they yield a significant cognitive effect at a reasonable processing cost (Sperber & Wilson 1995; Wilson & Sperber 2012; Carston 1998).

There is by now a sizable body of experimental research addressing the opposing predictions of these two major theories of the way scalar implicatures arise. This is not the place to review, let alone evaluate, the outcomes of this voluminous work. It is fair to say, however, that the basic debate has not been conclusively settled in either direction. While some recent psycholinguistic experiments have been argued to disfavor the defaultist view (Noveck & Posada 2003; Bott & Noveck 2004; Breheny, Katsos & Williams 2006; Katsos 2006; Huang & Snedeker 2009; Bonnefon, Feeney & Villejoubert 2009; Zondervan 2010), this conclusion has been contested forcefully (Bezuidenhout & Cooper Cutting 2002; Feeney et al. 2004; Degen et al. 2009; Grodner et al. 2010; but see also Zondervan's 2010, Hartshorne & Snedeker's 2014, and Huang & Snedeker's 2018 methodological criticism of some of the experiments that have been interpreted as supporting the contextualist view).

The controversy extends to the scalar implicature associated with disjunction, namely the exclusivity implicature in (1b). The effect of context on this inference was examined in a reading study reported in Breheny et al.'s (2006) seminal paper. In this experiment (run in Greek) participants read the disjoined NPs (e.g., *meat or fish*) more slowly in contexts that support the scalar implicature than in contexts that do not support it. The authors took this outcome to suggest that the calculation of the exclusivity implicature (reflected in slower processing) is affected by context, in line with predictions of contextualist approaches. However, as Hartshorne & Snedeker (2014) point out, the two conditions also differed substantially in their lexical and propositional content; therefore, the task was confounded with factors that are known to affect reading speed, such as cloze probability, syntactic complexity, lexical repetition, and semantic priming. As Breheny et al. provided no evidence that participants in fact calculated the exclusivity implicature, there is no way of knowing whether or not the reading time difference was in fact due to scalar implicature processing. In short, it cannot be concluded from this experiment that the implicature associated with disjunction is affected in fundamental ways by the context.

Pijnacker et al.'s (2009) study is also related to the role of context in the exclusive interpretation of or. These authors report that in a neutral context normal controls derive the exclusive implicature of disjunction at a rate of 54% (see also Evans & Newstead 1980 for a comparable result). The interpretation of results like this requires caution: enforcing the lack of a discourse context in an experimental stimulus is notoriously difficult. When no disambiguating context is given, subjects are free to "project" contexts of their own in the course of processing sentence interpretation.[1]

The main aim of this chapter is to contribute to this general discussion by investigating the possible contribution of two aspects of context to the calculation of the exclusivity implicature of disjunction.[2] Experiment 1 studies how

---

[1] See also Paris (1973), whose study contains results from the testing of the (offline) interpretation of disjunction in adult controls. The disjunctions tested by Paris linked two complete propositions rather than two phrases.

[2] The term "context" is used in a broad sense, including properties of pragmatic relevance as determined by the communicative situation and information structure, but excluding semantic properties of the syntactic environment. A semantic feature of the syntactic context that is

the radical lack of its contextually induced relevance affects the generation of *or*'s scalar implicature. The experiment involves a task that only requires "shallow" processing, in the course of which target sentences do not necessarily receive a complete semantic and pragmatic analysis (Ferreira, Bailey & Ferraro 2002; Sanford & Sturt 2002). The task is designed to block any contextual influences as much as possible. Our interest here lies not with the issue whether scalar implicature calculation is effortful, nor with the time course of its processing – two closely interrelated and central questions addressed in much recent work in psychopragmatics (see Bott & Noveck, 2004; Chevallier et al. 2008; Chierchia et al. 2001; De Neys & Schaeken, 2007; Feeney et al. 2004; Huang & Snedeker 2009, 2011; Noveck & Posada 2003; Pouscoulous et al. 2007; Sedivy et al. 1999; Sedivy 2003; Grodner et al. 2010; Degen & Tanenhaus 2011; Breheny, Ferguson & Katsos 2013 for diverging conclusions). Rather, the aim of Experiment 1 is to investigate whether or not a scalar implicature gets calculated in a "shallow" processing task, using an experimental setting in which the influence from context, including the relevance of the implicature itself, is maximally reduced.

In the second part we consider the potential role of another well-studied aspect of contextual meaning in *or*'s exclusive interpretation, namely focus structure. Highlighting by focus is a means to indicate the contextual relevance of alternatives to the focused item. The particular question we seek to answer is whether focusing affects the exclusivity implicature of disjunction, a claim advanced in prior literature (Chevalliear et al. 2008; Zondervan 2010). Experiment 2 addresses this issue using a Truth Value Judgment (TVJ) task based on sentences similar to the target items of Experiment 1.

In Section 2 we present and discuss the outcomes of our "shallow" processing experiment (Experiment 1). In Section 3 we critically review some prior psycholinguistic studies that sought to investigate the role of focus in the interpretation of disjunction, before turning to our TVJ experiment gauging the effect of focus (Experiment 2) in Section 4. Section 5 concludes with a summary of the main results.

---

known to systematically affect scalar implicatures is downward entailingness. In particular, SIs arise with a relatively low likelihood in downward entailing syntactico-semantic contexts, such as the antecedent of conditional and the scope of negation (Chierchia et al. 2001; Noveck et al. 2002; Chierchia, Frazier & Clifton, 2009; Schwarz, Clifton & Frazier, to appear).

2 The role of contextual relevance in the exclusive interpretation of disjunction (Experiment 1)

2.1 Method

2.1.1 The paradigm

Empirical studies in the realm of the psychopragmatics often seek to selectively reduce the likelihood of implicatures through an experimentally increased processing load, which restricts the cognitive resources available to generate implicatures (e.g., de Neys & Schaeken 2007). The experiment to be presented in this section shares the essential rationale behind this type of paradigms; however, it employs a different strategy. In particular, our experiment investigates how a decrease in cognitive effort due to the irrelevance of the scalar implicature at issue affects its computation.

The specific paradigm we employed only requires a form of "shallow" processing, in the course of which sentences do not necessarily receive a complete semantic and pragmatic analysis (cf. the concepts of "good enough", or "shallow" cognitive representations in experimental work by Ferreira, Bailey and Ferraro (2002) and Louwerse & Jeuniaux (2010), respectively). Participants were presented with stimuli that involved isolated, decontextualized sentences with a neutral word order. The experimental task required participants to perform a relatively easy sentence–picture verification task that was completely unrelated to the calculation of implicatures. This setting helped reduce the likelihood of participants projecting a context of their own for the test sentences; therefore it contributed to minimizing any possible contextual impact of context. As in this task the exclusivity implicature is not supported by contextual relevance (the presence or absence of the implicature is irrelevant to performing the task itself), on contextualist assumptions it is predicted not to arise.[3] By contrast, on the defaultist view (whether the strong or the weak version is considered) the implicature associated with disjunction is expected to be generated automatically, whether or not it is contextually relevant.

Our experimental task is similar to that used in the mental simulation literature, for instance, by Stanfield & Zwaan (2001) (cf. also Zwaan, Stanfield & Yaxley 2002). These authors asked participants to decide whether or not pictures

---

[3] See also Swets et al. (2008) for experimental evidence for a broadly similar syntactic analogue of the same reasoning. We thank an anonymous reviewer for a pointer to this work.

depicted the objects described in previously presented sentences. These actions involved an object with either a vertical or horizontal orientation, such as a nail that was either driven into the wall or into the ceiling. The results showed that subjects responded more quickly to the pictures in which the object was represented in the same orientation as in the previously described action. The general conclusion from this line of work that is significant from our current perspective is the following. Even in "shallow" processing tasks rather subtle properties of the visual stimuli, which are in fact irrelevant to the experimental task, do get processed, and they may cause delays in responses in those cases in which they represent a mismatch with another stimulus presented within the same trial (Richardson et al. 2003; Kaschak et al. 2005; Scorolli & Borghi 2007, a.o.).

2.1.2 Method and design

We tested the processing of the connectives *és* ('and') and *vagy* ('or') in Hungarian in a sentence–picture verification task. Each picture was preceded by a sentence that describes a scenario involving two physical objects. These objects appeared as object NPs conjoined either by *and* or by *or* (Connective Type), for example, *John peeled the orange and/or the banana*. The state of the two objects either matched or mismatched the scenario explicitly described in the previous sentence (Congruence). To continue with the previous example, in the mismatching condition of *and*-sentences only one of the two fruits was peeled (incongruently with the entailment of *and*), while in the matching *and*-condition, both fruits were peeled in the picture. In the case of *or*-sentences, both fruits were peeled in the mismatching condition (incongruently with the exclusivity implicature of *or*), and only one of them was peeled in the matching *or*-condition (in accordance with the exclusive reading of *or*). Figure 1 illustrates the crucial manipulation of the objects in our experiment. The first column represents conditions involving *and*-sentences, with a matching picture above a mismatching picture. In the right-hand-side column of the two *or*-sentence conditions, the upper picture is consistent with the implicature of *or*, viz. "but not both", while the one below it is consistent with the logical meaning of *or* ("or maybe both"), but not with *or*'s implicature.

The participants' task was unrelated to both Connective Type and Congruence. They had to decide if both of the two physical objects had been mentioned in the previous sentence or not (without considering the states of the objects depicted). The dependent measure was response time to picture stimuli. In all four of the test conditions, both objects depicted in the picture are mentioned in the prior sentence

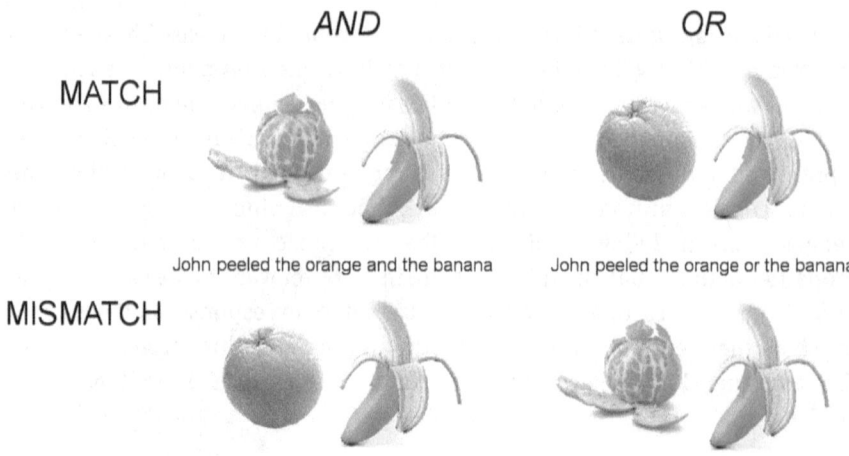

Figure 1: Examples of the four critical conditions in Experiment 1.

stimulus. Thus all critical trials were designed to elicit an affirmative response, allowing the response times to be directly compared across the four conditions.

Assuming that mismatches are not ignored (see Section 2.1.1), they are generally expected to slow down reaction times compared to the corresponding matching conditions. Thus, the *and*-mismatch condition is expected to induce significantly slower responses than *and*-match trials. Beyond that point, however, defaultist and contextualist predictions diverge sharply with regard to the expected outcomes. If the exclusivity implicature is obtained independently of contextual relevance, as hypothesized by the defaultist approach, then we expect significantly slower responses in the *or*-mismatch condition, in which the picture is at variance with this implicature, then in the *or*-match condition, in which there is no such disparity.

On the other hand, on contextualist assumptions, the exclusivity implicature has no relevance whatsoever in this task, and therefore it is expected not to be generated at all. Thus the *or*-mismatch condition is not predicted to differ from the *or*-match condition in terms of reaction times. Connective Type and Congruence are expected to exhibit a clear interaction.

2.1.3 Participants

Seventy-seven Hungarian students from Budapest participated in the experiment for course credit (mean age: 22.5, age range: 17–32; 33 female and 44 male participants). All the participants were native speakers of Hungarian.

2.1.4 Stimuli

Thirty-two critical sentences and 64 filler sentences were constructed. The 64 filler sentences did not contain either of the two critical connectives, instead, they included either of the two temporal connectives "then" or "next", as in the sentence "Bandi [Andy] set up the tent, and then he sharpened the knife". Filler sentences that required a negative response were presented with picture stimuli in which one of the objects was not mentioned in the sentence.

All 32 critical trials (a pair of a picture stimulus and a sentence containing either a disjoined or a conjoined NP) required an affirmative response to an yes–no question, while filler sentences required a negative response in 48 trials, and in 16 trials an affirmative response. In other words, in half of the trials the picture stimuli required a positive response, and in the other half a negative response. None of the sentences was ambiguous either lexically or structurally.

The critical sentences were counterbalanced in four between-subject lists. These four lists, each with a pseudo-randomized order, were created in order to counterbalance items and conditions (incomplete counterbalancing). Each list included one of the four possible versions of a sentence–picture stimulus pair illustrated in Figure 1, with 19 or 20 participants assigned to each list randomly. Each participant saw only one list, and each participant read each sentence once. Each sentence was presented with each Connective Type (*and/or*) across the experiment. Each item was tested equally often in each condition, and each subject received an equal number of items in each condition. Because lists were included only to reduce error variance, effects involving lists will not be discussed.

2.1.5 Procedure

Participants were first presented with an instruction screen. They were asked to read the sentences that appeared on the computer screen and press the SPACE key when they had read the sentence. They were told that after every sentence they would see a picture with two objects, and their task was to decide if both of the objects had been mentioned in the previous sentence or not. They were also instructed not to pay attention to the state of the objects. Each participant was tested individually in one session lasting approximately 12 min. Participants first completed a practice phase, in which they were familiarized with the logic of the experiment. One trial consisted of a sentence and a picture stimulus. The sentence appeared in the center of the computer screen. After the participant read the sentence, a picture appeared. The mean response times to the picture stimuli were collected. The trials appeared one after the other, with a fixation cross appearing between trials for 1,000 ms in the center of the screen. No time limit was set for responses to pictures or sentences; however, subjects were asked to react to picture stimuli as quickly as possible because verification time was measured at the point when the pictures were shown. The trials were presented in random order within every participant. The E-Prime 2.0 software (Psychology Software Tools) was used to run the experiment.

2.2 Results and discussion

The practice trials were excluded from the analyses, as were the filler items. Erroneous trials – in which a factually wrong, that is, negative, response was given to the picture stimulus – were also excluded. The corresponding reaction time values were not replaced.[4] The data of seven participants were discarded in toto on account of their overall accuracy being lower than 75%. The median response times of the critical trials per condition entered analysis.[5] Table 1 illustrates the mean picture verification times (and SDs) in the four conditions.[6]

Table 1: Mean verification times (ms) of the picture stimuli in the four test conditions (means with standard deviations in parentheses).

		Connective Type	
		AND	OR
Picture Congruence	Match	1,124 (295)	1,194 (347)
	Mismatch	1,270 (445)	1,170 (346)

---

[4] These occasional errors, which come from four participants, may represent genuine errors, lapses of attention and/or guessing behavior. Independently of what may underlie incorrect responses, it is prudent not to mix reaction time data from negative responses with reaction time data from affirmative responses in any statistical analysis.

[5] Mean accuracy rate for the critical trials for the entire subject sample before excluding outliers was 0.92 (SD: 0.13). After the exclusion of outliers, mean accuracy rate for the critical trials was 0.97 (SD: 0.05). Median reaction times per condition were used as the starting point for the analysis for three reasons. First, median is relatively insensitive to non-Gaussian outliers, that is, it is less susceptible to departures from normality. Second, when using medians, no valid data on the left end of the scale are lost (unlike when using means, in which case trimming the data becomes necessary). Third, when there is large variability among subjects, the median has more power (Whelan 2008).

[6] We also analyzed the mean reading times of the sentences before the picture stimuli to check if the two Connective Types are processed differently during reading. It was found that the *and*-sentences (Mean: 1953 ms, SD: 600 ms) were not read differently from the *or*-sentences (Mean: 2038 ms, SD: 607 ms), $t(65) = -1.837$, $p > 0.05$).

Mean picture verification times were first analyzed in a participant-based 2*2 ANOVA model with Connective Type (two levels: *and/or*) and Picture Congruence (two levels: match/mismatch) as within-participant factors. We found a significant interaction between Connective Type and Picture Congruence, $F(1,65) = 12.224$, $p < 0.001$, $\eta_p^2 = 0.158$, indicating that the two connectives are affected differently by Congruence. The main effect of Congruence is significant, $F(1,65) = 6.825$, $p = 0.011$, $\eta_p^2 = 0.095$. However, Connective Type does not reveal a significant main effect; $F(1,65) = 0.358$, $p = 0.552$, $\eta_p^2 = 0.005$.[7]

Simple effects were also examined, comparing the *and*-match condition with *and*-mismatch, *or*-match with *or*-mismatch, *and*-match with *or*-match, and *and*-mismatch with *or*-mismatch (applying Bonferroni correction; below we report the corrected *p*-values).[8] Figure 2 depicts the mean picture verification times in the four conditions, and summarizes the significant differences found:

First, it was revealed that pictures after *and*-sentences were verified significantly faster in the matching picture condition than in the mismatching picture condition, $t(65) = -3.628$, $p = 0.004$. Crucially, the same effect was not found in the set of *or*-sentences, $t(65) = 0.487$, $p > 0.99$. As noted in Section 2.1.2, mismatches are generally expected to slow down reaction times compared to the corresponding matching conditions. As we have just seen, this is indeed what happened after *and*-sentences. Yet the same was not the case after *or*-sentences. The lack of a slowdown after *or*-sentences is expected if the exclusive implicature of *or* was not generated.

The lack of the exclusive implicature is predicted on the contextualist view, since it was not licensed by contextual relevance. On (both strong and weak) defaultist approaches, however, the implicature is expected to be generated even in such cases. Our findings therefore support contextualist theories over defaultist accounts.

Pictures in the *and*-mismatch condition were reacted to significantly more slowly than those in the *or*-mismatch condition, $t(65) = 2.638$, $p = 0.02$. This difference is explained straightforwardly if there was an actual mismatch between the

---

[7] Since we found a significant interaction between Connective Type and Congruence with the picture, the possibility that no semantic processing took place in the experimental task at all, or that participants just scanned the nouns in the sentences, skimming over the connectives, can be ruled out. That Congruence affected the processing of *or*-sentences differently from that of *and*-sentences is also clearly revealed by the results of the pairwise comparisons presented below.

[8] The alpha level of every comparison was adjusted according to the Bonferroni formula, which in our case is tantamount to multiplying the alpha level by four because we carried out four planned comparisons. Pairwise comparisons are based on those participants who are included in the ANOVA.

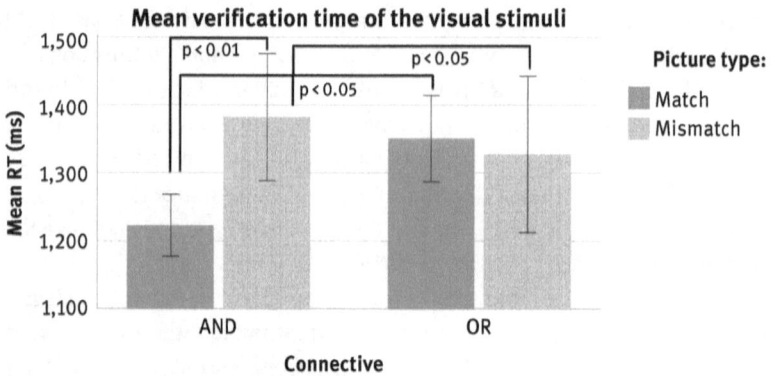

Figure 2: Mean verification times (ms) of the picture stimuli with significant pairwise comparisons (error bars: ±1 SE).

picture stimulus and the interpretation assigned by the participants to the sentence only in the *and*-mismatch condition, but not in the *or*-mismatch condition. There was no genuine discrepancy between the sentence and the picture stimulus in the latter condition if, as we are assuming, the exclusive implicature of the disjunction did not get generated in this task.

On defaultist approaches, according to which the exclusive implicature must have been generated in the *or*-sentences, the longer response time associated with the *and*-mismatch conditions than with the *or*-mismatch conditions is difficult to account for. Perhaps one possibility for defaultists would be to assume that in some sense the *and*-mismatch conditions, in which the mismatch is due to a semantic entailment of the conjunction, lead to a stronger discrepancy than does the implicature of the disjunction. But that assumption rests on dubious grounds in that both the entailments of conjunction and the exclusivity implicature of disjunction are arguably part of the truth conditions of the respective sentence types (see Carston 2004 for a forceful defense of this position; see also Levinson 2000; Recanati 2003; Chierchia et al. 2012). Once enriched with the implicature, the exclusive disjunction is contradicted by the mismatching picture in the same way as conjunction is contradicted by its own mismatching picture. Any difference between the mean response times incurred by the two types of mismatches may only arise from the amount of processing resources the exclusivity implicature takes to compute, or to cancel.[9] But even if either of these latter processes induce extra processing, that would predict the opposite

---

[9] For experimental investigations of the processing costs incurred by the computation of scalar implicatures, see Noveck & Posada (2003), Bott & Noveck (2004), Breheny, Katsos & Williams

of what we found. Namely, due to the extra processing load the *or*-mismatch condition should have incurred longer, rather than shorter, response times than the *and*-mismatch condition.

The last pairwise comparison, namely that between the two match conditions, is also of potential interest. Pictures in the and-match condition were verified faster than those in the or-match condition, $t(65) = -2.556$, $p = 0.05$. Concentrating on just this difference, one could take it to suggest that the scalar implicature was in fact generated in the or-match condition, contrary to our interpretation of the data. Specifically, the longer reaction time in this condition compared to the and-match condition could be attributed to the extra processing cost incurred by generating scalar implicatures (the latter assumption is compatible with weak defaultism, but not with strong defaultism, according to which implicature generation is not only automatic, but also has no cost; e.g., Levinson 2000). However, this interpretation of the data is hard to maintain in view of the fact that, as it was just discussed, the mismatch of the allegedly generated implicature with the picture had no effect.

We suggest that the longer verification times for the or-match condition may be due to an independent factor: logical complexity. In particular, there is a major difference in complexity between the meanings of the conjunction "and" and the disjunction "or". In order to capture the interpretation of disjunctions in modal environments, several recent studies have analyzed disjunction as having a more complex semantics than conjunction. For instance, Simons (2005) and Alonso-Ovalle (2006) have argued that disjunctions introduce sets of propositional alternatives into the semantic derivation. Assuming this type of semantic approach, the more complex meaning of the disjunction may be more taxing to process than that of an ordinary conjunction (for processing effects of semantic complexity, see, e.g., McKoon & MacFarland 2000, 2002; Gennari & Poeppel 2003).[10] Since the disjoined NPs (as well as their conjoined counterparts) were in

---

(2006), De Neys & Schaeken (2007), and Huang & Snedeker (2009) (cf. also Shetreet et al.'s 2014 fMRI study).

10 The semantic complexity of disjunction is characterized differently on Zimmermann's (2000) account, according to which natural language disjunction is interpreted as a conjunction of (possibility) modal propositions. Thus, informally speaking, a disjunctive sentence such as "A or B" amounts to "Possibly A and possibly B". The alleged complexity of disjunction can also be approached from the perspective of "interpretation entropy". In the case of *or*, interpretation entropy can be characterized as the uncertainty regarding the interpretation of the disjoined NP. The entropy of disjunction is larger than that of conjunction (the set of possible choices of interpretation for a disjoined NP, with different probability distributions, is larger than that for a conjoined NP). Such differences in entropy during language processing have been shown to incur extra processing costs (e.g., Moscoso del Prado Martín, Kostic & Baayen 2004).

a sentence-final position in all test sentences, this potentially caused a spillover effect in the picture-verification phase of trials.

2.3 Interim conclusion

To sum up the main results of Experiment 1, a clear asymmetry was found between conjunction and disjunction: incongruence of the picture paired with the test sentence led to longer reaction times in *and*-trials, while incongruence had no such effect in *or*-trials. This finding points to the conclusion that, as opposed to the entailments of conjunction, the scalar implicature associated with disjunction is not calculated if the experimental task only requires "shallow" processing of the sentence and thus the potential effects of context(ualization) are minimized. This finding furnishes support for contextualism over defaultism.

To make the argument complete, however, it remains to be shown that when relevant, disjunction does in fact normally lead to exclusivity implicatures in the syntactico-semantic context in which it was tested. This was one of the objectives of Experiment 2. The issue whether or not disjunction normally gives rise to an exclusive interpretation in the target sentences involved in Experiment 1 is real, since the scalar implicature associated with *or* is known not to arise equally under all information structural conditions. A notable factor at play, and one that is relevant to our present concerns, is focus. What makes the focus structure of the target sentences of Experiment 1 potentially critical is the special sensitivity of the grammar of Hungarian to focus structure.

3 The relevance of focus

3.1 The potential relevance of focus in Experiment 1

Focusing indicates that the alternatives to the focused item are relevant to the interpretation of the sentence in context (Rooth 1992; Krifka 2008). Focusing a *scalar* item draws attention to the speaker's use of a particular term on a scale of alternatives: it is highlighted that the term used contrasts with its scalar alternatives. As a result, in the case of some scalar implicatures, the implicature is computed more frequently when the scalar element is in focus than when it is not (or according to some accounts, it becomes obligatory; see Hirschberg 1985; van Kuppevelt

1996; Tomlinson & Bott 2013; for a grammar-based analysis of the relation between scalar implicatures and exhaustification by focus, see Chierchia 2004; Fox & Katzir 2009).

As noted earlier, the focus structure of the target sentences in Experiment 1 is of potential significance because the grammar of Hungarian exhibits special sensitivity to focus structure. In particular, Hungarian has obligatory syntactic marking of focus: a narrow focus is routinely placed in an immediately preverbal position (with some systematic exceptions, for which see É. Kiss 2002). This can be illustrated with the case of so-called exclusive adverbs (Kiefer 1967; É. Kiss 1987) of degree (e.g., "barely"), manner (e.g., "badly"), time (e.g., "late"), or frequency (e.g., "rarely"). These adverbs denote values lower on a scale than an expected value or norm, and therefore they are a natural focus of the sentences they are contained in. In Hungarian such adverbs mandatorily appear in the preverbal focus position, that is, their narrow focus status must be marked by word order.[11]

(2) a. *A kislány   meg-látogatja   ritkán   a nagymamát.
       the little.girl PRT-visits   rarely   the grandmother.ACC

   b. A kislány   ritkán látogatja meg   a nagymamát.
      the little.girl rarely visits   PRT   the grandmother.ACC
      "The little girl rarely visits the grandmother."

Of specific relevance to the issue of the relation between the generation of scalar implicatures and the presence versus absence of syntactic focus marking is the case of bare numeral NPs. In particular, an NP like "three cafés" must be syntactically focused if the interpretation is to be unambiguously restricted to no more than three cafés, that is, if higher values on the scale of natural numbers are to be blocked. Consider the minimal pair in (3). (3a), a broad focus sentence with neutral word order, easily licenses an interpretation in which John knows three or more good cafés in town; the scalar implicature "not more than n" arises only optionally. By contrast, according to (3b), in which the numeral phrase is syntactically fronted to a preverbal position, John knows no more than three good cafés, that is, the upward boundedness implicature is practically obligatory (see Gerőcs & Pintér 2014 for an empirical investigation of this difference).

---

[11] For a different explanation for why "exclusive" adverbials are focused by default, see É. Kiss (2009).

(3) a. János ismer három jó kávézót a városban.
   John knows three good café.ACC the town.in

b. János három jó kávézót ismer a városban.
   John three good café.ACC knows the town.in
   "John knows three good cafés in town."

Recall now that in Experiment 1 the critical coordinated nominals appeared in a postverbal position in target sentences that had an unmarked word order associated with a neutral, broad focus interpretation. Thus, word order unambiguously marked the disjunctive NP as not being a focus. In order to be able to draw conclusions from the results of Experiment 1, it needs to be ascertained whether and to what extent the exclusivity implicature of disjunction normally gets calculated in this type of syntactico-semantic context.[12] This is tested in Experiment 2.

At the same time Experiment 2 also serves a second objective. Namely, by comparing disjoined NPs in a nonfocus position to disjoined NPs in a focus position it investigates whether or not focusing enhances the exclusivity implicature of disjunction. In the remainder of this section we briefly review some previous treatments of this question, and formulate our predictions.

3.2 The apparent effect of focus on the exclusivity of disjunction

Whether and how focus (or more generally, prominence) affects the exclusivity of disjunction has been investigated by Chevalliear et al. (2008), Schwarz, Clifton & Frazier (to appear), and Zondervan (2010). These authors unanimously conclude that focal prominence boosts the exclusivity inference associated with *or*. In the remainder of this section we offer a brief critical assessment of their arguments.

As opposed to restraining any facilitating role context may play, the strategy of Chevallier et al.'s (2008) and Schwarz, Clifton & Frazier (to appear)

---

[12] An anonymous reviewer prompts us to demonstrate that the basic meaning of the disjunction *vagy* 'or' in Hungarian is indeed inclusive. This is revealed in downward entailing contexts (though not in the direct scope of negation, because *vagy* is a positive polarity item in Hungarian, see Szabolcsi 2004), as illustrated below:

Mindenki, aki ismeri Marit vagy Annát, meg van hívva a buliba.
Everyone who knows Mary.ACC or Ann.ACC PRT is invited the party.to
"Everyone who knows Mary or Ann is invited to the party."

experiments was to try to facilitate implicatures by adding prominence to disjunction. Chevallier et al. (2008) carried out TVJ experiments involving existential sentences (e.g., *There is an A or a B.*) in which the critical manipulation was whether or not the word *or* was emphasized (by typographic or prosodic means, depending on the nature of the stimulus). In these TVJ experiments, narrow focus on *or* (whether it was expressed typographically or prosodically) significantly increased the proportion of exclusive readings.[13] According to Chevallier et al., this shows that focus on disjunction can increase the rate at which it gives rise to a scalar implicature.

Unfortunately, we cannot conclude from these data that it is *or*'s exclusivity implicature that receives a boost from focus (hence we also cannot draw the more general inference that *or*'s exclusivity implicature itself is due to contextual triggers). The result no doubt demonstrates that focus on *or* ultimately yields a higher rate of "A or B but not both" readings. However, as Zondervan (2010: 90) remarks, it is not clear in this design whether focus increased the rate at which *disjunction* gives rise to a scalar implicature. This is because contrastive focus comes with its own implicature of exhaustivity (focus on the disjunction can only be interpreted contrastively in Chevallier et al.'s test sentences). According to the exhaustivity implicature of focus, while the sentence containing the focused item is true, alternative propositions with relevant alternatives to the focused item replacing the focus are false. As *and* is an obvious relevant alternative lexical item to focused *or*, the increase in the rate of readings with an exclusive interpretation of disjunction follows *even without calculating the exclusivity implicature of disjunction itself.*[14]

Zondervan (2010) offers a book-length treatment of the relation between focus and the exclusivity implicature of disjunction. The basic question addressed by Zondervan's study is not whether the defaultist or the contextualist account of the scalar implicature of *or* is correct, but rather, whether (and how) focus affects this implicature. Nevertheless, a resolution of this latter question also bears on the debate between defaultism and contextualism insofar as if it is demonstrated that focus affects a scalar implicature SI, then a fortiori an aspect of context is

---

13 For the relation between prosodic prominence and focus, see the references in De Kuthy & Stolterfoht (this volume).
14 Schwarz, Clifton & Frazier (to appear) ran a paraphrase selection experiment similar to those in the Chevallier et al. study. In their Experiment 1, prosodic emphasis was added to a disjunction relating to NPs, and this case was compared to a case in which the disjoined NPs were in background of a (verum) focus. Similar comments apply to this experiment as to the Chevallier et al.'s study.

shown to be able to modulate SI, which would be predicted by contextualism without further ado.[15]

Zondervan carried out three types of experiments to gauge the effect of focus on the exclusive interpretation of disjunction: three versions of a TVJ experiment, four versions of an experiment involving what is termed a Possible World Judgment (in which participants are asked about a possibility rather than about truth), and two versions of a self-paced reading experiment. In difference to Chevallier et al. (2008) and Schwarz, Clifton & Frazier (to appear) (see Note 14), Zondervan's experiments involve focus on the disjoined NP "A or B" rather than on the disjunction itself. Unfortunately, none of the experiments that found an effect directly compared a condition with a disjoined NP functioning as a narrow focus to a condition with a disjoined NP having neutral information structural status (i.e., appearing in a broad focus sentence).

The self-paced reading experiment 9 (which detected a slowdown at an anaphoric pronoun in a sentence following the disjoined NP) and the Possible World Judgment experiments 5 and 6 did not discriminate between the effect of focus and the effect of the relevance of the alternative "A and B" in the context: the relevant conditions simultaneously differed with regard to both of these factors.[16] Well aware of this, Zondervan only took his TVJ experiments to demonstrate the effect of focus per se.[17] However, those experiments did not directly compare minimally different conditions either: the condition with the disjoined NP in focus was compared not to a condition in which the disjoined NP was neutral (part of a sentence-wide broad focus), but rather, to a condition in which it was in the background of another focus, hence having a *given* information structural status.[18] The difference between these two latter information structural scenarios is far

---

15 Note that the reverse does not hold. Namely, if focus is shown not to affect SI, then this is not necessarily a blow to contextualism: the claim of contextualism is not that *all* aspects of context affect all scalar implicatures in the same way.
16 Specifically, "A and B" was made relevant as an alternative by "at least two" in the preceding context in the Focus condition, and "A and B" was made irrelevant as an alternative by an inclusively interpreted disjunction "A or B" (appearing in an antecedent of a conditional) in the preceding context.
17 In these TVJ experiments, the size of the difference between the critical focus and nonfocus conditions was relatively small, which Zondervan offers three possible explanations for: (i) chance performance in the nonfocus condition, (ii) a mismatch between implicit and explicit question in the context, and (iii) the default position of information focus at the end of the sentence.
18 In fact, the stories that were provided as a context-setter for this latter sentence type might have even licensed a focus-in-background (aka Second Occurrence Focus, Partee 1991) interpretation to the disjoined NP.

from innocuous, since it is unknown whether and how the scalar implicature of disjunction is affected either simply by givenness, or by being in the background of an information focus. As far as the latter case is concerned, it is not unreasonable to expect that the rate of inclusive readings of disjunction is higher than in neutral cases, at least on an approach to information focus according to which it presupposes an information question in the context, sometimes called Question Under Discussion (QUD, Roberts 1996; in fact, a *wh*-interrogative corresponding to the QUD explicitly appeared in the context preceding the target sentence in Experiments 1 and 2). For instance, a sentence like *PAULA took an apple or a pear* presupposes the QUD "Who took an apple or a pear?" Questions, however, are known to be a type of semantic context in which disjunction gives rise to few exclusive interpretations (Chierchia et al. 2001; Noveck et al. 2002; Chierchia, Frazier & Clifton 2009; Schwarz, Clifton & Frazier, to appear). This could then have a priming effect on the rate of exclusive interpretations when a disjoined NP is in the background of an information focus, which was the case in all three of Zondervan's TVJ experiments.

It can be concluded that the evidence offered so far to support the idea that focus on the disjoined NP enhances the scalar implicature associated with disjunction is inconclusive at best. In view of this it is worth reconsidering whether the expectation of such a boosting effect of focusing is well founded in the first place.

The prediction that focusing a disjoined NP will enhance *or*'s exclusive reading rests on the assumption that the set of relevant focus-alternatives to disjoined NPs and the set of scalar alternatives to disjoined NPs both contain (the denotation of) a conjoined counterpart of the disjoined NP (i.e., "an apple and a pear" in the case of the disjoined NP *an apple or a pear*). If the highlighting of alternatives achieved by focus is potentially stronger than the level of activation normally associated with the scalar alternatives of the item at hand, then the conjoined alternative may be more likely to get excluded in the course of sentence interpretation. However, the correctness of the assumption that the relevant focus-alternatives to a disjunction of two NPs include a conjunction of the same NPs is doubtful. It has been argued that the set of alternatives {A, B, A and B} forms part of the semantic interpretation of a disjoined NP *A or B* (see Simons 2005; Alonso-Ovalle 2006). Given that "A and B" is included in the semantics of *A or B*, "A and B" cannot be among the pragmatically excludable focus alternatives to the denotation of *A or B*. What focusing *A or B* can exclude by exhaustification are alternatives like "C", "A and C", and "A and B and C". If "A and B" is not among the excludable alternatives for exhaustification by focus, then focusing *A or B* simply cannot enter its exclusion. Therefore, if the scalar exclusivity implicature is not triggered independently of focus, focusing the disjoined NP will not trigger it. In short, focus on *A or B* should not have an effect on the rate at which disjunction is interpreted exclusively. In order to investigate this prediction, Experiment 2, to be reported below, compares broad focus sentences containing a disjoined NP to sentences in which the disjoined NP is a narrow focus.

4 Experiment 2

4.1 Objectives

In this experiment we tested whether focusing a disjoined NP has an effect on the rate of exclusivity implicatures. In particular, we compared broad focus sentences containing a disjoined NP to sentences in which the disjoined NP was syntactically unambiguously marked as a narrow focus. Such a comparison is different from the comparison made in Zondervan's (2010) TVJ experiments: the latter compared a focused disjoined NP to a given disjoined NP in the background of another focus (see Section 3.2, cf. also note 18). As explained at the end of the preceding section, we expected focus on the disjoined NP not to affect the likelihood of exclusive interpretations.

4.2 Method

4.2.1 Method and design

Participants performed a computer-based sentence–picture matching task by rating the pictures on a five-point Likert scale with regard to the extent of their match with the sentences. We opted for a five-point scale to allow for neutral ratings (i.e., 3), with 5 representing best and 1 corresponding to worst match.[19]

At the beginning of the experiment, the following story frame was provided. A girl at a party that took place some time ago claimed to be a witch, and to be able to see into the future. To prove this, she made predictions as to what other people at the party will do in the near future. In each trial participants read a sentence (which was a prediction that the girl had made) and saw a picture (which depicted what the person actually did). The experimental task in each trial was

---

[19] For a discussion of the use of Likert-scale-based judgments in investigations of sentence interpretation, see Gerbrich et al. (this volume).

to judge the correctness of the prediction. Specifically, participants had to decide to what extent the prediction that had been made corresponds to what happened later in reality.

Stimulus sentences contained a disjoined NP, and pictures depicted the two objects corresponding to the disjoined nouns. Either one or both of the objects were depicted either as having undergone the event denoted by the verb, or as not having undergone it, similarly to Experiment 1 (see Section 2.1.2). As independent variables, we varied the focus status of the disjoined NP in the sentence (focused or neutral) and the targeted interpretation of the disjunction according to the picture depiction (exclusive or inclusive). The dependent variable was the rating score.

The reason why we based this TVJ task on participants' evaluation of the truth of *predictions* (call this PTVJ) is that this modality carries an important benefit for the purposes of testing the interpretation of disjunction. Based on Gricean reasoning, a simple disjunctive assertion amounting to $p \vee q$ should give rise to what has been called an "ignorance" implicature, namely that the speaker is not sure that p and she is not sure that q. If the context is such that the speaker is supposed to know whether p and whether q, then the assertion of $p \vee q$ may be perceived as infelicitous. This potential infelicitiousness may enter experimental participants' judgments of disjunctive statements describing straightforward pictures. In our PTVJ, in which stimulus sentences are predictions about the future rather than statements made about here and now, this problem of infelicitousness does not arise.

2×2 sets of critical sentence–picture pairs were created (neutral-inclusive, neutral-exclusive, focused-inclusive, focused-exclusive). The two variables (Picture Type: exclusive / inclusive and Sentence Type: neutral / focused) were within-subject factors. The sentences were split into four lists of 20 test items (5 items per condition), to which 20 fillers were added. Four counterbalancing lists were created to which participants were assigned at random, with the critical and the filler items on a list also randomized per person. Each target item was tested equally frequently in every Sentence Type and Picture Type condition across the four between-subject counterbalance lists. As list did not have a significant effect, the four lists were collapsed in the course of the statistical analyses. Therefore, the two independent variables were not treated as single within-item factors.

4.2.2 Participants

A total of 91 Hungarian undergraduates participated in the web-based experiment after giving informed consent. They were all monolingual speakers of Hungarian and received money for their participation. No participant was excluded from the analyses.

4.2.3 Stimuli

The stimulus sentences in which the disjoined NP was not focused were neutral, broad focus sentences with canonical word order: they had the disjoined NP in a postverbal position. On the other hand, in stimulus sentences in which the disjoined NP was focused, this was marked by noncanonical word order, with the disjoined NP in an immediately preverbal position (see Section 3.1). The two word orders are illustrated in (4). The preverbal versus postverbal position of the disjoined NP was balanced across target sentences.

(4) a. Mari majd kettévágja a dinnyét vagy
 Mari FUT into.two.cuts the melon.ACC or
 a paradicsomot. (neutral)
 the tomato.ACC
 "Mary will cut the melon or the tomato into two."

 b. Mari majd a dinnyét vagy a paradicsomot vágja
 Mari FUT the melon.ACC or the tomato.ACC cuts
 ketté. (focused)
 into.two

The same type of (color) picture stimuli was used as in Experiment 1. Pictures were counterbalanced in terms of the arrangement of the two objects they depicted in the exclusive conditions. That is, in half of the cases the object that was affected by the event denoted by the verb appeared on the right, while in the other half of the cases the object appeared on the left. For example, in the exclusive picture associated with the sentences in (4) the cut object either appeared on the left or on the right. This latter type of variation was balanced in the survey.

4.2.4 Procedure

The experimental items were presented on a computer screen using the Inquisite software. The participants first read the instructions. Four practice items were part of the instructions. In every trial the task was to read a sentence, inspect a picture, and judge its match with the sentence. After the practice phase, the experimental trials were presented one by one. The participants' responses were recorded, transcribed, and scored.

4.3 Results and discussion

Data were analyzed using the R software (R Development Core Team, 2013, version 3.3.2). On the scale from 1 to 5 the focused-inclusive condition received a median rating of 3.00 (Min: 1, Max: 5) compared to the focused-exclusive condition with a median rating of 5 (Min: 1, Max: 5). In the neutral-inclusive condition we find a median score of 3 (Min: 1, Max: 5) compared to the neutral-exclusive with a median rating of 5 (Min: 1, Max: 5) (Figure 3).

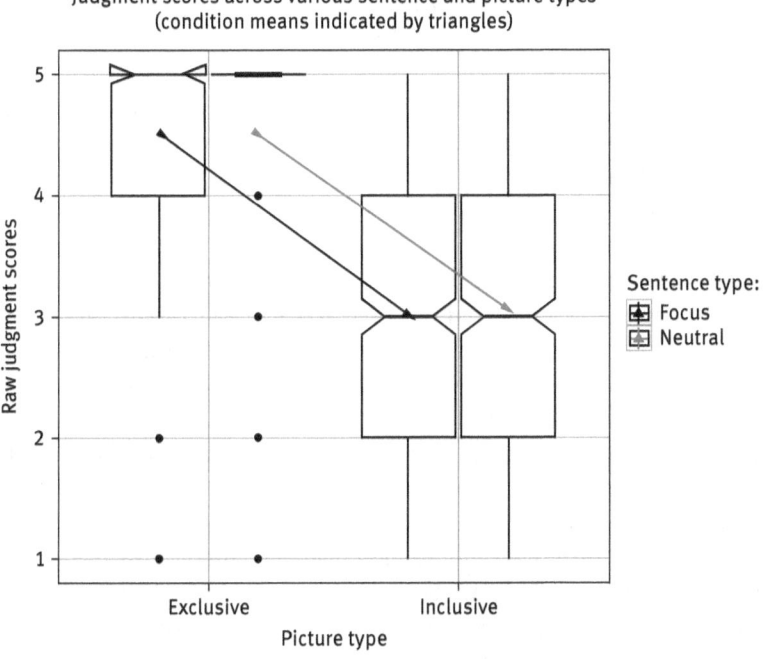

Figure 3: Boxplot of rating score medians with interaction plot of rating score means.

The R package *ordinal* (Christensen 2015) was used to perform cumulative link mixed models (CLMM) on the ordinal-scale data to model both participant and item variabilities, that is, to simultaneously model differences between participants and items. The raw scores as primary outcomes (i.e., item ratings per participant and condition) were entered into the statistical analyses. Sentence Type (neutral/focused), Picture Type (inclusive/exclusive), and their interaction served as fixed factors in the model, including random intercepts for participant and item. Inclusion of random effects was assessed by comparing the Akaike information criterion values of fitted models (Akaike 1974) using likelihood ratio tests.

We first contrast coded the two levels of Sentence Type and the two levels of Picture Type to allow for testing the overall effect of the two fixed factors. Additionally, we calculated the interaction in order to assess whether the Picture Type violation has a different impact on the two levels of Sentence Type. We started out with a model that had a single random factor and then added additional random factors and random slopes. Our best-fitting model contained random intercepts for participant and item. The CLMMs were fitted with the Laplace approximation (Pinheiro & Bates 1995) using the probit link function and the "equidistant" threshold option.

The CLMM analysis revealed a significant main effect of Picture Type ($\beta = -1.9813$, $se = 0.1813$, $Z = -10.925$, $p < 0.001$). The main effect of Sentence Type was not significant ($\beta = -0.0041$, $se = 0.1896$, $Z = -0.022$, $p = 0.983$), and neither was the interaction of the two factors ($\beta = 0.0359$, $se = 0.1126$, $Z = 0.318$, $p = 0.750$).[20]

In other words, the exclusive interpretation of the disjunctive NP was accepted at close to ceiling levels and was unaffected by focus status, while the non-exclusive interpretation received ratings averaging around the center of the 5-point scale, again without exhibiting any influence of focus status.

First, these results point to the following conclusion with regard to postverbal disjoined NPs appearing in a neutral, broad focus information structural context. When relevant, the exclusivity implicature is routinely calculated for such NPs, and their exclusive reading is strongly preferred compared to their inclusive reading. From that, in turn, we can conclude that the pattern of results of the *or*-conditions in Experiment 1 cannot be due to a general, context-independent lack (or sporadicity) of exclusivity implicatures in the postverbal, nonfocus position, but rather, it must be due to the experimental manipulation, namely, the radical irrelevance of the implicature in the task.

---

20 The use of a CLMM analysis is based on the assumption that our judgment data are ordinal in nature. In view of the long-standing controversy regarding the ordinal or interval nature, and the admissible statistical analyses, of Likert-scale data of the kind we are concerned with (see Carifio & Perla 2007, Norman 2010), we also analyzed the collected ratings as interval data. Performing a repeated measures ANOVA, with Sentence Type and Picture Type as within-subject factors, yielded the same results for main effects and interaction as those derived from the main text CLMM analysis.

Second, the fact that focusing had no significant effect and it showed no significant interaction with the targeted interpretation of disjunction confirms our prediction that focus on the disjoined NP should have no effect on the likelihood of an exclusive implicature. As argued in Section 3, this pattern is expected if in the case of a focused disjoined NP *A or B*, "A and B" is not among the excludable focus alternatives

5 Conclusions

In this chapter, we reported on the results of two experiments examining the scalar implicature associated with disjunction. Experiment 1 employed a task only requiring "shallow" processing, which made the exclusivity implicature of *or* contextually maximally irrelevant. Overall, the results suggest that in such a task, while the entailment of the connective *and* was computed automatically, the implicature of *or* was not calculated. This finding speaks against (both strong and weak versions of) defaultism, according to which scalar implicatures are generated by default (in which they are unaffected by context), and it favors contextualist approaches. From a broader perspective, our results indicate that "shallow" processing tasks are a valuable experimental tool for psycholinguistic experimental research at the semantics–pragmatics interface more generally.

A further TVJ study (Experiment 2) confirmed that the absence of the exclusivity implicatures in Experiment 1 was indeed due to its contextual irrelevance, rather than to an overall lack of exclusivity implicatures in the neutral word order that was employed. In addition, a comparison of broad focus and narrow focus sentences in Experiment 2 casts serious doubt on previous claims that the focus status of the disjoined NP, a contextual property of the sentence in which it occurs, boosts the likelihood of the exclusivity implicature. The lack of such an effect is expected if in the case of the disjunction *A or B*, "A and B" is not among the excludable alternatives for exhaustification by focus.

Acknowledgments: The authors are grateful to Anna Babarczy and Mátyás Gerőcs for helpful discussion. This work was supported by a Momentum grant to the first author (#2011–013, Hungarian Academy of Sciences), and by grant #KAP19-14014-1.2-BTK of PPCU.

References

Akaike, H. 1974. A new look at the statistical model identification. IEEE Transactions on Automatic Control 19(6): 716–723.

Alonso-Ovalle, L. 2006. Disjunction in alternative semantics. PhD diss., University of Massachusetts.

Bezuidenhout, A. & J.C. Cutting 2002. Literal meaning, minimal propositions, and pragmatic processing. Journal of Pragmatics 34(4). 433–456.

Bonnefon, J.-F., A. Feeney & G. Villejoubert. 2009. When some is actually all: Scalar inferences in face-threatening contexts. Cognition 112(2): 249–258.

Bott, L. & I.A. Noveck. 2004. Some utterances are underinformative: The onset and time course of scalar inferences. Journal of Memory and Language 51(3): 437–457.

Breheny, R., N. Katsos & J. Williams. 2006. Are generalised scalar implicatures generated by default? An on-line investigation into the role of context in generating pragmatic inferences. Cognition 100(3): 434–463.

Breheny, R., H.J. Ferguson & N. Katsos. 2013. Investigating the timecourse of accessing conversational implicatures during incremental sentence interpretation. Language and Cognitive Processes 28(4): 443–467.

Carifio, J. & R.J. Perla. 2007. Ten common misunderstandings, misconceptions, persistent myths and urban legends about Likert scales and Likert response formats and their antidotes. Journal of the Social Sciences 3(3): 106–116.

Carston, R. 1998. Informativeness, relevance and scalar implicature. In: (R. Carston & S. Uchida, eds) Relevance Theory: Applications and Implications, 179–236. Amsterdam: John Benjamins.

Carston, R. 2004. Truth-conditional content and conversational implicature. In: (C. Bianchi, ed) The Semantics/Pragmatics Distinction, 18–48. Stanford: CSLI Publications.

Chierchia, G. 2004. Scalar implicatures, polarity phenomena and the syntax/pragmatics interface. In: (A. Belletti, ed) Structures and Beyond: The Cartography of Syntactic Structures, Vol. 3, 39–103. Oxford: Oxford University Press.

Chierchia, G., S. Crain, M.T. Guasti, A. Gualmini & L. Meroni. 2001. The acquisition of disjunction: evidence for a grammatical view of scalar implicatures. In: Proceedings of the 25th Annual Boston University Conference on Language Development. Somerville, MA: Cascadilla Press.

Chierchia, G., D. Fox & B. Spector. 2012. Scalar implicature as a grammatical phenomenon. In: (C. Maienborn, K. von Heusinger & P. Portner, eds) Semantics: An International Handbook of Natural Language Meaning, Vol. 3, 2297–2331. Berlin: Mouton de Gruyter.

Chierchia, G., L. Frazier & C. Clifton, Jr. 2009. When basic meanings are (not) enough: Processing scalar implicatures in adult comprehension. In: (M. Biezma & J.A. Harris, eds) UMOP 39: Papers in Pragmatics, 21–39. Amherst, MA: GLSA Publications.

Chevallier, C., I.A. Noveck, T. Nazir, L. Bott, V. Lanzetti & D. Sperber. 2008. Making disjunctions exclusive. Quarterly Journal of Experimental Psychology 61(11): 1741–1760.

Christensen, R.H.B. 2015. Analysis of ordinal data with cumulative link models – estimation with the R-package ordinal. https://cran.r-project.org/web/packages/ordinal/vignettes/clm_intro.pdf

Degen, J., P.A. Reeder, K. Carbary & M.K. Tanenhaus. 2009. Using a novel experimental paradigm to investigate the processing of scalar implicatures. Paper presented at the Experimental Pragmatics Conference 2009, Lyon, April 23 –25, 2009.

Degen, J. & M.K. Tanenhaus. 2011. Making inferences: The case of scalar implicature processing. In: (L. Carlson, C. Hölscher & T. Shipley, eds) Proceedings of the 33rd Annual Conference of the Cognitive Science Society, 3299–3304. Austin, TX: Cognitive Science Society.
De Neys, W. & W. Schaeken. 2007. When people are more logical under cognitive load: Dual task impact on scalar implicature. Experimental Psychology 54(2): 128–133.
É. Kiss, K. 1987. Configurationality in Hungarian. Dordrecht: Foris.
É. Kiss, K. 2002. Syntax of Hungarian. Cambridge: Cambridge University Press.
É. Kiss, K. 2009. Scalar adverbs in and out of focus. In: (É. Kiss, K., ed) Adverbs and Adverbial Adjuncts at the Interfaces, 297–316. Berlin: Mouton de Gruyter.
Evans, J.S.B. & S.E. Newstead, 1980. A study of disjunctive reasoning. Psychological Research 41(4): 373–388.
Feeney, A., S. Scafton, A. Duckworth & S.J. Handley. 2004. The story of some: Everyday pragmatic inferences by children and adults. Canadian Journal of Experimental Psychology 58(2): 121–132.
Ferreira, F., K.G.D. Bailey & V. Ferraro. 2002. Good-enough representations in language comprehension. Current Directions in Psychological Science 11(1): 11–15.
Fox, D. & Katzir, R. 2009. On the characterization of alternatives. Manuscript. Cambridge, MA. MIT.
Gennari, S. & D. Poeppel. 2003. Processing correlates of lexical semantic complexity. Cognition 89(1): 27–41.
Gerőcs, M. & L. Pintér. 2014. How do Hungarian preschoolers interpret number words? In: M. Kohlberger, K. Bellamy & E. Dutton (eds.), ConSOLE XXI, 104–122. Leiden: Leiden University.
Geurts, B. 2011. Quantity Implicatures. Cambridge: Cambridge University Press.
Grodner, D.J., N.M. Klein, K.M. Carbary & M.K. Tanenhaus. 2010. 'Some', and possibly all, scalar inferences are not delayed: Evidence for immediate pragmatic enrichment. Cognition 116(1): 42–55.
Hartshorne, J.K. & J. Snedeker. 2014. The speed of inference: Evidence against rapid use of context in calculation of scalar implicatures.
Hirschberg, J. 1985. A theory of scalar implicature, Ph.D. thesis, Pennsylvania State University.
Huang, Y. & J. Snedeker. 2009. On-line interpretation of scalar quantifiers: Insight into the semantic-pragmatics interface. Cognitive Psychology 58(3): 376–415.
Huang, Y. & J. Snedeker. 2011. 'Logic & conversation' revisited: Evidence for a division between semantic and pragmatic content in real time language comprehension. Language and Cognitive Processes 26(8): 1161–1172.
Huang, Y. & J. Snedeker. 2018. Some inferences still take time: Prosody, predictability, and the speed of scalar implicatures. Cognitive Psychology 102: 105–126.
Kaschak, M.P., C.J. Madden, D.J. Therriault, R.H. Yaxley, M. Aveyard, A.A. Blanchard & R.A. Zwaan. 2005. Perception of motion affects language processing. Cognition 94(3): B79–B89.
Katsos, N. 2006. Experimental investigations of the effects of structure and context on the generation of scalar implicatures. Ph.D. diss. Cambridge, UK, University of Cambridge.
Kiefer, F. 1967. On Emphasis and Word Order in Hungarian. (Uralic and Altaic Series 76.) Bloomington, Indiana University: Mouton VII. Indiana University Publications.
Krifka, M. 2008. Basic notions of information structure. Acta Linguistica Hungarica 55: 243–276.
Kuppevelt, J. van. 1996. Inferring from topics. Scalar implicatures as topic dependent inferences. Linguistics and Philosophy 19(4): 393–443.
Landman, F. 2000. Events and Plurality. Dordrecht: Kluwer.

Levinson, S.C. 2000. Presumptive Meaning: The Theory of Generalized Conversational Implicature. Cambridge, MA: MIT Press.
Louwerse, M.M. & P. Jeuniaux. 2010. The linguistic and embodied nature of conceptual processing. Cognition 114(1): 96–104.
Magri, G. 2009. A theory of individual-level predicates based on blind mandatory scalar implicatures. Natural Language Semantics 17(3): 245–297.
Magri, G. 2011. Another argument for embedded scalar implicatures based on oddness in downward entailing environments. Semantics and Pragmatics 4: 1–51.
McKoon, G. & T. Macfarland. 2000. Externally and internally caused change of state verbs. Language 76(4): 833–858.
McKoon, G. & T. Macfarland. 2002. Event templates in the lexical representations of verbs. Cognitive Psychology 47(1): 1–44.
Moscoso del Prado Martín, F., A. Kostíc & R.H. Baayen. 2004. Putting the bits together: An informational theoretical perspective on morphological processing. Cognition 94(1): 1–18.
Norman, G. 2010. Likert scales, levels of measurement and the "laws" of statistics. Advances Health Sciences Education Theory Practical 15(5): 625–632.
Noveck, I.A., G. Chierchia, F. Chevaux, R. Guelminger & E. Sylvestre. 2002. Linguistic-pragmatic factors in interpreting disjunctions. Thinking and Reasoning 8(4): 297–326.
Noveck, I.A. & A. Posada. 2003. Characterizing the time course of an implicature: An evoked potentials study. Brain and Language 85(2): 203–210.
Noveck, I.A. & D. Sperber. 2007. The why and how of experimental pragmatics: The case of 'scalar inferences'. In: (N. Burton-Roberts, ed) Pragmatics, 184–212. Basingstoke, UK: Palgrave Macmillan.
Paris, S.G. 1973. Comprehension of language connectives and propositional logical relationships. Journal of Experimental Child Psychology 16(2). 278–291.
Partee, B. 1991. Topic, focus and quantification. Semantics and Linguistic Theory 1: 159–187.
Pijnacker, J., P. Hagoort, J. Buitelaar, J.-P. Teunisse & B. Geurts. 2009. Pragmatic inferences in high-functioning adults with autism and Asperger Syndrome. Journal of Autism and Developmental Disorders 39(4): 607–618.
Pinheiro, J.C. & D.M. Bates. 1995. Approximations to the log-likelihood function in the nonlinear mixed-effects model. Journal of Computational and Graphical Statistics 4(1): 12–35.
Pouscoulous, N., I.A. Noveck, G. Politzer & A. Bastide. 2007. A developmental investigation of processing costs in implicature production. Language Acquisition 14(4): 347–376.
Psychology Software Tools, Inc. 2017. E-Prime: Documentation Article. https://support.pstnet.com
R Core Team. 2013. R: A language and environment for statistical computing. R Foundation for Statistical Computing, Vienna, Austria. http://www.R-project.org/
Recanati, F. 2003. Embedded implicatures. Philosophical Perspectives 17(1): 299–332.
Richardson, D.C., M.J. Spivey, L.W. Barsalou & K. McRae. 2003. Spatial representations activated during real-time comprehension of verbs. Cognitive Science 27(5): 767–780.
Roberts, C. 1996. Information Structure in discourse: Towards an integrated formal theory of pragmatics. In: J. Yoon & A. Kathol (eds.) Ohio State University Working Papers in Linguistics Volume 49. (Reprinted in the 1998 version with a new afterword in Semantics and Pragmatics Vol. 5, 2012.)
Rooth, M.E. 1992. A theory of focus interpretation. Natural Language Semantics 1(1): 75–116.
Sanford, A. J., & Sturt, P. 2002. Depth of processing in language comprehension: not noticing the evidence. Trends in Cognitive Sciences 6(9),382–386.

Sauerland, U. 2004. Scalar implicatures in complex sentences. Linguistics and Philosophy 27(3): 367–391.
Schwarz, F., C. Clifton Jr. & L. Frazier. to appear. Strengthening 'or': Effects of focus and downward entailing contexts on scalar implicatures. In: (J. Anderssen, K. Moulton, F. Schwarz & C. Ussery, eds) Semantics and Processing (UMOP 37). Amherst, MA: GLSA Publications.
Scorolli, C. & A.M. Borghi. 2007. Sentence comprehension and action: Effector specific modulation of the motor system. Brain Research 1130(1): 119–124.
Sedivy, J.C. 2003. Pragmatic versus form-based accounts of referential contrast: Evidence for effects of informativity expectations. Journal of Psycholinguistic Research 32(1): 3–23.
Sedivy, J.C., M.K. Tanenhaus, C.G. Chambers & G.N. Carlson. 1999. Achieving incremental semantic interpretation through contextual representation. Cognition 71(2): 109–147.
Shetreet, E., G. Chierchia & N. Gaab. 2014. When 'some' is not 'every': Dissociating scalar implicature generation and mismatch. Human Brain Mapping 35(4): 1503–1514.
Simons, M. 2005. Dividing things up: The semantics of or and the modal/or interaction. Natural Language Semantics 13: 271–316.
Sperber, D. & D. Wilson. 1995. Relevance: Communication and Cognition. 2nd ed. Cambridge: Blackwell.
Stanfield, R.A. & R.A. Zwaan. 2001. The effect of implied orientation derived from verbal context on picture recognition. Psychological Science 12(2): 153–156.
Swets, B., T. Desmet, C. Clifton Jr. & F. Ferreira. 2008. Underspecification of syntactic ambiguities: Evidence from self-paced reading. Memory and Cognition 36(1): 201–216.
Szabolcsi, A. 2004. Positive polarity – negative polarity. Natural Language and Linguistic Theory 22(2). 409–452.
Tomlinson, J.M. Jr. & L. Bott. 2013. How intonation constrains pragmatic inference. In: (M. Knauff, M. Pauen, N. Sebanz & I. Wachsmuth, eds) Proceedings of 35th Annual Conference of the Cognitive Science Society, 3567–3574. Austin, TX: Cognitive Science Society.
Van Rooij, R. & K. Schulz. 2004. Exhaustive Interpretation of Complex Sentences. Journal of Logic, Language and Information 13(4): 491–419.
Whelan, R. 2008. Effective analysis of reaction time data. The Psychological Record 58(3). Article 9. http://opensiuc.lib.siu.edu/tpr/vol58/iss3/9
Wilson, D. & D. Sperber. 2012. Meaning and Relevance. Cambridge: Cambridge University Press.
Zimmermann, T.E. 2000. Free choice disjunction and epistemic possibility. Natural Language Semantics 8(4): 255–290.
Zondervan, A. 2010. Scalar Implicatures or Focus: An Experimental Approach. Utrecht: LOT Publications.
Zwaan, R.A., R.A. Stanfield & R.H. Yaxley. 2002. Language comprehenders mentally represent the shapes of objects. Psychological Science 13(2): 168–171.

Andreas Konietzko and Karen Lidzba
The processing of argument structure: A comparison between patients with early left-hemispheric brain lesions and healthy controls

1 Introduction

In this study, we report a series of experiments on the linguistic competence of patients with pre- or perinatally acquired unilateral left-hemispheric brain lesions in comparison to well-matched healthy controls. We focus on the syntactic competence and test various types of noncanonical word order and noncanonical argument realizations such as topicalization, passivization, and psych-verbs. Research on this patient group has revealed a mixed picture with regard to the overall linguistic competence. Concentrating mainly on standardized tests, early work on this patient group has shown that patients reach an unremarkable competence in grammar by the age of 5 (Stiles et al. 1998) or 10 (Reilly et al. 1998) although the language acquisition process may be delayed (Eisele & Aram 1995, Chilosi et al. 2005) in comparison to healthy controls. However, some studies also report that the mean length of utterance is shorter in patients and syntactic complexity may be reduced in language production, that is, production may contain less embedded structures. Eisele & Aram (1994) report differences in imitation but no differences in language comprehension.

However, there are also studies that report clear differences in language competence between patients and healthy controls. MacWhinney et al. (2000) report that patients perform worse than controls in some parts of the CELF-R language test (Semel et al. 1987). In particular, differences were detected in the subparts *oral directions* (OD) and *formulating sentences* (FS). FS tests syntactic, semantic, and pragmatic competence in the formation of sentences out of given words and OD contains complex oral directions. MacWhinney et al. also report longer reaction times with verbal tasks in the patient group. By contrast, no significant differences were detected in the IQ-Tests (cf. also Staudt et al. 2002). More recently, Schwilling (2012) and Schwilling et al. (2012) report for German speakers that patients perform significantly worse with respect to more complex syntactic structures such as object topicalization and object relative clauses in comparison to healthy controls. These findings have also been confirmed in detailed experimental settings for complex syntax in German (Lidzba et al. 2013), and also for verbal morphology (Knecht & Lidzba 2016).

https://doi.org/10.1515/9783110623093-011

Although syntactic deficits have been reported for various types of constructions, the precise source of these deficits is still unclear. In particular, it is unclear whether these deficits have one common source, such as for instance a general computational deficit having to do with increasing syntactic complexity or whether there are multiple sources for these deficits. Different syntactic constructions, such as relative clause formation, passivization, and topicalization might each come with their own construction-specific requirements responsible for deficits in the patients group. Also, it is not clear whether the deficits are to be located within the syntactic domain or whether it is rather a problem of the interfaces where representations of one domain have to be mapped onto representations of another domain. For instance, in the case of object topicalization in German, which has been reported to be particularly problematic for patients with left-hemispheric brain lesions (Schwilling 2012; Schwilling et al. 2012; Lidzba et al. 2013), the problem could lie in the computational component or at the interface to argument structure. Under the first assumption, one could assume that filler-gap dependencies, which involve movement, are particularly difficult to process for patients because movement imposes a higher computational burden on the processor. A somewhat different assumption would be to assume that movement per se is not a problem. Rather, the mapping between different grammatical representations, such as syntax and argument structure, could be affected in the patient group leading thus to processing difficulties. In this chapter, we investigate the hypothesis that the deficits are best analyzed as being located at the interface between syntax and argument structure. In particular, we propose the following hypothesis for the processing of noncanonical word order in patients with language reorganization:

(1) Default mapping hypothesis:
    The mapping between syntax and argument structure in patients with left hemispheric brain lesions prefers direct linking over indirect linking.

We will couch our approach within the extended argument dependency model (eADM) (Bornkessel & Schlesewsky 2006). Empirical evidence will be drawn from the investigation of three different types of construction such as object topicalization (2a,b), passivization (2c), and psych-verbs (2d):[1]

---

[1] Throughout the paper, we mark NPs with syncretic case by providing all potential case values for the NP. Since our test material did not contain structurally ambiguous sentences, the ambiguity only arises when the NP is first encountered during incremental processing.

(2) a. Das Buch   lobt   der Kritiker.
       the$_{nom/acc}$ book praises the$_{nom}$ critic
    b. Den Autor   lobt   der Kritiker.
       the$_{acc}$ author praises the$_{nom}$ critic
    c. Das Buch   wird von dem Kritiker gelobt.
       the$_{nom/acc}$ book aux by the$_{dat}$ critic praised
    d. Dem Kritiker gefällt das Buch.
       the$_{dat}$ critic pleases the$_{nom/acc}$ book

All three constructions pose a challenge for the parser with respect to argument structure. For instance, in topicalization, given in (2a), there is a reordering of the arguments of the verb. If the topicalized object DP is case ambiguous as in (2a), the parser runs into a garden path and realizes only when it encounters the nominative *der Kritiker* that the sentence-initial DP *das Buch* bears accusative case. Consequently, the sentence has to be reanalyzed. But even when the sentence-initial DP is case unambiguous, as in (2b), it might still be misinterpreted as a nominative. In the passive in (2c) there is an argument alternation induced by the passivization. In this case, the sentence-initial nominative is not assigned the Agent role, as would be the case in the equivalent active sentence, rather it bears the Theme role and the Agent is realized in the *von*-PP. In the psych-verb construction in (2d), the sentence contains an initial dative, which is presumably base generated in this position; hence, no reordering of arguments is involved (cf. Haider 1993; Fanselow 2000). In this example, the highest argument role, here the Experiencer, is associated with the dative case, while the nominative is assigned to the Theme-bearing DP *das Buch*. The chapter is structured as follows: Sections 2 and 3 provide the theoretical background on argument structure and the eADM. Section 4 introduces the main hypotheses of the chapter regarding the processing of argument structure: The Strong Morphosyntactic Hypothesis, the Cumulativity Hypothesis, and the Cue Strength Hypothesis. In Section 5, these hypotheses are tested against experimental evidence from object topicalization, psych-verbs, and passivization. Section 6 summarizes and discusses the results.

2 Argument structure

Argument structure (a-structure) refers to a lexical representation of a predicate's grammatical information (Grimshaw 1990: 1). It mediates between the lexical meaning of a predicate and the syntactic component of the grammar. The core component of argument structure is to represent the prominence relations between the arguments of a predicate (Grimshaw 1990: 4). For instance, the representation of the argument structure of a verb such as *announce* would be the following (Grimshaw 1990: 4):

(3) announce(Agent (Goal (Theme)))

The bracketed structure mirrors the prominence relations between the arguments. The Agent is the most prominent argument and the Goal argument is more prominent than the Theme. Thematic hierarchy is the "organizing principle of a-structure" (Grimshaw 1990: 7). Grimshaw proposes the following hierarchy of thematic prominence (cf. also Jackendoff 1972):

(4) (Agent (Experiencer (Goal/Source/Location (Theme))))

Under this view, the Agent is the highest-ranked argument, followed by the Experiencer. Goal, Source, and Location are equally ranked and less prominent than the Experiencer. The Theme is the least prominent argument.

Let us now see how the approach sketched so far can be applied to the data in (2). The verb *loben* ('praise') is a two-place predicate, which assigns an Agent role to the subject DP (someone who does the praising) and a Theme role to the object DP (the entity that is praised). The argument structure of *loben* is exemplified in (5):

(5) loben(x (y))
     x = Agent y = Theme

In the syntax, the Agent role of *loben* is mapped onto the subject, which is assigned nominative case, the Theme is mapped onto the object which bears the accusative. In the case of *gefallen* ('please'), the argument structure is different. Here, the verb is associated with an Experiencer role, which is assigned to the dative bearing DP *dem Kritiker*. The second role is a Theme, which is assigned to the subject DP *das Buch*. Verbs that assign an Experiencer theta role are referred to as psychological predicates (or psych-verbs) in the literature (cf. Belletti & Rizzi 1988, Scheepers et al. 2000). The argument structure is shown in (6):

(6) gefallen(x (y))
     x = Exp. y = Theme

Note, that the linking between the theta roles and the DPs in the syntax is quite different in the two cases. In (5), the highest ranked argument (the Agent) is linked to the subject DP and, as (2a-b) shows, the less prominent Theme is associated with the object DP. In the case of *gefallen* (cf. 2d) the highest ranked argument, the Experiencer, is associated with the dative object, while the less prominent Theme is linked to the subject DP. We will come back to this behavior in Section 3. Let us now turn to the processing of argument structure. In particular, let us consider how argument structure is mapped onto syntactic structure during sentence processing.

3 The extended argument dependency model

The eADM (Bornkessel & Schlesewsky 2006) offers an approach to sentence processing with a very explicit idea about how argument structure is mapped onto syntactic structure. The core idea is that sentence processing proceeds in three separate phases in a serial fashion, as shown in Figure 1.

The first phase includes the activation of syntactic templates. The core idea is that the templates represent basic verb-complement patterns of a given language. These templates are then assigned phrasal category labels that are identified by morphological information. For a transitive agentive verb such as *loben*, the output of the first phase would look as shown in (8):

(8)

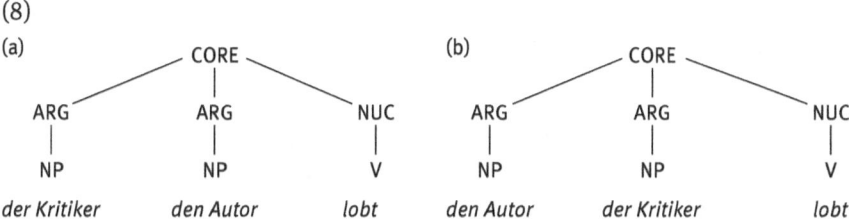

As German exhibits a relatively free word order, the phrasal category labels would be the same for canonical word orders, as in (8a), or nonbase structures such as (8b). The critical step during sentence processing with respect to word order happens during the second phase where thematic hierarchies as in (4) are activated and assigned to the NPs on the basis of case information. Moreover, verbal morphology responsible for agreement and voice is considered to compute the correct sentence structure. In the third phase, the computed sentence structure is validated and wellformedness is checked. If necessary, repair mechanisms may apply. Let us now consider the mapping mechanism between the syntactic structure and the thematic hierarchies. Bornkessel & Schlesewsky (2006) distinguish two types of mapping. The first case is found in unmarked word orders where the highest argument is mapped onto the highest syntactic DP position, as in an SVO word order in German where the subject is assigned the Agent theta role. This is the case of "direct linking" between argument structure and syntactic structure. The second case is found in marked word orders, as in topicalization structures. In this case, the highest syntactic NP position (which may be derived by topicalizing the object DP to the prefield position) is mapped onto the less prominent argument as, for example, the Theme. The two instances of argument linking are shown in (9). Instead of Agent and Theme, Bornkessel & Schlesewsky use the labels Actor and Undergoer:

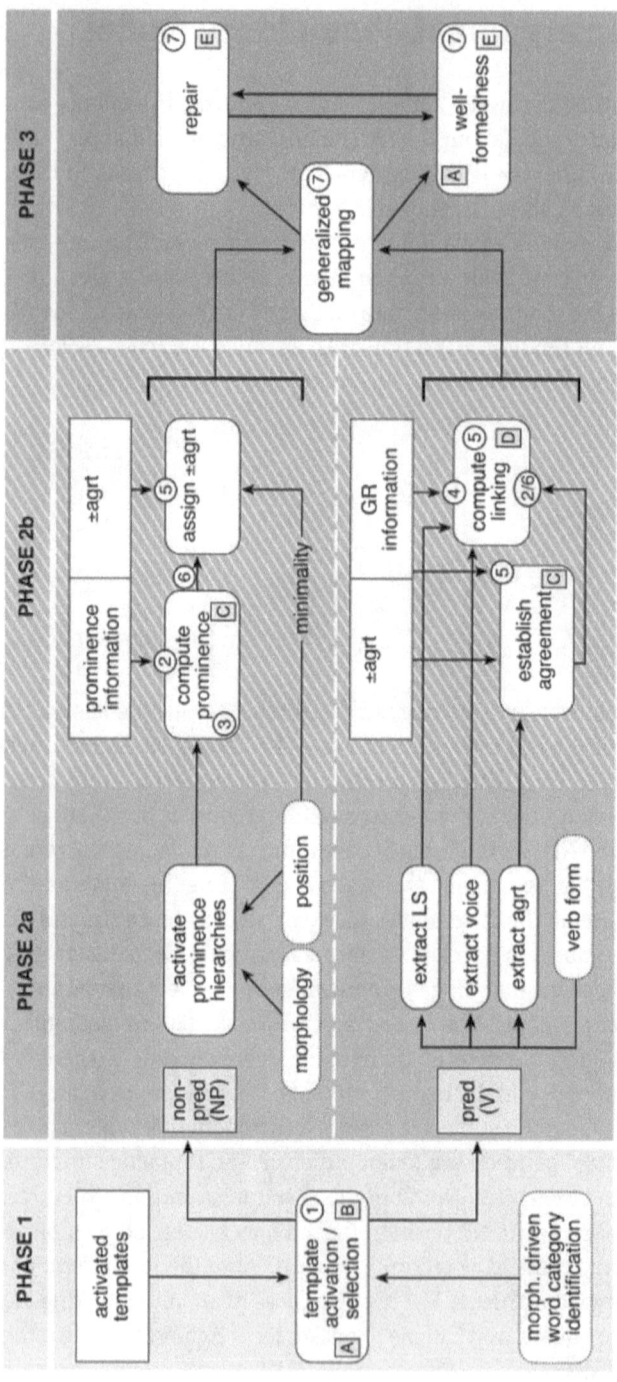

Figure 1: Extended argument dependency model of Bornkessel & Schlesewsky (2006).

(9)

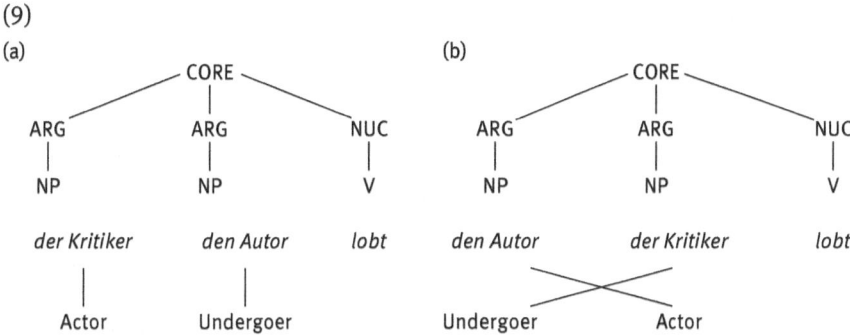

These two cases of linking apply in syntactic structures that contain agentive two-place predicates. In German, these verbs typically assign accusative case to their internal arguments. Let us now turn to a different class of verbs, which does not fall under the linking rules described earlier. Based on evidence from work on the dative case (Silverstein 1976; Chomsky 1981; Helbig & Buscha 1996; Van Valin & LaPolla 1997), Bornkessel & Schlesewsky (2006) propose that datives are not subject to the linking in (9). Instead they assume that dative-marked arguments "receive their interpretation directly from the LS [logical structure] of the verb" (p. 792). Let's take a stative psychological predicate such as *gefallen* ('to like') to illustrate the linking rules for dative verbs. Bornkessel & Schlesewsky assume only two thematic proto roles ('Actor' and 'Undergoer'). We will depart from their convention and assume the thematic roles shown in (4). Under these assumptions, the linking rule for *gefallen* would be as given in (10), slightly adapted from Bornkessel & Schlesewsky (2006: 801). The dative argument is linked directly to the lexical semantic representation of the verb:

(10)

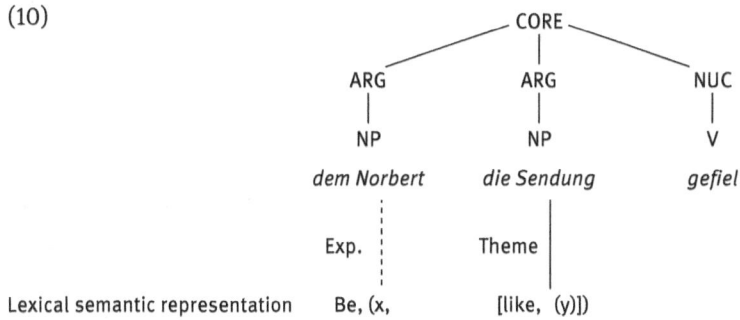

Having introduced the eADM model, let us now turn to atypical populations again and discuss how this model can be applied to patients with left-hemispheric brain lesions.

4 Hypotheses

In this section, we will apply the eADM to patients with early left-hemispheric brain lesions and develop several hypotheses with respect to the precise nature of the deficits observed in this patient group. The eADM in combination with the Default Mapping Hypothesis makes the following predictions with respect to the processing of noncanonical word order and nondefault argument realizations which will be tested on the basis of evidence from topicalization (Experiment 1), psych-verbs (Experiment 2), and passivization (Experiment 3). The default mapping hypothesis locates the processing difficulty at the interface between stage 1 and stage 2 of the eADM. If mapping is default the hypothesis would be that indirect linking should be globally dispreferred in comparison to direct linking. Moreover, phase two of the eADM contains two stages. Stage 2a is concerned with the activation of thematic prominence hierarchies and the extraction of morphological information such as case, voice, and agreement. Stage 2b is concerned with the computation of this information. Under the assumption that these types of information may facilitate processing in patients, as agreement provides a second cue (in addition to unambiguous case marking) for processing word order, we would expect that patients perform better in structures where the disambiguation of the structure toward OVS is also supported by agreement.

Let us now consider passives. Passivization exhibits the same order of thematic roles as object topicalization. The initial constituent corresponds to the Theme argument while the Agent may be suppressed or be realized in an optional PP. The two constructions, however, differ completely from a morphosyntactic point of view. In the case of passives the Theme is realized as the subject of the clause and an auxiliary, which encodes voice, is added, while topicalization involves a reordering of constituents without morphosyntactic modifications. The two constructions lead to an interesting hypothesis with respect to the mapping between syntax and argument structure in the patient group. We hypothesized earlier that indirect linking is dispreferred in patients. But what is the reason for this behavior? Within the eADM, linking is governed by morphosyntactic information such as case, agreement, and voice. The preference for direct linking in patients would follow from the processing of these morphosyntactic cues. If, for instance, the processing of morphosyntactic cues is generally impaired, it would follow that the parser simply does not have enough evidence to support indirect linking (cf. Knecht & Lidzba 2016, for deficits in the morphological component in this patient group). We will call this assumption the "morphosyntactic hypothesis". A strong version of this hypothesis would predict that the processing of morphosyntax is impaired globally. Under the strong morphosyntactic hypothesis we would expect that passives should be dispreferred just like OVS word orders.

A weaker version of this hypothesis would mean that the cues interact cumulatively. This would mean that the more cues there are, the more evidence the parser has to establish indirect linking. We will refer to this version of the weak hypothesis as the "cumulativity hypothesis". A slightly different version of the weak morphosyntactic hypothesis could be formulated if one combines some aspects of the competition model by MacWhinney et al. (2000) and the eADM. MacWhinney et al. argue that the strength of morphosyntactic cues varies across languages. Under this view one could assume that the deficit with respect to the processing of morphosyntax varies across different types of cues. The processing of voice, for example, could be less affected than the processing of case in a language in which voice is a stronger cue than case. This pattern could be governed by the frequency of different types of cues in a given language. We will refer to this version as the "cue strength hypothesis". We will discuss these different options in more detail as we go along. Generally speaking, the weak hypothesis would predict a difference with respect to indirect linking depending on the additive behavior of cues or the strength of cues. Passivization would then be predicted to push indirect linking on the basis of agreement and the presence of the auxiliary. Moreover, indirect linking in OVS should also be pushed if the disambiguation toward SVO is supported not only by case but also by agreement.

Let us now turn to psych-verbs. We will concentrate here on psych-verbs that exhibit an unmarked word order where the highest DP bears dative or accusative case. Psych-verbs of this class include verbs such as *schmecken* 'like' (as in *Peter liked the soup.*), which assigns dative case to the Experiencer DP and *beeindrucken* 'impress' where the Experiencer is associated with accusative case. Let us concentrate on accusative psych-verbs first. With respect to linking, these types of verbs should be subject to direct linking. This is due to the fact that the unmarked word order is ACC > NOM and the initial ACC-DP is also associated with the highest ranked thematic role, in this case the Experiencer. The type of linking and a simplified lexical semantic representation (without causality) is given in (11):

(11)

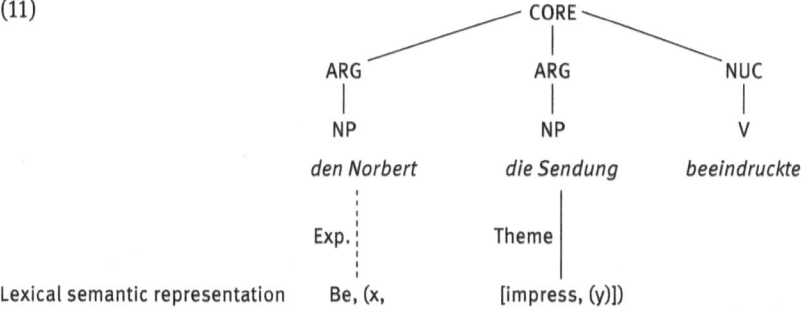

The default mapping hypothesis in (1) would predict that these types of psych-verbs should not be a problem for the patient group because indirect linking is not involved. However, if morphosyntactic impairment is involved, processing deficits would be predicted, at least to some extent, under any version of the morphosyntactic hypothesis.

Let us turn to datives next. Recall that the dative is assigned a special status in the eADM. Hence, it is not subject to the linking rules discussed with respect to accusative bearing arguments. If this is the case, the hypotheses discussed above would make different predictions. The strong morphosyntactic hypothesis and the cumulativity hypothesis would predict no difference between datives and accusatives. The cue strength hypothesis would predict a difference under the assumption that dative case marking is a stronger cue than accusative case marking, an assumption that is supported by the theoretical literature and which is also part of the eADM.

To summarize this section, we have developed three different hypotheses, summarized in (13). Each of them seeks to provide a morphosyntactic explanation for the default mapping hypothesis:

(13) (i) Strong Morphosyntactic Hypothesis
        The processing of morphosyntax is globally impaired
     (ii) Cumulativity Hypothesis
        The impaired processing of morphosyntactic cues is additive
     (iii) Cue Strength Hypothesis
        The impaired processing of morphosyntactic cues is relativized according to the respective cue strength in a given language

The strong morphosyntactic hypothesis states that the processing of morphosyntax is globally impaired, independent of the type of morphosyntactic marking. It makes the strongest possible prediction with respect to why default linking should be preferred. Two weaker versions of the morphosyntactic hypothesis have been developed. The cumulativity hypothesis states that nondefault linking is supported by different morphosyntactic cues showing an additive behavior. Although each cue might have equal strength, the availability of indirect linking is determined by the number of cues that the parser encounters. Finally, the cue strength hypothesis relativizes different morphosyntactic cues with respect to their strength. Under this hypothesis, morphosyntactic markings such as different types of case, agreement, and voice would affect the mapping between syntax and argument structure differently. Consequently, the availability of indirect linking would depend on the presence of specific cues in the linguistic input. In the next section we will discuss a series of experiments to test the hypotheses developed so far.

5 Experimental evidence

In this section, we will discuss a series of experiments designed to test the hypotheses in (13). The overall goal is to provide an explanation for the default mapping hypothesis. Experiment 1 will compare SVO word orders and OVS word orders to test the strong morphosyntactic hypothesis and the cumulativity hypothesis. Experiment 2 will investigate psych-verbs to test the cue strength hypothesis. Finally, Experiment 3 compares passives and OVS structures to test whether the morphosyntactic hypotheses proposed in this chapter provide a better explanation for the data than an Agent-first hypothesis. Before we do so, we will first introduce the patient group that participated in the experiments.

5.1 Participants

We tested 12 patients with focal early left-hemispheric brain lesions with an age at study ranging from 9 years to adulthood. In all patients, brain damage was detected at or shortly after birth, that is, lesions were acquired pre- or perinatally. The patient group consisted of five children (9–13 years old), four teenagers (14–17 years old), and three adults (18–30 years old). Nine patients exhibited a verbal IQ within normal range (i.e., verbal IQ > 85), three patients scored slightly below 85. However, their linguistic data did not differ from the other patients; hence, they were not excluded from the analysis. Verbal IQ was measured with the German version of the Wechsler intelligence scales for adults (WIE; von Aster, Neubauer & Horn 2006) and the German version of the Wechsler intelligence scales for children III (HAWIK-III; Tewes, Schallberger & Rossmann 1999). The experimental results from the patient group were compared to the results of a large cohort of controls of mixed age (ranging from 9 years to adulthood). This ensures that no confound with respect to age between patients and controls is expected. There were 35 controls altogether. All of them delivered data for Experiment 3; 27 of them delivered also data for Experiment 1; 24 controls remained for Experiment 2. The rise of the control groups differs for the three experiments due to time constraints during the experimental sessions and varying attention spans of the younger participants. All participants were native speakers of German.

5.2 Experiment 1: the processing of topicalization

The first experiment investigated object topicalization. The items contained agentive transitive verbs such as *schubsen* 'push'. Under the assumption made in the eADM, object topicalizations with these verbs are subject to indirect linking. The corresponding SVO counterparts are subject to direct linking.

5.2.1 Method

5.2.1.1 Design

The sentence-initial DP was always masculine, which in German ensures that the accusative case exhibits unambiguous case marking. The DP that appeared after the finite verb was either feminine or neuter. Since the nominative case marking for feminine and neuter nouns exhibits case syncretism with the corresponding accusative case for these nouns, it follows that if the sentence-initial accusative is read as a nominative, the sentence can still be interpreted since the following DP can then be interpreted simply as an accusative object. The sentences were constructed in such a way that there was no plausibility bias toward one or the other reading. For instance, in a sentence such as *Den Esel schubst das Schaf* 'The donkey$_{acc}$ shoves the sheep$_{nom}$', it is equally plausible that the donkey or the sheep does the shoving. The participants were instructed to accept these kinds of artificial settings. The design contained two kinds of morphosyntactic cues to disambiguate the overall structure. In one of the conditions, accusative case marking was the sole cue that disambiguated the structure. In a different condition, plural marking on the subject was added as a second cue. In this case the structure is also disambiguated by agreement. The experiment also contained the equivalent SVO structures as control conditions resulting in a 2 × 2 design with the factors "word order" (SVO vs. OVS) and "agreement" (singular vs. plural). The design is exemplified in (14):

(14) Experiment 1: Conditions

1. *Der Esel*   *schubst*   *das Schaf.*   SVO-sg
the$_{nom/sg}$ donkey shoves the$_{nom/acc/sg}$ sheep
2. *Der Esel*   *schubst*   *die Schafe.*   SVO-pl
the$_{nom/sg}$ donkey shoves the$_{nom/acc/pl}$ sheep
3. *Den Esel*   *schubst*   *das Schaf.*   OVS-sg
the$_{acc/sg}$ donkey shoves the$_{nom/acc/sg}$ sheep
4. *Den Esel*   *schubsen*   *die Schafe.*   OVS-pl
the$_{acc/sg}$ donkey shoves the$_{nom/acc/pl}$ sheep

5.2.1.2 Materials

Sixteen experimental items were constructed according to the design given in (14). The items were distributed on four different lists according to the Latin square design such that each participant saw one item only in one condition. To increase the number of trials in the patient group, most patients were retested on the experiment in two different experimental sessions. In the second session, patients did a different list than in the first one.

5.2.1.3 Procedure
The experiment was conducted using a truth-value judgment task. The experiment was run on the e-prime software. The task consisted of a short movie that displayed the action described by the target item. After watching the short film sequence, participants heard the target sentence. The task was to state whether the target sentence matched the film sequence or not. In half of the cases, the film sequence matched the target item, in the other half there was a mismatch. Items were presented in a randomized order. To minimize the effort for the patients, the experimenter pressed the corresponding button on the key board that matched the answer given by the participant. The procedure, with the film sequence being played prior to the target item, was chosen to decrease the processing effort for the patients. Participants could give the answer immediately after hearing the auditory stimulus. This decreased the overall memory effort for the target item.

5.2.1.4 Predictions
The design allows us to test strong morphosyntactic hypothesis, which states that the processing of morphosyntax is globally impaired. Under this hypothesis we would not expect that participants benefit from additional morphosyntactic information in condition 4. Thus the results should show a main effect of "structure". Moreover, the experiment also tests the cumulativity hypothesis since two different morphosyntactic markings were used: case and agreement. The cumulativity hypothesis predicts that if both morphosyntactic cues are present in the data, the structure should be easier to disambiguate toward OVS than if only one cue is present. This suggests that we should see less errors in condition 4 than in condition 3. Overall, we should observe more difficulty with OVS in the patient group than in the control group.

5.2.2 Results

The data was analyzed using a repeated measures ANOVA with the within factors "word order" and "agreement" and with "group" as a between factor and "accuracy" as a dependent variable. Accuracy refers to correctly identifying whether the target item matched the film sequence or not. The results reveal that the patient group differs significantly from the control group [$F_1(1,37) = 4.64, p < 0.05$; $F_2(1,23) = 16.82, p < 0.001$]. Both within factors revealed highly significant main effects [word order: $F_1(1,37) = 26.98, p < 0.001$; $F_2(1,23) = 132.22, p < 0.001$; agreement: $F_1(1,37) = 22.24, p < 0.001$; $F_2(1,23) = 43.28, p < 0.001$]. The results show that OVS word orders are more difficult to process than SVO word orders. The main effect of "agreement" provides evidence that subjects benefit from agreement information to disambiguate the structure towards OVS. Moreover, there is also a significant interaction of "word order" and "agreement" [$F_1(1,37) = 26.57, p < 0.001$; $F_2(1,23) = 48.79, p < 0.001$], indicating that agreement shows a stronger effect in the OVS conditions than in the SVO conditions (cf. Figure 2a and 2b). Crucially, we also observe an interaction of "word order" and "group" [$F_1(1,37) = 4.62, p < 0.05$; $F_2(1,23) = 16.49, p < 0.001$]. This shows that OVS word orders are more difficult to process for patients than for controls. The interaction of "agreement" and "group" missed significance because controls also benefited from agreement information. There was also no three-way interaction.

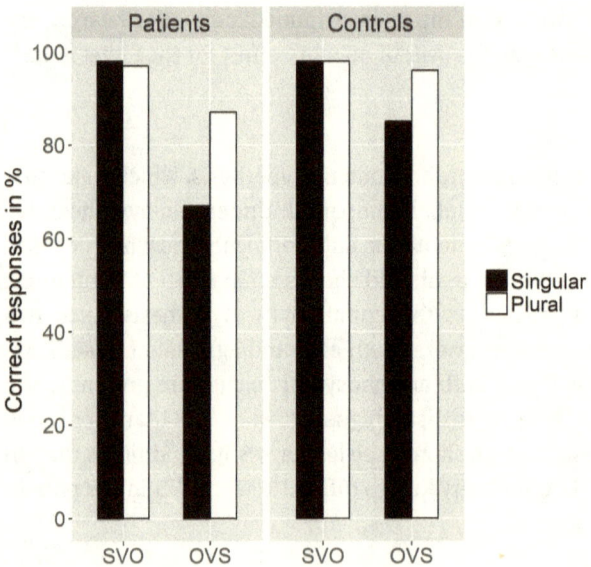

Figure 2: Correct responses of patients and controls in Experiment 1

5.2.3 Discussion

The data provide evidence that patients have more difficulty to establish indirect linking than controls. This is supported by the interaction of "group" and "word order". With respect to the effect of specific disambiguating cues, this result shows that case information on the initial object DP is a better cue for controls than for patients. Moreover, the data provide evidence for the cumulativity hypothesis. The main effect of "agreement" shows that conditions with plural agreement are easier to process than conditions with singular agreement. The interaction of "word order" and "agreement" shows that the additional cue provided by plural agreement is operative especially in the OVS conditions, which provides support for the assumption that it helps to establish indirect linking. This is true for both experimental groups. The data thus provide direct evidence against the strong morphosyntactic hypothesis, which does not predict that cues behave additively. In this experiment we have provided evidence for the cumulativity hypothesis, by showing that "case" and "agreement" add up in their effect to support indirect linking. We will investigate in Experiment 2 whether a stronger version of this hypothesis, the cue strength hypothesis, can be established. This hypothesis predicts that different cues support noncanonical argument realization in a different way. This will be tested with different cases (accusative vs. dative).

5.3 Experiment 2: the processing of psych-verbs

The second experiment included different types of psych-verbs to test the cue strength hypothesis. Psych-verbs are particularly interesting in this respect since, depending on the verb, the Experiencer role may be realized as an accusative DP or a dative DP. At the same time, the Theme is assigned to the nominative subject DP. These types of verbs are therefore particularly revealing with respect to the cue strength hypothesis because they exhibit parallel argument structures but different case patterns. This allows us to test whether different cases are processed the same way and whether they exhibit the same cue strength to support canonical argument structures.

5.3.1 Method

5.3.1.1 Design
We compared psych-verbs that assign the Experiencer role to the accusative DP as, for instance, *beeindrucken* ('impress') to psych-verbs that realize the Experiencer in the dative, for example, *gefallen* ('like'). Accusative psych-verbs occurred in two different conditions. For instance, verbs of the *impress*-type occurred with an animate and an inanimate nominative subject. This manipulation has the effect that if the initial accusative DP is misanalyzed as a nomina-

tive, the sentence still has a grammatical continuation if the nominative subject is also animate (cf. condition 1 in (15)). If, by contrast, the subject is inanimate, the sentence does not have a plausible continuation (cf. condition 2). This type of semantic garden pathing was included in the design to investigate whether patients would benefit from this type of semantic cue during sentence processing. The dative-type psych-verbs came with a similar manipulation. Here we chose verbs that have a grammatical continuation if the initial dative is misinterpreted as a nominative, such as *schmecken* ('like'). In this case, the grammatical continuation would result in a different meaning of the sentence, since the meaning of the verb would change from "like" to "taste" (cf. condition 3). The other dative condition did not allow a grammatical continuation (cf. condition 4). The idea behind this manipulation is that participants should produce less errors if the sentence does not have a grammatical continuation when they misinterpret the initial DP as a nominative. The fact that the sentence cannot be assigned a well-formed structure might provide a cue for reanalysis. This type of manipulation could be particularly effective in the accusative cases since verbs like "impress" are plausible in both directions; hence, there is no plausibility shift if the initial accusative is read as a nominative. In addition to the four psych-verb conditions, the design also included an SVO condition, as baseline.

(15) Experiment 2: Conditions

1. *Den Peter*   *beeindruckte*   *die Lehrerin*
   the$_{acc/sg}$ Peter   impressed   the$_{nom/acc/sg}$ teacher-FEM
   in der Schule.   acc/+anim
   in the school

2. *Den Peter*   *beeindruckte*   *die Vorstellung*
   the$_{acc/sg}$ Peter   impressed   the$_{nom/acc/sg}$ performance
   in der Schule.   acc/−anim
   in the school

3. *Dem Tobias*   *schmeckte*   *das Gewürz*
   the$_{dat/sg}$ Tobias   liked   the$_{nom/acc/sg}$ spice
   in der Suppe.   dat/type 1
   in the soup

4. *Dem Norbert*   *gefiel*   *die Sendung*
   the$_{dat/sg}$ Norbert   liked   the$_{nom/acc/sg}$ show
   im Fernsehen.   dat/type 2
   on TV

5. Der Lehrer   begrüßte   die Schülerin
   the_nom/sg teacher   impressed   the_nom/acc/sg teacher-FEM
   auf dem Schulhof.   SVO
   in the school

5.3.1.2 Materials

The experiment contained a total of 46 items. Twelve items with accusative psych-verbs, 10 items dative psych-verbs and 24 SVO sentences. The different amount of items in the psych-verb class results from the fact that the number of psych-verbs is limited. In particular, dative psych-verbs that allow a grammatical continuation, as shown in condition 3, are very rare. The accusative psych-verbs used in conditions 1 and 2 were distributed on two different lists according to the Latin square design, since both conditions contain the same psych-verb. Each list additionally contained five items in condition 3, and five items in condition 4, and 24 SVO items. The items used in conditions 3–5 were identical in both lists.

5.3.1.3 Procedure

For this experiment, we chose the sentence repetition task. The reason was that psych-verbs are difficult to display in a film sequence since they often denote mental states. Participants first heard the target sentence auditorily and were then asked to provide a precise repetition of the sentence. Participants' productions were recorded and afterwards analyzed with respect to whether the initial DP was reproduced correctly or not.

5.3.2 Results

The data was analyzed using a repeated measures ANOVA with "structure" as within factor and "group" as between factor.[2] The dependent variable was "accuracy", which measured whether the initial DP was reproduced correctly or not. The results reveal a main effect of "group" [$F_1(1,34) = 6.47$, $p < 0.05$] which shows that overall, patients performed significantly worse than controls. There is also a main effect of "structure" [$F_1(4,136) = 11.33$, $p < 0.001$], which did not interact with "group". This result indicates that the tested structures differed with

---

[2] Since the verbs necessarily differed between some of the conditions, it was impossible to implement a consistent repeated measures design. Instead, the conditions were realized partly within items and partly between items and we therefore computed only an F_1 analysis of the data.

respect to all participants' performance alike, although the patterns in Figure 3 suggest that patients suffered more in the accusative conditions compared to the dative conditions than the controls.

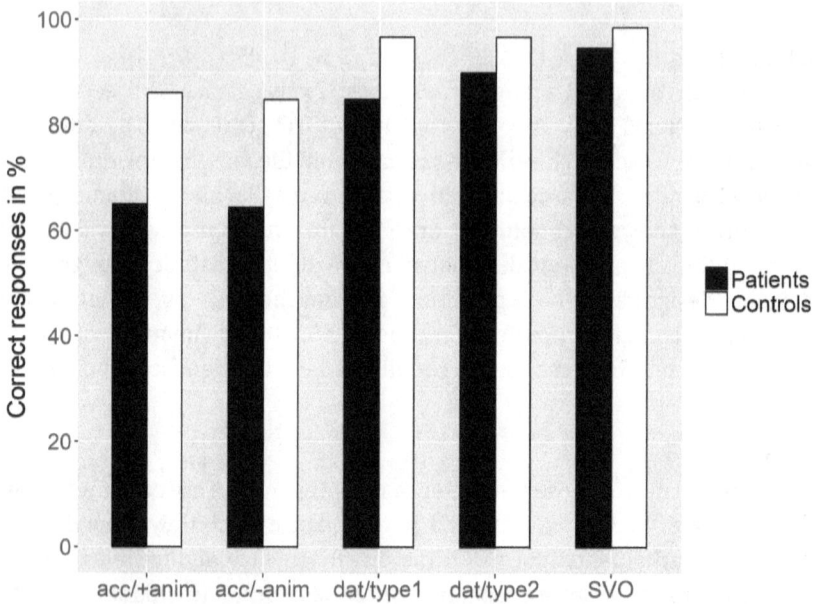

Figure 3: Accuracy in percentages for patients and controls in Experiment 2

For the five-level factor "structure" we specified four orthogonal contrasts: The first contrast compared the SOV condition against the two dative conditions (condition 5 vs. conditions 3/4) and the second contrast compared the two dative conditions against the two accusative conditions (conditions 3/4 vs. conditions 1/2). This allows us to make conclusions about the processing of dative Experiencers and of accusative Experiencers in general. The third and fourth contrast compared between the two dative conditions (condition 3 vs. 4) and the two accusative conditions (condition 1 vs. 2), respectively. These comparisons will show whether a grammatical continuation matters for processing after a potential misanalysis of the initial DP as a nominative.

The comparisons reveal the following result: Only one of the four contrasts reaches significance, namely the second one, which compares the two dative conditions against the two accusative conditions $[F_1(1,34) = 14.35, p < 0.001]$. This shows that the dative is easier to process than the accusative. This holds true for both groups as the contrast does not significantly interact with "group".

5.3.3 Discussion

The significant difference between datives and accusatives provides direct evidence for the cue strength hypothesis. Both types of psych-verbs exhibit parallel argument structures but different case realizations for the Experiencer. The fact that participants produce less errors with datives than with accusatives suggests that the dative case is a stronger cue than the accusative case. This finding is in line with the eADM, which assigns a special status to the dative case. Moreover, we did not find differences between the two accusative conditions and the two dative conditions, respectively. This finding is particularly interesting in the accusative conditions, since participants produced generally more errors here than in the dative conditions. In the accusative conditions, it did not matter for patients and controls whether the sentence had a plausible and grammatical continuation or not. If this was a decisive factor, we would expect less errors in condition 2 because participants might be led to reanalyze the sentence. The absence of an effect suggests that there is an overall strong tendency for a subject-first strategy in the patient group. We will come back to this later when we interpret the psych-verb data within the eADM. The two dative conditions did also not differ. For the controls this is simply due to the fact that they performed at ceiling in the dative conditions anyway. The patient group, by contrast, shows a numerical difference in the dative conditions. In fact, patients produced numerically less errors in condition 4, which does not have a grammatical continuation if the initial DP is misinterpreted as a nominative.[3] It is interesting that this effect shows up in combination with the dative case because the dative is semantically more prominent than the accusative. We will leave this point aside here because the difference is only numerical, but this might be an interesting point for further investigation. Before we close this section, let us address the question why the preference for direct linking is not reflected in the processing of psych-verbs. Note that object-Experiencer psych-verbs are subject to direct linking because the highest thematic role, the Experiencer, is assigned to the highest DP, under the assumption that the unmarked order with these verbs is ACC > NOM. Consequently, indirect linking is not at issue here. Under the cue strength hypothesis, processing difficulty with accusative case is independently predicted, and the data have shown that accusative case is a weaker cue than dative case. These results suggest the conclusion that default mappings, as predicted by the default mapping hypothesis, are merely a consequence of the cue strength hypothesis

---

[3] The direct comparison of conditions 3 and 4 within the patient group revealed a marginal effect ($t_1(11) = 1.89$, $p < 0.09$). The marginality might be due to the small sample size of this cohort.

and that the mapping is driven by the processing of morphosyntax. This line of reasoning is supported by the eADM which assumes that theta role assignment in German is driven by case marking (Bornkessel, Schlesewsky & Friederici 2002, 2003). Finally, let us briefly discuss the processing of condition 2 in this experiment. Note that participants did not perform better in this condition compared to condition 1. However, under the assumption that the initial DP was misanalyzed as a nominative, there is no grammatical continuation in condition 2. Under this view, participants could notice when they encounter the second DP *die Vorstellung* ('the performance') that they have to reanalyze the sentence. However, such a reanalysis in a garden path does not seem to count as a cue during sentence processing in the patients group. There is independent evidence that patients typically do not recover from a garden-path. Lidzba et al. (2013) provide evidence that agreement information alone is the weakest cue for establishing OVS order in patients (compared to case and case + agreement). Such sentences (e.g. *Die Giraffe*$_{acc/sg}$ *jagen die Löwinnen*$_{nom/pl}$ 'The lionesses are hunting the giraffe') typically exhibit a garden path if the initial DP is misanalyzed as a subject. These results suggest that patients have problems to recover from a garden path and that reanalysis is not easily available. Note also that conditions 1 and 2 involve a manipulation of animacy, which is an important factor in processing word order in the eADM framework. Our results do not provide evidence for the assumption that animacy helped patients to establish the correct parse for condition 2. The reason might be that patients do not easily recover from a garden path, as mentioned earlier or that psych-verbs are less sensitive to animacy in comparison to agentive verbs.

5.4 Experiment 3: the processing of passives

In the previous experiments we have established that the processing of noncanonical word order and noncanonical argument realization is governed by two processing principles: cue additivity and cue strength. The distribution of cues and cue types governs the availability of indirect linking and the processing of psych-verbs with object experiencers. In the following experiment, we will discuss the processing of passives. Passivization could pose a problem for the patient group because the subject position is associated with a nonprominent theta role. Thus, if patients pursue an Agent-first strategy passivization might be problematic. On the other hand, if patients pursue the model developed so far, we would predict that passivization should not be a problem. The reason is that passives are subject initial; hence, the morphological marking on the initial DP is default. Second, passives exhibit a series of cues that should support the assignment of the patient role to the subject DP. This follows from the cumulativity hypothesis. In addition, cue strength might also play a role. Standard passives in German are constructed with the auxiliary *werden* plus past participle. The auxiliary, however, is also used for future tense and may also be used as a copula verb in the sense of English *become*; hence, it is not clear whether the auxiliary alone serves as a cue for passivization. However, the combination of the auxiliary plus participle is an unambiguous cue for passivization and the *von*-PP (*by*-phrase) also serves as a cue if it occurs in a passive context. Moreover, an Agent-first strategy in the patient group would also predict that patients and controls should differ with respect to passivization.

5.4.1 Method

5.4.1.1 Design
Overall, the design contained four conditions, two of which are irrelevant for the present discussion. Here, we report the comparison of a passive (condition 2) to a clause with a topicalized object (condition 1), for which we have independent evidence that it is difficult to process for patients (cf. Experiment 1).

(16) Conditions:
1. *Den Esel schubst das Schaf.* (OVS)
   the donkey$_{acc/sg}$ shoves the sheep$_{nom/sg}$
2. *Der Esel wird von dem Schaf geschubst.* (Passive)
   the donkey$_{nom/sg}$ is by the sheep$_{dat/sg}$ shoved

5.4.1.2 Materials
The whole experiment contained 24 items in four conditions. The items were distributed on four different lists according to the Latin square design.

5.4.1.3 Procedure
We used the same procedure (truth-value judgment task) as in Experiment 1. The reader is referred to Section 5.2.3 for a detailed description.

5.4.1.4 Results
The results were analyzed using a one-factorial repeated measures ANOVA with the within-factor "structure" (OVS vs. passive) and the between-factor "group". The data reveal a main effect of 'structure' [$F_1(1,45) = 24.17$, $p < 0.001$;

$F_2(1,23) = 59.63$, $p < 0.001$]. Participants produced significantly less errors in the passive condition than in the OVS condition. The interaction of "structure" and "group" missed significance. This suggests that patients and controls show the same pattern in the data (cf. Figure 4).

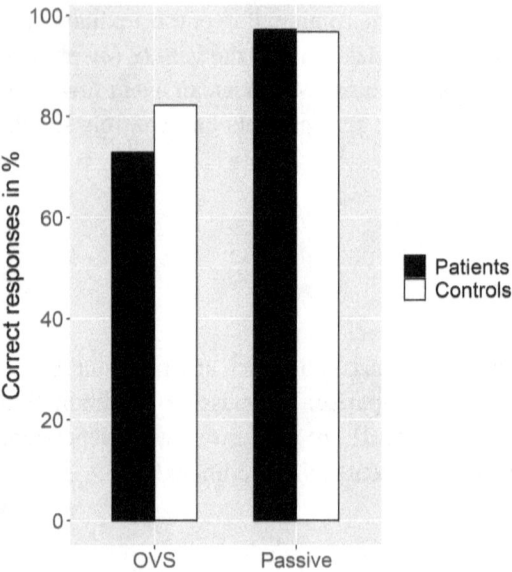

Figure 4: Accuracy in percentages for patients and controls in Experiment 3

5.4.2 Discussion

The experiment was designed to test whether the hypotheses developed in this chapter provide a better explanation for the data discussed in the two previous experiments than a hypothesis which states that patients pursue an Agent-first strategy. We predicted that the Agent-first assumption should render passives difficult to process. Moreover, the two experimental groups should differ in the processing of passives since Agent first is only relevant for the patient group. The results suggest that an Agent-first strategy in the patient group need not be assumed to explain the data. First, patients and controls do not differ with respect to the processing of passives. Moreover, we have discussed earlier that passives provide a series of morphosyntactic cues to support the linking between syntax and argument structure in this construction. Thus, the cumulativity hypothesis would predict that passives should be less problematic than OVS, which is only supported by case, and this is exactly what we observe in the data.

6 General discussion and conclusion

In this chapter we have investigated the processing of noncanonical word order and noncanonical argument realization in patients with early left-hemispheric brain lesions and in healthy controls. The goal of this study was to provide an explanation for the finding that patients with early left-hemispheric brain lesions exhibit difficulty in processing these structures. This observation led to the default mapping hypothesis, which states that patients prefer direct linking over indirect linking in the mapping between syntax and argument structure. We have provided two hypotheses to explain the preference for direct linking. The cumulativity hypothesis states that morphosyntactic cues behave additively in the linguistic input to support indirect linking. This hypothesis was supported by the results from the processing of object topicalization. The results show that patients are more successful with indirect linking if the disambiguation towards OVS is supported by case and agreement as opposed to only by case. We have also provided evidence for a stronger hypothesis: the cue strength hypothesis. This hypothesis states that individual cues affect the disambiguation of the linguistic input in a different way. For instance, dative case in German proved to be a stronger cue than accusative case. In the third experiment, we discussed the role of processing strategies such as "Agent-first". We have argued that such an assumption is superfluous to explain the experimental results. Rather, the observed effects follow directly from the mapping assumptions made by the eADM in connection with the strength of different cues, as proposed by the competition model (MacWinney 1987, 1989). The basic assumption is that the processing is driven by morphosyntactic cues. The number and the strength of these cues determine the mapping between syntax and argument structure. The difficulty with noncanonical word order is thus best explained as a subject-first strategy caused by the processing difficulty of morphosyntactic cues. One question that arises from these results is why accusative case is more difficult to process than dative case. This difference is of course reminiscent of the traditional distinction between structural and lexical cases. Within the eADM, the assumption is that datives are not part of the linking relation, but are linked directly to the lexical-semantic representation of the verb. Another way of thinking about this would be to assume that the dative has more semantic content than the accusative. Under this assumption, patients would more strongly rely on semantic information, given the fact that purely structural relations seem to be subject to impairment. What about the computational component of structure building? We did not find evidence that computational operations such as movement are unavailable to patients. Movement can be computed if there is enough morphosyntactic evidence in the linguistic input to support it. If this hypothesis is correct, the impairment in patients could be reduced to the processing of morphosyntactic cues. This assumption would mean that sentence processing in patients is driven by the processing of morphosyntax, that is, surface information. If the processing of morphosyntax is impaired everything else follows from interface conditions. Finally, the question arises why patients do not exhibit communicative difficulties in everyday conversation. In the eADM, the well-formedness of structures is checked in the third phase of the model. This is also the phase where repair mechanisms apply. Repair mechanisms can be triggered by plausibility or context information. The data discussed in this study focused mainly on the processing relevant for the first two phases of the eADM. In cases where plausibility played a role, for example, in the garden-path condition in accusative psych-verbs (condition 2 of Experiment 2), we did not observe any improvement. The reason might be that recovery from a garden-path is particularly difficult in patients. What hasn't been studied yet is the role of context information and information structure in sentence processing with patients. The eADM, being a syntax driven model, locates this type of information in the third phase of processing. Although we have to leave this question open at this point, the role of context and information structure deserves a more thorough treatment in future research.

Acknowledgments: This research was conducted within the SFB 833, Project B5 "The Syntax and Semantics of Reorganized Language and its Neuronal Architecture" funded by the German Research Foundation (Deutsche Forschungsgemeinschaft, DFG). We are grateful to two anonymous reviewers and the volume editors for valuable comments and suggestions.

References

Aster, M. von, A. Neubauer & R. Horn. 2006. Wechsler Intelligenztest für Erwachsene WIE. Übersetzung und Adaptation der WAIS-III von David Wechsler. Frankfurt/Main: Harcourt Test Services.
Belletti, A. & L. Rizzi. 1988. Psych-verbs and θ-theory. Natural Language and Linguistic Theory 6(3): 291–352.
Bornkessel, I. & M. Schlesewsky. 2006. The extended argument dependency model: A neuro-cognitive approach to sentence comprehension across languages. Psychological Review 113(4): 787–821.
Bornkessel, I., M. Schlesewsky & A.D. Friederici. 2002. Beyond syntax: Language-related positivities reflect the revision of hierarchies. Neuroreport 13(3): 361–364.
Bornkessel, I., M. Schlesewsky & A.D. Friederici. 2003. Eliciting thematic reanalysis effects: The role of syntax-independent information during parsing. Language and Cognitive Processes 18(3): 268–298.
Chomsky, N. 1981. Lectures on government and binding. Dordrecht: Kluwer.

Chilosi, A.M., C. Pecini, P. Cipriani, P. Brovedani, D. Brizzolara, G. Ferretti, L. Pfanner & G. Cioni. 2005. Atypical language lateralization and early linguistic development in children with focal brain lesions. Developmental Medicine & Child Neurology 47(11): 725–720.
Eisele, J.A. & D.M. Aram. 1994. Comprehension and imitation of syntax following early hemisphere damage. Brain and Language 46(2): 212–231.
Eisele, J.A. & D.M. Aram. 1995. Lexical and grammatical development in children with early left hemisphere damage: A cross-sectional view from birth to adolescence. In: (P. Fletcher & B. MacWhinney, eds) Handbook of child language, 664–689. Oxford: Basil Blackwell.
Fanselow, G. 2000. Optimal exceptions. In: (B. Stiebels & D. Wunderlich, eds) Lexicon in focus, 173–209. Berlin: Akademie Verlag.
Grimshaw, J. 1990. Argument Structure. Cambridge, MA: MIT Press.
Haider, H. 1993. Deutsche Syntax – Generativ: Vorstudien zur Theorie einer projektiven Grammatik. Tübingen: Narr.
Helbig, G. & J. Buscha. 1996. Deutsche Grammatik. Leipzig: Verlag Enzyklopädie Langenscheidt.
Jackendoff, R. 1972. Semantic interpretation in generative grammar. Cambridge, MA: MIT Press.
Knecht, M. & K. Lidzba. 2016. Processing verbal morphology in patients with congenital left-hemispheric brain lesions. Brain and Language 157–158: 25–34.
Lidzba, K., A. Konietzko, E. Schwilling, I. Krägeloh-Mann & S. Winkler. 2013. Processing of non-canonical word-order: A case-series on lesion-induced reorganized language and age-effects in typical development. Brain and Language 127: 377–387.
MacWhinney, B. 1987. The competition model. In: (B. MacWhinney, ed) Mechanisms of language acquisition, 249–308. Hillsdale, NJ: Lawrence Erlbaum.
MacWhinney, B. 1989. Competition and lexical categorization. In: (R. Corrigan, F.R. Eckman & M. Noonan, eds) Linguistic categorization, 195–242. Amsterdam / Philadelphia: Benjamins.
MacWhinney, B., H. Feldman, K. Sacco & R. Valdes-Perez. 2000. Online measures of basic language skills in children with early focal brain lesions. Brain and Language 71(3): 400–431.
Reilly, J.S., E.A. Bates & V.A. Marchman. 1998. Narrative discourse in children with early focal brain injury. Brain and Language 61(3): 335–375.
Scheepers, C., B. Hemforth & L. Konieczny. 2000. Linking syntactic functions with thematic roles: Psych-verbs and the resolution of subject-object ambiguity. In: (B. Hemforth & L. Konieczny, eds) German sentence processing, 95–135. Dordrecht: Kluwer Academic Press.
Schwilling, E. 2012. Sprachreorganisation nach angeborenen linkshemisphärischen Läsionen. Tübingen: Universität Tübingen Dissertation.
Schwilling, E., I. Krägeloh-Mann, A. Konietzko, S. Winkler & K. Lidzba. 2012. Testing the language of German cerebral palsy patients with right hemispheric language organization after early left hemispheric damage. Clinical Linguistics and Phonetics 26(2): 135–147.
Semel, E., E. Wiig & W. Secord. 1987. Clinical evaluation of language fundamentals. Revised (CELF-R). San Antonio, TX: The Psychological Corporation.
Silverstein, M. 1976. Hierarchy of features and ergativity. In: (R.M.W. Dixon, ed) Grammatical categories in Australian languages, 112–171. Atlantic Highlands, NJ: Humanities Press.
Staudt, M., K. Lidzba, W. Grodd, D. Wildgruber, M. Erb & I. Krägeloh-Mann. 2002. Right hemispheric organization of language following early left-sided brain lesions: Functional MRI topography. NeuroImage 16(4): 954–967.
Stiles, J., E.A. Bates, D. Thal, D. Trauner & J. Reilly. 1998. Linguistic, cognitive and affective development in children with pre- and perinatal focal brain injury: A ten year overview from the San Diego Longitudinal project. In: (C. Rovee-Collier, L.P. Lipsitt & H. Hayne, eds) Advances in infant research 12: 131–163. Stamford, CT: Ablex.

Tewes, U., U. Schallberger & P.r Rossmann. 1999. Hamburg-Wechsler-Intelligenztest für Kinder III (HAWIK III). Bern: Huber.
Van Valin, R.D., Jr., & R. LaPolla. 1997. Syntax: Form, meaning and function. Cambridge, MA: Cambridge University Press.

Hannah Gerbrich, Vivian Schreier and Sam Featherston
Standard items for English judgment studies: Syntax and semantics

1 Background: experimental grammar research

Chapters like those in this volume testify to the increasing attention to empirical data collection. The use of experimental methods in grammar research has gone from strength to strength and has established itself as one of the key ways to investigate linguistic patterning among words, phrases, and clauses up to the sentence level.

This is to be welcomed: many linguists have a feeling of unease about the thin ice of weak validity that work in syntactic and semantic theory sometimes skates upon when it is done without reasonable attention to its evidential base. In particular, if linguists can radically disagree about the underlying architecture of the grammar that they are attempting to describe without it being clear who is wrong and who is right, then this is a sign that the data basis used is insufficient (either in quantity or quality or both) to uniquely determine the system to be described. That an improved data basis is desirable is of course fairly uncontroversial; the challenge is to obtain this without disproportionate additional work being necessary. In this chapter we present a tool that aims at achieving exactly this.

Experimental linguists take the view that both hypothesis building and hypothesis testing can be improved by the use of finer-grained data and the use of multiple lexical variants of structures. This permits us to make wider generalizations about what speakers of a language do in general. Collecting data from groups of informants instead of relying on individual judgments helps enable us to make these stronger claims. The use of experimental procedures has thus brought us some way forward, both by hardening up the data basis of syntax to make wider, falsifiable statements, and by providing a far more exact picture of what well-formedness tells us about the grammar.

That picture turns out to be very interesting. The two most important new insights into the nature of the grammar concern the effect that a grammatical constraint violation has and how constraint violations interact with each other; neither of these is as often assumed in the traditional literature. The first observation is that the violation of a particular constraint triggers a constant cost in terms of perceived well-formedness. A corollary of this is that different violation types have different amplitudes of cost, so there are stronger and weaker constraints.

https://doi.org/10.1515/9783110623093-012

This means that an empirically adequate model of grammar must have a parameter of violation cost strength; put differently, grammatical constraints must have specific weightings.

The second observation is that multiple constraint violations affect our perception of well-formedness in a cumulative fashion, so that an example sentence that breaks two rules is worse than one which breaks only one rule. Furthermore, both the violations appear to affect the violating example sentence independently and additively, so that their violation costs remain constant (Keller 2000).

These two findings are very robust and can be formulated as in (1) and (2), which are parts of the Decathlon Model (Featherston 2005, 2011).

(1) *Weighting and cumulativity rule 1*
Given a sentence *S* and a sentence *SA*, which is a minimal pair to *S* but contains the grammatical constraint violation *A*, then the difference in perceived acceptability between *S* and *SA* will be *a*, the specific violation cost of *A*, all other things being equal.

(2) *Weighting and cumulativity rule 2*
Given the following sentences:
- a sentence *S*,...
- a sentence *SA*, which is a minimal pair to *S* but contains the grammatical constraint violation *A* with the violation cost *a*,...
- a sentence *SB*, which is a minimal pair to *S* but contains the grammatical constraint violation *B*, with the violation cost *b*,...
- a sentence *SAB*, which is a minimal pair to both *SA* and *SB* but contains both grammatical constraint violations *A* and *B*,...
then the difference in perceived acceptability between *S* and *SAB* will be the sum of the violation costs *a* + *b*, all other things being equal.

The differential weightings of constraint violations and the fact of their cumulative effect have become very clear, so that these characteristics are a fundamental component of our understanding of any realistic grammar model (Keller 2000). Interestingly, some syntacticians had in fact come to this view independently by merely considering their own judgments, but these views were not sufficiently influential to cause them to be more widely adopted (e.g., Uszkoreit 1986; Jacobs 1988). It is more surprising that Chomsky's *Barriers* (1986), which also contains the seeds of cumulativity, did not have this effect either.

But there is one more apparent feature of the grammar which we have not dealt with yet but which follows from the previous findings. Every linguist who has collected data relating to well-formedness will know that robust distinctions are obtained between conditions, but there is no binary opposition between absolutely good and absolutely bad. Instead, we usually find a *continuum* representing degrees of perceived well-formedness.

This is sometimes due to the nature of the task assigned: most experimental procedures gather data points along a scale in some form or other. This task itself is likely to produce results in the form of a continuum, but this is not only due to the task type; informants generally perceive well-formedness as a gradient phenomenon. This is, for example, apparent when we consider the results of the speeded judgments task used by the research team Markus Bader and Jana Häussler (2010) and the chapter by Andreas Konietzko and Karen Lidzba in this volume. This method also produces gradient data even though participants are only given a binary differentiation task. The gradience comes from the frequencies with which informants choose one or other option, so that an integrated scale combining a (binary) well-formedness judgment and scalar frequency of choice is derived. The effect is not merely task-related, therefore, but seems to be inherent in our perception.

The traditional model of grammatical and ungrammatical structures, sometimes with the addition of a marginal class in between with a question mark, is thus insufficient: we must distinguish not only good and bad, but also good from better, and bad from worse. A re-reading of Chomsky's *Aspects* (1965) makes it clear that he is aware that this was a simplifying assumption: "Obviously, acceptability will be a matter of degree, along several dimensions. [...] it is clear that we can characterize unacceptable sentences only in terms of some 'global' property of derivations and the structures they define – a property which is attributable, not to a particular rule, but rather to the way in which rules interact [...]" and then: "Like acceptability, grammaticalness is no doubt a matter of degree (Chomsky 1955, 1957, 1961)" (Chomsky 1965: 10–11). In the light of this it can appear more surprising that syntax has spent the last 30 or 40 years assuming that well-formedness is a binary opposition, especially since first, the raw data of gradient well-formedness is available to every speaker of a language, and second, the additional information is rich and useful.

This greater degree of differentiation offers much more information and real additional insights into the way that our grammars work, but this comes at a cost in additional complexity: it prevents us from giving a simple categorization of a sentence as well-formed or ill-formed, since experimental judgment studies offer us *relative* data, rather than *absolute* data. This can sometimes be a problem: linguists want to be able to make a clear statement about the status of a particular example. Relative data alone does not permit this; we can only say that example A is significantly better or worse than example B. It is for this reason that we developed *standard items* for inclusion in judgment experiments. We have previously made available standard items for German (Featherston 2009), in this chapter we supply standard items for experiments on English. This tool provides in accessible form something very close to absolute well-formedness standards, anchored with carefully selected example sentences.

2 The uses of standard items

Standard items are sets of filler sentences that should be included in any judgment experiment. They are carefully selected and tested to represent the whole of the accessible scale of syntactic well-formedness. When the results of an experiment are evaluated, the scores given to the standard items should be evaluated in the same way. They thus provide a basis for comparison so that the judgment score of a given sentence can be more nearly given an absolute interpretation. The values given to the standard items thus function as anchor points on the scale of perceived naturalness. We distinguish five such points and label them from A (good) to E (bad).

In order to function as fixed points relative to which comparisons can be made, standard items should ideally represent known values on a familiar scale. The reason for this is that we are better at judging where a new stimulus is located on a scale if we have close and familiar reference points. An example would be that of temperature. If you ask people how warm it is outside, they can usually guess it to within few degrees. People know that below 18 °C you need to put something over your t-shirt, below 12 °C you need a coat, and below 6 °C you could put on gloves. If on the other hand we present people with water between 40 and 80 °C and ask them to estimate its temperature, their guesses will be much less exact. People know that boiling water will scald them; they know that 40 °C is a nice warm bath, but they have few points of reference between these, so they will judge it much less accurately.

Unfortunately, there is as yet no recognized scale of linguistic well-formedness beyond the division of sentences into those with stars, which are thought of as "ungrammatical", and those without stars, which are thought of as "grammatical". Although this is a start, linguists are notorious for disagreeing about whether specific examples should receive a star or not. Part of the problem is that the categories "grammatical" and "ungrammatical" refer to ranges of values, not just single points, so absolute values that could act as anchors are lacking. The system of standard items provides a multipoint scale of perceived well-formedness, relative to which other examples can be more exactly and definitely located.

In order to be maximally useful, a system of anchor points should have as many scale points as possible, because more points provide more distinctions. One approach to the size of the scale would be to match it to the number of degrees of well-formedness that speakers are able to distinguish. Informally our observation is that individual informants can distinguish perhaps ten different degrees of well-formedness, but the results of groups yield far more distinctions, perhaps as many as 20 (see Section 4.2)

We do not need standard items that distinguish quite so many points on the scale, however. Practical considerations dictate that the standard items should be as few as possible, since these items must be included in every experiment. Each anchor point must be exemplified by (ideally) three items in order to establish a reasonably reliable value; a scale with ten points would then require 30 sentences to be inserted into every experiment. We therefore decided on five as the optimal number of degrees of well-formedness in the standard items. In practice this gives more than five different degrees on the scale as positions between the points are also identifiable. The use of our standard items thus requires the inclusion of 15 standard items in every experiment, which seems a reasonable trade-off between desirable detail and undesirable experiment bloating.

The use of standard items in experiments also permits comparisons across experiments. If we include the same 15 items in every experiment, we can realistically state how good the scores from one experiment were compared to the scores in an entirely different experiment. This is useful and often provides intriguing results, because the correspondences between structure types are not always as expected.

This can be taken further by using the standard items as the basis for a direct calculation of equivalences across experiments. When we analyze the results of a judgment experiment, it is often useful to normalize the data in order to remove the variation in the use of the scale by the participants: some people give better scores, others worse; some utilize a wider spread of scores, other use only a narrow range. In order to compensate for this, researchers often transform experimental judgments into z-scores. This manipulation involves subtracting from each score the participant's mean score and dividing the result by the participant's standard deviation of scores. Thus the scores of each participant have the mean value zero and the standard deviation 1, which removes a degree of irrelevant inter-participant variation.

This method can be built upon to provide a quantified comparison across experiments using the standard items. Instead of using the participant's mean of all scores and standard deviation of all scores, we can use just their mean of the standard items and standard deviation of the standard items. This provides a firm basis of comparison even across experiments, as long as the standard items were included in both, and the procedure and context of the two experiments were reasonably similar.

Since the five values on the well-formedness scale are used again and again, they thus provide something approaching absolute values of well-formedness. If every linguist measured their examples against these standard items, then they would exactly become an inter-subjective standard, which would allow comparison of well-formedness judgments between any two linguists. Linguist A would say: "I find this one quite good, a little better than a B, perhaps." To which linguist B might reply: "I think you are being a bit kind there. I'd say it's more like a B minus." And each would know exactly what degree of well-formedness the other meant.

Another way of thinking about the absolute values of the five points is as representatives of the degrees of well-formedness that linguists have traditionally used. We can think of both A and B grades are grammatical, but C is something like the intermediate degree often given a question mark (?), D is worth two question marks (??), and E is the fully ungrammatical asterisk (*).

An additional advantage of the use of standard items is that they fill out the accessible range of syntactic well-formedness. We should perhaps briefly clarify what we mean by this term. Experimental sentences fall within the accessible range of well-formedness if the informant knows what they are intended to mean and can analyze them within their grammar. Informants are able to judge word strings that do not have these qualities, but such examples do not produce evidence relevant to syntactic computation. A couple of examples should make this clearer.

(3) a. The seven cows in the field eat grass happily all afternoon.
    b. The seven cows in the field eat happily grass all afternoon.
    c. The seven cows in the field eats grass happily all afternoon.
    d. Seven happily the cows field the grass in all afternoon eat.

Example (3a) can be regarded as fully acceptable and provides an anchor point. Example (3b) will be judged worse than (3a) by exactly the violation cost of the requirement for objects to directly follow their subcategorizing verbs. Again the comparison of (3a) and example (3c) will show the violation cost of a verb agreement violation. The violation costs are quantifiable because all of these are recognizable faulty structures. But (3d) consists just of word salad. It is not possible for us to say what is wrong with it or indeed what it is intended to mean and thus how it should be structured. It therefore falls outside the range of well-formedness judgments because it is not a faulty structure whose fault can be uniquely identified. It is no single structure, rather it exhibits a lack of structure. Such examples will show us how bad we perceive word mixtures to be but they can tell us nothing about the effects of specific constraints within the grammar.[1]

3 The selection of standard items

We went about choosing the items for English in the same way that we selected the standard items for German, with multiple judgment experiments using the Thermometer Judgments procedure (Featherston 2009). Since we shall report several studies using this technique here, we shall briefly outline this collection method. This is a procedure for obtaining judgments from naive informants with the greatest possible degree of differentiation and the least possible distortion.

This method is a development from Magnitude Estimation (Bard et al. 1996). It varies from the simple elicitation of standard categorical judgments ("Is this grammatical or not?") in several ways. First, informants are asked to provide purely relative judgments: at no point is an absolute criterion of grammaticality applied. Judgments are relative to two reference examples and the informant's own previous judgments. Second, all judgments are proportional; that is, subjects are asked to state how much better or worse sentence A is than the reference examples. Next, the scale along which judgments are made is open-ended: subjects can always add an additional higher or lower score. Additionally, the scale has no minimum division: participants can always place a score between two previous ratings. Last of all, two reference examples, one of which is quite good and the other quite bad, are given the values 20 and 30. These are sufficiently far from zero to avoid the known problem of scale end distortion there (Poulton 1989).

The instructions have the form "Look at example A. It is worth 20. Look at example B. It is worth 30. Relative to these reference items, how much would you give this one?" The result is that subjects are able to produce judgments that distinguish all the differences in well-formedness they perceive with no interference

---

[1] It is a moot question whether an example can be *too good* to be properly judged within the range of accessible structures. There does seem to be an intuition that there is such a thing as a perfect structure, but there still seem to be distinctions within perfectness. One relevant factor is length. Shorter examples, like (i), are judged better than longer ones, like (ii), because they require less processing effort, even though both are perfect.
i. Cows eat grass.
ii. The seven cows in the field happily eat grass all afternoon.

from an imposed scale. This approach can produce judgment data of higher definition than traditional techniques such as a seven-point scale and thus affords us a clearer picture of the factors that affect perceived well-formedness.

In order to select standard items for English we carried out a total of five experiments with the aim of finding sets of appropriate standard sentences. The procedure has two steps: first, we collect experimental judgments from English native speakers of example sentences that seem to us to span the full range of naturalness. These items should be evenly distributed across the full range of well-formedness, so that all areas are well represented. We choose possible exemplars from sentences with a wide range of characteristics, so that no particular sort of markedness appears more frequently than any other. These are tested, and adjustments made to some examples, while other items are replaced. The new set is then retested. This process continues until they appear to provide a continuum of perceived well-formedness. When we have a nice set of examples that covers the full range of values, we can divide the range of judgments exhibited into five equal areas. The values located in the middle of these areas become our five degrees of well-formedness.

We carried out several studies in which we elicited judgments using Thermometer Judgments (see above). We repeated this step several times in order to be sure that the distribution of items across the scale of naturalness was even and that it extended as far as possible up and down. We illustrate the approximate range of naturalness in (4) and the three sentences judged best and worst in (5).

(4) a. The sales assistant went to ask if she could permit a discount.
 b. You can't say that to me, who does most of the work round here!
 c. Who do you doubt that will complete his degree in three years?
 d. Alice is looking for something which for her to give her brother.
 e. The Spartans brave stood in line fight for freedom.

(5) a. There's a statue in the middle of the square.
 b. The patient fooled the dentist by pretending to be in pain.
 c. It's nice to eat pizza and watch a film.
 d. Historians wondering what cause is disappear civilization.
 e. Student must read much book for they become clever.
 f. Old man he work garden grow many flowers and vegetable.

Between these studies we discarded some items that had a lot of judgment variance as this would make them unsuitable as standard items. A lot of variance suggests that an item has more than one readily accessible reading, so that people are processing it differently. We also excluded some others when there were more items than necessary at the same level, and added items in places where there were too few. The final distribution is shown in Figure 1. For the purposes of establishing a set of standard examples only the vertical axis is the measure that we are interested in, so the bumps in the line do not matter. The continuum in Figure 1 thus represents the range of well-formedness, which is accessible to speakers (or perhaps to this methodology).

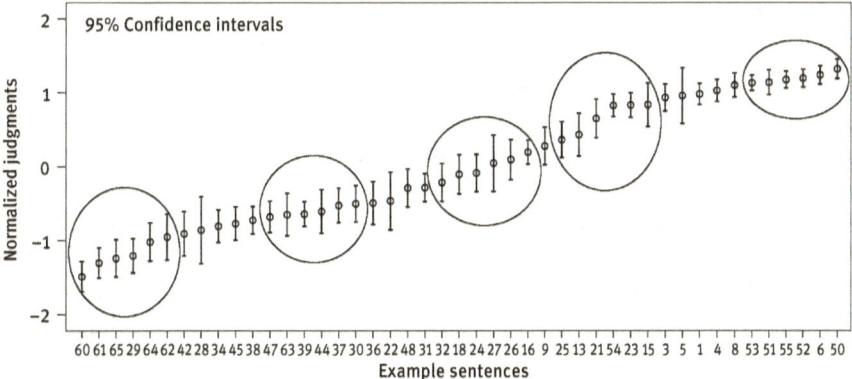

Figure 1: The results of our judgment collection (Exps 1–3) show the distribution of example sentences and the areas that exemplify the five degrees of naturalness.

The second step in this process is to find good exemplars of the five values. These standard items should be fairly consistently assigned the same or similar scores, so that we can be sure speakers agree about them, and they should be approximately half-way between the items selected for the adjacent values above and below. We next tested which of these are most reliably assigned to their group.

To do this we carried out a new type of experiment. We first choose six possible candidate examples for each naturalness value, on the basis of their scores so far. Participants in this experiment have the naturalness groups presented to them and are instructed that their task is to assign examples to the correct group. They have the opportunity to practice this in a practice stage. From the six sentences from each of the five groups we select one example sentence; these become the comparison items for the groups. Participants then see the other 25 examples one after another and are instructed to assign each of them to the group whose naturalness level the example best matches.

This experiment took place in three forms. These varied only in which example sentence from the group was used as comparison item for that group. An example may make this clearer. If we label the six candidate examples for a given naturalness level *a* to *f*, in the first version of the experiment, the informants received example *a* as the reference item and were presented with examples *b* to *f* to assign to the groups. In the second version *b* was the reference example, and *a, c, d, e, f* were to be assigned, and so on. The results give us a good idea how reliably the examples are matched to their groups.

The results of this experiment are presented in Figure 2. In order to make the accuracy of the assignments to groups visually accessible, we must treat the standard values A to E as numerical values 5 to 1. We then encode the group assignments as numerical values and calculate a mean value: an example from well-formedness group 1 (=A) should have the mean value 5.0 an example from group 3 (=C) should have the mean value 3.0. The squares mark the expected – or rather intended – value if an item is a perfect representative for a naturalness group. The error bars thus give a good idea of how an example was assigned; if the mean value is further from the square, the item was assigned more often wrongly. If the error bar is long, there was less consistency in assignment. In an ideal world, the means of the error bars would all lie exactly on the rows of squares; in fact there is a degree of error. In particular, the best examples tend to be rated worse than the 5.0 value, while the worst are rated better than the 1.0. This is perhaps inevitable, given that errors on these items can only occur in the one direction.

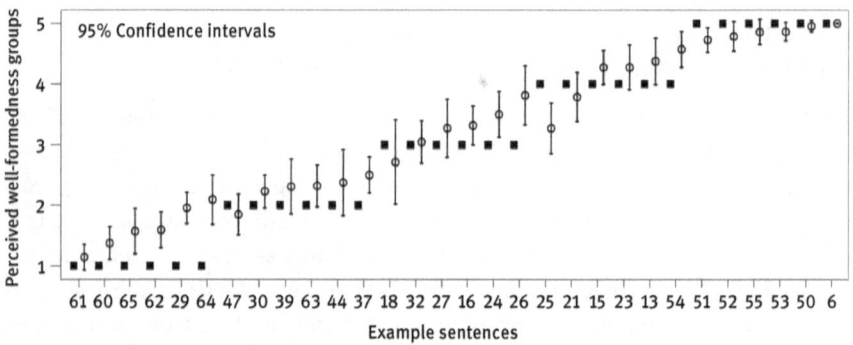

Figure 2: The results of our group assignment experiment. The squares mark the expected results, and the error bars show the mean values and 95% confidence intervals of the assignments.

It will be noted that almost no items are always correctly assigned. The fact that there is a degree of random noise in human language performance is reflected in the Decathlon Model (Featherston 2005). This has sometimes been interpreted as unreliability in the data type (for extensive discussion see Schütze 1996), but while individual single judgments are noisy, groups of informants can consistently give judgments with very fine distinctions (Featherston 2007). The noise in individual judgments partly explains why linguists provided contrasting judgments in the days of the armchair linguist.

We chose those items that are most consistently assigned correctly to become members of our final set of standard items. The full set of examples tested is in the Appendix, but the final set of standard items is listed here in (6). The sentence numbers are those given in Figure 2.

(6) a. *Standard items for naturalness value A*
   6: The patient fooled the dentist by pretending to be in pain.
   50: There's a statue in the middle of the square.
   53: The winter is very harsh in the North.

   b. *Standard items for naturalness value B*
   13: Before every lesson the teacher must prepare their materials.
   15: Jack doesn't boast about his being elected chairman.
   21: Jack cleaned his motorbike with which cleaning cloth?

   c. *Standard items for naturalness value C*
   24: Hannah hates but Linda loves eating popcorn in the cinema.
   16: Most people like very much a cup of tea in the morning.
   32: The striker must have fouled deliberately the goalkeeper.

   d. *Standard items for naturalness value D*
   44: Who did he whisper that had unfairly condemned the prisoner?
   63: The old fisherman took her pipe out of mouth and began story.
   30: Which professor did you claim that the student really admires him?

   e. *Standard items for naturalness value E*
   65: Historians wondering what cause is disappear civilization.
   60: Old man he work garden grow many flowers and vegetable.
   61: Student must read much book for they become clever.

We would recommend the use of these standard items in all studies that involve measuring well-formedness, especially when it is beneficial to be able to make reference to the approximation to an absolute standard of acceptability that they provide. The use of standard items in studies of syntax has amply demonstrated its usefulness in studies on German (Featherston & Winkler 2009), so we are pleased to offer an English set for general use.

It is best to include all 15 items in any and every study, randomized among all the other example sentences being investigated. As such they additionally offer a basic set of fillers that distract participants from the point of the investigation. These items will generally be found to produce a continuum of five roughly equally spaced points, though there are a number of factors that can distort this. For example, if the well-formedness values of the experimental sentences fall disproportionately often between two specific values, then the scores of these values will tend to be pushed further apart. We can imagine that the participants are trying to "make space" for the many judgments. For more details of known distortion effects, see Poulton (1989). Note however that the simple use of standard items in an experiment will help reduce the general level of distortion by providing values across the full range of accessible well-formedness values.

4 Example study: binding into adverbial clauses

In order to show how the standard items work in practice we shall present a recent experiment using them. It comes from our series of studies on the syntactic integration of adverbial clauses. As the experiment is fairly complex, we will present it in two parts, for clarity of exposition. We reflect on the relevance of the standard items after each part.

4.1 Example experiment part I

There has recently been considerable interest in the question how dependent clauses are attached to matrix clauses. Can the full range of these apparently diverse relationships be captured with the mechanisms and categories of standard models of syntax? To investigate this question we have been looking at examples of adverbial subordinate clauses where the identical surface form can have two different grammatical and interpretive statuses. For example, the adverbial *while* clause in (7a) is a temporal specification and it modifies the matrix clause event. The superficially identical *while* clause in (7b) on the other hand expresses a separate proposition that contrasts with the first.

(7) a. While Jean runs in the park in the morning she mentally prepares her lectures.
    b. While Jean runs in the park in the morning, she mentally relaxes in the evening.

These two types of subordinate clauses are dubbed central adverbial clauses (CACs) and peripheral adverbial clauses (PACs) by Haegeman (2003). They are frequently referred to as *integrated* and *less integrated* clause types (e.g., Reis 1997). The assumption is that their integration status derives from the fact that they are attached to the syntactic tree of the matrix clause at different points, though there is no consensus about what that point might be (Reis 1997; Frey 2011). Our experiment uses variable binding, a fairly standard test of constituency, to investigate whether or not the two clause types behave as if they were a part of the core clause, perhaps the VP structure. If they are, then they would be c-commanded from the subject position in the matrix clause and thus variable binding could occur from that position into the clause. This therefore is the criterion we use.

While many authors have used quantifier variable binding as evidence, the sorts of structures that have been used and the choice of quantifier has been very varied. This chapter was part of our research program aiming to find out if all quantifiers and context structures produced the same results. In order to do this, the experiment contrasted four quantifiers: *nobody*, *no NP*, *hardly anyone*, and *an NP*. Three of these quantifiers were negative because it is often felt that negative quantifiers produce the most valid data (cf. Pauly 2013). We also varied the position of the quantifier and main clause: it could either precede or follow the adverbial clause. Since the aim was to investigate whether this structural test could yield worthwhile data about the difference between CACs and PACs, we contrast these two adverbial clause types in our experiment.

We may thus distinguish three parameters in the 4 × 2 × 2 design:
- Quantifier: *nobody, hardly anyone, no NP, an NP*
- Clause order: matrix > adverbial, adverbial > matrix
- Adverbial clause type: CAC, PAC

The materials had the following form. In these sentences the quantifier was always in the matrix clause, the variable always in the adverbial clause.[2] Notice too that speakers increasingly find a singular – and therefore gender-specific – pronoun awkward in today's English when the person referred to can be of either gender. It is therefore very common to hear examples as in (8a), whereas (8b) is felt to sound unnatural (cf. Huddlestone & Pullum 2002).

(8) a. A teacher must prepare their material before the lesson.
    b. A teacher must prepare ?his/?her material before the lesson.

We therefore used the genderless *they* in all items.

(9)   Temporal adverbial clause: CAC
   a. Matrix clause > adverbial clause (Mq Av)
      {Nobody/hardly anyone/no Italian} wants to go to church while they still have sins on their conscience.

---

[2] Note that the examples with a positive existential quantifier are omitted here for reasons of space. They require the insertion of a negative particle into the clause in order for the sentences to make sense. So *No Italian wants to go to church* ... becomes *An Italian doesn't want to go to church* ...

b. Adverbial clause > matrix clause (Av Mq)
While they still have sins on their conscience, {nobody/hardly anyone/ no Italian} wants to go to church.

(10) Adversative adverbial clause: PAC
a. Matrix clause > adverbial clause (Mq Av)
{Nobody/hardly anyone/no Italian} wants to go to church while they readily claim to believe in God.
b. Adverbial clause > matrix clause (Av Mq)
While they readily claim to believe in God, {nobody/hardly anyone/no Italian} wants to go to church.

This was a judgment study, which used the Thermometer Judgments method as above and which was made accessible online on our server at Tübingen University in four counterbalanced versions. The 36 participants were collected by advertising the study in Linguistics departments in universities in the UK. Three prizes of £50 were distributed by lottery among the participants.

The judgment scores are normalized to z-scores in order to reduce the inter-judger variation. Each person's scores then have the mean value zero and the standard deviation 1. The results are illustrated in Figure 3.

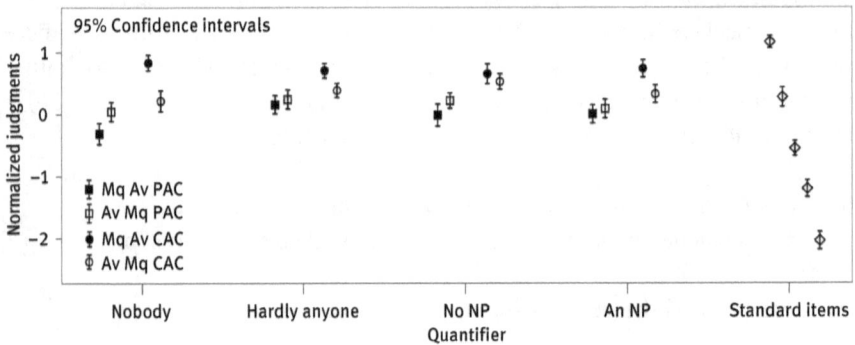

Figure 3: Results of experiment on quantifier variable binding into adverbial clauses.
CAC, temporal adverbial clause; PAC, adversative adverbial clause;
Mq Av, matrix clause with quantifier > adverbial clause with variable;
Av Mq, adverbial clause with variable > matrix clause with quantifier.

The four quantifiers are along the horizontal axis, and the normalized naturalness judgments are on the vertical axis. Higher scores indicate judgments that a structure is more natural. The error bars show the means and 95% confidence intervals of the normalized judgment scores by condition. The conditions are grouped by the type of quantifier on the x-axis. Within each group, the pair on the left (with square mean markers) is PAC conditions and the pair on the right (round mean markers) is CACs. Within the pairs, the left-hand error bar (with filled mean marker) shows the matrix > adverbial clause order, while the right-hand error bar (with empty mean marker) shows the adverbial > matrix clause order. On the right-hand end of the chart we see the standard items, whose mean points are marked with diamond shapes.

What therefore do these results show us? Above all, the PACs behave differently to the CACs, which was the core question in the experiment. Consistently across the different quantifiers, the PAC pairs of bars with squares are always judged clearly weaker than the CAC pairs of bars with circles. Within these pairs, the relationship between the filled and hollow markers is also different: while for the PACS, the bars with filled markers are never better than the bars with hollow markers, the reverse is true for the CACS.

These results support several observations. First, that our informants permit variable binding differentially into integrated and less integrated clauses, which would support the claim that they have different attachment points, if we assume that binding is dependent on a structural relation such as c-command. Since the CACs are judged consistently better, it seems natural to assume that these subordinated clause types are embedded below the quantifier in the matrix clause. This does not appear to be the case in the PACs, which are judged clearly worse.

Second, that the CACs and PACs respond differently to the order of the clauses. This is an effect that we have observed in other experiments contrasting temporal and adversative *while*: there is an ordering preference asymmetry. Temporal *while* seems to be preferred following its main clause, adversative *while* preceding it. Given some thought, this effect appears plausible. Temporal *while* merely modifies a main clause event, adding the specification when it takes place. It is essentially subordinate information, which does not require the salient preceding position. Adversative *while*, on the other hand, structures the discourse and tells us how to interpret that which follows, namely as a contrasting pair of facts. It is credible that it eases the processing of the discourse if this information is provided early on.[3] Relating this to our examples in (7), this would mean that the preferred versions are as in (11). If this interpretation is correct, it is further evident that informants process CACs and PACs differently, in this case in terms that we might think of as relating to information structure.

---

[3] Interestingly, this effect seems to be specific to English. It does not visibly appear in German with the equivalent connector *während*.

(11) a. CAC: *while* clause preferred following
   Jean mentally prepares her lectures while she runs in the park in the morning.
   b. PAC: *while* clause preferred preceding
   While Jean runs in the park in the morning, she mentally relaxes in the evening.

There are further distinctions in the data, in particular across the quantifiers, which we shall mention though we cannot here discuss them in detail (von Wietersheim 2016 for discussion). Roughly, we may say that the data from the different quantifiers behave in a parallel but not identical manner, so if our aim is to distinguish CACs from PACs, we may use any of these quantifiers. In fact there is a tendency for the differences to reduce as the semantic content of the quantifier becomes less exclusively negative. *Nobody* produces the most polarized results, *hardly anyone* slightly less so, and *no NP* less again. *An NP* is similar to this last one.

To see this, we look first at the results for quantifier *nobody*. The condition predicted to best permit variable binding is *Mq Av CAC*, which is the first in (9), and in fact it is judged better than the equivalents with the quantifier phrases *hardly anyone* and *no NP*. But the minimally different condition with the adverbial clause preceding the matrix clause *Av Mq CAC* is relatively worse for *nobody* than for the other quantifiers. The PAC conditions too are worse for the quantifier *nobody*. Nevertheless, the basic patterns are the same across the quantifiers: *nobody* produces not different results, but more extreme results.

One way of accounting for this effect, which we have found for German negative quantifiers too, would be in terms of pragmatic preferences on antecedents. It has been observed at least since Sag & Pollard (1992) that specific, nonabstract, and animate antecedents are preferred in binding constructions. The effect observed here may be related to this, but unfortunately we cannot discuss this further here, since it takes us too far from our main aim in this chapter.

4.2 Standard items I

We are reporting this study here as an example of the use of the standard items, so it is to this that we now turn. How do they behave in this study? The standard items are on the right-hand side of Figure 3. We should first note that they form a pleasingly regular pattern – our attempts to produce five equally spaced reference points have thus apparently been successful. There are also no experimental conditions that lie beyond the standard items, so we have no reason to think that our scale does not cover the whole range of accessible values.

What therefore is the added value of the scale? One advantage of having the scale is to demonstrate that the differences between the conditions are fairly minor: nothing is as bad as the C value on the scale and nothing is as good as A. This restricted range of the results only becomes apparent when we have an external comparison scale that shows the full range available.[4]

4.3 Example experiment part II

We mentioned above that this experiment had some more conditions that we have so far omitted for clarity of exposition. All the conditions up to now had the quantifier in the matrix clause, but in fact we also tested some conditions in which the quantifier was in the subordinate clause. In our experiments on binding as a diagnostic of clause integration (e.g., von Wietersheim 2016) we normally include this additional condition, but it is not easy to achieve with negative quantifiers because the relocation of the quantifier relocates the negation too, and this changes the meaning radically. For example, changing the position of the negative quantifier in (12) alters the meaning completely, so that neither (12b) nor (12c) can be minimal pairs to (12a).

(12) a. No student lies in bed when they could go to the library.
 b. They lie in bed when no student could go to the library.
 c. When no student could go to the library, they lie in bed.

For this reason we do not test this additional condition with the negative quantifiers, but only with the existential quantifier *an NP*. The full set of conditions with the existential quantifier thus looks like this – (13), (14).

(13) Temporal adverbial clause: CAC
 a. Matrix clause + quantifier > adverbial clause + variable (Mq Av)
 An Italian doesn't want to go to church while they still have sins on their conscience.

---

[4] We might note in this context that result charts like Figures 3 and 4 also demonstrate the fine granularity of differences detectable by this methodology. The lengths of the error bars show the degree of accuracy of group judgments; the standard items show the accessible range of perceived well-formedness that these judgments can be given over. We might estimate on the basis of this data that group judgments can distinguish 15–20 different degrees of well-formedness, a much higher figure than is generally assumed for introspective judgments, the ugly ducklings of psycholinguistic study.

b. Adverbial clause + variable > matrix clause + quantifier (Av Mq)
   While they still have sins on their conscience, an Italian doesn't want to go to church.
c. Matrix clause + variable > adverbial clause + quantifier (Mv Aq)
   They don't want to go to church while an Italian still has sins on their conscience.
d. Adverbial clause + quantifier > matrix clause + variable (Aq Mv)
   While an Italian still has sins on their conscience, they don't want to go to church.

(14) Adversative adverbial clause: PAC
   a. Matrix clause + quantifier > adverbial clause + variable (Mq Av)
      An Italian doesn't want to go to church, while they readily claim to believe in God.
   b. Adverbial clause + variable > matrix clause + quantifier (Av Mq)
      While they readily claim to believe in God, an Italian doesn't want to go to church.
   c. Matrix clause + variable > adverbial clause + quantifier (Mv Aq)
      They don't want to go to church, while an Italian happily claims to believe in God.
   d. Adverbial clause + quantifier > matrix clause + variable (Aq Mv)
      While an Italian happily claims to believe in God, they don't want to go to church.

The full result set is illustrated in Figure 4. The only changes are to the group of the *an NP* quantifier.

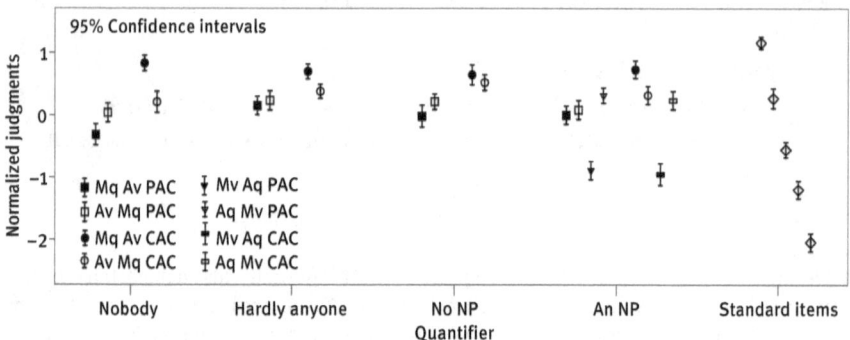

Figure 4: The full set of results of our experiment on quantifier variable binding into adverbial clauses. This shows the same results as in the previous graphic but with the addition of the conditions with the quantifier in the subordinate clause.

The additional conditions with the quantifier in the subordinate clause pattern rather differently to those we have looked at so far. Their error bars have triangles and rectangles, filled and hollow. The *Mv Aq PAC* and *Mv Aq CAC* conditions in which the quantifier is not only in the subordinate clause but also follows the variable (filled triangle and rectangle) are the worst of all by some way, below standard item C. The cases where the quantifier precedes the variable (hollow triangle and rectangle) are much better, roughly at level B, about the same as the PAC conditions (squares). We would highlight this as illustrating the importance of linear ordering, when – and only when – the parser is attempting to pragmatically repair failed binding. If we look at the CAC conditions across the quantifiers, we see that the order *Mq Av*, in which the quantifier precedes the variable, is judged more natural than the inverse order. But crucially the difference is not all that large. The error bars with filled and hollow mean markers are between the A and B standard items. It is easier for us to process sentences with quantifiers preceding variables, but syntactic binding is quite possible in the other direction too.

This is very different from the conditions that we have newly introduced, where syntactic binding is quite impossible. In these conditions, the linear order of quantifier and potentially bound variable makes a very large difference: the error bars with filled and hollow triangles and rectangles are far apart. This finding is an indication that these examples are being dealt with as best as possible by a process of pragmatic repair. For syntactic binding, what counts is the hierarchical relationship; for pragmatic repair processing, factors such as linear order play a large role too.

4.4 Standard items II

These additional examples are intended to show further aspects of the usefulness of the scale of standard items. We have been able to label degrees of well-formedness in absolute terms by using the standard values. We have also been able to show varying degrees of difference between conditions. Being able to recognize degrees of perceived well-formedness in absolute terms permits us to put forward arguments such as the distinction between syntactic and pragmatic effects that we advance here.

5 Standard items in semantic studies?

A question often raised about the use of standard items is their applicability to studies concerning factors other than syntactic well-formedness. These items were originally developed for use within the field of syntax and the range of well-formedness that they cover is that which is accessible to syntactic intuitions (Featherston 2009). Can they therefore sensibly be used in studies where the variable at issue is one of semantic coherence or pragmatic felicity? Can we map intuitions of coherence and semantic feasibility onto the same scale? This is an interesting question, because it seems fairly uncontroversial that syntactic well-formedness (often termed, for better or worse: "grammaticality") is not the same as semantic felicity. In many cases, the two are clearly distinguishable: there is nothing wrong in strictly syntactic terms with "a married bachelor/spinster", "I am in the process of loving you", or "the old man died the oak tree", but their (potential) meanings do not fit our world. These examples would thus appear to contain semantic mismatches. On the other hand, we can readily make sense of "You should can swim after all these lessons", "I'm afraid I seen't the problem", and the question "Go you home now?" but we cannot phrase them that way in current English. These therefore would seem to be problems of the syntactic form, not the semantic or pragmatic content. Since this is the case, it must be clear that the two types of adverbial clauses can in principle be distinguished. Given that they can in some cases be distinguished, they cannot be the same thing. It might well therefore be expected that syntactic well-formedness and semantic coherence and/or felicity should not be mapped onto the same scale.

Nevertheless, we argue here that it can indeed be useful to include the set of standard items into experiments that address issues of interpretation. One reason is simple: the boundary between form and interpretation is highly permeable, so that the two depend on each other. Work on judgment studies has made it clear that introspective judgments are sensitive to both: a well-formedness judgment is always a judgment of a structure *in* a certain interpretation. Speakers are quite incapable of giving judgments of strings that they do not understand, and judgments of ambiguous structures with multiple roughly equally accessible readings will show more variability. The problem is thus less acute than it might at first glance appear. In fact the study reported above is not purely syntactic, but rather addresses an issue with both syntactic and semantic features. Binding, particularly variable binding, appears to have syntactic structural preconditions, but it relates to an aspect of interpretation. So the example study we have advanced here is itself partly a semantic one, but the standard items produce the usual tidy pattern, which would seem to confirm that the participants in the experiment had no problems judging them.

All the same, experience has shown that there is a difference between syntactic and semantic studies in the use of the standard items, and it lies in the absolute values that the standards represent. In semantic studies, the well-formedness judgments rarely descend to the lower values on the scale – as we observed in the example study reported above and Konietzko, Radó & Winkler (this volume). This might appear puzzling, but we have a suggestion why this might be the case: whereas a syntactic violation produces a form that is impossible, a semantically ill-formed example can generally (perhaps: always?) be repaired by changing our perspective on the world or imagining a figurative interpretation. For example, "a married bachelor" could be a husband with a BA, and "a married spinster" could be a wife who has characteristics that are conventionally associated with spinsters. Similarly, the statement "I am in the process of loving you" could be uttered by an over-rational robot such as Star Wars' C-3PO. Semantic failures can thus often be saved by an act of imagination. For this reason, we hypothesize these examples tend not to be judged as entirely unacceptable on the standard scale. The absolute values of the scale therefore might require re-anchoring when we use them in semantic studies.

This may not matter particularly; we have used these same items in studies testing the appropriateness of statements in given contexts. However, it would be desirable to have a specific set with which to test semantic and/or pragmatic felicity. What will probably not work is to attempt to model this with the core semantic concept of contradiction because this will hardly allow degrees of felicity. A more promising approach would be to vary the felicity of an utterance in context. Here we can readily imagine multiple degrees of appropriateness that could be captured with sets of examples that could gain intersubjective agreement. We imagine using sentences that are all in themselves fully acceptable, with only their fit to their context providing the gradations in apparent semantic acceptability. These would therefore represent effects purely of interpretation and not of form. We are currently thinking about how to construct these items; since they require a stimulus and response pair, there are certain difficulties about making them fit into all experiment types. We must however leave this to further work.

Appendix

The candidate examples we tested were the following. The numbers refer to the sentence numbers in Figure 2.

Candidates for standard item group A
6:   The patient fooled the dentist by pretending to be in pain.
50: There's a statue in the middle of the square.
53: The winter is very harsh in the North.
55: The tired teacher drank a cup of tea in the staff room.

52: It's nice to eat pizza and watch a film.
51: A hammer is a useful thing in a tool box.

Candidates for standard item group B
54: The best thing about a sister is you can borrow her clothes.
13: Before every lesson the teacher must prepare their materials.
23: What I need to know is which witness identified which defendant.
15: Jack doesn't boast about his being elected chairman.
21: Jack cleaned his motorbike with which cleaning cloth?
25: A thousand dollars are a lot of money to pay for a flight.

Candidates for standard item group C
26: What I want to know is which exam which student failed.
24: Hannah hates but Linda loves eating popcorn in the cinema.
16: Most people like very much a cup of tea in the morning.
27: You can't say that to me, who does most of the work here!
32: The striker must have fouled deliberately the goalkeeper.
18: The estate agent revealed him the whole plan to build a gas works.

Candidates for standard item group D
37: That boy had run away from home, who we saw in the bus.
44: Who did he whisper that had unfairly condemned the prisoner?
63: The old fisherman took her pipe out of mouth and began story.
39: In southern Spain heavy rain falling only in the mountains.
30: Which professor did you claim that the student really admires him?
47: The author looked in the dictionary up the word.

Candidates for standard item group E
64: Crossing the wild seas Odysseus was meet some monster.
29: Who did you wonder when Michael will introduce to his parents?
62: The Spartans brave stood in line fight for freedom.
65: Historians wondering what cause is disappear civilization.
60: Old man he work garden grow many flowers and vegetable.
61: Student must read much book for they become clever.

Acknowledgments: This work took place within the project C6 Expressions of Extrapropositional Meaning: Synchrony and Diachrony of the SFB 833 Constructing Meaning, and was supported by the Deutsche Forschungsgemeinschaft. Many thanks to the staff of the SFB 833 in general and project C6 in particular.

References

Bader, M. & J. Häussler. 2010. Toward a model of grammaticality judgments. Journal of Linguistics 46(2): 273–330.
Bard, E., D. Robertson & A. Sorace. 1996. Magnitude estimation of linguistic acceptability. Language 72(1): 32–68.
Chomsky, N. 1965. Aspects of the Theory of Syntax. Cambridge, MA: MIT Press.
Chomsky, N. 1986. Barriers. Linguistic Inquiry Monograph 13. Cambridge, MA: MIT Press.
Featherston, S. 2005. Universals and grammaticality: Wh-constraints in German and English. Linguistics 43(4): 667–711.
Featherston, S. 2007. Data in generative grammar: The stick and the carrot. Theoretical Linguistics 33(3): 269–318.
Featherston, S. 2009. A scale for measuring well-formedness: Why linguistics needs boiling and freezing points. In: (S. Featherston & S. Winkler, eds) The Fruits of Empirical Linguistics. Vol.1 Process. Berlin: Mouton de Gruyter.
Featherston, S. 2011. Three types of exceptions – and all of them rule-based. In: (H. Simon & H. Wiese, eds) Expecting the Unexpected: Exceptions in Grammar. Berlin: de Gruyter.
Frey, W. 2011. Peripheral adverbial clauses, their licensing and the prefield in German. In: (E. Breindl, G. Ferraresi & A. Volodina, eds) Satzverknüpfung – Zur Interaktion von Form, Bedeutung und Diskursfunktion, 41–77. Berlin: de Gruyter.
Haegeman, L. 2003. Conditional Clauses: External and Internal Syntax. Mind & Language 18(4): 317–339.
Huddlestone, R. & G. Pullum. 2002. The Cambridge Grammar of the English Language. Cambridge, MA: CUP.
Jacobs, J. 1988. Probleme der freien Wortstellung im Deutschen. In: Arbeitsbericht Nr. 5 des Forschungsprogramms Sprache und Pragmatik, 8–37. Lund.
Keller, F. 2000. Gradience in grammar: Experimental and computational aspects of degrees of grammaticality. PhD Thesis, University of Edinburgh.
Pauly, D. 2013. Grenzfälle der Subordination: Merkmale, Empirie und Theorie abhängiger Nebensätze. Phd dissertation, University of Potsdam, urn:nbn:de:kobv:517-opus-70275
Poulton, E. 1989. Bias in Quantifying Judgements. Hove: Erlbaum.
Reis, M. 1997. Zum syntaktischen Status unselbständiger Verbzweit-Sätze. In: (C. Dürscheid, K.-H. Ramers & M. Schwarz, eds) Sprache im Fokus. Festschrift für Heinz Vater zum 65. Geburtstag, 121–144. Tübingen: Niemeyer.
Sag, I. & C. Pollard. 1992. Anaphors in English and the Scope of Binding Theory. Linguistic Inquiry 23(2): 261–303.
Schütze, C. 1996. The empirical base of linguistics: Grammaticality judgments and linguistic methodology. Chicago: University of Chicago Press.
Uszkoreit, H. 1986. Constraints on order. Linguistics 24(5): 883–906.
von Wietersheim, S. 2016. Variable binding as evidence for clausal attachment. In: (I. Reich & A. Speyer, eds) Co- and subordination in German and other languages, Linguistische Berichte, Sonderheft 21, 319–345. Hamburg: Buske.

Index

accent
- ~ placement 2, 7–10, 57–69, 76, 86, 136
- deaccenting 76–77, 80, 86, 92, 99, 101, 113, 136
- pitch ~ 2, 4, 8–11, 57–69, 115, 118, 129–150
- topic ~ 78, 80

acceptability 12, 14, 59, 68, 72, 82, 111–112, 116, 124, 134, 159, 171, 173, 185, 213, 216, 306, 315, see also grammaticality

acceptability judgments 5–6, 11, 13, 62, 64, 68, 153, 157, 171–177, 183–204, 210, 213, 220–225, 227, 231, 242
- continuous ~ scores 183, 185–190, 192–195, 203–205

accessibility 93–95, 105–106, 109, 124, 135
accommodation 23, 51, 82, 157
active voice 12, 190–205, 281
adverbial clause 316–322, 324
agreement 87–88, 217, 219, 238, 283, 286–288, 290–293, 298, 301, 310
ambiguity 4, 9, 57–69, 107, 110, 281, 324
argument realization 13, 185, 197, 279–302
at issue information 17, 20, 22

British National Corpus 73

canonical order 13–14, 64, 154, 156–157, 161, 166, 209, 210–218, 223–227, 231–239, 242, 270, 281, 283

case 14, 108, 153–155, 215, 233–234, 280–302
- nominative 209–212, 217, 219, 233, 281–282, 287, 290, 293–298
- accusative 13, 190–191, 281–282, 285, 287–288, 290, 293–297, 301–302
- accusative-dative order 209–243
- dative 190–192, 202–203, 293–297, 301
- ~ syncretism 214, 217, 280–281, 290

CELF-R 279
coherence 9, 18–19, 23–24, 30, 49, 51–52, 120–121, 123, 147, 324
common ground CG 1, 10, 17–23, 26, 30, 38–43, 49–52, 93, 95, 129, 158

competence and performance 13, 183, 185–186, 279, 314
constraint violation 185–186, 198–199, 305–306
contextual licensing 1, 5–7, 9, 10–13, 77, 86, 106, 134, 153–179, 203, 216
contrast 11, 27–28, 44, 50–52, 106, 110, 117–119, 122, 124, 155, 171, 177, 262, 265, 316, 319
conversational crisis 20–24, 49–52
copula 10–11, 69, 71–101, 157, 160, 163–166, 178, 299
corpus frequency 6, 10, 19, 24, 29, 30–45, 47, 49–51, 54, 149, 169, 184–187, 191, 193–196, 199, 215

Decathlon Model 12, 184, 186–189, 204–205, 306, 314
definiteness 11, 73, 78, 89–90, 93–94, 96, 100, 129, 132–134, 138–139, 141, 143–144, 147–150, 162, 209
deWaC corpus 193
Direct Mapping Model 12, 184, 187–189, 192
disambiguation 286–287, 290–293, 301
discourse commitment 17, 20–23, 42–43, 49
discourse relation 10, 18, 19, 24–52, 55
discourse status 1, 11–12, 129–150, 158, 160, 162, 164, 166, 168, 178, 204
Dutch 134, 212

English 2, 7, 9, 12, 57, 61, 71–101, 131, 133–134, 153–179, 209, 211, 234, 299, 305–324
entailment 17, 21–23, 253, 255, 260, 262, 264, 273
equatives 72–75, 96–97
ERP 13, 210, 216, 219–242
exclusivity implicature 13, 251–273
extended Argument Dependency Model 280–281, 283–288, 290, 297–298, 301–302

F-marking 57–59
Finnish 153

focus 1, 2–4, 6–8, 10–11, 13, 57–69, 71–101, 106, 109–110, 112, 115–124, 129, 136, 138, 209, 253, 262–273
– ~ alternatives 3, 13, 82, 92, 112, 262, 265–267, 273
– ~ vs. background 72, 76, 86, 91–97, 136, 138, 265–268
– broad vs. narrow ~ 4, 6–8, 11, 13, 57–69, 263, 266, 268–273
– contrastive ~ 1, 10, 62–63, 112, 117–118, 124, 265
– narrow ~ 77–78, 81, 83, 85–86, 100–101
– postcopular ~ 76, 80–83, 85, 87
– prosodic ~ 110
forced-choice selection 19, 195, 204
functional interpretation 72, 82, 86, 91, 96, 98, 100

garden-path 281, 294, 298, 302
German 2, 4, 9, 11–13, 17–52, 57–69, 87, 90, 105, 108–114, 117–124, 129–150, 153–156, 159–161, 163, 165–179, 184, 190–193, 196–205, 209–244, 279–285, 289–302
given-before-new order 134, 158–160, 162, 168–169, 178
givenness 1, 9, 29, 76, 93, 97–98, 110, 112–114, 118, 123, 129–150, 157–169, 178–179, 266–267, see also newness
grammar vs. processing 154, 184
grammaticality 9, 13, 183–185, 188–205, 210, 213, 220, 225, 231, 241–242, 307
– ~ and frequency 12, 184–187, 190–205
grammaticality rating 174, 183–205, 310–311
gradient judgments 12, 14, 183–205, 220, 307, 325

Hungarian 13, 97, 100, 255–256, 262–264, 269–270

incremental processing 1, 204, 217, 219, 232–233, 280
information structure 1, 3, 4, 9, 11, 14, 57, 62, 72, 76–77, 86, 92, 96, 105–106, 109, 124, 136, 179, 252, 262, 266, 272, 302, 319

intonation 4, 10, 57, 61–63, 69, 72, 77–81, 83, 86, 135–136, 142, 149
inversion 11–12, 71–72, 75–77, 86–101, 134, 153–179, see also word order, canonical, noncanonical, OVS
island violation 106–107, 110–111, 114–117, 121, 124
Italian 87

Japanese 209
judgment study 60, 191–192, 198–199, 213, 266, 308–309, 311, 318

Likert scale 184, 188, 268, 272

Magnitude Estimation 183–184, 187, 190, 192–195, 198, 311
markedness 1–15, 20, 61–62, 68–69, 76–77, 81–83, 85, 99, 101, 106, 111–112, 121, 124, 133–135, 137, 141, 146–150, 153–179, 203, 210, 212, 217, 235, 243, 264, 283, 287, 297, 312, see also noncanonical
middle field 13, 64, 210–211, 213, 216, 234
morphosyntactic cue 13, 238–239, 286–293, 300–301

naturalness rating 81, 83–84, 308, 312–315
newness 23, 27, 39, 51, 112–114, 129, 142, 147, 149–150, 158, 161 see also givenness
noncanonical 13–14, 153, 156–157, 203, 209–243, 270, 279–280, 286, 293, 298, 300–301 see also inversion, markedness, OVS order
nonreferential 72–73, 82, 86, 91, 96

OVS order 171–172, 176, 286–287, 289–293, 298–301

passive 12–13, 134, 190–205, 279–281, 286–287, 289, 298–300
perception experiment 10, 57, 59–64, 68, 136
picture verification task 13, 163, 254–255, 258
poset licensing 169–171, 177–178

pragmatics 13–14, 17, 43, 57, 58, 135, 157,
    158–159, 179, 251–273, 279, 320,
    323–324
prefield 133, 141–142, 283
production study 11, 60, 137, 147, 150,
    166, 185
pronoun 11, 13, 76, 87, 89–90, 98–99,
    113, 118–119, 141–142, 169, 209–243,
    266, 317
prosody 2, 6, 9, 57–58, 60–62, 68, 71–101,
    112, 115, 124, 135–136, 149, 265
psych-verb 13, 279–282, 285–289,
    293–298, 302

quantifier 317–323
question, concealed 72, 76, 90, 94, 98
QUD 18, 267

rapid serial visual presentation 120
rating study 10–11, 13–14, 62–68, 72, 77,
    81–85, 100, 116–117, 120–123, 154,
    171–177, 183–205, 221, 224–225, 231,
    241, 268–269, 271–272, 311, see also
    grammaticality rating, naturalness rating
relative clause 11, 90, 105–124, 141–143,
    279–280

salience 10, 13, 21–22, 73, 110, 115–117, 239
schon 46–48
scrambling 213, 242–243
self-paced reading 6, 154, 159–160, 163–165,
    171–177, 266
semantics 41, 72, 88, 92, 96, 98, 108,
    120, 191–192, 197–199, 219, 225, 232,
    238–239, 252–254, 259–262, 267, 273,
    279, 285, 287, 294, 297, 301, 305, 320,
    323–325
Sentence Accent Assignment Rule 53, 57, 63

sentence-picture matching 268
sentence repetition task 295
set-subset relation 7, 10, 170–171
shallow processing 13, 253–255, 262, 273
SOV order 64, 65, 154, 296
speeded grammaticality judgment 114,
    116, 307
Stuttgart-Tübingen Tagset 30
subject, underlying vs. surface 73, 75,
    87–89, 91, 96, 98
SVO order
– in English 153, 155–156, 171–176
– in German 283, 287, 289–290, 292,
    294–295
syntactic deficit 13, 280, 286–288
syntactic template 231–238, 240, 242, 283

thematic role 179, 211, 235, 282–283,
    285–287, 297–298
thermometer method 188, 311, 318
topic 12, 85, 97, 136, 138, 148, 196–203
– aboutness ~ 74, 149
topicalization 12–13, 153–179, 279–281,
    283, 286, 289–293, 299, 301
truth value judgment 253, 261, 266, 291, 299

Vietnamese 68

Wechsler intelligence scales 289
well-formedness 12–14, 183–205, 231,
    239–241, 294, 302, 305–326
word order 1–2, 7–8, 11–13, 65, 129,
    132–139, 141–150, 153–179, 209–243,
    263–264, 270, 279–280, 283,
    286–287, 289–293, 298, 300–301,
    see also OVS, SOV, SVO, canonical,
    noncanonical, inversion, markedness,
    scrambling

www.ingramcontent.com/pod-product-compliance
Lightning Source LLC
Chambersburg PA
CBHW031756220426
43662CB00007B/419